# HOMELESSNESS AND HEALTH IN CANADA

D1281884

# HOMELESSNESS AND HEALTH IN CANADA

## EDITED BY

Manal Guirguis-Younger

Ryan McNeil

Stephen W. Hwang

University of Ottawa Press
2014

The University of Ottawa Press acknowledges with gratitude the support extended
to its publishing list by Heritage Canada through the Canada Book Fund, by the
Canada Council for the Arts, by the Federation for the Humanities and Social
Sciences through the Awards to Scholarly Publications Program and by the
University of Ottawa.


Copy editing: Trish O'Reilly-Brennan
Proofreading: Joanne Muzak
Typesetting: Infographie CS
Cover illustration and design: Johanna Pedersen

**Library and Archives Canada Cataloguing in Publication**

Homelessness & health in Canada / edited by Manal Guirguis-Younger,
Ryan McNeil, Stephen W. Hwang.

Includes bibliographical references.
Issued in print and electronic formats.
ISBN 978-0-7766-2143-2 (pbk.).-- ISBN 978-0-7766-2148-7 (pdf).--
ISBN 978-0-7766-2147-0 (epub)

1. Homelessness--Health aspects--Canada. 2. Homeless persons--
Health and hygiene--Canada. 3. Homeless persons--Medical care--Canada.
4. Homeless persons--Government policy--Canada. 5. Homeless persons--
Canada--Social conditions. I. Guirguis-Younger, Manal, 1967- author,
editor of compilation II. McNeil, Ryan, 1982- author, editor of compilation
III. Hwang, Stephen, editor of compilation IV. Title: Homelessness and
health in Canada.

RA564.9.H63H64 2014      362.1'0425      C2014-901278-0
                                         C2014-901279-9

MIX
Paper from
responsible sources
FSC   FSC® C100212
www.fsc.org

# Table of Contents

# List of Figures

# List of Tables

# Introduction

Manal Guirguis-Younger, PhD
Faculty of Human Sciences, Saint Paul University

Ryan McNeil, PhD
British Columbia Centre for Excellence in HIV/AIDS
Faculty of Health Sciences, Simon Fraser University

Stephen W. Hwang, MD
Centre for Research on Inner City Health, St. Michael's Hospital

## Why This Book?

Stereotypical images of homeless persons, such as those of 'junkies', 'squeegee kids' or 'bag ladies', shape popular understandings of homelessness but obscure the scope and diversity of Canada's homeless population. Over the past thirty years, the retreat of the federal government from social housing, along with reforms to social welfare programs and health care, has contributed to a growing homelessness crisis that affects tens of thousands of people every year (Hulchanski et al. 2009). This steady growth in Canada's homeless population has been accompanied by greater awareness that this population is highly heterogeneous (Gaetz 2010; Laird 2007). Although some groups are overrepresented among the nation's homeless population due to wider social inequities embedded in Canadian society, notably people of Aboriginal ancestry (Hwang 2001), homelessness does not discriminate on the basis of age, gender, sexuality or race. In turn, Canada's homeless population reflects the country's overall diversity.

Increased recognition of the diversity of Canada's homeless population has led to greater acknowledgement that homelessness encompasses a wide range of living situations (Canadian Homelessness Research Network 2012). Recently, Canadian researchers have advanced a definition of homelessness that recognizes this diversity by situating homelessness along a continuum of living arrangements, including: (1) living outside or in places not fit for human habitation; (2) staying in temporary or emergency accommodations (e.g., emergency and transition shelters); (3) living in accommodations without security of tenure (e.g., 'couch surfing' or staying with friends or acquaintances); and (4) living at risk of homelessness due to lack of financial security or other factors (e.g., intimate partner violence, separation or divorce, etc.) that may compromise housing (Canadian Homelessness Research Network 2012). In many regards, this definition underscores the fact that *homelessness is experienced differently by different people,* often in accordance with the unique constellation of individual, social and structural factors that shape their lives (see, for example, Karabanow 2004; Menzies 2009; Walsh, Rutherford and Kumak 2009). For example, women and their children escaping intimate partner violence by staying in a transition shelter, street-involved youth sleeping on a friend or acquaintance's sofa and an individual staying in an emergency shelter or sleeping outside may all be characterized as homeless, in that they lack access to secure and stable housing.

While these diverse categories of homelessness underscore the varied needs and experiences of Canada's homeless population, more than two decades of research indicates that one factor linking this population is poor overall health (Dunn 2000; Frankish, Hwang and Quantz 2005; Hwang 2001). Homelessness is associated with high levels of morbidity and mortality (Hwang 2000; Hwang et al. 2009; Street Health Toronto 2007), with homeless populations in Canada experiencing higher incidences of alcohol and drug use (Grinman, Chiu and Rederlmeier 2010; Kerr et al. 2009; Torchalla, Strehlau and Krausz 2011), mental illness (Stergiopoulos et al. 2010) and infectious diseases, such as HIV/AIDS and hepatitis C (Corneil et al. 2006; Roy, Haley and LeClerc 2001), than their housed counterparts. In addition, an array of chronic health problems are common among homeless populations, including but not limited to diabetes (Hwang and Bugeja 2000), cardiovascular disease (Lee et al. 2005) and respiratory illnesses (Raoult, Foucault and Brouqi 2001). Unsurprisingly, the cumulative disease burden experienced by homeless persons, when combined with high levels of suicide, fatal injury and homicide, results in some of the highest all-cause mortality rates of any population in Canada (Cheung and Hwang 2004; Hwang, 2000; Hwang et al. 2009).

Paradoxically, whereas homeless populations have high levels of health services utilization, especially emergency department and in-patient care (Hwang et al. 2011; Palepu et al. 1999), they frequently have unmet health needs due to the barriers that they face to accessing care and adhering to treatment (Hwang et al. 2010; Khandor et al. 2011; McNeil and Guirguis-Younger 2012). The reasons for this are complex and, to a great extent, largely the product of the challenges experienced by homeless persons. For example, the daily struggle for survival, such as addressing immediate needs (e.g., food, shelter etc.), often takes precedence over health needs, leading homeless persons to delay seeking treatment (Gelberg et al. 1997). Furthermore, researchers have found that homeless persons often feel unwelcome in health care settings due to discrimination and subsequent to these experiences are less likely to seek care (Wen, Hudak and Hwang 2007).

Against this backdrop, homelessness has been increasingly characterized as Canada's most significant public health challenge (Frankish, Hwang and Quantz 2005; Hulchanski et al. 2009; Hwang 2001; Layton 2000) and yet no book or edited collection has unpacked the relationship between homelessness and health to identify potential solutions. This book seeks to remedy this by bringing together, for the first time, contributions by leading and emerging Canadian researchers exploring the relationship between homelessness and health. In doing so, it signifies an important step towards advancing our understanding of this relationship and identifying future directions. While fully accounting for the impact of homelessness on health lies beyond the scope of any one project, this book disentangles many important dimensions of this relationship. Accordingly, it has considerable potential to inform the response to one of Canada's enduring social challenges and, to that end, contributors have linked their chapters to policy and practice recommendations. The chapters in this book have been organized into three distinct but complementary sections that address a range of topics, spanning from youth homelessness to hospice and palliative care, and together constitute a blueprint for improving the health of homeless persons in Canada.

## The Organization of This Book

Part 1 of this book highlights the diversity of Canada's homeless population by exploring the health needs and experiences of particular populations. Researchers have increasingly turned their attention toward how individual characteristics intersect with social and structural factors to shape the health of *particular* homeless populations (i.e., women, persons of Aboriginal ancestry, etc.) and, in many cases, increase their vulnerability to adverse health outcomes (see, for example, Gelberg et al. 2004; Reading and Wien 2010). The chapters in this section of the book expand on this literature, while providing policy and practice recommendations that aim to mitigate these health disparities within the larger homeless population.

The first two chapters explore the experiences of homeless youth. In Chapter 1, Jeff Karabanow and Sean Kidd review social and structural factors that contribute to youth homelessness, while highlighting the diversity of homeless and street-involved youth. Given that the lived experiences of homeless youth vary in accordance with their age, gender, sexuality and race, Karabanow and Kidd argue that it is critical that interventions to address youth homelessness account for this diversity. Importantly, this chapter seeks to inform the response to youth homelessness by outlining policy and practice recommendations that take into consideration the needs and experiences of homeless youth. In Chapter 2, Danielle Schwartz and her colleagues provide an overview of the individual, social and structural factors that shape sexual health outcomes among homeless and street-involved youth. In light of epidemiological data indicating that homeless youth experience adverse sexual health outcomes (see, for example, Marshall et al. 2009; Shields et al. 2004), this chapter contributes to the literature by outlining how homelessness constrains the ability of youth to adhere to risk reduction strategies.

Chapters 3 and 4 situate the disproportionate levels of homelessness and unstable housing experienced by people of Aboriginal ancestry within the context of Canada's history of colonialism and racism. In Chapter 3, Billie Allan and Izumi Sakamoto report findings from the Coming Together project, a community-based participatory research project that explored how Aboriginal women and transwomen negotiate and survive the many challenges of homelessness and unstable housing. This chapter highlights the severe marginalization that Aboriginal women and transwomen encounter in Canadian society and presents recommendations for policymakers and service providers that seek to empower these women. In Chapter 4, Nathanael Lauster and Frank Tester report findings from a survey that explored the impact of residential crowding on Inuit people in Nunavut, focusing in particular on the implications for population health. Lauster and Tester link the shortage of safe, affordable housing to high levels of residential crowding and self-reported health problems.

In Chapter 5, Fran Klodawsky and her colleagues explore how homelessness impacts self-reported health status and health care access among immigrants and refugees. Klodawsky and her colleagues draw upon data from the Ottawa Panel Study on Homelessness, a longitudinal study that examined changes in housing status and health among a cohort of homeless persons in the Greater Ottawa region. This study found that immigrants and refugees experienced better physical and mental health than their Canadian-born counterparts. However, Klodawsky and her colleagues note that, given that health and social service utilization increased among immigrants and refugees over time, greater attention is needed to how well existing services meet the needs of this population.

Part 2 explores potential policy and programmatic responses to improve health access and outcomes among homeless populations. Over the past two decades, greater attention to the impact that homelessness has on health has been accompanied by calls to implement policy and programmatic reforms to increase access to affordable housing and health care services (Frankish, Hwang and Quantz 2005; Hwang 2001). To date, policy approaches to addressing the intersection of homelessness and health have been lacking, with Canada being notably without a national housing strategy. In many regards, this section of the book adds an important dimension to this ongoing discussion by mapping policies and programs that have the potential to improve our overall response to homelessness at the local, regional and national level.

Chapters 6 and 7 explore innovative housing policies and interventions with the potential to improve health outcomes among homeless populations. In Chapter 6, Brandon Marshall and Thomas Kerr review the relationship between housing and HIV/AIDS among people who inject drugs. They explore policy and programmatic reforms that have the potential to minimize HIV risks and increase support among this population. Importantly, Marshall and Kerr suggest that integrating housing interventions with addictions treatment, health services and other evidence-based interventions have the potential to achieve the greatest possible benefits. In Chapter 7, Tim Aubry and his colleagues present findings of a review exploring the impact of supported housing initiatives on people with severe and persistent mental illness. They link the history and impact of deinstitutionalization to high levels of homelessness among people with severe and persistent mental illness. Aubry and his colleagues demonstrate that supported housing has been shown to be effective in helping people with severe and persistent mental illness achieve housing stability and should be considered as a central plank of the larger response to homelessness.

The remaining chapters in Part 2 explore policy and programmatic strategies with the potential to improve health services delivery to homeless populations. In Chapter 8, Bruce Wallace and his colleagues explore the oral health care needs of homeless populations, which have been largely overlooked by researchers. This chapter reviews barriers that homeless populations encounter to accessing oral health care services, linking unmet oral health needs to poor overall health outcomes. Wallace and his colleagues examine how community dental clinics, and in particular those integrated into existing community health clinics, have the potential to minimize barriers that homeless populations encounter to accessing oral health care services and thus improve oral health outcomes. In Chapter 9, Bernadette Pauly explores how nurse–patient interactions shape health care access among homeless and street-involved populations. Drawing on ethnographic fieldwork, including participant observation in community health clinics and an urban emergency department, Pauly reports that by adopting non-judgmental, harm reduction approaches, nurses are able to establish trust with homeless and street-involved populations and thereby facilitate access to health care services. This chapter argues that the widespread adoption of these approaches is critical to increasing health equity. In Chapter 10, Ryan McNeil and Manal Guirguis-Younger draw on qualitative interviews conducted with health and social services professionals to examine factors that influence the siting and design of community and shelter-based health facilities for homeless populations. Given that community and shelter-based health facilities occupy an increasingly prominent role in health services delivery to homeless populations, this chapter outlines important recommendations to inform the continued development of these services across Canada and internationally.

The final section of this book highlights innovative programs that have emerged to address the unmet health needs of homeless populations. Across Canada, communities have developed programs responsive to the needs of local homeless populations that, in many cases, represent innovative service delivery models. While, in many respects, these programs are tailored to the unique social, structural and environmental factors that shape health access and outcomes among homeless persons in these communities, they may be adapted and implemented elsewhere to respond to similar challenges. In Chapter 11, Susan Farrell and her colleagues present findings from research conducted at Ottawa's managed alcohol program, an innovative shelter-based harm reduction program for homeless persons with alcohol dependency. This chapter reviews this innovative service delivery model, which has since been replicated in several Canadian cities, and evaluates the integration of psychiatric services into this program. Farrell and her colleagues found that program participants experienced improvements in mental health outcomes, thereby underscoring the significant potential of integrating housing, harm reduction and mental health services.

In Chapter 12, Vicky Stergiopoulos discusses Toronto's Inner City Health Associates, a program funded by the Ontario Ministry of Health and Long Term Care that aims to improve access to health care services for homeless persons by placing physicians in homeless health care settings (e.g., emergency shelters and drop-in shelters). This program has been critical in the development of innovative health care programs, such as shelter-based collaborative mental health care teams and interdisciplinary mental health outreach teams. Accordingly, this chapter provides many insights that could inform the development of similar approach in other provinces. Finally, in Chapter 13, Guirguis-Younger and McNeil discuss the dynamics that shaped the development of the Ottawa Mission Hospice, a shelter-based hospice that provides end-of-life care to homeless persons. Drawing on qualitative fieldwork, they discuss the complexities of delivering compassionate palliative care in the context of homelessness. Guirguis-Younger and McNeil contend that the development of shelter-based palliative services required a higher level of integration across the health and social care system and map the relationships between the Ottawa Mission Hospice and its partnering organizations, notably Ottawa Inner City Health. By focusing on the planning and implementation of this program, this chapter presents a framework for those who wish to adapt this model to their community.

## References

Canadian Homelessness Research Network. 2012. "Canadian Definition of Homelessness." [on-line]. Homeless Hub. www.homelesshub.ca/ CHRNhomelessdefinition/ [consulted June 30, 2012].

Cheung, A. M. and S. W. Hwang. 2004. "Risk of Death among Homeless Women: A Cohort Study and Review of the Literature." *Canadian Medical Association Journal*, 170(8): 1243–47.

Corneil, T. A., L. M. Kuyper, J. Shoveller et al. 2006. "Unstable Housing, Associated Risk Behaviour, and Increased Risk for HIV Infection among Injection Drug Users." *Health & Place*, 12(1): 79–85.

Dunn, J. R. 2000. "Housing and Health Inequalities: Review and Prospects for Research." *Housing Studies*, 15(3): 341–66.

Frankish, C. J., S. W. Hwang and D. Quantz. 2005. "Homelessness and Health in Canada: Research Lessons and Priorities." *Canadian Journal of Public Health*, 96: S23–S29.

Gaetz, S. 2010. "The Struggle to End Homelessness in Canada: How We Created the Crisis, and How We Can End It." *The Open Health Services and Policy Journal*, 3: 21–26.

Gelberg, L., C. H. Browner, E. Lejano and L. Arangua. 2004. "Access to Women's Health Care: A Qualitative Study of Barriers Perceived by Homeless Women." *Women & Health*, 40(2): 87–100.

Gelberg, L., T. C. Gallagher, R. M. Andersen and P. Koegel. 1997. "Competing Priorities as a Barrier to Medical Care among Homeless Adults in Los Angeles." *American Journal of Public Health*, 87(2): 217–20.

Grinman, M., S. Chiu, D. A. Rederlmeier et al. 2010. "Drug Problems among Homeless Individuals in Toronto, Canada: Prevalence, Drugs of Choice, and Relation to Health Status." *BMC Public Health*, 10: 94.

Hulchanski, D. J., P. Campsie, S. Chau, S. W. Hwang and E. Paradis. 2009. "Homelessness: What's in a Word?" In *Finding Home: Policy Options for Addressing Homelessness in Canada*, ed. D. J. Hulchanski, P. Campsie, S. Chau, S. W. Hwang and E. Paradis. Toronto: Cities Centre, University of Toronto, 1–16.

Hwang, S. W. 2001. "Homelessness and Health." *Canadian Medical Association Journal*, 164(2): 229–33.

——. 2000. "Mortality among Men Using Homeless Shelters in Toronto, Ontario." *Journal of the American Medical Association*, 283(16): 2152–57.

Hwang, S. W. and A. L. Bugeja. 2000. "Barriers to Appropriate Diabetes Management among Homeless People in Toronto." *Canadian Medical Association Journal*, 163(2): 161–65.

Hwang, S. W., J. M. Ueng, S. Chiu et al. 2010. "Universal Health Insurance and Health Care Access for Homeless Persons." *American Journal of Public Health*, 100(8): 1454–61.

Hwang, S. W., J. Weaver, T. Aubry and J. S. Hoch. 2011. "Hospital Costs and Length of Stay among Homeless Patients Admitted to Medical, Surgical, and Psychiatric Services." *Medical Care*, 49(4): 350–54.

Hwang, S. W., R. Wilkins, M. Tjepkema, P. J. O'Campo and J. R. Dunn. 2009. "Mortality among Residents of Shelters, Rooming Houses, and Hostels in Canada: 11 Year Follow-up Study." *British Medical Journal*, 339: b4036.

Karabanow, J. 2004. *Being Young and Homeless: Understanding How Youth Enter and Exit Street Life*. New York: Peter Lang.

Kerr, T., B. D. L. Marshall, C. Miller et al. 2009. "Injection Drug Use among Street-Involved Youth in a Canadian Setting." *BMC Public Health*, 9: 171.

Khandor, E., K. Mason, C. Chambers, K. Rossiter, L. Cowan and S. W. Hwang. 2011. "Access to Primary Health Care among Homeless Adults in Toronto, Canada: Results from the Street Health Survey." *Open Medicine*, 5(2): E94.

Laird, G. 2007. *Homelessness in a Growth Economy: Canada's 21st Century Paradox*. Calgary: Sheldon Chumir Foundation for Ethics in Leadership.

Layton, J. 2000. *Homelessness: The Making and Unmaking of a Crisis*. Toronto: Penguin.

Lee, T. C., J. G. Hanlon, J. Ben-David et al. 2005. "Risk Factors for Cardiovascular Disease in Homeless Adults." *Circulation*, 111: 2629–35.

Marshall, B. D. L., T. Kerr, J. Shoveller et al. 2009. "Homelessness and Unstable Housing Associated with an Increased Risk of HIV and STI Transmission among Street-Involved Youth." *Health & Place*, 15(3): 753–60.

McNeil, R. and M. Guirguis-Younger. 2012. "Illicit Drug Use as a Challenge to the Delivery of End-of-Life Care Services to Homeless Persons: Perceptions of Health and Social Services Professionals." *Palliative Medicine*, 26(4): 350–59.

Menzies, P. 2009. "Homeless Aboriginal Men and the Effects of Intergenerational Trauma." In *Finding Home: Policy Options for Addressing Homelessness in Canada*, ed. D. J. Hulchanski, P. Campsie, S. Chau, S. W. Hwang and E. Paradis. Toronto: Cities Centre, University of Toronto, 1–25.

Palepu, A., S. A. Strathdee, R. S. Hogg et al. 1999. "The Social Determinants of Emergency Department and Hospital Use by Injection Drug Users in Canada." *Journal of Urban Health*, 76(4): 409–18.

Raoult, D., C. Foucault and P. Brouqi. 2001. "Infections in the Homeless." *Lancet Infectious Diseases*, 1(1): 77–84.

Reading, C. L. and F. Wien. 2010. *Health Inequalities and Social Determinants of Aboriginal Peoples' Health*. Prince George, BC: National Collaborating Centre for Aboriginal Health.

Roy, E., N. Haley, P. LeClerc et al. 2001. "Risk Factors for Hepatitis C Virus Infection among Street Youths." *Canadian Medical Association Journal,* 165(5): 557–60.

Shields, S.A., T. Wong, J. Mann et al. 2004. "Prevalence and Correlates of Chlamydia Infection in Canadian Street Youth." *Journal of Adolescent Health,* 34(5): 384–90.

Stergiopoulos, V., C. Dewa, J. Durbin, N. Chau and T. Svoboda. 2010. "Assessing the Mental Health Service Needs of the Homeless: A Level-of-Care Approach." *Journal of Health Care for the Poor and Underserved,* 21(3): 1031–45.

Street Health Toronto. 2007. *The Street Health Report.* Toronto: Street Health.

Torchalla, I., V. Strehlau, K. Li, M. Krausz. 2011. "Substance Use and Predictors of Substance Dependence in Homeless Women." *Drug and Alcohol Dependence,* 118(2–3): 173–79.

Walsh, C. A., G. Rutherford and N. Kumak. 2009. "Characteristics of Home: Perspectives of Women Who Are Homeless." *The Qualitative Report,* 14(2): 299–317.

Wen, C. K., P. L. Hudak and S. W. Hwang. 2007. "Homeless People's Perceptions of Welcomeness and Unwelcomeness in Healthcare Encounters." *Journal of General Internal Medicine,* 22(7): 1011–17.

PART I

# HOMELESSNESS & HEALTH IN CANADIAN POPULATIONS

# CHAPTER 1

# Being Young and Homeless: Addressing Youth Homelessness from Drop-in to Drafting Policy

Jeff Karabanow, PhD
School of Social Work, Dalhousie University

Sean Kidd, PhD
Psychological Services, Centre for Addiction and Mental Health

*I met this chick that I was squeegeeing with two years ago. We were squeegeeing together. And I don't know how it happened but she got in this fight with this lady and this bitch took her garbage out of her car and threw it in the chick's face and said "Here's a bunch of trash for street trash like you" or something like that. And this girl had just left home, and she was like 16 or 17 or something, maybe a year older than me, she was just dealing with the whole leaving home situation, and this happened, and the car drove away and she came back to the sidewalk and she was like "fucking bitch blah blah blah", and then she just lost it. She started crying.*

– 19-year-old girl, Toronto,
interviewed between squeegee runs

## Introduction

Street youth populations are increasingly understood as being diverse, complex and heterogeneous. The generic terms *street youth* and *homeless youth* are made up of a number of intersecting subcultures including hardcore street entrenched young people, squatters, group home kids, child welfare kids, softcore twinkies, in-and-outers, punks, runaways, throwaways, refugees and immigrants, young single mothers and those who are homeless because their entire family is homeless. Within these makeshift categories are numerous labels that tend to be associated with street activities, such as *gang bangers, sex trade workers, drug dealers, drug users, panhandlers* and *squeegees*. While these labels may denote some of the actions of young people on the street, for the purposes of this chapter, street youth or homeless youth (terms used interchangeably throughout the text) are defined as young people between the ages of 12 and 24 who do not have a permanent place to call home and who instead spend a significant amount of time and energy on the street, in squats (abandoned buildings), at youth shelters and centres and/or with friends (referred to as *couch surfers*) (Karabanow 2004a; Kidd and Scrimenti 2004).

While many estimates have been made regarding the number of homeless youth at city and national levels in Canada, to date there have been no enumerations that might be considered definitive. This is due to the tremendous difficulty identifying youths who do not regularly use youth services and ambiguity regarding the definition of homelessness. A generally accepted estimate for all homeless persons in Canada is 150,000 (National Homelessness Initiative 2006), with youth between the ages of 16 and 24 considered the fastest growing segment of the homeless population in Canada.

In the following literature review, we draw upon the North American literature, a large proportion of which is American. While there are clearly marked differences in the homeless child and youth experiences in South America and Africa (two other substantial bodies of literature), findings across studies in Canada and the United States are very similar. As such, we draw on a wider literature to frame this discussion highlighting key issues specific to the Canadian context. With research into the determinants of youth homelessness having largely run its course and a policy landscape that is, in most contexts, inadequate to take on the task of effectively addressing this pervasive social problem, it would seem timely to 'take a step back' and consider the knowledge gathered to date. We have sought, through this comprehensive review, to consolidate the research base and highlight domains where research and action needs to turn if we are to make inroads into this problem that compromises the health and lives of so many young people and has major impacts on their families and our communities.

## Shifting Conceptualizations of Youth Homelessness

By far the most common question asked in both research and public commentary is, why are these young people living on the street? As is the case with many social problems, the answers to these questions tend to be totalistic, with a range of themes waxing and waning as a function of the cultural norms in a given time. For instance, early 19th-century labelling referred to street youth as "petty thieves", "street sinners", "street urchins" and "begging impostors", while in the early 20th century, street youth were commonly branded as "young barbarians" and "street wandering children". In the late 19th century, an official from the Children's Aid Society commented:

> Enjoying the idle and lazzaroni life on the docks, living in the summer almost in the water, and curling down at night, as the animals do, in any corner they can find . . . this is without a doubt in the blood of most children—as an inheritance, perhaps from some remote barbarian ancestor—a passion for roving. (Rivlin and Manzo 1988: 27–28)

By the 1950s, popular perceptions of this same population were influenced by notions of psychological deviance, and street youth were thought to be mentally disturbed (Rivlin and Manzo 1988). Robertson (1992: 288) describes the common psychiatric understanding of homeless youth that helped shape the image of this population in the 1950s and 1960s, during a period when psychoanalysis was at the forefront of accepted wisdom:

> Individuals characteristically escape from threatening situations by running away from home for a day or more without permission . . . typically they are immature and timid and often feel rejected at home, inadequate, friendless. They often steal furtively.

The present day image of street kids is that of the sexually and/ or physically abused runaway. Ruddick's (1996) comprehensive analysis of homeless youth in Hollywood highlights a series of changes from the 1970s onward that were responsible for the shift away from the image of the street youth as a *juvenile delinquent* and *criminal*. The deinstitutionalization of the runaway from the juvenile penal system, combined with an increase in public recognition of the reality of abuse within dysfunctional families and the lack of employment and shelter opportunities, all played central roles in the transformation of the popular perception of street youth (Karabanow 2000). A crucial outcome of those changes was the novel awareness that these children had been forgotten or had 'slipped through the cracks' of the conventional child welfare system. The street kid/homeless youth of today evokes varied images that include young mothers, runaways, immigrant youth and squeegee kids. A single, though significant, element binding these perceptions together is the growing acceptance that youth are homeless because of reasons beyond their own control. A study of street youth in Halifax found that over 60 percent of public citizens interviewed perceived the root causes of youth homelessness as other than individual pathology (Karabanow 2004b). Today's street kid is often thought to be fleeing an abusive, dysfunctional family life or a miserable institutional situation and finding refuge on the street or in a short-term emergency shelter.

## Etiology

In the past 20 years, a consensus has emerged around the pathways to youth homelessness. There is growing agreement that for the most part, homeless youth are 'running away' from problematic and traumatic environments rather than 'running towards' street cultures (Karabanow 2003). The major commonality lies in various forms of troubled/strained family histories. High rates of drug and alcohol abuse and criminality are found among the parents of many homeless youth (Hagan and McCarthy 1997; MacLean, Embry and Cauce 1999). Poverty is a prominent finding with a high percentage of the families on social assistance (Ringwalt, Greene and Robertson 1998) and disrupted families are common, with few homeless youth reporting having lived with both biological parents (Hagan and McCarthy 1997). Also common are reports of marital discord (Dadds et al. 1993), domestic violence and a greater than average number of household moves involving frequent changes of school (Buckner and Bassuk 1997; Karabanow 2004a). Reports of childhood physical and sexual abuse are consistently high, as are histories of emotional abuse and neglect (Karabanow 2003, 2004a; Kidd 2006; MacLean, Embry and Cauce 1999; Molnar et al. 1998; Ringwalt, Greene and Robertson 1998). These negative home experiences intersect with a host of other problems, including poor performance in school, conflict with teachers and other adults in positions of authority and conduct problems (Feitel et al. 1992; Hagan and McCarthy 1997; Rotheram-Borus 1993).

Another disturbing finding is that street youth populations in numerous studies speak to problematic child welfare placements as a major reason for their entry into street life (Karabanow 2003, 2004a, 2008; Kurtz, Jarvis and Kurtz 1991; van der Ploeg 1989). These experiences were most often described as uncaring, exploitative and unstable (Michaud 1989; Raychaba 1989). Numerous moves from group home to group home or between foster parents, coupled with feelings of being treated as 'criminals', 'delinquents' or 'unwanted', shaped young people's transition to street life (Edney 1988a, 1988b; Morrisette and MacIntyre 1989). Child welfare settings were routinely described by young people as unresponsive to their needs and perceived as 'prison' environments rather than loving and home-like structures (Raychaba 1989). Street life became an enticing option for young people who either experienced episodes of 'running away' from or graduating from child welfare placements. Finally, in line with the above body of research, most homeless youths with mental illness on the streets report that their mental illness began prior to their leaving home and, not surprisingly, was exacerbated by street living (Craig and Hodson 1998; Karabanow et al. 2007).

One topic that has been largely absent throughout the discussion of youth homelessness in the media and in research is diversity. Similar to other subcultures, the culture of street life is diverse and complex. Street youth are equally diverse in terms of background, present experiences and future aspirations. Labels such as *squeegee kids, punks, street-entrenched, group-home, in-and-outers, runaways* or *shelter youth* are used in the literature as an attempt to make sense of the diverse population and to organize analytical discussions (see, e.g., Kufeldt and Nimmo 1987; McCarthy 1990; Morrisette and McIntyre 1989; Shane 1989; van der Ploeg 1989). Only a few studies have addressed the implications and outcomes of various subgroups of homeless youth. Kipke and colleagues (1997) typologized homeless youths into five groups: punks, gang members, loners, hustlers (sex trade involved youth) and druggies, with the participants indicating which group they most strongly identified with. It was found that group affiliation had a major impact on residential status (e.g., punks are more likely to live on the streets or in an abandoned building), subsistence pattern (e.g., gang members are more involved in drug dealing) and service use (e.g., hustlers are most often accessed by outreach workers). In line with Kipke's work, studies looking at the experiences of sex trade involved youth have highlighted the unique risks and heightened discrimination experienced by these youth (Cusick 2002; Kidd and Kral 2002; Kidd and Liborio 2011; Yates et al. 1991). Those who use the sex trade as a primary source of income and become associated with it as an identity have markedly poorer mental health and far worse trajectories of risk than most other youth.

Some studies in the past few years have also started to take a closer look at gender and sexual orientation on the streets. It has been found that, relative to boys, girls have more extensive sexual abuse histories, are more often sexually victimized on the streets and have a harder time subsisting on the streets (Cauce et al. 2000; Karabanow 2004a; O'Grady and Gaetz 2004). Youth with lesbian, gay, bisexual or transgendered (LGBT) sexual orientation are in many cases homeless because of abuse and rejection by family who are intolerant of their revealing and exploring their sexual orientation (Karabanow 2008). LGBT youth have more often been abused at home, are victimized more often on the streets and generally have poorer mental health and greater involvement in risk activities relative to other homeless youth (Noell and Ochs 2001; Kruks 1991; Cochran et al. 2002).

In sum, the vast majority of youth become homeless due to external circumstances. For the most part, these are young people who have rarely experienced a stable, loving family unit—rarely did they feel loved, cared for, supported or experience a sense of belonging. As such, it is of little wonder why street life is consistently perceived by the vast majority of the street youth population as a safer and more stable environment than home.

## Street Contexts and Cultures

Complementing the large body of work documenting pathways to homelessness, a substantial body of work has developed in recent years documenting risks and subsistence strategies on the streets. This line of work has revealed diverse, complex and, at times, contradictory narratives of survival among homeless youth. While street life may be perceived initially as a place of freedom, community and relative security, these feelings quickly fade or become demystified (Karabanow 2006, 2008; Visano 1990). As such, street cultures present complex and often dichotomous narratives; they can be sites of excitement, belonging and acceptance as well as exploitation, violence, hunger, boredom and stress (Karabanow 2003, 2006; Karabanow et al. 2007). Much of the literature has focused upon these negative attributes of street culture. More recent focus of academic investigations has explored street youth survival strategies (Karabanow et al. 2009; O'Grady and Greene 2003).

To support themselves, homeless youth engage in numerous activities including employment seeking, seeking money from family/ friends, panhandling, prostitution, survival sex (sex for food, shelter etc.), dealing drugs and theft (Greene, Ennett and Ringwalt 1999; Hagan and McCarthy 1997; Kipke et al. 1997). The difficulty of surviving on the streets is evident in the large number of homeless youth who regularly lack shelter and go hungry (Antoniades and Tarasuk 1998). Moreover, street life presents numerous dangers and stresses in the form of physical and sexual assaults and other types of victimization (Karabanow et al. 2007; Whitbeck, Hoyt and Bao 2000). Drug abuse is a common way of coping with these stressors (Adlaf, Zdanowicz and Smart 1996; Karabanow et al. 2007), and addiction is a major problem among this population (Greene and Ringwalt 1996). There is a high incidence of mental disorders among homeless youth, with depression, post-traumatic stress disorder and suicidal behaviours highlighted as common problem areas (Karabanow et al. 2007; Kidd 2004; Whitbeck, Hoyt and Bao 2000; Yoder 1999). Mortality rates for these youth have been found to be 12 to 40 times that of the general population (Shaw and Dorling 1998), with suicide and drug overdose having been found as the leading cause of death among Canadian homeless youth (Roy et al. 2004). In general, it has been found that victimization and decline in physical and mental health on the streets would seem to occur as a function of the degree of victimization in the lives of homeless youth prior to coming to the streets.

Youths characterize their lives on the streets, for the most part, as unhealthy, difficult, boring, requiring an unrelenting effort to meet basic needs, violent and dangerous and lonely and exploitative (Karabanow et al. 2007; Karabanow 2004a; Kidd 2004). However, the street continues to be seen by many as the best option in their lives, especially within the context of their youth, poverty, low self-esteem/ confidence, instability, lack of education and lack of employment/life skills (Karabanow 2008). They are consistently in survival mode— spending much of their talents, energies and resources securing food, shelter, clothing, emotional support and some form of formal or informal employment. Travel makes up some of their activity—moving from place to place, city to city, province to province—for the most part searching for, first, better supports; second, a new environment (in order to clean up, escape problematic situations, etc.); and, third, building different communities (punk, squatter, squeegee) (Karabanow 2006; Karabanow et al. 2007). While the majority of these young people work in informal or formal sectors, employment tends to be sporadic, fluid and uncompromising (Karabanow et al. 2009). Some seek out jobs as day labourers, others squeegee/pan to survive, others perform on the street (playing music), others act as drug peddlers, while others sell their bodies. Work is important to this population, providing a means to survive and/or a means to feel good about themselves (Karabanow et al. 2009).

Finally, youths describe extensive experiences with social stigma. Most regularly experience insulting interactions with the general public based upon their appearance and homeless status, and stigmatization extends to difficulty finding work and housing and to criminalization (Kidd 2003, 2004; Karabanow 2004a; Karabanow et al. 2009; Schissel 1997). Numerous studies have highlighted how street youth feel outside of civil society, alienated from mainstream culture and without a sense of belonging or acceptance (e.g., Kidd and Davidson 2007). This stigma is particularly salient for visibly homeless youth and youths who face multiple forms of stigma based on other aspects of identity (e.g., sexual minorities) and activities (e.g., sex trade involved youth) and has been linked to a greater risk of suicide and negative mental health outcomes (Kidd 2006).

The topics of resilience, strength and survival have increasingly been addressed in the North American youth homelessness literature. The coping literature has highlighted several themes which emerged in this study including self-reliance, the support of other youth, spirituality and caring for others (Karabanow 2003, 2004a, 2008; Kidd 2003; Lindsey et al. 2000; Rew and Horner 2003; Williams et al. 2001). There has also been some emerging work addressing the deeper identity and cultural shifts that determine how homeless youth understand and experience their world which, in turn, defines and drives their coping efforts (Karabanow 2006; Visano 1990). In a large study examining the experiences of youth in New York City and Toronto, Kidd and Davidson (2007) highlighted the manner in which coping efforts were framed within youths testing, adopting and rejecting the various meaning systems made available in the street context. This adaptation, or the particular version of 'normal' used, has major implications for their trajectories on and off the streets. For youths who don't take on street value systems and norms, the streets are far more difficult to survive in and these youth are much more motivated to make use of services to exit the street. For those who take on one or more of the value systems/subcultures on the streets, they might experience a better quality of life in the street context but also face far greater risks and are more difficult to engage in interventions (e.g., youths for whom sex trade work has become the norm). Such meaning systems are typically challenged many times over the course of youths' time on the streets in the face of any number of contradictions: friends prove untrustworthy, serious criminal charges arise, health fails, assaults occur, addictions take over, caring and respected supports describe other ways of living that are more meaningful and healthier. However it is described, be it shift in worldview, value systems, or culture, it is the person's own view of their world that sets the nature and parameters of their coping, efforts to survive and sources of happiness.

## Street Disengagement

While much of the literature concerning street youth has focused upon trajectories onto the streets and youths' efforts to survive in street contexts, there have been few systematic analyses of strategies employed by this population to disengage from homelessness. Karabanow and colleages (2005) and Karabanow (2006, 2008) explored how Canadian street youth successfully and unsuccessfully disengaged from street culture through in-depth qualitative interviews with youth and service providers in Halifax, Montreal, Ottawa, Toronto, Calgary and Vancouver. A comprehensive portrait of street exiting involves numerous stages or dimensions:

> 1. *Precipitating Factors:* The precipitating factors that propel contemplation of street disengagement tend to include the experience of a traumatic event (such as physical/sexual assault, drug overdoses, witness of street violence or involvement with the criminal justice system), becoming disenchanted with street culture and/or becoming worn down, physically, emotionally and/or spiritually, by daily street existence.

2. *Courage to Change:* Layer two involves the individual's courage to change and this was highly influenced by such factors as increased responsibility (becoming pregnant, having an intimate partner or recognition that someone was dependent on them), having someone who cares, having support from family and/or friends and being internally motivated and committed to street transitioning. Young people talked about having "strong will power" to combat impressive obstacles like drug addiction, trauma and lack of supports. Knowing someone truly cares for you, or having steady support builds motivation.

3. *Seeking Support:* The third step is highly interrelated with layer two and involves seeking available support (primarily in relation to housing and employment) within the initial stages of street disembarking. This aspect is about asking for help—being able to use available services and being able to articulate one's needs, in many instances, to service providers.

4. *Transitioning away from the Street:* Layer four deals with transitioning away from the street and entailed physically leaving the downtown core, reducing ties with street culture and street friends and constructing or reconstructing relationships with mainstream society. Cutting street ties meant leaving friends, surrogate families and a culture associated with the downtown core. Participants expressed that it was as difficult leaving the street culture/street friends as it was entering into the more mainstream society and building new relationships. Despite the emotional strains of leaving relationships with people who had helped support them on the street, building new relationships outside of street culture was highlighted as essential for healthy transitioning. New friends and communities tended to be seen by participants as "good influences" in their day-to-day living. But this transitional time was also characterized by feelings of loneliness and uncertainty.

5. *Restructuring:* Next there is a clear restructuring of one's routine in terms of employment, education and housing; a shift in thinking about future aspirations; and the ability to acquire some form of financial assistance to support one's transitioning. During this stage, young people highlighted a renewed sense of health/wellness, self-confidence and personal motivation. Participants described both physical

and psychological shifts occurring in their lives, such as sleeping better, feeling healthier and experiencing increased self-esteem and self-confidence. Such changes tended to be linked to young people having more stability and consistency in their lives. Shifts in routine were commonly seen as interwoven with the notion of building new communities and tended to focus upon replacing street activities with formal employment and returning to school. However, subtle day-to-day shifts in routine (such as waking up and making some coffee or coming home and watching television) were as celebrated as more tangible elements such as living in one's own apartment or going to work each day. These transitions allowed many youth to reflect upon their past experiences, and for the majority of participants, this meant perceiving the street as an unhealthy and destructive environment. Along with a healthier sense of self, young people were more ready to develop longer-term plans and envision some control in their futures.

6. *Successful Exiting:* The final stage primarily embodies young people's emotional and spiritual sense of identity. "Successful exiting" was exemplified by a sense of "being in control" and "having direction" in one's life. The majority of participants spoke of feeling proud of their movements out of street life, being able to finally enjoy life on their own terms, having healthy self-esteem and self-confidence, being able to take care of themselves and feeling stable in terms of both housing/security and wellness. "Getting off the street" translated into more than simply finding an apartment and physically removing oneself from a street lifestyle. Truly becoming an "ex-street youth" entailed emotional and spiritual shifts within the individual.

Challenges and obstacles pepper young people's travels throughout these layers of street exiting. Structural and personal barriers include drug and alcohol addictions, past and present traumas, mental health issues, discrimination, lack of reasonable employment, a dearth of affordable housing stock, loneliness and isolation and the often difficult process of breaking ties with street culture and street friends. At times, these challenges appear monumental and young people are forced back to the street an average of six times; however, with the support of innovative and caring service providers throughout the country, each exiting attempt creates greater distance, both physically and emotionally, between them and street culture (Karabanow 2008).

## Intervention

There exists a vast array of shelters, drop-ins, clinics and other emergency services that do primary basic-needs support, some outreach/ prevention and short term counselling. Unfortunately, relative to the large body of research literature describing homeless youth and their various risk trajectories, there are very few studies and informal descriptions of services, their strengths and limitations. The literature developed to date tends to cluster around the following areas.

### Basic Needs and Physical Health

Many researchers recommend that the first priority is to ensure that youths are provided with the basic necessities of life in an immediate fashion (Cauce et al. 1994; Karabanow and Clement 2004; Terrell 1997). This includes assistance with obtaining adequate food, shelter and attention to physical ailments. Assessment of needs in this area is crucial, with many suffering from multiple health problems, including poor nutrition (Antoniades and Tarasuk 1998; Yates et al. 1991). Related to health issues, there is a need to ensure that youth are educated regarding the risks of communicable diseases, unprotected sex and sharing needles, by both peers and trusted workers or other individuals whose opinions are respected (Booth, Zhang and Kwiatkowski 1999; Ensign and Gittelsohn 1998; Greene and Ringwalt 1996). Of the intervention strategies that focus on interventions to reduce sexually transmitted disease, peer-based strategies have been found to increase street youths' HIV knowledge (Podschun 1993). Tenner and colleagues (1998) described an intensive case management approach with HIV-positive youth, noting the importance of a flexible and responsive service system that responds to both the medical and other social service needs of its clients. A recent study has also shown that cognitive behavioural intervention that focuses on skill building and education was more effective than treatment as usual in increasing condom use (Slesnick and Kang 2008). Lastly, researchers have highlighted the importance of making prenatal education and care available given the high rates of pregnancy among street-involved youth (Greene and Ringwalt 1998).

### Drug Use and Addiction

Assessment of substance use is regarded as a necessary aspect of services for homeless youths given the extremely high rates of alcohol and drug use (Baron 1999). It is important to recognize that the mechanisms underlying substance abuse may differ greatly from youth to youth. MacLean, Embry and Cauce (1999) have found different motives for drug use as a function of gender and other factors such as affect regulation. Several researchers caution, however, that too heavy a focus on drug use alone is ineffective and that drug use is likely a symptom of other problems that need to be addressed just as urgently (Adlaf, Zdanowicz and Smart 1996; Sibthorpe et al. 1995). With respect to specific interventions, Natasha Slesnick has done a considerable amount of work in the area of family therapy. She has found that ecologically based family therapy, with both family and individual sessions focused on decision-making, emotion regulation or other intrapersonal factors, results in greater reductions in substance use when compared with treatment as usual (Slesnick and Prestopnik 2005). Several studies in this area have also discussed motivational intervention as a model for working with substance-using street youth (Baer, Peterson and Wells 2004), with findings indicating a sustained reduction in substance use following a brief group-based motivational enhancement intervention (Peterson et al. 2006). Lastly, peer-led groups have also been cited as more effective for substance-using homeless youths than adult-led groups (Fors and Jarvis 1995). While concurrent mental illness and addictions problems are undoubtedly present in this group, integrated treatment models have yet to receive substantial attention in the research literature.

### Mental Health

Many researchers stress the importance of screening for symptoms of mental health problems. Specifically, it has been suggested that workers screen for suicidality, depression and histories of maltreatment and abuse, which are potentially indicative of increased vulnerability (Kidd 2006; Kurtz, Jarvis and Kurtz 1991; Ringwalt, Greene and Robertson 1998; Rotheram-Borus 1993; Stiffman 1989; Yoder 1999; Yoder et al. 1998). It has also been recommended that interventions be tailored to specific subpopulations of youth. For example, Cauce and colleagues (2000) recommended that service providers working with males who have experienced physical violence and are more likely to have conduct-related problems develop interventions that focus on limit setting and impulse control. Other recommendations include training in a wide range of best practice approaches to mental health intervention for staff (Cauce et al. 2000), the integration of peers as supports (Fisk, Rowe and Brooks 2000) and the importance of providing effective interventions for trauma in mental health counselling with this population (McManus and Thompson 2008). Outcome research on specific mental health interventions for this group are, however, very rare. One exception is an evaluation of the Community Reinforcement Approach (CRA), which used a cognitive behavioural approach to address the systematic challenges faced by youth and demonstrated better outcomes than treatment as usual across a number of domains (Slesnick et al. 2007).

### Housing

The most common housing service for street youth is short-term emergency shelters that provide basic sleeping arrangements and often case management support/guidance. These shelters proliferated in the seventies and eighties due to the growing number of runaways and street kids in need of a safe refuge. Alleva (1988) and Karabanow (1999, 2000, 2004) argue that these shelters were portrayed as alternatives for youth who mistrusted traditional services. While street youth have objected to particular sets of rules and structures within shelters, for the most part, they have perceived such settings as surrogate families and its workers as highly supportive (Alleva 1988; Karabanow 2004a). Karabanow (2003, 2008) has argued that the vast diversity of street youth shelters are for the most part "symbolic spaces" for troubled and alienated youth to find acceptance/belonging, satisfy immediate basic needs, explore options for street exiting, manage personal traumas and structural challenges and gain self esteem and confidence. However, access is generally more complicated for youths with addictions who do not view abstinence-focused shelters as a viable option (Krusi et al. 2010).

### Service Provider Perspectives

With respect to service provider perspectives on their work, a study of the narratives of 15 youth workers in Toronto suggested that what they viewed as effective revolved mostly around their relationships with clients (Kidd et al. 2007). Themes included a need to have a versatile approach that can be tailored to an individual youth's circumstances and establishing a connection based upon valuing, respecting and 'liking' youths. This trusting relationship was, in turn, essential; youths are drawn to that rare experience of trust, which serves as a platform for effective work. Youth workers also described the challenges associated with working with street-involved youth. These challenges included the complexity of the needs of youths, the various barriers that exist as a function of social stigma and marginalization and the minimal resources available to do the work. These challenges can readily lead to burnout and high staff turnover, both of which can negatively affect the services provided.

## Policy

Of the range of factors involved in youth homelessness, socio-cultural and policy issues have arguably received the least attention in the literature. This circumstance exists despite emerging evidence that social stigma at both public (e.g., insults, physical assaults, etc.) and structural levels (e.g., multiple arrests, inadequate funding for services, etc.) have a profound impact on the health and well-being of this population (Karabanow 2004a; Kidd 2003; Kidd and Carroll 2007; Schissel 1997). Specific difficulties present in the Canadian context include, first, difficulty accessing income support, unemployment insurance and disability payments; second, increasing criminalization and disproportionate arrests; third, declines in affordable housing, difficulty accessing socially supported housing and increasing evictions; fourth, breakdowns in continuity of care due to child welfare service age cutoffs (ranging from 16 to 19) and youth services age cutoffs (typically 24); and, finally, a lack of services specific to the needs of homeless youths, such as adequate discharge planning from health care and criminal justice systems (Kidd and Davidson 2006). Additionally, prevention efforts, which are almost ubiquitously called for across all forums, have yet to materialize and be evaluated in a substantive manner.

At the policy level, there are a range of approaches that might serve to reduce both the extent of youth homelessness and the degree of risk faced by homeless youths. Such strategies might include reducing criminalization of minor non-violent and victimless crimes (e.g., panhandling), as this serves to hamper access to public assistance and supported housing. Underlying such an argument is the need to initiate preventive structures that tap into the true reasons for youth homelessness: child welfare failures, poverty, family distress, abuse and neglect and violence. We need thoughtful educational strategies (such as runaway prevention programs carried out by numerous street youth organizations) to disentangle myths and stereotypes as to why these young people enter street life and remain on the street.

Another need area is the provision of sustained funding that is commensurate with both the extent of the problem in terms of number of homeless youth and the complexity of their needs. At present, most services operate within budget restrictions that markedly hamper their ability to provide the sorts of comprehensive approaches highlighted in the review above. Furthermore, the fierce competition that exists for the small amount of funding available in a given city can impede inter-agency cooperation. Numerous scholars have argued for the emergence of thoughtful long-term structural development initiatives including supportive and independent housing and meaningful employment opportunities (see, for example, Karabanow 2008; Kidd and Davidson 2006). There are many case examples throughout North America of innovative linkages between government, business and non-profit sectors to build such initiatives (e.g., Montreal's Dans La Rue, Toronto's Covenant House and Eva's Place and Calgary's Open Door). Young people have been unequivocal about the need for safe and sustainable housing in order to seek out employment opportunities.

## Conclusion

The last twenty years have witnessed a more sympathetic perspective on homeless youth in both the academic literature and popular media. Rather than being seen as social misfits, increasingly they are understood as victims of social structures. The academic literature reviewed makes it clear that street youth are a highly marginalized and alienated population, and forms of intervention that attempt to support, care for and show genuine interest towards these adolescents have the best chance of proving successful.

We conclude that youth homelessness is fundamentally a systemic problem that requires a systemic response. We highlight the key domains that would form such a response, but how such an effort might be undertaken in a coherent and coordinated manner is less clear. We suggest that, following the example of the Mental Health Commission of Canada, a body be formed that cuts across research, policy and practice sectors to facilitate a coordinated response to youth homelessness and stimulate partnerships. Until such a response is developed, we will continue to have young people funnelling through pathways of inadequate supports onto our streets—at profound personal and social cost.

## References

Adlaf, E. M., Y. M. Zdanowicz and R. G. Smart. 1996. "Alcohol and Other Drug Use among Street-Involved Youth in Toronto." *Addiction Research & Theory,* 4(1): 11–24.

Alleva, F. 1988. "Youth at Risk, Systems in Crisis: A Dialogue with Youth who Needed Shelter." PhD dissertation, Education, Boston University.

Antoniades, M. and V. Tarasuk. 1998. "A Survey of Food Problems Experienced by Toronto Street Youth." *Canadian Journal of Public Health,* 89: 371–75.

Baer, J., P. Peterson and E. Wells. 2004. "Rationale and Design of a Brief Substance Use Intervention for Homeless Adolescents." *Addiction Research and Theory,* 12: 317–34.

Baron, S. W. 1999. "Street Youths and Substance Use: The Role of Background, Street Lifestyle, and Economic Factors." *Youth & Society,* 31: 3–26.

Booth, R. E., Y. Zhang and C. F. Kwiatkowski. 1999. "The Challenge of Changing Drug and Sex Risk Behaviors of Runaway and Homeless Adolescents." *Child Abuse & Neglect,* 23: 1295–1306.

Buckner, J. C. and E. L. Bassuk, 1997. "Mental Disorders and Service Utilization among Youths from Homeless and Low-Income Families." *Journal of the American Academy of Child & Adolescent Psychiatry,* 36(7): 890–900.

Buckner, J. C., E. L. Bassuk, L. F. Weinreb and M. G. Brooks. 1999. "Homelessness and Its Relation to the Mental Health and Behavior of Low-Income School-Age Children." *Developmental Psychology,* 35: 246–57.

Cauce, A. M., C. J. Morgan, V. Wagner, E. Moore, J. Sy, K. Wurzbacher, K. Weeden, S. Tomlin and T. Blanchard. 1994. "Effectiveness of Intensive Case Management for Homeless Adolescents: Results of a 3-Month Follow-Up." *Journal of Emotional and Behavioral Disorders,* 2: 219–27.

Cauce, A. M., M. Paradise, J. A. Ginzler, L. Embry, C. Morgan, Y. Lohr and J. Theofolis. 2000. "The Characteristics and Mental Health of Homeless Adolescents: Age and Gender Differences." *Journal of Emotional and Behavioral Disorders,* 8: 230–39.

Cochran, B. N., A. J. Stewart, J. A. Ginzler and A. M. Cauce. 2002. "Challenges Faced by Homeless Sexual Minorities: Comparison of Gay, Lesbian, Bisexual, and Transgender Homeless Adolescents with

Their Heterosexual Counterparts." *American Journal of Public Health,* 92: 773–77.

Craig, K. J. T. and S. Hodson. 1998. "Homeless Youth in London: I. Childhood Antecedents and Psychiatric Disorder." *Psychological Medicine,* 28(6): 1379–88.

Cusick, L. 2002. "Youth Prostitution: A Literature Review." *Child Abuse Review,* 11: 230–51.

Dadds, M., D. Braddock, S. Cuers, A. Elliott and A. Kelly. 1993. "Personal and Family Distress in Homeless Adolescents." *Community Mental Health Journal,* 29: 413–22.

Edney, R. 1988a. "The Impact of Sexual Abuse on Adolescent Females Who Prostitute." In *Dead End,* ed. M. Michaud. Calgary: Detselig Enterprises Ltd., 25–36.

Edney, R. 1988b. "Successful Experiences." In *Dead End,* ed. M. Michaud. Calgary: Detselig Enterprises Ltd., 67–72.

Ensign, J. and J. Gittelsohn. 1998. "Health and Access to Care: Perspectives of Homeless Youth in Baltimore City, U.S.A." *Social Science & Medicine,* 47: 2087–99.

Feitel, B., N. Margetson, J. Chamas and C. Lipman. 1992. "Psychosocial Background and Behavioral and Emotional Disorders of Homeless and Runaway Youth." *Hospital and Community Psychiatry,* 43: 155–59.

Fisk, D., M. Rowe and R. Brooks. 2000. "Integrating Consumer Staff Members into a Homeless Outreach Project: Critical Issues and Strategies." *Psychiatric Rehabilitation Journal,* 23: 244–52.

Fors, S. and S. Jarvis. 1995. "Evaluation of a Peer-Led Drug Abuse Reduction Project for Runaway/Homeless Youths." *Journal of Drug Education,* 25: 321–33.

Greene, J. M. and C. L. Ringwalt. 1998. "Pregnancy among Three Samples of Runaway and Homeless Youth." *Journal of Adolescent Health,* 23(6): 370–77.

_____. 1996. "Youth and Familial Substance Use's Association with Suicide Attempts among Runaway and Homeless Youth." *Substance Use & Misuse,* 31(8): 1041–58.

Greene, J. M., S. T. Ennett and C. L. Ringwalt. 1999. "Prevalence and Correlates of Survival Sex among Runaway and Homeless Youth." *American Journal of Public Health,* 89: 1406–09.

Hagan, J. and B. McCarthy. 1997. *Mean Streets: Youth Crime and Homelessness.* Cambridge, UK: Cambridge University Press.

Karabanow, J. 2008. "Getting Off the Street: Exploring Young People's Street Exits." *American Behavioral Scientist,* 51(6): 772–88.

_____. 2006. "Becoming a Street Youth: Uncovering the Stages to Street Life." *Journal of Human Behavior in the Social Environment,* 13(2): 49–72.

_____. 2004a. *Being Young and Homeless: Understanding How Youth Enter and Exit Street Life*. New York: Peter Lang.

_____. 2004b. *Exploring Salient Issues of Youth Homelessness in Halifax, Nova Scotia*. Human Resources Development Canada Report.

_____. 2003. "Creating a Culture of Hope: Lessons from Street Children Agencies in Canada and Guatemala." *International Social Work*, 46(3): 369–86.

_____. 2000. "A Place for All Seasons: Examining Youth Shelters and The Youth-in-Trouble Network in Toronto." PhD dissertation, Social Work, Wilfrid Laurier University.

_____. 1999. "Creating Community: A Case Study of a Montreal Street Kid Agency." *Community Development Journal*, 34(4): 318–27.

Karabanow, J. and P. Clement. 2004. "Interventions with Street Youth: A Commentary on the Practice-Based Research Literature." *Brief Treatment and Crisis Intervention*, 4(1): 93–108.

Karabanow, J., P. Clement, A. Carson and K. Crane. 2005. *Getting Off the Street: Exploring Strategies Used by Canadian Youth to Exit Street Life*. Halifax: The National Homelessness Initiative, National Research Program.

Karabanow, J., S. Hopkins, S. Kisely, J. Parker, J. Hughes, J. Gahagan and L. A. Campbell. 2007. "Can You Be Healthy on the Street?: Exploring the Health Experiences of Halifax Street Youth." *The Canadian Journal of Urban Research*, 16(1): 12–32.

Karabanow, J., J. Ticknor, J. Hughes, S. Kidd and D. Patterson. 2009. *Working within Formal and Informal Economies: How Homeless Youth Survive in Neo-liberal Times*. Human Resources and Social Development Canada Report.

Kidd, S. A. 2007. "Youth Homelessness and Social Stigma." *Journal of Youth and Adolescence*, 36: 291–99.

_____. 2006. "Factors Precipitating Suicidality among Homeless Youth: A Quantitative Follow-Up." *Youth & Society*, 37: 393–422.

_____. 2004. "'The Walls Were Closing in and We Were Trapped': A Qualitative Analysis of Street Youth Suicide." *Youth & Society*, 36: 30–55.

_____. 2003. "Street Youth: Coping and Interventions." *Child and Adolescent Social Work Journal*, 20: 235–61.

Kidd, S. A. and M. Carroll. 2007. "Coping and Suicidality among Homeless Youth." *Journal of Adolescence*, 30: 283–96.

Kidd, S. A. and L. Davidson. 2007. "'You Have to Adapt Because You Have No Other Choice': The Stories of Strength and Resilience of 208 Homeless Youth in New York City and Toronto." *Journal of Community Psychology*, 35: 219–38.

_____. 2006. "Youth Homelessness: A Call for Partnerships between Research and Policy." *Canadian Journal of Public Health*, 97: 445–47.

Kidd, S. A. and M. J. Kral. 2002. "Street Youth Suicide and Prostitution: A Qualitative Analysis." *Adolescence*, 37: 411–30.

Kidd, S. A. and R. Liborio. 2011. "Sex Trade Involvement in Sao Paulo, Brazil and Toronto, Canada: Narratives of Social Exclusion and Fragmented Identities." *Youth & Society,* 43(3): 982–1009.

Kidd, S. A. and K. Scrimenti. 2004. "The New Haven Homeless Count: Children and Youth." *Evaluation Review,* 28: 325–41.

Kidd, S. A., S. Miner, D. Walker and L. Davidson. 2007. "Stories of Working with Homeless Youth: On Being 'Mind-Boggling.'" *Children and Youth Services Review,* 29: 16–34.

Kipke, M. D., J. B. Unger, S. O'Connor, R. F. Palmer and S. R. LaFrance. 1997. "Street Youth, Their Peer Group Affiliation and Differences According to Residential Status, Subsistence Patterns, and Use of Services." *Adolescence,* 32: 655–69.

Kruks, G. 1991. "Gay and Lesbian Homeless/Street Youth: Special Issues and Concerns." *Journal of Adolescent Health,* 12: 515–18.

Krusi, A., D. Fast, W. Small, E. Wood and T. Kerr. 2010. "Social and Structural Barriers to Housing among Street Involved Youth Who Use Illicit Drugs." *Health and Social Care in the Community,* 18: 282–88.

Kufeldt, K. and M. Nimmo. 1987. "Youth on the Street." *Child Abuse & Neglect,* 11(4): 531–43.

Kurtz, P. D., S. V. Jarvis and G. L. Kurtz. 1991. "Problems of Homeless Youth." *Social Work,* 36(4): 309–14.

Lindsey, E. W., D. Kurtz, S. Jarvis, N. R. Williams and L. Nackerud. 2000. "How Runaways and Homeless Youth Navigate Troubled Waters: Personal Strengths and Resources." *Child and Adolescent Social Work Journal,* 17: 115–40.

MacLean, M. G., L. E. Embry and A. M. Cauce. 1999. "Homeless Adolescents' Paths to Separation from Family: Comparison of Family Characteristics, Psychological Adjustment, and Victimization." *Journal of Community Psychology,* 27: 179–87.

McCarthy, W. 1990. "Life on the Streets." PhD dissertation, Sociology, University of Toronto.

McManus, H. and S. Thomson. 2008. "Trauma among Unaccompanied Homeless Youth: The Integration of Street Culture into a Model of Intervention." *Journal of Aggression, Maltreatment, and Trauma,* 16: 92–109.

Michaud, M. 1989. *Dead End.* Calgary: Detselig Enterprises Ltd.

Molnar, B. E., S. B. Shade, A. H. Kral, R. E. Booth and J. K. Watters. 1998. "Suicidal Behavior and Sexual/Physical Abuse among Street Youth." *Child Abuse & Neglect,* 22: 213–22.

Morrissette, P. and S. McIntyre. 1989. "Homeless Youth in Residential Care." *Social Casework,* 20: 165–88.

Noell, J. W. and L. M Ochs. 2001. "Relationship of Sexual Orientation to Substance Use, Suicidal Ideation, Suicide Attempts, and Other Factors in a Population of Homeless Adolescents." *Journal of Adolescent Health,* 29: 31–36.

National Homelessness Initiative. 2006. "A Snapshot of Homelessness in Canada." [on-line]. www.homelessness.gc.ca [consulted June 10, 2010].

O'Grady, B. and S. Gaetz. 2004. "Homelessness, Gender and Subsistence: The Case of Toronto Street Youth." *Journal of Youth Studies,* 7(4): 397–416.

O'Grady, B. and C. Greene. 2003. "A Social and Economic Impact Study of the Ontario Safe Streets Act on Toronto Squeegee Workers." *Online Journal of Justice Issues,* 1(1): 1–8.

Peterson, P., J. Baer, E. Wells, J. Ginzler and Sharon Garrett. 2006. "Short-Term Effects of a Brief Motivational Intervention to Reduce Alcohol and Drug Risk among Homeless Adolescents." *Psychology of Addictive Behaviors,* 20: 254–64.

Podschun, G. 1993. "Teen Peer Outreach-Street Work Project: HIV Prevention Education for Runaway and Homeless Youth." *Public Health Reports,* 108: 150–55.

Raychaba, B. 1989. "Canadian Youth in Care." *Children and Youth Services Review,* 11: 61–73.

Rew, L. and S. D. Horner. 2003. "Personal Strengths of Homeless Adolescents Living in a High-Risk Environment." *Advances in Nursing Science,* 26: 90–101.

Ringwalt, C. L., J. M. Greene and M. J. Robertson. 1998. "Familial Backgrounds and Risk Behaviors of Youth with Throwaway Experiences." *Journal of Adolescence,* 21: 421–52.

Rivlin, L. G. and L. Manzo. 1988. "Homeless Children in N.Y. City: A View from the 19th Century." *Children's Environment Quarterly,* 5: 26–33.

Robertson, J. 1992. "Homeless and Runaway Youth: A Review of the Literature." In *Homelessness: A National Perspective,* ed. M. Robertson and M. Greenblatt. New York: Plenum Press, 287–97.

Rotheram-Borus, M. J. 1993. "Suicidal Behavior and Risk Factors among Runaway Youths." *American Journal of Psychiatry,* 150: 103–07.

Roy, E., N. Haley, P. Leclerc, B. Sochanski, J. Boudreau and J. Boivin. 2004. "Mortality in a Cohort of Street Youth in Montreal." *Journal of the American Medical Association,* 292: 569–74.

Ruddick, S. 1996. *Young and Homeless in Hollywood.* New York: Routledge.

Schissel B. 1997. *Blaming Children.* Halifax: Fernwood.

Shane, P. 1989. "Changing Patterns among Homeless and Runaway Youth." *American Journal of Orthopsychiatry,* 59(2): 208–14.

Shaw, M. and D. Dorling. 1998. "Mortality among Street Youth in the UK." *Lancet,* 352: 743.

Sibthorpe, B., J. Drinkwater, K. Gardner and G. Bammer. 1995. "Drug Use, Binge Drinking and Attempted Suicide among Homeless and

Potentially Homeless Youth." *Australian and New Zealand Journal of Psychiatry*, 29: 248–56.

Slesnick, N. and M. J. Kang. 2008. "The Impact of an Integrated Treatment on HIV Risk Behavior among Homeless Youth: A Randomized Controlled Trial." *Journal of Behavioral Medicine*, 31(1): 45–59.

Slesnik, N. and J. Prestopnik. 2005. "Ecologically Based Family Therapy Outcome with Substance Abusing Runaway Adolescents." *Journal of Adolescence*, 28: 277–98.

Slesnick, N., J. L. Prestopnik, R. J. Meyers and M. Glassman. 2007. "Treatment Outcome for Street-Living, Homeless Youth." *Addictive Behaviors*, 32(6): 1237–51.

Stiffman, A. R. 1989. "Suicide Attempts in Runaway Youths." *Suicide and Life Threatening Behavior*, 19: 147–59.

Tenner, A., L. Trevithick, V. Wagner and R. Birch. 1998. "Seattle YouthCare's Prevention, Intervention, and Education Program: A Model of Care for HIV-Positive, Homeless, and At-Risk Youth." *Journal of Adolescent Health*, 23: 96–106.

Terrell, N. E. 1997. "Aggravated and Sexual Assaults among Homeless and Runaway Adolescents." *Youth & Society*, 28(3): 267–90.

van der Ploeg, J. D. 1989. "Homelessness: A Multidimensional Problem." *Children and Youth Services Review*, 11: 45–56.

Visano, L. 1990. "The Socialization of Street Children: The Development and Transformation of Identities." *Sociological Studies of Child Development*, 3: 139–61.

Whitebeck, L. B., D. R. Hoyt and W. N. Bao. 2000. "Depressive Symptoms and Co-occurring Depressive Symptoms, Substance Abuse, and Conduct Problems among Runaway and Homelss Adolescents." *Child Development*, 71(3): 721–32.

Williams, N. R., E. W. Lindsey, D. Kurtz and S. Jarvis. 2001. "From Trauma to Resiliency: Lessons from Former Runaway and Homeless Youth." *Journal of Youth Studies*, 4: 233–53.

Yates, G. L., R. G. Mackenzie, J. Pennbridge and A. Swofford. 1991. "A Risk Profile Comparison of Homeless Youth Involved in Prostitution and Homeless Youth Not Involved." *Journal of Adolescent Health*, 12: 545–48.

Yoder, K. A. 1999. "Comparing Suicide Attempters, Suicide Ideators, and Nonsuicidal Homeless and Runaway Adolescents." *Suicide and Life-Threatening Behavior*, 29: 25–36.

Yoder, K. A., D. R. Hoyt and L. B. Whitbeck. 1998. "Suicidal Behavior among Homeless and Runaway Adolescents." *Journal of Youth and Adolescence*, 27: 753–77.

# CHAPTER 2

# Sexual Risk Behaviours and Sexual Health Outcomes among Homeless Youth in Canada

Danielle R. Schwartz, PhD candidate
Department of Psychology, Ryerson University

Carolyn A. James, PhD candidate
Department of Psychology, Faculty of Health, York University

Anne C. Wagner, PhD candidate
Department of Psychology, Ryerson University

Trevor A. Hart, PhD
Department of Psychology, Ryerson University

## Introduction

Homeless youth are a high-risk population that experiences a range of adverse sexual health outcomes. This chapter provides an overview of the sexual health of homeless youth in Canada, describing the various factors that contribute to sexual risk behaviours and poor sexual health outcomes and offering suggestions for future research and clinical interventions. This chapter first reviews the prevalence of sexual risk behaviours and poor sexual health outcomes among homeless youth. It then examines the various determinants of sexual risk behaviours and highlights the structural barriers influencing poor sexual health in this population. The chapter concludes by examining how knowledge of these risk factors can be implemented toward the development of intervention strategies and policy changes in order to improve the sexual health of homeless youth in Canada.

## Prevalence of Sexually Transmitted Infections, HIV and Pregnancy

In 2006, the Public Health Agency of Canada (PHAC) published find-ings from the Enhanced Surveillance of Canadian Street Youth (E-SYS), a three-year cross-sectional study examining the sexual health of homeless youth (ages 15–24) in seven urban centres across Canada (PHAC 2006a, 2006b). The goal of E-SYS was to obtain national data on the sexual health and sexual behaviours of this high-risk population in order to guide the development of disease prevention programs. To date, E-SYS is the largest and most comprehensive Canadian study of homeless youth. A summary of major E-SYS findings across the three-year study period is presented in Table 2-1.

According to E-SYS, the overall proportion of homeless youth reporting a lifetime sexually transmitted infection (STI) ranged from 20.8 percent to 26.6 percent (PHAC, 2006b). Lifetime STI prevalence was even higher in a separate sample of Montreal street youth (ages 13–25), in which 31.7 percent reported a past STI (Roy et al. 2000). These rates appear significantly higher than the STI prevalence among the general Canadian youth population (ages 15–24), which has been estimated at 4 percent (Rotermann 2005).

### Table 2-1.  Overview of major E-SYS findings in 1999, 2001 and 2003

|  | Prevalence Rates/Mean | | |
|---|---|---|---|
|  | 1999 (n = 1645) | 2001 (n = 1427) | 2003 (n = 1656) |
| **Sexual Health Outcomes** | | | |
| Chlamydia | 8.6% | 11.5% | 11.0% |
| Gonorrhoea | 1.4% | 1.4% | 3.1% |
| Syphilis | — | 0% (< 0.01%) | 0.7% |
| HSV-2 | — | 14.2% | 18.8% |
| Hepatitis B | 2.5% | 2.1% | 2.3% |
| Hepatitis C | 4.0% | 3.6% | 4.5% |
| HIV | < 1.0% | < 1.0% | < 1.0% |
| **Sexual Behaviours** | | | |
| Lifetime sexual partners* | 19.0 | 21.5 | 22.5 |
| Past STI | 20.8% | 22.7% | 26.6% |
| Lifetime involvement in sex trade | 20.2% | 20.9% | 22.6% |

*Mean of male and female lifetime sexual partners is reported as no overall mean was provided.

Prevalence rates are also higher for specific STIs and HIV. In E-SYS, the prevalence of chlamydia ranged from 8.6 percent to 11.5 percent, approximately 10 times higher than the prevalence among youth in the general population (PHAC 2006a). Other Canadian studies of homeless youth have reported similar chlamydia rates of 6.6 percent (Haley et al. 2002) and 8.6 percent (Shields et al. 2004). In E-SYS, the prevalence of gonorrhea was 20 to 30 times higher than rates in the general youth population and increased significantly over the study period (PHAC 2006a). Prevalence rates were also high for hepatitis B and herpes simplex virus 2 (HSV-2), the primary cause of genital herpes. Studies in Toronto, Montreal and Vancouver have reported high HIV prevalence among homeless youth, ranging from 1.9 percent to 2.8 percent (DeMatteo et al. 1999; Marshall et al. 2008; Roy et al. 2000). Comparable data on HIV prevalence rates among youth in the general population are not available, likely because this age group makes up an extremely small proportion (approximately 3.5%) of the total number of HIV cases in Canada (PHAC 2007).

Unintended pregnancy is also common among homeless youth. In one Canadian study of homeless youth ages 13–25, 47.1 percent of the females reported at least one past pregnancy and 35.6 percent of the males reported having impregnated a female (Roy et al. 2000). This is markedly higher than rates from a national sample of Canadian students in grades 9 and 11, in which 3.0 percent of females reported lifetime pregnancy and 1.7 percent of males reported having impregnated a female (Boyce et al. 2006).

## Sexual Risk Behaviours among Canadian Homeless Youth

Results from E-SYS and the aforementioned studies highlight that poor sexual health among homeless youth is a significant public health concern in Canada. A full discussion of the factors influencing these high rates of sexual risk behaviours will be discussed later in the chapter. Compared to youth in the general population, homeless youth are more likely to be sexually active and more likely to engage in specific sexual behaviours known to be related to negative outcomes. In Canadian studies, nearly all homeless youth (> 95%) report having ever engaged in sexual intercourse, and the average age of first intercourse was approximately 14 (PHAC 2006a; Roy et al. 2000). This is notably younger than the average age among the general population in Canada (16.8 years; Hansen et al. 2004).

Homeless youth are more likely to engage in unprotected sex than youth in the general population. Among Montreal homeless youth, 86.8 percent who had engaged in vaginal intercourse and 67.6 percent who had engaged in anal intercourse did not always use a condom (Roy et al. 2000). In an analysis of sexually active youth in E-SYS, 41–51 percent reported not using a condom with a female partner and 47–56 percent reported not using a condom with a male partner at their last sexual encounter (PHAC 2006a). These proportions are higher than those reported in two nationally representative studies of Canadian youth, in which 26.4 percent of sexually active youth who had been with multiple partners in the past year and/or who were not married reported not using a condom at last intercourse (Rotermann 2008).

Homeless youth also report high numbers of sexual partners. Across the three years of E-SYS, male youth reported an average of 21–23 lifetime sexual partners and female youth reported an average of 17–22 lifetime sexual partners. Male youth who reported same-sex sexual activity reported an average of 45 lifetime sexual partners (PHAC 2006a). Roy and colleagues (2000) found that 20.6 percent of sexually active youth reported between 6 and 20 sexual partners in the past six months, and 7.6 percent reported more than 20 sexual partners. High proportions of youth in E-SYS engaged in sexual activity with high-risk sexual partners, including partners who had an STI, partners who were involved in sex trading and partners who were under the influence of drugs during their sexual encounter. On average, 21.2 percent of homeless youth reported lifetime involvement in sex trade (PHAC 2006a). Other Canadian studies have reported similar or higher rates of lifetime sex trade involvement (25.9% and 27% respectively; Roy et al. 2000; Weber et al. 2002).

## Predictors of Poor Sexual Health among Homeless Youth in Canada

In light of these findings, a substantial amount of research has been conducted examining why homeless youth demonstrate such poor sexual health. For the purpose of this chapter, risk factors for poor sexual health will be broadly broken down into multiple categories. These categories include socio-demographic factors, family environment and early life experiences and individual/psychological factors. Further, an exploration of the structural barriers associated with street life is critical for a comprehensive understanding of why homeless youth may demonstrate poor sexual health.

### Socio-Demographic Risk Factors

**Gender and sexual orientation.** Although both male and female homeless youth are at considerable risk for STIs, HIV and pregnancy, there are gender differences in disease prevalence as well as reported frequency and nature of sexual risk behaviours. In studies from Canada and the United States, females had higher STI prevalence rates (excluding HIV), were less likely to report consistent condom use, were more likely to report having had a sexual partner with an STI history and were more likely to report past sex trading. Males reported more frequent intercourse with regular and casual partners and more lifetime sex partners and were also more likely to have engaged in anal sex (Halcón and Lifson 2004; PHAC 2006a; Roy et al. 2000; Solorio et al. 2006; Tevendale, Lightfoot, and Slocum 2009). HIV prevalence was also higher among males than females (DeMatteo et al. 1999; Roy et al. 2000).

One possible explanation for these gender disparities is that male and female homeless youth have different life experiences and are thus differentially predisposed to engage in certain behaviours. For example, female homeless youth are more likely than male homeless youth to report childhood sexual abuse and sexual victimization (e.g., Rew, Taylor-Seehafer and Fitzgerald 2001; Tyler et al. 2004), which are known risk factors for sexual risk behaviours such as sex trading and unprotected sex (Senn, Carey, and Vanable 2008). Further, from a sociological perspective, it has been proposed that gender-based power imbalances play an important role in determining individuals' sexual behaviours (e.g., Amaro 1995). In several studies of non-homeless females from diverse ethnic backgrounds, individuals who were low in relationship power (e.g., decision-making abilities, assertiveness, control) demonstrated an increased risk of sexual risk behaviours and poor sexual health outcomes, including unprotected sex and HIV (e.g., Bralock and Koniak-Griffin 2007; Campbell et al. 2009; Jewkes et al. 2010). This power differential may make it difficult for girls and women to assert themselves sexually and to resist coercion in sexual situations (Tyler and Johnson 2006). Future studies would benefit from investigating the ways in which gender-based power dynamics interact with factors related to homelessness to influence youths' sexual behaviour and health.

When examining HIV specifically, its relatively high prevalence among male homeless youth may be accounted for by the large proportion of HIV-positive homeless youth who identify as gay or bisexual (DeMatteo et al. 1999), since Canadian gay and bisexual males have disproportionately high HIV prevalence (PHAC 2007). The high number of male gay and bisexual youth involved in sex trading (Tyler 2009) and the higher number of sexual partners among lesbian, gay and bisexual (LGB) youth (Cochran et al. 2002) may also explain higher prevalence of HIV among LGB youth. However, there is a clear need for more research examining how sexual orientation is associated with sexual health among homeless youth.

**Age.** Greater age has consistently been identified as a predictor of sexual risk behaviours and poor sexual health among homeless youth (e.g., DeMatteo et al. 1999; Ennett, Federman, Bailey, Ringwalt, and Hubbard 1999; Linton et al. 2009). In E-SYS, the prevalence of gonorrhea and infectious syphilis were higher among older youth (ages 20–25) compared to younger youth (ages 15–19). Older youth had a higher prevalence of HIV infection and HSV-2 and a higher prevalence of hepatitis B and C (PHAC 2006a). Similarly, two studies of homeless youth in Toronto found that HIV prevalence was significantly higher among older youth compared to younger youth (DeMatteo et al. 1999; Linton et al. 2009). Greater age is also associated with sex trading, with one study reporting that homeless youth were 37 percent more likely to have traded sex with each additional year of age (Tyler 2009). There are several explanations for the association between older age and increased HIV risk. First, youth who are older in age have had more years and greater opportunity to engage in sexual risk behaviours and may therefore have increased exposure to HIV or other STIs (Linton et al. 2009). As all youth age, they gain more freedoms that allow them to engage in risky behaviours, and such behaviours are considered a natural part of the maturation process. However, these freedoms are likely to be exaggerated among homeless youth, who may be forced to make many decisions about their sexual behaviour without the cognitive maturity to do so (Milburn et al. 2007).

Linton and colleagues (2009) examined predictors of HIV in a Toronto sample of youth (ages 18–30) and noted that homeless youth under age 25 have an easier time accessing preventive health and social service support networks and in obtaining welfare assistance.

They indicated that, in Ontario, the network of health and social service organizations that are available to youth under 25 are not available to individuals over this age. Further, in order to receive financial assistance for unemployment through welfare agencies, individuals over age 25 require proof of address (Linton et al. 2009). Finally, there may be a lag in time between exposure to an infection or virus, seroconversion (in the case of HIV) and manifestation of symptoms. Therefore, some younger youth may be unaware that they have contracted an STI or HIV or may demonstrate negative test results (Linton et al. 2009).

**Ethnicity.** Canadian studies that have examined ethnic differences in sexual heath have primarily compared non-Aboriginal youth to Aboriginal youth (e.g., Marshall et al. 2008; Miller et al. 2006; Shields et al. 2004). Studies have consistently reported that Aboriginal youth demonstrate more sexual risk behaviours and higher prevalence rates of STIs and HIV. In Vancouver, Aboriginal homeless youth were nearly three times more likely to be HIV positive than non-Aboriginal youth (Marshall et al. 2008). In Toronto, a higher proportion of Aboriginal youth (5.0%) and black youth (4.3%) self-reported their HIV status as positive compared to white youth (3.0%; Linton et al. 2009). Further, in a cross-sectional study of homeless youth across seven Canadian urban centres, higher chlamydia prevalence was found among Aboriginal youth (13.7%) compared to non-Aboriginal youth (6.6%; Shields et al. 2004). Aboriginal individuals are more likely to experience a range of adverse health outcomes, including substance abuse, trauma, poverty and discrimination (Pearce et al. 2008). These factors, coupled with common stressors experienced by all homeless youth, may predispose Aboriginal homeless youth towards poor sexual health outcomes.

### Family Environment and Early Life Experiences
Past studies have demonstrated that a large proportion of homeless youth are raised in troubled and disorganized family environments (Cauce et al. 2000; Ringwalt, Greene and Robertson 1998). Youth who have grown up in unsupportive, neglectful or abusive family environments may resort to homelessness as an escape from their adverse living situations. Once on the street, they may be more susceptible to negative influences, as they have not developed the social support, coping skills or resources to protect them from adverse health

consequences (PHAC 2006b; Tyler 2006; Tyler et al. 2004). In one qualitative study, many participants reported parental substance misuse and criminal activity (Tyler 2006). Childhood abuse and neglect are also identified as primary reasons for leaving home (Ringwalt, Greene and Robertson 1998; Tyler 2006). Across studies of homeless youth, 38–70 percent of females and 23–24 percent of males reported childhood sexual abuse, and 35–51 percent of males and females reported childhood physical abuse (Cauce et al. 2000; Molnar et al. 1998; Noell et al. 2001; Rew, Taylor-Seehafer and Fitzgerald 2001).

Childhood sexual abuse has been particularly emphasized as a risk factor for poor sexual health outcomes, including unprotected sex, high numbers of sexual partners, early age of first intercourse and sex trading (Johnson, Rew and Sternglanz 2006; Rotheram-Borus et al. 1996; Senn, Carey and Vanable 2008; Simons and Whitbeck 1991). LGB homeless youth, who report even higher rates of childhood sexual abuse compared to heterosexual homeless youth (Tyler and Cauce 2002), have been found to engage in sex trading at the same rate as heterosexual female homeless youth and at a higher rate than heterosexual male homeless youth (Gangamma et al. 2008). Childhood physical and emotional abuse are also correlates of sexual risk behaviours and poor sexual health among homeless youth, including sex trading (Greene, Ennett and Ringwalt 1999) and unintended pregnancy (Thompson et al. 2008).

### Individual/Psychological Factors

Past research has demonstrated that certain cognitive, perceptual and behavioural factors may predict sexual health outcomes among homeless youth. In one study of homeless youth, Rew, Fouladi and Yockey (2002) examined the association between a range of cognitive-perceptual and behavioural factors and sexual health practices. Results of a path analysis indicated a direct link from safe sex behaviours to future time perspective (i.e., concern about future consequences), intention to use condoms and self-efficacy to use condoms. Further, an indirect association was found between safe sex behaviours and social support, connectedness, perceived health status and assertive communication. Other studies have further highlighted the importance of social support networks in reducing sexual risk behaviours such as sex trading (Ennett, Bailey and Federman 1999; Milburn et al. 2007) and unprotected sex (Tevendale, Lightfoot and Slocum 2009).

Findings from Tevendale, Lightfoot and Slocum's (2009) study provided additional evidence for the importance of social support and future time perspective as protective factors among homeless youth. Specifically, having positive expectations for the future was associated with fewer sex partners, and, among females, having a mentor (i.e., an individual to go to for support and guidance) reduced the risk of having unprotected sex. In terms of future time perspective, the authors suggested that youth who have future-oriented goals (e.g., family, career) may be less inclined to engage in certain sexual risk behaviours as they might interfere with their long-term goals. Conversely, individuals without such goals may be less concerned with the long-term implications of their actions. Other protective factors that emerged from this study include goal setting and decision-making skills, which presumably assist youth to manage stress and make more health-conscious and future-oriented decisions. In addition, self-esteem appeared to reduce the likelihood of engaging in unprotected sex among females (Tevendale, Lightfoot and Slocum 2009).

Although homeless youth demonstrate elevated rates of mental health problems (Cauce et al. 2000), limited research has examined their association with sexual health in this population. One study demonstrated that depressive symptoms were a risk factor for sex trading among homeless youth (Tyler 2009). Another study found that conduct disorder, which is highly prevalent among homeless youth (Cauce et al. 2000), is associated with a range of HIV-risk behaviours including sex trading, multiple sexual partners and drug use (Booth and Zhang 1997). Emotional dysregulation models have been applied to explain various risk behaviours among homeless youth, including substance use (MacLean, Paradise and Cauce 1999) and self-mutilation (Tyler et al. 2003). However, future studies are needed to examine the impact of emotional dysregulation on sexual health in this population.

Substance use is also a key variable to explore when examining the sexual health of homeless youth. According to E-SYS, among injection and non-injection drug users, 36.3 percent reported sex trading in the past three months. Compared to non-injection drug users, injection drug users were more likely to have had sex with a high-risk partner, to have been involved in sex trading, to have had unprotected sex during their last sexual encounter and to have had more lifetime sexual partners. Similarly, a study of homeless youth in Vancouver found that the use of non-injection crack and crystal methamphetamine increased the odds of engaging in survival sex (i.e., sexual activities to meet subsistence needs such as acquiring food, shelter or money) 3.45 and 2.02 times, respectively (Chettiar et al. 2010). These findings are consistent with US studies of homeless youth showing that substance use is associated with sex with multiple partners, inconsistent condom use and lifetime involvement in sex trade (Greene, Ennett and Ringwalt 1999; Halcón and Lifson 2004; Solorio et al. 2008). Substance use is also associated with higher STI rates among homeless youth (PHAC 2006a). In E-SYS, the prevalence of chlamydia and gonorrhea was higher among crystal methamphetamine users compared to non-users, and the prevalence of genital herpes was significantly higher among youth who reported any (injection or non-injection) drug use compared to no drug use. Compared to non-injection drug users, injection drug users were more likely to have had an STI (PHAC 2006a).

Although the higher prevalence of STIs among injection drug users may be partially accounted for by intravenous transmission, other important contextual variables likely account for sexual risk behaviours and poor sexual health among drug users in general relative to non-drug users. Drug users may engage in sexual risk behaviours such as sex trade as a means of obtaining drugs or money to purchase drugs (Tyler and Johnson 2006). Further, being under the influence of drugs may increase vulnerability to sexual coercion or assault. In a qualitative study, Bungay and colleagues (2010) reported that gendered power dynamics diminished the sexual safety of women who used crack cocaine. Specifically, the women reported that men waited for them to be in a position of heightened vulnerability while under the influence of drugs to sexually assault or coerce them.

## Structural Barriers

Homeless youth face significant barriers to obtaining stable housing. Many landlords will not rent to youth who are on welfare, and alternative and affordable housing options such as single-room occupancy hotels are often viewed as unsafe by youth. Additionally, such accommodations may be considered undesirable by youth, as single-room occupancy hotels are often viewed as a last resort and the domain of adults who are homeless (Krüsi et al. 2010). Youth who engage in substance use are particularly disadvantaged in finding stable housing, as the majority of shelters require abstinence, often an unfeasible task for youth with competing needs. Collectively, structural and societal barriers, such as the presence of enforcement-based policies and a lack of affordable options, make finding stable housing for street-involved youth extremely challenging (Krüsi et al. 2010).

Research has found that not having a regular, safe place to stay has implications for the sexual health of homeless youth. In one study, male and female homeless youth who had ever spent the night in public places or with strangers engaged in a greater number of sexual risk behaviours (e.g., no condom use, sex with a high-risk partner) than those who had not experienced such circumstances (Ennett et al. 1999). Additionally, in a Vancouver study examining housing status and sexual risk among street-involved youth, youth living on the streets were more likely to report inconsistent condom use than were youth who were stably housed (i.e., in an apartment, house or single-room occupancy hotel), adjusting for socio-demographic and drug-related variables (Marshall, Kerr, Shoveller, Patterson et al. 2009). On the streets, there is likely limited access to sexual health resources such as condoms that might be available in shelters. However, despite greater amenities in shelters versus sleeping on the streets, youth living in a shelter had more sexual partners in the past six months compared to youth who were stably housed. The authors posited that high turnover rates at shelters and sharing of unstable sleeping quarters may encourage multiple sexual partnerships (Marshall, Kerr, Shoveller, Patterson et al. 2009).

The context of street life may also limit homeless youth's access to social and health services, which may influence sexual health practices (Kelly and Caputo 2007; Marshall, Kerr, Shoveller, Montaner et al. 2009). In Canada, not having a fixed address makes it challenging to get a provincial health card, which may lead to denied access to health services (Kelly and Caputo 2007). Additionally, street-involved youth may fear discrimination and may distrust adult service providers, creating further barriers to accessing services (Geber 1997). For youth who are not utilizing health care and social services, it may be difficult to obtain contraceptives, information regarding safe sex skills and the social support systems to encourage safe sex behaviours (Rew, Chambers and Kulkarni 2002). Enforcement-based policies resulting in the criminalization of street youth may also strongly contribute to sexual risk behaviours in this population (Marshall, Kerr, Shoveller,

Montaner et al. 2009). For example, in a study of female homeless crack users, individuals described using dangerous, secluded locations, such as alleys, for drug use in order to avoid detection by police. These locations often increased their vulnerability to sexual assault (Bungay et al. 2010). Furthermore, homeless youth who are engaging in illegal activity such as sex trading or illicit drug use may fear contact with police or social service agencies and thus be deterred from accessing health care services (Chettiar et al. 2010; Kelly and Caputo 2007).

Duration of homelessness has consistently shown associations with increased sexual risk (Milburn et al. 2005; Rew, Fouladi, and Yockey 2002; Rew et al. 2008). The longer youth remain homeless, the more likely they are to become part of marginalized subcultures that may encourage increasingly dysfunctional risk behaviours (Tyler et al. 2001). For example, youth who had been homeless for more than one year engaged in more sexual risk behaviours and fewer safer-sex behaviours than those who were homeless for less than six months (Rew et al. 2008). Given that many homeless youth enter the streets as a result of family conflict and poor social support, they are likely to form new social networks involving other homeless youth (PHAC 2006b). Although these networks may be beneficial in providing youth with the social support they previously lacked, they may also lead youth to engage in risky behaviours. Homeless youth often become embedded in criminal street networks and gain exposure to criminal mentors who pass on information and skills that facilitate criminal involvement. This form of mentorship may also promote and normalize behaviours such as sex trading or survival sex (Hagan and McCarthy 1997).

Survival sex is a sexual risk behaviour that appears strongly linked to the context of street life (Greene, Ennett and Ringwalt 1999). In a recent study of Canadian street youth, only 10 percent were working a consistently paid job, and these formal positions offered considerably less income than illicit activities, such as selling drugs or trading sex (Benoit, Jansson and Anderson 2007). Gwadz and colleagues (2009) qualitatively examined homeless youths' initiation into the street economy, including sex trading. The authors identified five factors that influenced youths' involvement in these illicit activities: (1) social control (i.e., decreased attachment to conventional society and increased attachment to unconventional society), (2) barriers to the formal economy (i.e., no fixed address, educational deficits,

perceived stigma and past incarceration), (3) benefits to street economy (i.e., immediate financial support, emotional gratification, sense
of empowerment, independence and flexibility), (4) severe/immediate
economic need (i.e., need for food, clothing and shelter) and (5) active
recruitment into the street economy by predatory adults or homeless
peers. In another qualitative study, Tyler and Johnson (2006) found
that, although youth generally did not want to engage in sex trading, most did so in a desperate attempt to gain access to resources
they deemed necessary for survival (i.e., money, shelter, food, drugs).
Further, in some circumstances, youth's involvement in sex trading
was involuntary. A number of youth stated that they likely would not
have traded sex if not for pressure from others. Furthermore, several
youth explained that although they did not engage in sex trading,
they had friends who did. Evidently, sex trading is considered a
relatively normative behaviour among homeless youth and therefore
a viable strategy for fulfilling subsistence needs (Gwadz et al. 2009;
Tyler and Johnson 2006).

## Limitations and Future Directions

When describing the current status of sexual health among homeless youth in Canada, several limitations are noteworthy. First, for
certain sexual risk behaviours and STIs, incidence rates are more
likely to be reported than prevalence rates, making cross-study comparisons inappropriate. Furthermore, there is a lack of large-scale
Canadian studies comparing the sexual health in homeless youth to
youth in the general population. E-SYS (PHAC 2006a, 200b) provides
detailed information regarding the sexual health of homeless youth
in Canada; however, findings are only released once every few years,
provide retrospective data and do not statistically compare homeless
youth to the general population. In addition, E-SYS does not compare
the sexual health of homeless youth on important socio-demographic
variables such as ethnicity or sexual orientation, which are known
correlates of sexual risk (Halcón and Lifson 2004; Tyler 2009). Studies
that do examine ethnicity typically use broad and often dichotomous ethnic categories and do not provide a detailed exploration of
sexual health differences among individuals of varying ethnicities.
Given the considerable ethnic diversity in most urban centres in
Canada, ethnic differences in sexual health outcomes should be better
addressed in the literature. Future large-scale studies of Canadian

homeless youth should consider examining socio-demographic risk factors, including detailed information on youths' ethnic identities and comparative data from normative youth samples, in order to ascertain how much more at risk this population is relative to youth in the general Canadian population.

Another limitation of this literature is that certain sexual health variables may be strongly correlated, which could potentially lead to inaccurate reporting of results. For example, many studies examine sex trading as a dichotomous variable without assessing the number of sexual partners youth have had within the context of sex trading versus outside of sex trading. Therefore, if an individual has traded sex with multiple sexual partners, this may increase the overall sample mean of lifetime sexual partners and give the impression that high numbers of sexual partners are common to all homeless youth. Another example is the reporting of age at first intercourse. Given that many homeless youth experience childhood sexual abuse (Molnar et al. 1998; Rew, Taylor-Seehafer and Fitzgerald 2001; Rew et al. 2001), it is possible that they are reporting age of childhood sexual abuse rather than age of first consensual intercourse. This could decrease the overall mean and give the impression that most youth first engaged in consensual intercourse at a young age.

Gender biases in reporting of sexual risk behaviours may also limit the research in this area. For example, as a result of social norms and expectations, males may be less likely than females to report certain behaviours (e.g., involvement in sex trading) whereas females may be less likely than males to report other behaviours (e.g., high numbers of lifetime sexual partners). Throughout the literature, males consistently report higher numbers of sexual partners than females (e.g., Halcón and Lifson 2004; PHAC 2006a). However, in theory, if males are engaging in sexual behaviours with female partners, then males and females should report roughly similar numbers of sexual partners. It is possible that these differences may be partially due to the fact that many homeless male youth identify as gay or bisexual; however, this is not clarified in the literature. Although these concerns are important to underscore, there is ample evidence to demonstrate that homeless youth, in general, are a very high-risk population who engage in a wide range of sexual risk behaviours. Nevertheless, future studies should make efforts to clearly differentiate sexual health variables and avoid reporting bias in order to ensure that an accurate picture of homeless youth is being presented.

Finally, it is important to highlight that various studies define 'youth' differently, making it difficult to draw direct comparisons between studies. For example, the Linton and colleagues (2009) study defined youth as ages 18–30, whereas other studies have used age groupings of 15–24 (PHAC 2006a) and 13–25 (Roy et al. 2000). Thus, although many studies indicate that they are using youth samples, it is unlikely that the same populations are being compared across studies. Future research would benefit from developing more consistent guidelines as to what age groups constitute youth.

## Implications for Intervention Strategies and Policy Changes

Canadian homeless youth demonstrate elevated rates of sexual risk behaviours compared to youth in the general population, placing them at risk for a host of adverse sexual health outcomes. An examination of the risk factors for poor sexual health within this population highlights the complexity of this problem. Homeless youth represent a group of individuals who have experienced inordinate life stressors. Many use homelessness as an escape from a family environment that is unsupportive, neglectful and abusive. Once on the streets or in shelters, homeless youth become immersed in a culture that promotes high-risk behaviour as a normative way of life. Without adequate social support, coping skills and access to education and health care, these youth are vulnerable to a range of poor health outcomes.

Effective interventions to reduce aversive sexual health consequences among homeless youth in Canada must be based upon comprehensive models that take multiple factors into account. Harm reduction strategies are effective ways to prevent risk for poor sexual health and should be applied in both school systems and community-based programs (PHAC 2006b). These strategies should include information on the importance of safe sex strategies and condom use, as well as behavioural skills training to ensure that youth are aware of how to use condoms correctly and consistently. This type of intervention should be accessible through community-based programs to ensure that homeless youth are receiving this information regardless of whether or not they are attending school. At the school level, prevention programs can be applied, not only by enforcing sexual education programs, but also by identifying youth who may be at an increased risk of leaving their homes and applying individualized interventions to prevent them from becoming homeless. Community-based programs should also include outreach services that provide sti screening and treatment programs to prevent transmission of stis (phac 2006b). These programs should adopt youth-friendly, sex-positive policies that reduce barriers to traditional health care environments (e.g., using street-based sti testing as part of outreach services) (Marshall, Kerr, Shoveller, Montaner et al. 2009). Incorporating these preventative activities into the health care strategy for street-involved youth could increase health care utilization and uptake beyond traditionally mandated programs.

Changes at the structural and policy levels must also be considered in the development of effective sexual health interventions for homeless youth. Policy changes promoting safe, affordable and harm-reduction focused, as opposed to abstinence-requiring, housing options would allow for easier access to a fixed address. Marshall, Kerr, Shoveller, Patterson and colleagues (2009) proposed that future policies should implement rent and subsidy programs that provide safe and stable housing for homeless youth. Increased housing opportunities would help to improve barriers to formal employment, potentially reducing youths' involvement in the street economy, including sex trading (Gwadz et al. 2009). Given that many youth desire to be part of the formal economy but face significant barriers in obtaining employment, vocational counselling, job training programs and transitional support services would also help to re-connect youth with conventional society and encourage alternatives to the street economy. Overall, there is a clear emphasis in the literature for the need to target structural barriers preventing youth from accessing essential resources including housing, education, employment and health care (Zerger, Strehlow and Gundlapalli 2008).

In conclusion, homeless youth are at increased risk for a variety of sexual risk behaviours and poor sexual health outcomes. These sexual risk behaviours occur in a social context including lack of housing, formal employment and financial resources, low social support, mental health problems and other psychological outcomes related to their marginalization. Sufficient literature exists on the risk factors affecting homeless youth to create much-needed preventative and supportive interventions to decrease sexual health risk. These interventions should include strategies at the individual and structural levels to improve poor sexual health outcomes in this vulnerable population.

# References

Amaro, H. 1995. "Love, Sex, and Power." *American Psychologist,* 50: 437–47.

Benoit, C., M. Jansson and M. Anderson. 2007. "Understanding Health Disparities among Female Street Youth." In *Urban Girls Revisited: Building Strengths,* ed. B. J. Leadbeater and N. Way. New York: New York University Press, 321–37.

Booth, R. E. and Y. Zhang. 1997. "Conduct Disorder and HIV Risk Behaviors among Runaway and Homeless Adolescents." *Drug and Alcohol Dependence,* 48: 69–76.

Boyce, W., M. Doherty-Poirier, D. MacKinnon, C. Fortin, H. Saab, M. King and O. Gallupe. 2006. "Sexual Health of Canadian Youth: Findings from the Canadian Youth, Sexual Health, and HIV/AIDS Study." *Canadian Journal of Human Sexuality,* 15(2): 59–68.

Bralock, A. R. and D. Koniak-Griffin. 2007. "Relationship, Power, and Other Influences on Protective Sexual Behaviors of African American Female Adolescents." *Health Care for Women International,* 28: 247–67.

Bungay, V., J. Johnson, C. Varcoe and S. Boyd. 2010. "Women's Health and Use of Crack Cocaine in Context: Structural and 'Everyday' Violence." *International Journal of Drug Policy,* 21: 321–29.

Campbell, A. N. C., S. Tross, S. L. Dworkin, M-C. Hu, J. Manuel, M. Pavlicova and E. V. Nunes. 2009. "Relationship Power and Sexual Risk among Women in Community-Based Substance Abuse Treatment." *Journal of Urban Health,* 86: 951–64.

Cauce, A. M., M. Paradise, J. A. Ginzler, L. Embry, C. J. Morgan, Y. Lohr, and J. Theofelis. 2000. "The Characteristics and Mental Health of Homeless Adolescents: Age and Gender Differences." *Journal of Emotional and Behavioral Disorders,* 8: 230–39.

Chettiar, J., K. Shannon, E. Wood, R. Zhang and T. Kerr. 2010. "Survival Sex Work Involvement among Street-Involved Youth Who Use Drugs in a Canadian Setting." *Journal of Public Health,* 32: 322–27.

Cochran, B. N., A. J. Stewart, J. A. Ginzler and A. M. Cauce. 2002. "Challenges Faced by Homeless Sexual Minorities: Comparison of Gay, Lesbian, and Transgender Homeless Adolescents with Their Heterosexual Counterparts." *American Journal of Public Health,* 92(5): 773–77.

DeMatteo, D., C. Major, B. Block, R. Coates, M. Fearon, E. Goldberg . . . S. E. Read. 1999. "Toronto Street Youth and HIV/AIDS: Prevalence, Demographics and Risks." *Journal of Adolescent Health,* 25: 358–66.

Ennett, S. T., S. L. Bailey and E. B. Federman. 1999. "Social Network Characteristics Associated with Risky Behaviors among Runaway and Homeless Youth." *Journal of Health and Human Behavior,* 40: 63–78.

Ennett, S. T., E. B. Federman, S. L. Bailey, C. L. Ringwalt and M. L. Hubbard. 1999. "HIV-Risk Behaviors Associated with Homelessness Characteristics in Youth." *Journal of Adolescent Health,* 25: 344–53.

Gangamma, R., N. Slesnick, P. Toviessi and J. Serovich. 2008. "Comparison of HIV Risks among Gay, Lesbian, Bisexual and Heterosexual Homeless Youth." *Journal of Youth and Adolescence,* 37: 456–64.

Geber, G. M. 1997. "Barriers to Health Care for Street Youth." *Journal of Adolescent Health,* 21: 287–90.

Greene, J. M., S. T. Ennett and C. L. Ringwalt. 1999. "Prevalence and Correlates of Survival Sex among Runaway and Homeless Youth." *American Journal of Public Health,* 89: 1406–09.

Greene, J. M. and C. L. Ringwalt. 1998. "Pregnancy among Three National Samples of Runaway and Homeless Youth." *Journal of Adolescent Health,* 23: 370–77.

Gwadz, M. V., K. Gostnell, C. Smolenski, B. Willis, D. Nish, T. C. Nolan, M. Tharaken and A. S. Ritchie. 2009. "The Initiation of Homeless Youth into the Street Economy." *Journal of Adolescence,* 32: 357–77.

Hagan, J. and B. McCarthy. 1997. *Mean Streets: Youth Crime and Homelessness.* Cambridge, UK: Cambridge University Press.

Halcón, L. L. and A. R. Lifson. 2004. "Prevalence and Predictors of Sexual Risks among Homeless Youth." *Journal of Youth and Adolescence,* 33: 71–80.

Haley, N., E. Roy, P. Leclerc, G. Lambert, J. Boivin, L. Cedras and J. Vincelette. 2002. "Risk Behaviours and Prevalence of *Chlamydia trachomatis* and *Neisseria gonorrhea* Genital Infections among Montreal Street Youth." *International Journal of STD & AIDS,* 13: 238–45.

Hansen, L., J. Mann, S. McMahon and T. Wong. 2004. "Sexual Health." *BMC Women's Health,* 4(Suppl 1): S24.

Jewkes, R. K., K. Dunkle, M. Nduna and N. Shai. 2010. "Intimate Partner Violence, Relationship Power Inequity, and Incidence of HIV Infection in Young Women in South Africa: A Cohort Study." *Lancet,* 376: 41–48.

Johnson, R. J., L. Rew and R. W. Sternglanz. 2006. "The Relationship between Childhood Sexual Abuse and Sexual Health Practices of Homeless Adolescents." *Adolescence,* 41: 221–34.

Kelly, K. and T. Caputo 2007. "Health and Street/Homeless Youth." *Journal of Health Psychology,* 12: 726–36.

Krüsi, A., D. Fast, W. Small, E. Wood and T. Kerr. 2010. "Social and Structural Barriers to Housing among Street-Involved Youth Who Use Illicit Drugs." *Health and Social Care,* 18: 282–88.

Linton, A. B., M. D. Singh, D. Turbow and T. J. Legg. 2009. "Street Youth in Toronto, Canada: An Investigation of Demographic Predictors of HIV Status among Street Youth Who Access Preventive Health and Social Services." *Journal of HIV/AIDS & Social Services,* 8(4): 375–96.

MacLean, M. G., M. J. Paradise and A-M. Cauce. 1999. "Substance Use and Psychological Adjustment in Homeless Adolescents: A Test of Three Models." *American Journal of Community Psychology*, 27: 405–27.

Marshall, B. D., T. Kerr, C. Livingstone, K. Li, J. S. Montaner and E. Wood. 2008. "High Prevalence of HIV Infection among Homeless and Street-Involved Aboriginal Youth in a Canadian Setting." *Harm Reduction Journal*, 5(1): 35.

Marshall, B. D. L., T. Kerr, J. A. Shoveller, J. S. G. Montaner and E. Wood. 2009. "Structural Factors Associated with an Increased Risk of HIV and Sexually Transmitted Infection Transmission among Street-Involved Youth." *BMC Public Health*, 9: 1–9.

Marshall, B. D. L., T. Kerr, J. A. Shoveller, T. L. Patterson, J. A. Buxton and E. Wood. 2009. "Homelessness and Unstable Housing Associated with an Increased Risk of HIV and STI Transmission among Street-Involved Youth." *Health and Place*, 15: 783–90.

Milburn, N. G., M. J. Rotheram-Borus, P. Batterham, B. Brumback, D. Rosenthal and S. Mallett. 2005. "Predictors of Close Family Relationships over One Year among Homeless Young People." *Journal of Adolescence*, 28: 263–75.

Milburn, N. G., J. A. Stein, E. Rice, M. J. Rotheram-Borus, S. Mallett, D. Rosenthal and M. Lightfoot. 2007. "AIDS Risk Behaviors among American and Australian Homeless Youth." *Journal of Social Issues*, 63: 543–65.

Miller, C. L., S. A. Strathdee, P. M. Spittal, T. Kerr, K. Li, M. T. Schechter and E. Wood. 2006. "Elevated Rates of HIV Infection among Young Aboriginal Injection Drug Users in a Canadian Setting." *Harm Reduction Journal*, 3: 1–6.

Molnar, B. E., S. B. Shade, A. G. Kral, R. E., Booth and J. K. Watters. 1998. "Suicidal Behaviour and Sexual/Physical Abuse among Street Youth." *Child Abuse & Neglect*, 22: 213–22.

Noell, J., P. Rohde, J. Seeley and L. Ochs 2001. "Childhood Sexual Abuse, Adolescent Sexual Coercion and Sexually Transmitted Infection Acquisition among Homeless Female Adolescents." *Child Abuse & Neglect*, 25: 137–48.

Pearce, M. E., W. M. Christian, K. Patterson, K. Norris, A. Moniruzzaman, K. J. P. Craib . . . P. M. Spittal. 2008. "The Cedar Project: Historical Trauma, Sexual Abuse and HIV Risk among Young Aboriginal People Who Use Injection and Non-injection Drugs in Two Canadian Cities." *Social Science & Medicine*, 66: 2185–94.

PHAC (Public Health Agency of Canada). 2007. *HIV/AIDS Epi Updates*. Ottawa: Public Health Agency of Canada.

_____. 2006a. *Sexually Transmitted Infections in Canadian Street Youth: Findings from Enhanced Surveillance of Canadian Street Youth, 1999–2003*. Ottawa: Public Health Agency of Canada.

_____. 2006b. *Street Youth in Canada: Findings from Enhanced Surveillance of Canadian Street Youth, 1999–2003.* Ottawa: Public Health Agency of Canada.

Rew, L., K. B. Chambers and S. Kulkarni. 2002. "Planning a Sexual Health Promotion Intervention with Adolescents." *Nursing Research,* 51: 168–74.

Rew, L., R. T. Fouladi and R. D. Yockey. 2002. "Sexual Health Practices of Homeless Youth." *Journal of Nursing Scholarship,* 34: 139–45.

Rew, L., M. Grady, T. A. Whittaker and K. Bowman. 2008. "Interaction of Duration of Homelessness and Gender on Adolescent Sexual Health Indicators." *Journal of Nursing Scholarship,* 40: 109–15.

Rew, L., M. Taylor-Seehafer and M. L. Fitzgerald. 2001. "Sexual Abuse, Alcohol, and Other Drug Use, and Suicidal Behaviors in Homeless Adolescents." *Issues in Comprehensive Pediatric Nursing,* 24: 225–40.

Rew, L., M. Taylor-Seehafer, N. Y. Thomas and R. D. Yockey. 2001. "Correlates of Resilience in Homeless Adolescents." *Journal of Nursing Scholarship,* 33: 33–40.

Ringwalt, C. L., J. M. Greene and M. J. Robertson. 1998. "Familial Backgrounds and Risk Behaviors of Young with Thrownaway Experiences." *Journal of Adolescence,* 21: 241–52.

Rotermann, M. 2008. "Trends in Teen Sexual Behaviour and Condom Use." *Health Reports,* 19: 1–5.

_____. 2005. "Sex, Condoms, and STDs among Young People." *Health Reports,* 16: 39–45.

Rotheram-Borus, M. J., K. A. Mahler, C. Koopman and K. Langabeer. 1996. "Sexual Abuse History and Associated Multiple Risk Behavior in Adolescent Runaways." *American Journal of Orthopsychiatry,* 66: 390–400.

Roy, É., N. Haley, P. Leclerc, N. Lemire, J-F. Boivin, J-Y. Frappier and C. Claessens. 2000. "Prevalence of HIV Infection and Risk Behaviours among Montreal Street Youth." *International Journal of STD & AIDS,* 11: 241–47.

Senn, T. E., M. P. Carey and P. A. Vanable. 2008. "Childhood and Adolescent Sexual Abuse and Subsequent Sexual Risk Behavior: Evidence from Controlled Studies, Methodological Critique, and Suggestions for Research." *Clinical Psychology Review,* 28: 711–35.

Shields, S. A., T. Wong, J. Mann, A. M. Jolly, D. Haase, S. Mahaffey ... D. Sutherland. 2004. "Prevalence and Correlates of Chlamydia Infection in Canadian Street Youth." *Journal of Adolescent Health,* 34: 384–90.

Simons, R. L. and L. B. Whitbeck. 1991. "Sexual Abuse as a Precursor to Prostitution and Victimization among Adolescent and Adult Homeless Women." *Journal of Family Issues,* 12: 361–79.

Solorio, M. R., N. G. Milburn, M. J. Rotheram-Borus, C. Higgins and L. Gelberg. 2006. "Predictors of Sexually Transmitted Infection Testing among Sexually Active Homeless Youth." *AIDS and Behavior,* 10: 179–84.

Solorio, M. R., D. Rosenthal, N. G. Milburn, R. E. Weiss, P. J. Batterham, M. Gandara and M. J. Rotheram-Borus. 2008. "Predictors of Sexual Risk Behaviors among Newly Homeless Youth: A Longitudinal Study." *Journal of Adolescent Health,* 42: 401–09.

Tevendale, H. D., M. Lightfoot and S. L. Slocum. 2009. "Individual and Environmental Protective Factors for Risky Sexual Behavior among Homeless Youth: An Exploration of Gender Differences." *AIDS and Behavior,* 13: 154–64.

Thompson, S. J., K. A. Bender, C. M. Lewis and R. Watkins. 2008. "Runaway and Pregnant: Risk Factors Associated with Pregnancy in a National Sample of Runaway/Homeless Female Adolescents." *Journal of Adolescent Health,* 43: 125–32.

Tyler, K. A. 2009. "Risk Factors for Trading Sex among Homeless Young Adults." *Archives of Sexual Behavior,* 38: 290–97.

———. 2006. "A Qualitative Study of Early Family Histories and Transitions of Homeless Youth." *Journal of Interpersonal Violence,* 21: 1385–93.

Tyler, K. A. and A. M. Cauce. 2002. "Perpetrators of Early Physical and Sexual Abuse among Homeless and Runaway Adolescents." *Child Abuse & Neglect,* 26: 1261–74.

Tyler, K. A. and K. D. Johnson. 2006. "Trading Sex: Voluntary or Coerced? The Experiences of Homeless Youth." *Journal of Sex Research,* 43: 208–16.

Tyler, K. A., D. R. Hoyt, L. B. Whitbeck and A. M. Cauce. 2001. "The Impact of Childhood Sexual Abuse on Later Victimization among Runaway Youth." *Journal of Research on Adolescence,* 11: 151–76.

Tyler, K. A., L. B. Whitbeck, D. R. Hoyt and A. M. Cauce. 2004. "Risk Factors for Sexual Victimization among Male and Female Homeless and Runaway Youth." *Journal of Interpersonal Violence,* 19: 503–20.

Tyler, K. A., L. B. Whitbeck, D. R. Hoyt and K. Johnson. 2003. "Self-Mutilation and the Role of Family Abuse, Street Experiences, and Mental Disorders." *Journal of Research on Adolescence,* 13: 457–74.

Weber, A. E., J-F. Boivin, L. Blais, N. Haley and E. Roy. 2002. "HIV Risk Profile and Prostitution among Female Street Youths." *Journal of Urban Health,* 79: 525–35.

Zerger, S., A. J. Strehlow and A. V. Gundlapalli. 2008. "Homeless Young Adults and Behavioural Health." *American Behavioral Scientist,* 51: 824–41.

# CHAPTER 3

# Helpers, Not Helpless: Honouring the Strength, Wisdom and Vision of Aboriginal Women Experiencing Homelessness or Marginal Housing

Billie Allan, MSW, PhD candidate

Factor-Inwentash Faculty of Social Work, University of Toronto

Izumi Sakamoto, MSW, PhD

Factor-Inwentash Faculty of Social Work, University of Toronto

## Introduction

In reviewing the health of homeless persons in Canadian cities, Hwang (2001) estimates that the representation of Aboriginal peoples in urban homeless populations is approximately 10 times that of their relative proportion of the general populations of urban centres. Research on homelessness experienced by Aboriginal peoples is slowly increasing, but literature addressing the intersections of identities (e.g., Aboriginal women) that builds on a strengths-based model appears to be scarce. Homelessness does not occur in a vacuum (Jahiel 1992); creating effective solutions means moving far beyond narrow, deficit-based stereotypical constructions that paint homelessness as resulting from individual choices and personal characteristics (e.g., drug use, mental illness, unemployment) and effectively ignore underlying structural issues. For Aboriginal peoples, this means constructing an understanding of, and response to, the needs of those experiencing homelessness and marginal housing that acknowledges and resists the effects of colonization. We propose an Aboriginal approach to conceptualizing and advancing the health and well-being of Aboriginal women experiencing marginal housing or homelessness. This approach would be centred on the vision, voices, strengths and agency of Aboriginal women in determining their health and well-being and would honour their roles and contributions as helpers, not helpless.

Coming Together: Homeless Women, Housing and Social Support was a community- and arts-based, participatory action research project that explored how ciswomen build support networks with each other when experiencing homelessness or marginal housing. This chapter focuses specifically on the findings relating to the Aboriginal women who participated in the project. The project data were initially collected, coded and analyzed using a grounded theory approach (Charmaz 2006). Later in the research process, the research team focused on the Aboriginal sub-sample, drawing from Indigenous methodology (Smith 1999) in order to more fully understand the experiences of Aboriginal women in the context of an Aboriginal worldview. (While the research team would see this process as the second phase of the data analysis, this can be considered a secondary data analysis to some others.)

The findings from the subset of Aboriginal women participants revealed the kinds of marginalization and violence that they faced on the streets while attempting to access or maintain housing. At the same time, they were actively helping each other by offering social support, sharing stories and resources, accepting each other, promoting safety and volunteering. Moreover, these women offered significant insight into what was needed to improve their situations and the services they accessed and received. This chapter will focus on the recommendations for service providers and policy-makers offered by the participants. The results challenge health and social service providers, policy-makers, educators and researchers to revise discourses of housing and homelessness, to resist colonial history and practices and to instead honour the strength and agency of Aboriginal women.

## Context of the Research

### Aboriginal Health and Well-Being in Canada

Trying to capture a snapshot of the health and well-being of Aboriginal peoples generally is quite difficult (Health Council of Canada 2005), and that of Aboriginal women experiencing homelessness even more so. Indeed, the landscape of Aboriginal health statistics is not easily navigated. For example, census data gathered by Statistics Canada is impacted by incomplete enumeration or non-participation of several First Nations (Anderson et al. 2006). Health data collected through provincial and territorial health systems do not necessarily or consistently utilize markers for Aboriginal identity. Even where ethno-racial identification markers are included, Aboriginal peoples accessing health services may elect not to identify for fear of racism. Aboriginal health statistics may be gathered from one specific subpopulation, for example, First Nations (status or non-status Indians), and yet be generalized to Aboriginal peoples as a whole. Indeed, the majority of available information regarding Aboriginal peoples is drawn from data collected from the status Indian population (cihi 2004, as cited in Health Council of Canada 2005). As such, Aboriginal health data should be appreciated, with clear acknowledgement of all of its complications and challenges, for what it offers in helping to further our understanding.

There is a need for a general statement regarding the use of statistics (and other research data) relating to Aboriginal peoples, not only in terms of data collection (methods, sampling, generalizability, etc.), but in the responsibility to avoid inadvertently reinforcing stereotypes and systemic racism through the application of statistics. While this may seem like an obvious statement to some, the deeply painful history of both research and social policy directed towards Aboriginal peoples underlines the responsibility of researchers, educators, policy-makers, health professionals and community and social workers to gather, share and apply statistics in ways that disrupt stereotypical, one-dimensional ideas about Aboriginal peoples and instead advance the health, well-being and self-determination of Aboriginal communities. One means of responsibly utilizing statistics and other data derived from research is to ensure adequate discussion of the historical and ongoing colonial context faced by Aboriginal peoples. Another is to ensure the data is framed within the perspectives and voices of Aboriginal peoples. The purpose of including this statement here is to contextualize the challenges of engaging in and contributing to discussions of Aboriginal peoples' health and to stress the importance of doing so in ways that clearly identify limitations and actively move towards disrupting rather than reinforcing negative discourses of Aboriginal peoples. In the section that follows, we review available information on the health and well-being of Aboriginal women, as well as examining the impacts of historical and contemporary colonialism on Aboriginal women.

### Aboriginal Women: Looking at Our Past, in the Present, for the Future

To look at our past, in the present, for the future is a traditional teaching shared across many nations. In the case of Aboriginal women experiencing homelessness and marginal housing, this means looking at the history of colonization and its effects within the contemporary context, with an eye towards positively transforming their health and well-being and the social conditions they face.

**The past.** The effects of colonization on the lives of Aboriginal peoples are undeniable even though the colonial history of Canada receives limited attention in our public schools and public discourse (Kempf 2006). The intersectional effect of gender and racialization has amplified the impact of colonization on Aboriginal women. Attacking the roles of Aboriginal women was, in fact, a key strategy in destabilizing First Nations and establishing colonial control (Anderson 2004; Lawrence and Anderson 2005; Walters and Simoni 2002). Mohanram (1999) describes the fundamental role of women in building and maintaining a nation, in that women quite literally reproduce the nation through childbirth. She further highlights the patriarchal discourses of colonization that have and continue to portray women as existing without agency. The very idea of women without agency directly contravenes the status, roles and responsibilities of Aboriginal women on Turtle Island (North America) prior to European contact. Within the tremendous diversity of Aboriginal nations and their traditions across Turtle Island, Aboriginal women were understood as powerful and sacred; they held multiple and varying roles as helpers, healers, teachers, leaders, warriors, knowledge keepers and lifegivers (Walters and Simoni 2002). In matriarchal societies, Aboriginal women carried responsibilities for or control over property and leadership, for example, within the Haudenosanee Nations in which women held all property rights, and Clan Mothers were charged with selecting and deposing of leaders.

The colonial project of European settlers, aided by the work of Christian missionaries, undertook to 'civilize' Aboriginal peoples by upending traditional governance structures and cultural values and practices and by imposing and enforcing European values and norms, including patriarchy and the consequent subordination of women (Bourassa, McKay-McNabb and Hampton 2005; Lawrence and Anderson 2005). These efforts were ultimately institutionalized in the *Indian Act of 1876,* legislation that resulted in multiple human rights violations, including the political exclusion of women. The Act usurped the role of Aboriginal women in selecting and deposing leaders (i.e., the role of Clan Mothers) and prevented them from holding leadership positions themselves. The legislation instead inserted band chief and council structures in which only men were eligible for election and in which women held no right to vote (Blair 2005). The *Indian Act* further removed the real property rights of Aboriginal women and regulated their status such that women who married non-Aboriginal men (or non-status Aboriginal men) would lose their status, as would their children. This stood in contradiction to the treatment of status Aboriginal men who, upon marrying non-Aboriginal women, conferred their status on their wife and, subsequently, their children.

In response to activism and legal action by Aboriginal women, the federal government passed Bill C-31 in 1985, rescinding the 'enfranchisement' provisions of the *Indian Act* and reinstating those who had lost their status. Bill C-31 was meant to ensure the conformity of the *Indian Act* with the *Canadian Charter of Rights and Freedoms,* specifically section 15—the equality rights section. Using a 'gender neutral' approach, Bill C-31 removed the purely patrilineal eligibility for status, but it did not also provide Aboriginal women with the right to confer status onto their spouses and children. Instead, it situated status men in a position similar to that of status women, such that children of status women or men who married non-status or non-Aboriginal individuals could no longer confer their status on their own children if they too married a non-status or non-Aboriginal partner. The irony of Bill C-31, which was touted as a vehicle to restore gender equity for Aboriginal women and increase the number of people who qualify for Indian status, is that it actually works to speed the extinction of status Indians—since hundreds of thousands of descendants of today's status Indians will be excluded from status rights over the coming decades. This policy action has arguably significantly benefited the federal government by decreasing the status Indian population, for whom the government has a fiduciary duty to provide, thereby reducing associated obligations and costs (Daniels 1998).

The removal of property rights through the *Indian Act* continues to significantly impact Aboriginal women today. Provincial matrimonial real property laws do not apply to Aboriginal women living on reserve, as reserve land is a matter of federal jurisdiction and the use of reserve lands, including housing, is controlled directly by band councils (Blair 2005). This is especially problematic for women experiencing violence, which Blair (2005) has estimated to be approximately one in three among Aboriginal women. The violence faced by Aboriginal women is compounded by chronic and severe on-reserve housing shortages, such that the lack of matrimonial real property rights means that Aboriginal women experiencing violence may be forced to choose between fleeing at the cost of their housing or continuing to live in violence in order to maintain housing (Blair 2005). Violence is a well-documented force in the migration of Aboriginal women to urban centres (NAFC 2012; RCAP 1996). The federal government has been engaged in consultation around and the development of multiple (failed) bills for more than thirteen years, including Bill S-2. However, the legacy of this legal limbo and the continued strain of housing shortages will not simply disappear with one new piece of legislation.

The denigration of Aboriginal women was a central goal in the colonial project of European settlement (Walters and Simoni 2002), achieved through multiple means, including legislated and systemic oppression, social and economic exclusion, physical and sexual violence and the rupture and erosion of the role of Aboriginal women in having and caring for their children. This has included forced sterilization of Aboriginal women in both Canada and the United States (the division of which was only created through a colonial imposed border). In the 1970s, approximately 40 percent of Aboriginal women of childbearing age in the United States experienced non-consensual sterilization administered by the federally run Indian Health Services (Walters and Simoni 2002). This practice of eugenics also occurred here in Canada, although to a lesser degree and primarily in Alberta and British Columbia (Grekul, Krahn and Odynak 2004). More than 2,800 Aboriginal women underwent forced sterilization in Alberta alone between 1928 and 1972 (Truth Commission into Genocide in Canada 2001). Testimony provided to the Truth Commission into Genocide in Canada (2001), indicated that sterilization of Aboriginal women was in fact a standard practice in some places (i.e., provincial training schools). Additional testimonial evidence provided to the Commission suggests that the Department of Indian Affairs provided a financial reward to physicians for each Aboriginal woman sterilized, in particularly "if they weren't church-goers" (Truth Commission 2001: 13).

In addition to eugenics, the goals of cultural annihilation were enacted by the mass removal of Aboriginal children from their families, homes and communities, first in the era of residential schools and then through the assertion of child welfare authority in the lives of Aboriginal families, which saw thousands of children taken into foster care or placed in cross-cultural adoption. While some may wish to relegate residential schooling or invasive child welfare practices to the distant past, the last residential school in Canada closed in 1996, and recent data from the National Household Survey suggests that Aboriginal children presently constitute nearly half of the estimated 30,000 children in care in Canada (Woods and Kirkey 2013), despite the fact that Aboriginal peoples are thought to compose less than 5 percent of the Canadian population (Statistics Canada 2011). Residential schooling and child welfare involvement have been associated directly with adverse health outcomes, such as, increased risk and rates of HIV and hepatitis C (Pearce et al. 2008) as well as social determinants of poorer health, including homelessness (Baskin 2007; Sinclair 2009).

Colonization has had an undeniably devastating, intergenerational and collective impact on Aboriginal peoples, tearing at the fabric of Aboriginal ways of knowing and being, including substantive damage to roles of and respect accorded to Aboriginal women prior to contact and to family and community cohesion. In the context of decolonizing communities and improving Aboriginal health and well-being as a whole, the health and well-being, wisdom and vision of Aboriginal women is integral. An often cited Cheyenne saying states that "A Nation is not defeated, until the hearts of its women are on the ground", so that by caring for our women, honouring our women, raising their voices and raising their hearts, we are also caring for, honouring and renewing our nations.

**The present.** Subsequent to colonization, Aboriginal women face severe marginalization in Canadian society. Aboriginal women are more likely than their non-Aboriginal counterparts to experience poverty, under- or unemployment, under housing, homelessness or incarceration (Dion Stout, Kipling and Stout 2001; NWAC, 2007a). They are also more likely than non-Aboriginal women to have lower levels of educational achievement and to live with poorer community infrastructure and resources as a result of the persistent economic marginalization of Aboriginal peoples in Canada (Adelson 2005;

Benoit, Carroll and Chaudhry 2003; NWAC, 2007b; Smylie 2001; Loppie-Reading and Wien 2009). Aboriginal women experience substantial violence; those with status are five times more likely than non-Aboriginal women to die as a result of violence and eight times more likely to die by spousal homicide (CAEFS n.d.). The violence levelled at Aboriginal girls and women is painfully captured in the epidemic of missing and murdered Aboriginal women in Canada, an issue that has recently been identified as a subject of inquiry by the United Nations Committee on the Elimination of Discrimination Against Women (Talaga 2012). While the Native Women's Association of Canada (NWAC 2010) has verified nearly 600 cases of missing and murdered Aboriginal women, other activists suggest that the actual number may be much higher (Kraus 2011; Talaga 2012).

Aboriginal women experience alarming disparities in health, with higher rates of heart disease, hypertension, diabetes, multiple forms of cancer (including cervical and gallbladder), HIV/AIDS, mental illness, substance abuse and suicide (Dion Stout, Kipling and Stout 2001; Gatali and Archibald 2003; NWAC 2007b). They not only experience a shorter life expectancy and higher infant mortality rate than non-Aboriginal women (Statistics Canada 2006; Smylie, Fell and Ohlsson 2010) but also higher rates of chronic disease than Aboriginal men (Bourassa, McKay-McNabb and Hampton 2005). This disproportionate burden of ill-health reflects the inequities Aboriginal women face in foundational determinants of health, including housing, income, food security, education, violence and environmental degradation (NAFC 2012).

While recent census data estimates 54 percent of the overall Aboriginal population now resides in urban centres (Statistics Canada 2008), fully 78 percent of Aboriginal women live off-reserve (Statistics Canada 2006). Among Aboriginal women living off reserve, 52 percent have been diagnosed with a chronic health condition by a health professional (Vancouver Women's Health Collective 2006). Homelessness and marginal housing are in no way limited to urban contexts; however, the Coming Together Project was conducted in an urban centre (Toronto) and reflects the types of experiences and services accessed by Aboriginal women in a large, metropolitan city. As such, we focus our discussion and recommendations within the realm of urban housing and homelessness, while recognizing that homelessness and marginal housing are issues that abide by no geographical bounds. In fact, there is a need, beyond the scope of this chapter, to ensure more attention to issues of homelessness and marginal housing in rural, remote and Northern environments (see, for example, Qulliit Nunavut Status of Women Council 2007; Yukon Status of Women Council 2007).

Urban Aboriginal peoples earn substantially less than the median income of their non-urban counterparts and face higher rates of homelessness, tuberculosis, diabetes, HIV/AIDS, substance abuse and suicide than their non-Aboriginal peers (Benoit et al. 2003). Urban Aboriginal women are more likely than non-Aboriginal women to be lone mothers and to face difficulty in providing basic necessities for their children, including food, clothing and housing (UATF 2007). Homelessness statistics for the city of Toronto indicate that while Aboriginal peoples are estimated to compose less than 1 percent of the city's entire population, they account for approximately 15 percent of the homeless population but fully 26 percent of 'rough sleepers', meaning those who sleep outside (Novac et al. 2006; Khandor and Mason 2007).

## Methods

### Description of the Project

The research findings presented herein are part of a larger, multi-method community-based research project entitled Coming Together: Homeless Women, Housing and Social Support, which explored how ciswomen[1] and transwomen with experiences of homelessness build support networks with each other in Toronto, Canada. Adhering to the community-based research approach (e.g., Flicker and Savan 2006; Israel et al. 1998), the Coming Together Project was a collaborative effort between a university and two community agencies serving people who are homeless.

These findings were derived from a secondary analysis of the data, particularly focusing on the subset of the data comprising of Aboriginal ciswomen and transwomen participants, whose experiences were contrasted to that of the non-Aboriginal participants. Unlike what is typically seen when the term *secondary data analysis* is used, which typically involves an analysis of a large data set previously collected by a governmental body (e.g., Statistics Canada survey data sets, health utilization data from a provincial/territorial registries, etc.) or other researchers, this process involved a second phase analysis of our own data (from interviews and arts-based focus groups) with the intention of generating a deeper understanding of the experiences of Aboriginal participants through the application of a more 'Indigenized' approach to data analysis.

The analysis drew upon both a constructivist grounded theory approach (Charmaz 2006), where data collection and analysis are conducted hand-in-hand in a cyclical manner involving multiple reiteration of coding strategies, and upon Aboriginal/Indigenous knowledge and principles regarding the gathering and care of knowledge (research). Maori scholar Linda Tuhiwai Smith (1999) sets out several projects for Indigenous research, including 'reframing', which seeks to transform how social issues of Indigenous peoples are discussed and addressed. In the context of this project, reframing required continuous attention to the historical context of the lives and circumstances of the participants with an eye to what could be done now to disrupt the chronic, colonial marginalization of Aboriginal women and create change for our future.

The project's advisory board was comprised of seven ciswomen and transwomen who had experienced homelessness, including two Aboriginal members. During the project implementation and follow-up, two Aboriginal PhD students (Billie Allan and Rose Cameron) also became research assistants, helping with data collection, transcription, data management, data analysis and dissemination. The analysis presented herein was led by one of the Aboriginal researchers involved in the project (Billie) in consultation with the rest of the team, including the advisory board. She also integrated Indigenous research methodology (Smith 1999) during the analysis process so that we can understand and describe the experiences of Aboriginal women more fully.

As is often the case with community-based participatory research, the ethics approval process involved multiple steps to allow for flexibility in research design to reflect participants' opinions and increase the trustworthiness of research findings. In Phase I, in-depth face-to-face semi-structured interviews for both service providers and researchers as key informants ($n$ = 13) and service users (women and transwomen who were homeless; $n$ = 20) were conducted at either the participant's location or at a mutually designated location. For service user participants, each interview participant received a $25 honorarium and two transit tokens as a token of appreciation and partially to compensate for their time and contribution.

Of the 20 ciswomen and transwomen with experiences of homelessness interviewed, 11 were between the ages of 40 and 59 and nine were between 25 and 39 years old. Six identified as trans-women and 14 identified as women (ciswomen, non-transwomen). Nine of the ciswomen and transwomen with experiences of homelessness interviewed identified as Aboriginal or Metis, seven as white or of European descent and four identified as people of colour. At the time of their interviews, five ciswomen/transwomen had been homeless or marginally housed for over 10 years, two had been homeless or marginally housed between five and 10 years, six had been in similar situations between one and five years and seven had been without stable housing for up to a year. The living situations of the ciswomen and transwomen at the time of the study varied. Two ciswomen/transwomen were living on the street, two were living in subsidized housing, four were living in private housing, five were staying with relatives or friends and seven were accessing shelter or hostel services. Of 13 service providers interviewed, five service providers worked mostly with Aboriginal women, while one worked specifically with transwomen (including Aboriginal transwomen), and the rest worked with a range of ciswomen/transwomen who are marginally housed or homeless. While the experiences and insights of the service providers were a valuable part of our project, giving us a deeper understanding of the issues, due to space limitations, in this chapter we have chosen to focus mainly on the voices of ciswomen and transwomen who were actively experiencing homelessness or marginal housing themselves.

Based on the findings from Phase I, Phase II of the project was designed to be more participatory, action oriented and arts based. To ensure that this project was based on participatory, anti-oppressive and empowerment approaches (Gutiérrez and Lewis 1999; Ristock and Pennel 1996; Sakamoto and Pitner 2005), an advisory board was created consisting of women and transwomen who used their own experiences of being homeless and/or marginally housed to critically reflect on the information previously collected through interviews. These ciswomen/transwomen were recruited from the communities where the initial interviews had been conducted. Many of the members were asked to participate because of their reputations for supporting other homeless women. Out of seven advisory board members, three were transwomen, two were Aboriginal (one identified as a transwoman) and two were ciswomen or transwomen of colour. Advisory board members acted as consultants and peer researchers throughout the rest of the research process, participating

**Figure 3-1. Members of the advisory board and research team**

in the arts-making sessions, brainstorming the results with the rest of the team and helping the team make key decisions in analysis and dissemination strategies.

In Phase II, in order to examine and expand the earlier findings and generate more voices from ciswomen and transwomen who have experienced homelessness, the research team proposed to conduct arts-based group activities. Art has the power to bring people together in ways that verbal interaction alone may not be able. Further, the process of making art can allow for the creation of alternative and inclusive knowledge. To design and facilitate the process, a community artist, Natalie Wood, who had experience with art education, community organizing and working with ciswomen and transwomen who have experienced homelessness and poverty was hired to be as part of the research team.

The advisory board first met to review the project material and develop the key themes through discussion and brainstorming. In collaboration with the artist (Natalie), the advisory board members chose method of 'staged photography'[2] for the next phase of data collection. The artistic form was based on Natalie's experience teaching art with homeless and marginally housed women and her commitment to applying collaborative methodology and using a form of artistic expression in which all could participate. We also set a two-to-three-hour time limit for the discussion and distillation of ideas and experiences into visual form, because it was unlikely that exactly the same group of ciswomen and transwomen would return to the drop-in centres on a subsequent date had more than one session been required to complete the activity. The advisory board members were given a 'crash course' on the artistic form, collaborative methodology and how to transform the language of experience into visual metaphors that were unique and not stereotypical. The goal of this approach was to give voice to those individuals whose voices have been silenced, marginalized and socially isolated—in this case, ciswomen and transwomen who are homeless or marginally housed.

The advisory board and research team travelled to four drop-in centres across Toronto to engage groups of ciswomen/transwomen in the art-making sessions (overall $n$ = 50+). Through painting, costumes, theatre and photography, groups of ciswomen and transwomen who have experienced homelessness created scenes depicting their own visions and stories of inclusion, friendships and safe spaces. The preliminary findings were then followed by subsequent consultations with advisory board members and feedback sessions with ciswomen and transwomen at four drop-in sites. In addition to printing four posters depicting these four stories, a community research report was published to more fully capture the process and outcomes of research (Sakamoto et al. 2007). Dissemination of the research results included public exhibits of photos, distribution of posters and research reports, academic and community presentations and writing of journal articles (Sakamoto et al. 2009), followed by a larger synthesis report, joint exhibit and new website with seven other community-based, arts-informed research projects on homelessness in Toronto, entitled Homelessness: Solutions from Lived Experiences through Arts-Informed Research[3] (Sakamoto et al. 2008). For further description of the methodology, please refer to the project report, *Coming Together: Homeless Women, Housing and Social Support—With a special focus on the experiences of Aboriginal women and transwomen* (Sakamoto et al. 2010).

### An 'Indigenized' Approach to Grounded Theory Data Analysis

Building upon the grounded theory methodology employed in the broader research project, the analysis of the Aboriginal women's subset of data employed a methodology that drew upon both grounded theory and Indigenous knowledge practices regarding the gathering and care of knowledge (research). The challenge of bridging between these two ways of knowing and handling knowledge is not easy, and the limitations of Western approaches to organizing data in being able to generate a meaningful understanding of Indigenous experiences have been increasingly discussed by other Indigenous researchers (Absolon and Willett 2004; Kovach 2009; Lavallée 2009). Moreover, the considerable abuse, harm, loss and exploitation historically endured by Indigenous peoples in the name of scholarly research means that any kind of research method used with Indigenous peoples requires the utmost critical consciousness and attention to issues of power, domination and marginalization. As an Indigenous researcher [the first author of this article, Billie], this issue is particularly personal; I entered the process with a visceral understanding of all that has been stolen, misrepresented and used to create and enforce colonial policies and practices on our peoples (Absolon 2011; Smith 1999). Therefore, the process of engaging in data analysis involved a constant negotiation between the ideas of grounded theory, and the Western knowledge system from which it evolves, and Indigenous ways of conceptualizing and understanding all of existence. The process required a decolonizing lens in order that we all be cognizant of how both the process and the outcome of the research impacted the lives of the women: Did it further reinforce their marginalization and dehumanization or did it help to bring forward their voices, stories and wisdom? Was the analysis ignoring or embodying the values of Indigenous ways of knowing and caring for the stories the women had gifted us with?

The approach to coding and the subsequent themes and stories that emerged and are shared here reflect Smith's (1999) project of reframing, which acknowledges the power of framing not only in how an issue is understood, but whether and how it is responded to:

> The framing of an issue is about making decisions about its parameters, about what is in the foreground, what is in the background, and what shadings or complexities exist within the frame. The project of reframing is related to defining the problem or issue and determining how best to solve that problem. (153)

The use of grounded theory coding processes to stay close to the knowledge provided by each participant, positioned within an

Indigenous worldview that attends to the historical and contemporary contexts of Aboriginal women and to the project of reframing, follows what Cree scholar Margaret Kovach (2009) has referred to as a 'modified grounded theory' in which the researcher must attend to both the 'berry' (each small piece of knowledge) and the 'bush' (the context and relations in which each 'berry' exists). This 'grounding' of analysis in an Indigenous worldview aims to resist the fragmentation of Indigenous experience that may otherwise be caused by a grounded theory approach to data analysis as highlighted by Algonquin/Cree/Metis scholar Lynn Lavallée (2009).

## Results: Voices and Vision, Using Lived Experience to Create Change

The Aboriginal women participating in the project (both in the interviews and arts-making sessions) offered many recommendations to improve service provision based on their lived experiences, insight and the wisdom they carry inside of themselves—this wisdom could also then be understood as their *embodied knowledge*. Honouring the embodied knowledge of participants ruptures the discourse of *who* is understood to hold knowledge in the interactions between those accessing and and those providing services addressing the health and well-being of Aboriginal women experiencing homelessness. It also challenges *what kind* of knowledge is understood as valid. Centring the embodied knowledge of Aboriginal women honours their strengths, voices and visions, as well as their struggles, challenges and needs. It disrupts practices, intentional or unintentional, that position Aboriginal women as lacking understanding, insight or expertise of their very own lived experiences.

The recommendations offered by participants ranged from micro to macro practices, such as improving communication between and within agencies, increased outreach services, the development of services for women who are homeless with disabilities and efforts to remove structural barriers to service for women who are actively using drugs and alcohol. Themes within this part of the data included understanding/compassion, communication and transforming services. We explore these themes below, drawing linkages and discussing the implications for those involved in policy-making, programming (design, delivery and evaluation) and frontline services.

### Understanding and Compassion

Participants discussed the challenges of navigating systems of service and care and spoke directly to the need for deepened understanding and compassion on the part of staff at receiving agencies or services.

> *We shouldn't be treated like criminals or like we've done something bad and need to be punished. This humiliation is re-victimizing—we've already left abusive situations and now we get treated like this in the shelter . . . . When I arrived at the shelter I was told by one of the intake workers not to make friends with the other women. This goes to show how that worker regards the women staying in the shelter. And at the shelter, compassion is taking a second seat. It feels that the rules are more important to the shelter than each person as an individual.*
> — Dorene,[4] Ojibwe-European woman, 40–59 years old,
> residing in a shelter, following approximately
> one year of marginal housing

> *Don't blame it on you 'cause I find I get a lot of that 'It's your fault you're homeless', so more open-mindedness and understanding of where that person's coming from.*
> — Shelley, Ojibwe woman, 25–39 years old,
> residing in a shelter for the past five months
> after having lived on the streets for 1.5 years

These recommendations may seem small or even simple in terms of what is needed to create change. However, in light of the historical and contemporary conditions experienced by Aboriginal women previously discussed in this chapter, it is even more apparent why experiences of uncompassionate or even humiliating care could compound personal and societal experiences of colonization and racism. On the other hand, caring, genuine and accepting care can constitute a major element of accessibility of services.

### Improved Communication

Communication between agencies, and between staff within agencies, was a need clearly identified by the women. Increased communication was viewed as an essential piece of respect, and necessary to avoid humiliation or re-victimization:

*Share information amongst staff better so that we don't have to keep*
*telling our histories of abuse over and over. Women are shuffled around,*
*not helped. Once you've told your story, you shouldn't have to keep*
*reliving it. Direct and respectful communication is a key to building*
*trusting relationships between those seeking and providing services.*
— Dorene

Problematic communication can speak to underlying dynamics, as
discussed by a participant in the following passage:

*So there is a whole lack of understanding by social service workers who*
*try to speak a pretty language under the crisis management ideal as*
*opposed to speaking plain English and saying this is what I want from*
*you. Social services are very much about treating people like children.*
*If you're good I'll feed you and if you're bad you have to go home now—*
*even though you don't have a home. As opposed to 'this is an adult,*
*and I'm asking you to be respectful in my space', 'I have to work here*
*so you need to be respectful'. That's what is not happening in social*
*services. There is an 'us' and a 'them'. And they talk about boundaries.*
*'Boundaries' is another fake social services word. Boundaries are for*
*people who don't have the nuts to say 'no'.*
— Kim, Metis woman, 40–59 years old, residing
in subsidized housing with a history of both
homelessness and marginal housing

A focus on increased direct and positive communication could go a
long way towards uprooting and transforming unhealthy or harmful
power dynamics. Uprooting power dynamics is necessary to transforming the accessibility and experiences of health and social services for those who are homeless, where access and quality of these
services is understood as a determinant of health and well-being. For
Aboriginal women, open examination and transformation of power
dynamics can serve to honour their knowledge and contributions in
the process and contribute towards Aboriginal self-determination.

### Transforming Services
Participants offered concrete recommendations for transforming
services based on their lived experience and embodied knowledge.
These recommendations underline the importance of, as one participant stated, "a system in place to meet each woman's specific needs.

They need to realize that we are individuals and we have individual needs". Moreover, the following recommendations would all serve to decrease the marginalization of Aboriginal women (and women generally) experiencing homelessness. They make visible the interlocking nature of oppression where existing marginalization based on race, culture, gender and housing status are further compounded by additional factors.

**Figure 3-2. Example of Coming Together project dissemination posters**

For example, one participant spoke of the challenges she faced in navigating homelessness services with a disability. She suggested that

*There should be specific places/facilities for women with disabilities where women can get extra rest [and not be forced out during the day] and get special diet requirements met and have counsellors.*

– Dorene

Ensuring that services for those experiencing homelessness or marginal housing are not only physically accessible but also appropriate and responsive to the specific needs of women with disabilities should be considered a basic act of maintaining human rights. While the context of shelter services in particular tends to be marked by a lack of resources, high workloads and low staffing, a failure to recognize and respond to the needs of women with disabilities could be read as a symptom of a system that ignores the individual needs and context of each woman. Moreover, there is a need to deconstruct policies that require women to leave shelter services during the daytime, since these policies assume the ability to do so—and to do so without risk of harm to oneself or one's health.

Another participant spoke to the challenges and barriers to services faced by women who are actively using substances or alcohol. She advocated for a revision of policies that exclude women who are using from accessing services:

*These women need agencies even if they are smoking crack. They should be allowed to smoke crack inside agencies if that is what it takes to get them in the door 'cause even if they are stoned, at least they're sitting there* [in an agency] *talking. Giving them a place to cry if they need to and relieve themselves could mean more to them than even buying them a house.*

– Diane, Native/Black woman, 40–59 years old,
residing on the street for about five years

While allowing service users to smoke crack inside an agency may situate on the extreme end of a spectrum of options to make services more accessible to women who are using, the suggestion does highlight some important considerations. First, increasing the accessibility of services for women who are using should reflect a compassionate understanding of the reasons they are engaged in use in the first place. Secondly, it is arguable that women who are using, specifically Aboriginal women, may be at increased risk of harm in terms of violence and sexual assault. As such, policy and practice revision around substance and alcohol use could also increase safety.

Outreach services were a focus for one participant, who emphasized the role of outreach in decreasing isolation and making service utilization more viable for her:

> They should have more outreach support for loners like me. 'Cause a lot of the time I won't go searching for something. Either I'm too afraid, or nervous, so more outreach for women on the streets, and support.
> – Shelley

While another participant stressed the importance of having options in terms of service providers available to her:

> Where I go for support depends on how I'm feeling. For example, if I want a male or a female. Different days, different feelings—different people. Sometimes only females [service providers] will do. Some days a male [service provider] will ask me how I'm doing and I'll say 'fine', meanwhile my life could be falling apart. That's why it's important to have a lot of different people around you who can give you support, so you can pick and choose.
> – Ruth, Aboriginal woman, 40–59 years old, recently residing in rented room in private apartment after having been homeless for approximately three years

One participant shared from her experiences of having both been homeless and of providing 'frontline' services to women experiencing homelessness. She offered several powerful insights into needed transformation in how we deliver or even imagine services directed towards those experiencing homelessness:

> If you want to do anything to support street people, they have an incredible amount of grief. I have spent more time with my clients allowing them a safe place to grieve than anything else because it's not safe out there. The only thing you can do in social work is give them that space, because they are in a chronic state of loss.

*My advice to agencies is to get out of Dodge. Why are we pouring money into shelters? I don't want shelters. I refuse to do any activism around shelters. People are not dogs. I do not need a 20-year-old kid telling me when I can take a shower, when I can wash my hair, what clothes I can wear, when to go to bed, and, and, and, and. This is ludicrous. There's a whole political agenda to keeping people poverty ridden and homeless. We pump more and more money into shelters and we get more and more homeless. Hasn't somebody said 'What the fuck!!!' That has nothing to do with any of this, this is about land! There is enough empty land in this city and enough empty houses to house everybody in it . . . . There are a million creative ways to solve the problem that poor people already do all the time which is squat, break in, jump in, sleep on it, bring a friend into it, climb over the roof of it. Just give people a spot, they'll build a home, have a barrel and be perfectly happy. They don't need you, they don't need me. We have been conned that we're helpless. We're told we're psychologically unhealthy if we're independent.*

– Kim

Kim (not her real name) problematizes both the micro and macro understandings and responses to homelessness and the needs of those who are homeless. These passages highlight how current discourses of homelessness obscure, erase or ignore the agency of those who are homeless, resulting in services that can inadvertently imply to service users that they are helpless and reinforce feelings of grief, isolation and marginalization. In response, then, raising the voices of those who have or currently are experiencing homelessness and ensuring their active and meaningful involvement in policy, program and service development and delivery should transform both individual experiences and societal discourses of homelessness.

## Discussion

### *Looking Towards the Future*
The Aboriginal women who participated in the Coming Together project generously shared their voices and vision, clearly demonstrating their agency and wisdom in opposition to the negative stereotypical constructions of homeless Aboriginal women. They offer suggestions on how to move forward in a good way. While commonly housing, income, and service are understood as critical components

of addressing homelessness in Canada, the specific needs, history, strengths, and experiences of Aboriginal women need to be taken into account, considering when Aboriginal peoples are dispropor- tionately represented in homelessness in general. It is not enough just to address universal formula of resolving homelessness, but we need to step further to address particular issues, such as issues of colonialism, violence against Aboriginal women, and many other issues that affect Aboriginal women's lives differently than non- Aboriginal women's lives every day. Figure 3-3 (Sakamoto, Chin and Baskin 2010; Sakamoto et al. 2008) highlights this notion of needing to meaningfully include specific experiences of different identity/ social membership groups that go through homelessness differently in order to effectively address homelessness as a whole. Reflecting on the voices and vision of the Aboriginal women participants shared in this chapter, we propose the following implications for those working within systems associated with homelessness.

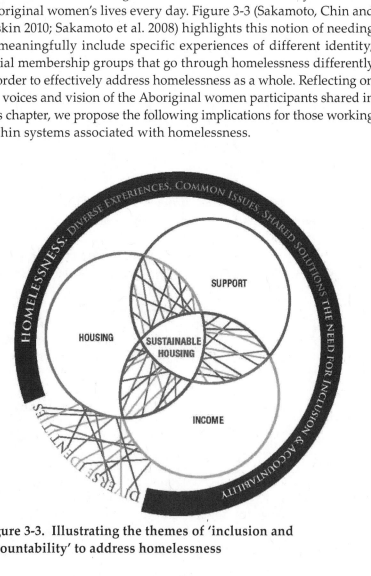

**Figure 3-3. Illustrating the themes of 'inclusion and accountability' to address homelessness**

### Reconstructing Ideas of Help and Helpers

There is a lot to be learned in here for how we think about, undertake, evaluate and plan the role of helping. Helping in the Western sense typically constructs the helper as one side of an equation, the powerful, normative, functional side. However, from an Aboriginal perspective a helper is an honoured role and responsibility. We all carry roles as helpers, but with different gifts to give. Aboriginal women, and particularly those experiencing homelessness, are not typically recognized for their gifts. They are situated among the lowest of the low in terms of marginalization in Canadian society. The racialized, sexualized violence levelled at Aboriginal women is starkly marked by the epidemic of missing and murdered women (e.g., NWAC 2010). We need system and service level responses that disrupt insidious societal stories of Aboriginal women experiencing homelessness as dependent, unworthy or helpless. Systems and services should honour the gifts and roles of these women as helpers, with important wisdom and experience to offer, in transforming their own safety, well-being and health and that of their families and communities. Honouring their voices and visions should occur in the creation, implementation or evaluation of policies, programs and services aimed at meeting their needs (including housing, shelter, health and social service systems). Aboriginal women who have or are currently experiencing homelessness should be well-represented in service organization boards of directors, community advisory panels, policy-making bodies, research teams and frontline service delivery and management.

### Decolonizing Systems, Services and Care

Decolonizing the education, practice and research of health and helping professions requires knowledge of Aboriginal histories prior to contact, of the history of colonization and cultural genocide and of the ongoing and intergenerational effects of colonization on both Aboriginal peoples and broader Canadian society today. Ignorance of the colonization and its effects enables the severe marginalization of Aboriginal women, their families, communities and nations to remain invisible and intact. As such, this should constitute mandatory content in the education and training of service providers and policy-makers. This education should also be delivered by Aboriginal peoples themselves.

In the context of policy development or change, decolonization efforts would include the involvement of Aboriginal women with direct experiences of homelessness, extending well beyond token-ism or one-off consultations, to ensure meaningful input and actual power to effect change. In the context of program development and delivery, decolonization would demand that programs are not sim-ply based in Western perspectives; indeed, Aboriginal approaches to helping would naturally fit with a decolonizing agenda. Reflecting notions of interconnectedness, interdependence and reciprocity, an Aboriginal approach would recognize all parties as sharing respon-sibility for health and well-being and each person having something to offer. In this way, Aboriginal women accessing services would be recognized as helpers just as much as those who are formally employed to serve them. This approach recognizes that formal ser-vice providers have just as much to learn and benefit as much from helping relationships as those accessing services. Interconnectedness and interdependence considers the relationships between all things, and in the context of the health and well-being this reflects an under-standing that the health of the collective is impacted by the health of the individual just as the health of the individual is impacted by that of the collective. If systems and providers of health social services moved away from an individualist stance (your health and well-being is *your* problem) to a collectivist stance, then we could operate as a society that understands how the illness and marginalization of some affects the health and well-being of all. Utilizing an Aboriginal approach also firmly recognizes and honours the agency of Aboriginal women in determining their own health and well-being and helps to foster a system in which seeking help does not equate with being helpless.

## Notes

1.  In this chapter, the terms *ciswomen*, *women*, and *non-transwomen* may be used interchangeably. For those unfamiliar with the term, "A cis-woman, shorthand for 'cissexual woman' or 'cisgender woman', is [a] non-transsexual woman—a woman whose assigned gender is female, and whose assigned female gender is more or less consistent with her personal sense of self. This distinguishes her from transwomen, short-hand for 'transsexual women'—women who were initially assigned a male gender, but have a female identity. If you identify as a woman but are not a transsexual woman, you're a ciswoman" (Head n.d.).

2. Traditionally, in 'staged' photography the artists take on the role of the director, creating or staging an image (McDonald 1999). They use models, props, costumes or lighting, often creating a sense of theatre that is then photographed. This kind of photography has ties to theatre, dance, sculpture, painting and literature. It is well suited to making stories from experiences because the images that are photographed are always coming out of context. The viewer is therefore invited to make the connections between the 'before' and 'after' sections of the story.
3. For more information about this project, visit www.artsandhomeless.com or www.homelesshub.ca/Topics/Arts-and-Homelessness-492.aspx.
4. All the participants' names shown here are pseudonyms, chosen to protect the anonymity and confidentiality of study participants.

## References

Absolon, K. E. 2011. *Kaandosswin: How We Come to Know.* Halifax: Fernwood.

Absolon, K. and C. Willett. 2004. "Aboriginal Research: Berry Picking and Hunting in the 21st Century." *First Peoples Child & Family Review,* 1(1): 5–17.

Adelson, N. 2005. "The Embodiment of Inequity: Health Disparities in Aboriginal Canada." *Canadian Journal of Public Health,* 96: s45–s61.

Anderson, K. 2004. *A Recognition of Being: Reconstructing Native Womanhood.* Toronto: Canadian Scholars' Press.

Anderson, M., J. Smylie, I. Anderson, R. Sinclair and S. Crengle. 2006. *First Nation, Métis, and Inuit Health Indicators in Canada,* Discussion Paper No. 18 [on-line]. Indigenous Peoples' Health Research Centre. http://www.iphrc.ca/Upload/canadian.pdf [consulted June 10, 2011].

Baskin, C. 2007. "Aboriginal Youth Talk about Structural Determinants as the Causes of Their Homelessness." *First Peoples Child & Family Review,* 3(3): 31–42.

Benoit, C., D. Carroll and M. Chaudhry. 2003. "In Search of a Healing Place: Aboriginal Women in Vancouver's Downtown Eastside." *Social Science & Medicine,* 56: 821–33.

Blair, P. J. 2005. *Rights of Aboriginal Women On- and Off-Reserve.* Vancouver: Scow Institute.

Bourassa, C., K. McKay-McNabb and M. Hampton. 2005. "Racism, Sexism and Colonialism: The Impact on the Health of Aboriginal Women in Canada." *Canadian Woman Studies,* 24(1): 55–58.

CAEFS (Canadian Association of Elizabeth Fry Societies). n.d. "Aboriginal Women." In Fact Sheets [on-line]. CAEFS Home Page. http://www.caefs.ca/wp-content/uploads/2013/04/Aboriginal-Women.pdf [consulted January 10, 2014].

Charmaz, K. 2006 *Constructing Grounded Theory: A Practical Guide through Qualitative Analysis*. London: Sage.

Daniels, H. W. 1998. "Bill C-31: The Abocide Bill." [on-line]. Congress of Aboriginal Peoples. http://www.abo-peoples.org/programs/C-31/Abocide/Abocide-6.html [consulted February 20, 2009].

Dion Stout, M., G. D. Kipling and R. Stout. 2001. *Aboriginal Women's Health Research Synthesis Project: Final Report*. Ottawa: Canadian Women's Health Network.

Flicker, S. and S. Savan. 2006. *A Snapshot of CBR in Canada*. Toronto: Wellesley Institute.

Gatali, M. and C. Archibald. 2003. "Women and HIV." In *Women's Health Surveillance Report*. Ottawa: Minister of Health, Canada.

Grekul, J., H. Krahn and D. Odynak. 2004. "Sterlizing the 'Feeble-Minded': Eugenics in Alberta, Canada, 1929–1972." *Journal of Historical Sociology*, 17: 358–84.

Gutiérrez, L. and E. Lewis. 1999. *Empowering Women of Color*. New York: Columbia University Press.

Head, Tom. n.d. "Ciswoman," *Civil Liberties* [online]. About.com. http://civil liberty.about.com/od/gendersexuality/g/Ciswoman-Cissexual-Woman. htm [consulted January 12, 2014].

Health Council of Canada. 2005. *The Health Status of Canada's First Nations, Métis and Inuit Peoples*. Toronto: Author.

Hwang, S. 2001. "Homelessness and Health." *Canadian Medical Association Journal*, 164(2): 229–33.

Israel, B. A., A. J. Schulz, E. A. Parker and A. B. Becker. 1998. "Review of Community-Based Research: Assessing Partnership Approaches to Improve Public Health." *Annual Review of Public Health*, 19: 173–202.

Jahiel, R., ed. 1992. *Homelessness: A Prevention-Oriented Approach*. Baltimore and London: Johns Hopkins University Press.

Kempf, A. 2006. "Anti-colonial Historiography: Interrogating Colonial Education." In *Anti-colonialism and Education: The Politics of Resistance*, ed. G. Dei and A. Kempf. Rotterdam: Sense Publishers, 129–58.

Khandor, E. and K. Mason. 2007. *Street Health Report*. [on-line]. Street Health. http://www.streethealth.ca/Downloads/SHReport2007.pdf [consulted August 30, 2013].

Kovach, M. 2009. *Indigenous Methodologies: Characteristics, Conversations and Contexts*. Toronto: University of Toronto Press.

Krauss, K. 2011 (April 7). "Activist Communique: 3,000 Missing Women Should Be an Election Issue." rabble.ca. [on-line]. http://rabble.ca/blogs/bloggers/krystalline-kraus/2011/04/activist-communiqu%C3%A9-3000-missing-women-should-be-election-i [consulted August 30, 2013].

Lavallée, L. 2009. "Practical Application of an Indigenous Research Framework and Indigenous Research Methods: Sharing Circles and Anishnaabe

Symbol-Based Reflection." *International Journal of Qualitative Methods*, 8(1): 21–40.

Lawrence, B. and K. Anderson. 2005. "Introduction to 'Indigenous Women: The State of Our Nations.'" *Atlantis*, 29(2): 1–10.

Loppie-Reading, C. and F. Wien. 2009. *Health Inequalities and Social Determinants of Aboriginal Peoples' Health*. Prince George, BC: National Collaborating Centre for Aboriginal Health.

McDonald, A. A. 1999. *Czech + Slovak Staged Photographs*. [on-line]. www.czechslovakphotos.com [consulted August 30, 2013].

Mohanram, R. 1999. *Black Body, Women, Colonialism and Space*. Minneapolis: University of Minnesota Press.

NAFC (National Association of Friendship Centres). 2012. *Urban Aboriginal Women: Social Determinants of Health and Well-Being*. National Association of Friendship Centres. [on-line]. http://www.laa.gov. nl.ca/laa/naws/pdf/NAFC-UrbanAboriginalWomen.pdf [consulted August 30, 2013].

NWAC (Native Women's Association of Canada). 2010. *What Their Stories Tell Us: Research Findings from the Sisters in Spirit Initiative*. Ottawa: Native Women's Association of Canada.

_____. 2007a. *Aboriginal Women and Homelessness: An Issue Paper*. Ottawa: Native Women's Association of Canada.

_____. 2007b. *Violence against Aboriginal Women and Girls: An Issue Paper*. Ottawa: Native Women's Association of Canada. Available at: http://www.nwac-hq.org/en/documents/nwac-vaaw.pdf [consulted June 10, 2011].

Novac S., J. Hermer, E. Paradis and A. Kellen. 2006. *Justice and Injustice: Homelessness, Crime, Victimization, and the Criminal Justice System*. Toronto: Centre for Urban and Community Studies, University of Toronto, and the John Howard Society of Toronto.

Qulliit Nunavut Status of Women Council. 2007. *The Little Voices of Nunavut: A Study of Women's Homelessness North of 60, Territorial Report*. Iqaluit: Qulliit Nunavut Status of Women Council.

RCAP (Royal Commission on Aboriginal Peoples). 1996. *Women's Perspectives*. [on-line]. Minister of Supply and Services Canada. http://www.ainc-inac.gc.ca/ap/pubs/sg/cg/cj2-eng.pdf [consulted March 4, 2009].

Ristock, J. L. and J. Pennel. 1996. *Community Research as Empowerment: Feminist Links, Postmodern Interruptions*. Toronto: Oxford University Press.

Sakamoto, I. and R. Pitner. 2005. "Use of Critical Consciousness in Anti-oppressive Social Work Practice: Disentangling Power Dynamics at Personal and Structural Levels." *British Journal of Social Work*, 35: 435–52.

Sakamoto, I., M. Chin, A. Chapra and J. Ricciardi. 2009. "A 'Normative' Homeless Woman?: Marginalisation, Emotional Injury, and Social Support of Transwomen Experiencing Homelessness." *Gay and Lesbian Issues and Psychology Review*, 5(1): 2–19.

Sakamoto, I., J. Ricciardi, J. Plyler and N. Wood. 2007. *Coming Together: Homeless Women, Housing and Social Support*. Toronto: Centre for Applied Social Research, Faculty of Social Work, University of Toronto.

Sakamoto, I., E. Khandor, A. Chapra, T. Hendrickson, J. Maher, B. Roche and M. Chin. 2008. *Homelessness—Diverse Experiences, Common Issues, Shared Solutions: The Need for Inclusion and Accountability*. Factor-Inwentash Faculty of Social Work, University of Toronto. [on-line]. Homelessness Hub. http://www.homelesshub.ca/ResourceFiles/id4katob.pdf [consulted January 12, 2014].

Sakamoto, I., J. Ricciardi, J. Plyler, N. Wood, A. Chapra, M. Chin, B. Allan, R. Cameron and M. Nunes. 2010. *Coming Together: Homeless Women, Housing and Social Support*. [on-line]. Wellesley Institute. http://www.wellesleyinstitute.com/research/coming-together-homeless-women-housing-and-social-support/ [consulted August 30, 2013].

Sinclair, R. 2009. "Identity or Racism? Aboriginal Transracial Adoption." In *Wicihitowin: Aboriginal Social Work in Canada*, ed. R. Sinclair, M. A. Hart and G. Bruyère. Halifax: Fernwood, 89–113.

Smith, L. T. 1999. *Decolonizing Methodologies: Research and Indigenous Peoples*. London: Zed Books.

Smylie, J. 2001. "SOGC Policy Statement: A Guide for Health Care Professionals Working with Aboriginal Peoples: Cross Cultural Understanding." *Journal of the Society of Obstetricians and Gynaecologists of Canada*, 100: 157–200.

Smylie, J., D. Fell and A. Ohlsson. 2010. "A Review of Aboriginal Infant Mortality Rates in Canada: Striking and Persistent Aboriginal/Non-Aboriginal Inequities." *Canadian Journal of Public Health*, 101(2): 143–48.

Statistics Canada. 2011. *Aboriginal Peoples in Canada: First Nations People, Métis and Inuit*. [on-line]. Statistics Canada. http://www12.statcan.gc.ca/nhs-enm/2011/as-sa/99-011-x/99-011-x2011001-eng.cfm [consulted August 30, 2013].

———. 2008. *Aboriginal Peoples in Canada in 2006: Inuit, Métis and First Nations*. [on-line]. Statistics Canada. http://www12.statcan.ca/english/census06/analysis/aboriginal/index.cfm [consulted August 30, 2013].

———. 2006. Chapter 8: Aboriginal Women. In *Women in Canada: A Gender-Based Statistical Report (5th ed.)*. [on-line]. Statistics Canada. http://www.statcan.gc.ca/pub/89-503-x/89-503-x2005001-eng.pdf [consulted August 30, 2013].

Talaga, T. 2012 (January 6). "UN to Investigate Missing Aboriginal Women." [on-line]. *Toronto Star*. http://www.thestar.com/news/insight/2012/01/

06/un_to_investigate_missing_aboriginal_women.html [consulted August 30, 2013].

The Truth Commission into Genocide in Canada. 2001. *Hidden from History: The Canadian Holocaust.* [on-line]. Truth Commission into Genocide in Canada, Justice in the Valley Coalition and International Human Rights Association of American Minorities. http://canadiangenocide. nativeweb.org/genocide.pdf [consulted August 30, 2013].

UATF (Urban Aboriginal Task Force). 2007. *Urban Aboriginal Task Force: Final Report.* Commissioned by the Ontario Federation of Indian Friendship Centres, the Ontario Métis Aboriginal Association, and the Ontario Native Women's Association.

Vancouver Women's Health Collective. 2006. "Titbits . . . on Women's Health: Facts on Aboriginal Women's Health." [on-line]. Vancouver Women's Health Collective. http://www.womenshealthcollective.ca/ PDF/aboriginal%20women%20and%20health%20titbit.pdf [consulted August 30, 2013].

Walters, K. L. and J. M. Simoni. 2002. "Reconceptualizing Native Women's Health: An 'Indigenist' Stress-Coping Model." *American Journal of Public Health,* 92(4): 520–24.

Woods, M. and S. Kirkey. 2013 (May 8). "'Tragic' Number of Aboriginal Children in Foster Care Stuns Even the Experts." *Montreal Gazette.* [on-line]. http://www.montrealgazette.com/life/Canada+young+aborig inals+grow+less+stable+homes+survey/8354098/story.html [consulted May 13, 2013].

Yukon Status of Women Council. 2007. *A Little Kindness Would Go a Long Way: A Study of Women's Homelessness in the Yukon Territory.* Whitehorse: Yukon Status of Women Council.

# CHAPTER 4

# Homelessness and Health in the Crowded Canadian Arctic: Inuit Experiences

Nathanael Lauster, PhD

Department of Sociology, University of British Columbia

Frank Tester, PhD

School of Social Work, University of British Columbia

## Introduction

The experience of homelessness for Inuit in the Eastern Arctic is the culturally mediated product of a history of displacement compounded by a serious shortage of affordable housing. Despite prominent photographs to the contrary in the national media (Paperny and Minogue 2009), homelessness in Nunavut is made most visible not by people sleeping in the streets but by extraordinarily high levels of residential crowding. However, key measurements of residential crowding only capture a portion of Inuit experiences of homelessness. In this chapter we explore Inuit experiences with four objectives. First, we present the cultural context and history of policy development relevant to housing in the Eastern Arctic. We then seek to better define what homelessness means, laying out different dimensions of homelessness and matching them to Inuit experiences. Third, we use the results of an innovative community-based survey, designed with local input, to estimate the prevalence of different types of homelessness in Nunavut and how these relate to more conventional measures. Finally, we establish relationships between homelessness and health issues in Nunavut, captured in the same community survey. Overall, we underscore the importance of housing as foundational in addressing a number of health-related problems in the Eastern Arctic. We also suggest that while conventional measures reveal some of the need for housing in Nunavut, they understate the overall experience of homelessness and miss important connections to health.

## Housing in Nunavut: Cultural Context and History of Policy

The following paragraphs provide a glimpse of what the transition to settlement life meant for many Inuit. They are presented as a composite of experiences, relayed to researcher Frank Tester in discussions with elders over years of researching the social history of Nunavut.

*The dogs were curled about in the snow, a slight north wind stretching across the Barrens. The entrance led down slightly, a tunnel through the walls he built two months earlier. The* kudlik, *or seal oil lamp, a base carved of soapstone and a wick from last summer's cotton grass was off to one side, frozen char and seal on the other, with a warm and familiar bench across the igloo's back, spread with several layers of skins from last fall's caribou hunt. Each family member had their designated spot, including hers, next to the kudlik, burning all day, all night, as long as there was seal oil to be had.*

*The bench was a place for games; for children to play with tiny bone and ivory carvings, some passed down from grandfather (*ataatattiq) *to child (*pariaq). *The next day, weather permitting, would be another at the floe edge; another day with dogs, raised from pups and harnessed to the* komatik (sled) *he'd made last winter with driftwood and pieces from the* Qallunaat's *(white person's) packing crates left behind the Hudson's Bay Post, three sleeps down the coast. It had been a tough winter. Bad storms (*uannaq) *had kept him away from the floe edge and the kudlik was burning low. It was a world, sometimes warm, but when not, still glowing with the satisfaction of things—skinning a seal or making new leads for the dog team—well done.*

*It was the winter before the plane came, skimming across what had, only a few weeks before, been a small bay (*ikirasaq) *full of floating ice. It carried the Reverend Father and the* RCMP *[Royal Canadian Mounted Police] Constable who had come to take Peter away to the Qallunaat school. He had to go. No choice in the matter. Neither he nor his wife could stand the thought of Peter, four, maybe five sleeps away, learning—what? To make a decent harness for the dogs? To set a successful fox trap? To find the right snow for building a home?*

*After a few months they followed where he'd gone. Now theirs was a government-supplied plywood home. The door didn't quite fit.*

*When it opened, the outside came in with a vengeance. The space heater fought the icy draft; a losing battle. The floor was cold, the ceiling sweaty. Money was needed for rent and fuel. The RCMP officer who provided family allowances and the social assistance that paid the bills was to be feared—and respected. He was surrounded by all that was no longer needed: his skill with a snow knife, her way of rolling cotton grass wicks, and dogs. What to do with a team that was hard to feed; confused in the presence of Inuit they'd never responded to before, and viewed with suspicion by a rifle-toting Mountie, threatening to shoot if some means was not found to tie them up.*

This scenario captures one of the circumstances that brought Inuit into settlements and the feelings of 'being useless' that often accompanied the move. Commencing in 1949, the federal government introduced a policy of providing Inuit children with an education designed to prepare them for entry into modern Canadian society. Through the 1950s, Inuit parents were increasingly pressured to send their children to federal day schools and church-run residential facilities. Inuit parents often followed their children, fearing what might become of them, and not willing to trust their children to the hands of strangers. Inuit also moved because they could no longer make a living on the land. Following the Second World War, the price of Arctic fox pelts and the trapping economy collapsed (Tester and Kulchyski 1994).

There were other reasons for moves to the settlements. Epidemics of disease, notably, tuberculosis and bouts of measles, whooping cough, diphtheria, chicken pox and influenza, made being in the vicinity of a nursing station useful. By the late 1960s, the migration of Inuit off the land was virtually complete. Inuit went from their homes—tents, igloos, *qamaqs* (sod homes) and a landscape they knew well—to clustered shacks made of scrap building materials, often gleaned from dumps at American-built radar stations. One energetic public health officer, in 1957, after touring the Eastern Arctic aboard the *C. D. Howe*, making its yearly visit with supplies and a party of physicians, nurses, dentists and X-ray technicians to check on 'Eskimo' health, compared what he saw to the worst slums of India, where he had served in the past (Tester 2006).

The northern administration introduced its first housing policy for Inuit in 1959, providing rigid frame, plywood one-room houses of 192 square feet. The rigid frame design (incorporating unnecessarily sloped roofs) was soon replaced by a variety of flat-roofed homes, affectionately known as matchboxes, a nickname reflecting their shape. The northern administration, fearing the 'dependency relations' that were imagined to develop should housing be given to Inuit, came up with a rent-to-own initiative. The houses cost about $1,500. Inuit were to pay $10 a month toward ownership, $500 being granted as a subsidy. Yet it cost about $50 a month to heat one of these units, and as a result few could keep up with the payments. As rent-to-own homes were converted to welfare units, record keeping became challenging. The units were poorly insulated and vented. They had no sanitary provisions other than a pail or 'honey bucket' lined with a green plastic garbage bag that was left outside when full. The water supply consisted of an indoor plastic tank that could be filled with water or ice to be melted down (Tester and Kulchyski 1994).

In Arviat (Eskimo Point), an epidemic of tuberculosis broke out in 1963 and was traced in large part to the appalling housing conditions (Moore 1964). Thirty-two percent of the community was ultimately evacuated to southern sanatoria for treatment. The cost was equivalent to providing the entire Eastern Arctic with three years' worth of housing. The rent-to-own policy was replaced in 1965 by the Eskimo Rental Housing Program. It provided Inuit with homes of up to three bedrooms with rent geared to income and house size and configuration to need. At the time, it was estimated that 1,600 homes were needed to properly house Inuit. In 1968, the federal government handed responsibility for the administration of social housing over to the Government of the Northwest Territories (GNWT). The GNWT integrated the initiative with a similar one in the Western Arctic and changed the name to the Northern Rental Housing Program.

Between 1968 and the present, housing policies in the Eastern Arctic have been marked by various attempts at encouraging home ownership. These policies have been costly, funnelling resources away from social housing (Hulchanski 1988), and have mostly failed to achieve their goals in the face of unsteady employment opportunities and low wages relative to the costs of housing. According to Statistics Canada 2006 census data, over 75 percent of households in Nunavut were renters. Commencing in 1981, Section 40 of the *National Housing Act* was used to fund public housing in the Northwest Territories. The Central Mortgage and Housing Corporation (CMHC) paid 75 percent of the capital costs of construction and 75 percent of the operating deficits. The capital cost provisions of this agreement were cancelled in 1993, and CMHC support for the maintenance of public housing is to decline to zero by the year 2037. Between 1992 and 1997, the GNWT spent $160 million on 1,435 social housing units in an attempt to address the growing housing shortage (Bourgeois 1997). Yet, by 1997, shortly before the new territory of Nunavut was carved out of the Northwest Territories, an estimated 4,350 new units were needed to meet the Northwest Territories' social housing needs, including the replacement of old stock (Northwest Territories Housing Corporation 1997). The response of the Northwest Territories' finance minister was to inject even more funding ($40–$50 million) into another home ownership program (Bourgeois 1998).

By 1999, the newly formed government of Nunavut had an estimated list of 1,231 households waiting for social housing. The Nunavut Housing Corporation (NHC) was created in 2000 to create, administer and coordinate housing programs in the territory. The 1,231 Inuit households on the wait list confronting the newly formed corporation were distributed among fewer than 5,600 existing households (5,665 households were enumerated in the 2001 Aboriginal census for Nunavut two years later). Given that all materials must be imported from the south and designs must address Arctic conditions, the costs of Arctic construction are considerable. In 2006, the federal government provided Nunavut with $200 million to build some 725 new units of affordable housing through the Nunavut Housing Trust (OAG 2008), at an average cost of $275,000 per unit. Unexpected labour and material costs added another estimated $75,000 to the cost of each (Windeyer 2010b). No funds were allocated for the operation and maintenance of the units. The $350,000 price tag of these dwellings compared to the $16,069 median income for Inuit aged 15 years and older (Statistics Canada 2006) provides insight into the reasons the severely limited stock of social housing dominates housing options for residents of Nunavut. By September of 2010, it was estimated that the $200 million Trust program set up to address the considerable social housing needs of Nunavummiut was $110 million over budget (Windeyer 2010a).

## Dimensions of Homelessness

Prominent definitions of homelessness, such as that offered by the United Nations, emphasize physical shelter from the elements in a unit meant for human habitation and a secure location for one's possessions so they need not be carried from place to place (Hill 1991;

Springer 2000; United Nations 1998). These often become working definitions for surveys of homelessness, focused on where people last slept or what services they've used (Peressini, McDonald and Hulchanski 1995). These definitions may be broadened to incorporate those living in inadequate shelter, usually defined with reference to tenure and physical security, privacy, space, basic services (water supply, sanitation, etc.) and affordability (Springer 2000).

In the Canadian context, being defined by CMHC as in "Core Housing Need" incorporates aspects of affordability, suitability (having enough bedrooms given household composition) and adequacy or state of repair (CMHC 2009a). Households are counted as being in core housing need if they do not meet the minimum thresholds for affordability, suitability and adequacy and are unable to afford local accommodation that meets these thresholds. According to these criteria an estimated 12.7 percent of households across all households in Canada and an estimated 44.7 percent of Inuit households in Nunavut in 20065 (CMHC 2009a) are in core housing need.[1] Those in core housing need and currently spending at least half their income on shelter costs have been identified as at risk of homelessness (Fiedler, Schuurman and Hyndman 2006).

While affordability drives the prevalence of core housing need in most parts of Canada, suitability is clearly the main driver in Nunavut. The measurement of suitability emphasizes privacy, home as a sanctuary and having a room of one's own (Lauster and Tester 2010). 'Home' has also acquired broad meanings as a symbol and stage for making claims to social belonging and inclusion (Hopper 1997; Mallett 2004). In this sense, acquiring a home may be related to the development of family and adult identity (Goldscheider and Goldscheider 1999; Lauster 2006). Together, the ideas of home as sanctuary and home as symbol relate to Goffman's notions of the back stages and front stages required for putting on successful social performances (Goffman 1959). In effect, people are always performing social roles for one another and they need spaces to both prepare their performances and to enact them. In this sense, home is a meaning-making tool. Correspondingly, being homeless means being unable to put on successful social performances, resulting in stigmatization and a sense of meaninglessness. Home as belonging is also tied to a sense of community and country, locating people in a homeland and way of life (Mallett 2004).

As varying definitions serve to indicate, the idea of 'home' used to define 'homelessness' remains highly subjective, often contested, malleable in definition and strongly dependent upon context (Hopper 1997; Kellett and Moore 2003; Mallett 2004). The ambiguity of the concept has driven at least one researcher to suggest replacing homelessness with 'houselessness' as a social problem, privileging more objective measures of shelter as definitional in order to enable cross-cultural comparisons (Springer 2000). Yet both what is seen as a problematic housing circumstance and what is seen as home are necessarily culturally specific. Consequently, we suggest that the best way to account for cultural difference in understandings of homelessness is not to ignore difference but to ask people in varying contexts about the problems they face in feeling at home throughout their daily lives.

In this sense we define homelessness as multidimensional, corresponding to problems in achieving various subjective experiences of feeling at home. From the literature reviewed above, we take the experiences of feeling at home to mean feeling: (1) sheltered from the elements, (2) physically secure, (3) secure in the storage of one's possessions, (4) secure in one's privacy, (5) a sense of belonging and meaning and (6) a connection to one's homeland. We define problems encountered in producing these feelings as problems of homelessness. Below we apply this understanding of dimensions of homelessness to the lived experience of Inuit in Nunavut, taking into account the crucial importance of cultural context, to estimate the prevalence and impact of homelessness.

### The Experience of Homelessness in the Eastern Arctic: The Kinngait Harvest Society Survey

Given the sketch of homelessness above, we use the results of a community-developed survey in Kinngait, Nunavut (formerly Cape Dorset) to estimate the prevalence of different forms of homelessness in the Eastern Arctic and to understand their relationships with health. Kinngait is one of 25 communities making up Nunavut, and in 2006 it contained just over 4 percent of the territory's population (1,236 people). It is located in the southwest corner of Baffin Island (Qikiqtani). According to the most recent census, over 90 percent of the community's population is Inuit. Approximately 85 percent of the housing is rented social housing. The official unemployment rate was high in 2006, at 25.3 percent, and the median annual income for Inuit members of the community, age 15 and older, was $12,672. Median household incomes were higher at $35,200, but still far below the median for the country as a whole ($52,634).

In 2005, researcher Frank Tester worked with community members from Kinngait to create and administer a questionnaire exploring the housing situations and the physical and mental health of residents. Sampling for the survey was stratified by categories of age, sex, family status (couple vs. single) and position on a housing waiting list. Households in the community were numbered and selected randomly until a household with a member meeting stratification criteria was found. That member was selected to be interviewed in the survey and the household was not replaced. As a result, some 91 residents of Kinngait (age 15 and older) were surveyed, reflecting 91 different households in the community. Overall, the sample is somewhat younger and more dominated by women than both the population of Kinngait and Nunavut as a whole, though it also has a slightly higher representation of residents over age 55. Census estimates for age–sex categories allow the sample to be re-weighted to correspond to the population distribution in Nunavut, and these results are reported in the analyses that follow, where indicated. The sample proportion in common-law and marital unions (49%) lies between the proportion reported in the 2006 census for Kinngait (47%) and for Nunavut as a whole (52%). Similarly, the sample proportion drawn from the waiting lists (14.3%) lies between that of the proportion of Inuit (15 years or older) on the waiting list estimated for Kinngait (12.2%), and the proportion estimated for Nunavut as a whole (using 1999 estimates, this would be approximately 15.9%).[2]

Community participation in the design of the survey incorporated local understandings of both the meaning of home and the related problems associated with feeling at home. Given the hunting culture of Inuit and that many Inuit lived on the land until the mid-1960s, we suggest a connection to one's homeland is especially important in the Eastern Arctic. The capacity to return to the land and a more traditional way of living away from settlements—spending summer and even long winter periods out of settlements and in cabins scattered along the coast in areas traditionally occupied—helps many Inuit "feel better" and "at home". Table 4-1 details the survey responses as they relate to these problems. The nature of the survey, based in local experience, helped avoid situations where language

**Table 4-1. Homelessness dimensions as measured by equivalent survey item responses**

| Homelessness Dimension | Equivalent Survey Responses |
|---|---|
| Lack shelter from elements | "I need a different house because it's too wet here" or "this house is cold or very cold, causing sickness or making us stay at someone else's house" |
| Lack physical security | "I do not sleep at home because of problems at home, or because I have nowhere to sleep there" or "violence is a problem related to my housing circumstance" |
| Lack security for possessions | "Someone sold furniture/appliances/equipment from house because of gambling, drug use, drinking, needing $ for food, etc." |
| Lack privacy | "I never have time alone or privacy" |
| Lack belonging | "Someone in my house needs to have a house of their own" or "I don't have a bedroom / sleep on the couch, etc." |
| Lack access to land | "I lack the equipment I need to get out on the land, and it is not okay" |

and concepts imported from southern Canada fail to make sense to local residents and broadened the range of topics considered, to include culturally specific concerns. A fuller description of the survey design is available in the report *Iglutaq: The Implications of Homelessness for Inuit* by Tester and the Harvest Society (2006).

### Measurement and Prevalence of Experiences of Homelessness

The extreme weather of the Arctic climate means that occupying a dwelling meant for human habitation, including a roof and walls, may not be enough to fully protect one from the elements, especially the cold and wet. Thirty-three percent of the respondents felt a lack of protection from the elements by these measurements, roughly matching the census estimates of 29 percent of occupied units in Kinngait needing major repairs in 2006 (Statistics Canada 2006). This compares to 23 percent of Nunavut's Aboriginal households as a whole needing major repairs in the CMHC estimate (CMHC 2009b).

We interpret physical security to mean having a stable place to stay, especially to sleep, where one can feel safe. Many Inuit reported sleeping away from home simply because they felt like it, reflecting the cultural flexibility of sleep arrangements for Inuit households and the difficulty of applying measurements of household suitability derived from elsewhere (Lauster and Tester 2010). But others reported sleeping away from home because of problems or lack of space, or they otherwise reported violence as a problem at home. Altogether, some 15 percent of the sample felt a lack of physical security according to these measurements. Given that recent data on the rate of violent crime in Nunavut is over eight times the Canadian average (Statistics Canada 2006), it may not be surprising that nearly one-sixth of the sample feels a lack of physical security in their housing situation.

Rates of breaking and entering are about four times higher in Nunavut than for Canada as a whole (Tester and the Harvest Society 2006), but we have little data on experience with breaking and entering from the survey. Instead, we have data on whether or not a household member has ever sold any "furniture, appliances, or equipment" from the respondent's house because of various immediate needs. Living in a household where household items needed for daily living might be sold at any time to cover costs for any of the items listed (and needing money for food was by far the most commonly reported reasons) constitutes a problem, leaving residents feeling insecure about their tenure. This possibility affected 32 percent of the sample respondents.

Given the widely acknowledged residential crowding in Nunavut, it is unsurprising that many Inuit reported feeling a lack of privacy. The survey asked those reporting that their housing situation was crowded, what problems this made for them. Those responding with "I never have time alone or privacy" as a problem were considered to be lacking in privacy, including 33 percent of the sample.

To measure lacking belonging, we focus on someone in a household being seen as needing a place of their own as a potential indicator of the lack of an opportunity to define oneself and, consequently, to belong to a family or community as both a member and contributing individual. Such individuals do not 'fit' in the household in some way, either because they are seen by other household members to be old enough to have their own place or because they make too much noise, they argue too much with a romantic partner, they are lazy, they disrespect their elders or some other reason. The sense of lack of belonging generated by this bad fit creates a feeling of homelessness, both for the household member who does not seem to fit, and for other household members who must deal with them, often being denied the respect they feel they should be accorded in the process. In the case of those old enough to have a place of their own, the lack of belonging is double-edged. By being denied a place of their own, they are also denied a place in the world of adults befitting their age. As a separate indicator of those not 'fitting' into a household, we include as lacking belonging those who do not have a clear space of their own in their housing situation, sleeping on the couch, the floor or some other location. In total, some 40 percent of the sample experienced a lack of belonging defined in these ways. This is the most prevalent form of homelessness we record, likely linked to the long waiting lists for public housing units across all Nunavut communities.

Finally, we consider the lack of access to the land as a dimension of homelessness for Inuit. Inuit are a hunting culture and despite attempts at acculturation, Inuit identity and social relations are still tied to hunting and 'life on the land'. Some 25 percent of the sample, mostly older respondents, indicated that they lived on the land before moving into the community. The land also supports a traditional way of life and the historic sources of food important to Inuit culture. Over 5 percent of Inuit reported returning to living on the land for a while since first moving to the settlement, either for better hunting, because they thought the traditional way of living was better or they missed it or because they simply wanted to get away from the community. However, it takes special equipment to get out onto the land. Respondents were asked whether or not they had the equipment needed to get out onto the land. Of the 36 percent of respondents who did not have the equipment, some reported feeling "okay" about not being able to go out. We considered those who did not feel "okay" about not having the equipment to get out on the land as lacking access to the land.

Table 4-2 provides estimates of the prevalence of homelessness by these various measures. An estimate of the percentage of households in core housing need is also included in this table. Data from the survey do not allow an easy calculation of affordability for the sample. But the *Canadian Housing Observer* estimates for core housing needs in Nunavut indicate that this is the least important criteria for the territory (despite being the most important criteria determining housing needs in every province in Canada). The sample estimate of core housing needs is drawn from questions about household

**Table 4-2.  Estimates of homelessness prevalence by dimension amongst those over age 15**

|  | Sample *n* | Sample % | Est. Nunavut % | Est. Nunavut *n* | 95% CI Low | 95% CI High |
|---|---|---|---|---|---|---|
| Lack shelter from elements | 30 | 33% | 35% | 5,429 | 3,768 | 7,477 |
| Lack physical security | 14 | 15% | 17% | 2,584 | 870 | 3,606 |
| Lack security for possessions | 29 | 32% | 36% | 5,638 | 3,925 | 7,753 |
| Lack privacy | 30 | 33% | 35% | 5,372 | 3,752 | 7,371 |
| Lack belonging | 36 | 40% | 42% | 6,446 | 4,357 | 8,119 |
| Lack access to land | 28 | 31% | 31% | 4,807 | 3,082 | 6,651 |
|  |  |  |  |  |  |  |
| Core housing need* | 40 | 44% | 44.7% | 2,600 | * | * |

*Core housing need refers to % of Inuit households rather than % of individuals. Estimated Nunavut data on core housing needs drawn from the *Canadian Housing Observer*.
Source: "Characteristics of Households in Core Housing Need, Nunavut, 2006" (CMHC, 2009b). No confidence intervals are provided, though estimates are based on approximately 1 in 5 household census sampling.

composition and bedroom numbers, taking a conservative estimate of the number of bedrooms required to meet Canadian National Occupancy Standards given the age and relationship status of household members (suitability), and questions about whether or not respondents need a new dwelling because of repair issues involving their current dwelling (adequacy). Overall, the sample estimate of those in core housing need matches well with the territorial estimates provided by the *Canadian Housing Observer* (CMHC 2009b).

Both estimates (sample and territorial) of core housing need suggest that the size of the at-risk-of-homelessness population, as may be currently considered by policy-makers, is higher than any single dimension of homelessness discussed above. However, considering that the coincidence of dimensions, as in Table 4-3, suggests that overall most Inuit—an astounding 87 percent—are likely to experience some dimension of homelessness, with about 30 percent experiencing three or more dimensions of homelessness. As a result, policy-makers are likely to underestimate the prevalence of homelessness amongst the Inuit. Notably, the dimensions of homelessness measured here tend to be positively correlated with one another, but

**Table 4-3. Coincidence of homelessness dimensions (homelessness index alpha = 0.396)**

|  | Sample $n$ | Sample % | Est. Nunavut % | Est. Nunavut $n$ |
|---|---|---|---|---|
| Lacking nothing | 11 | 12% | 13% | 1,956 |
| Lacking 1 item | 35 | 38% | 34% | 5,317 |
| Lacking 2 items | 20 | 22% | 22% | 3,440 |
| Lacking 3 items | 15 | 16% | 16% | 2,540 |
| Lacking 4 items | 4 | 4% | 6% | 953 |
| Lacking 5 items | 5 | 5% | 8% | 1,178 |
| Lacking all items | 1 | 1% | 1% | 126 |

the correlations are not high (the highest is 0.27). Creating an index of homelessness by combining dimensions provides an overall alpha that's relatively low (0.396) indicating that different dimensions are indeed being tapped by each indicator.

All homelessness dimensions except for 'Lacking shelter' and 'Lacking access to the land' are positively and significantly ($p < 0.05$) correlated with being in core housing need, but again the correlations are relatively low (the highest is 0.27). As in Table 4-4, combining all the dimensions into the single homelessness index yields a higher and statistically significant correlation of 0.38 to core housing needs, but the relationship between experiential measures of homelessness and core housing need measures indicates that much of the experience of homelessness in the Eastern Arctic is currently not being accounted for by CMHC measures. Other seemingly objective crowding measures (also included in Table 4-4) perform similarly or worse, failing to capture the full range of the homelessness problem in Nunavut, as described above. Survey respondents were asked directly about whether or not they subjectively felt they lived in a crowded house. For the 47 percent of respondents who felt they lived in crowded circumstances, over a third (35%) indicated they had no problems with it. A substantial minority (18%) of those experiencing crowding said they even liked having all the people around. Crowding is clearly a primary driver of the high prevalence of homelessness amongst Inuit, but the experience of homelessness is not entirely about crowding, nor is it fully captured by culturally ignorant measures of the phenomenon that fail to take into account Inuit experience (Lauster and Tester 2010).

**Table 4-4.  Other measures of housing need and crowding from survey (weighted to Nunavut age/sex distribution)**

|  | Mean | Std. Dev. | Min. | Max. | Correlation to Homelessness Index |
|---|---|---|---|---|---|
| Core housing need | 0.50 | 0.50 | 0 | 1 | 0.38*** |
| Bedrooms needed (cnos) | 0.60 | 1.17 | −2 | 4 | 0.43*** |
| Occupant to bedroom ratio | 1.95 | 0.82 | 0.5 | 5 | 0.32*** |
| Number sharing bedroom* | 1.13 | 1.01 | 0 | 4 | 0.15 |

*Other than partner.

## Homelessness and Health in the Eastern Arctic

A number of studies have linked crowding and aspects of housing situations in the Canadian North to health issues. Most prominently, researchers have linked tuberculosis (Clark, Riben and Nowgesic 2002; Lodge et al. 2006) and respiratory infections in children (Kovesi and Gilbert 2007) to housing circumstances and crowding. A larger literature has also linked psychological distress to crowding (Evans 2003). Here we extend this work by exploring the link between dimensions of homelessness and a more diverse set of health-related outcomes, as reported by respondents.

The survey asked, broadly, about various indicators of the health of Inuit respondents. In particular, the survey identified a set of ailments understood within the community to be health related and asked respondents whether or not they experienced them. The survey also asked about encounters with other key problems. Items are listed in Table 4-5. The separate items within each list were added together to create a health issue index (combining the former items, $\alpha = 0.7018$) and a more general problem index (combining the latter items, $\alpha = 0.4275$). Separate items and combined indices were subjected to a correlation analysis with dimensions of homelessness and the homelessness index, as well as with the indicator for core housing needs. Table 4-6 reveals the significant correlations emerging from this analysis corresponding to each measure of homelessness. In all cases, correlations to health issues and problems are positive.

Notably, every dimension of homelessness is significantly correlated with a set of health conditions and related problems. Moreover, each of the problem sets associated with different dimensions of homelessness is unique to that dimension. The problem index, obtained by

**Table 4-5. Items measuring health conditions and related problems**

| Health Conditions | Related Problems |
| --- | --- |
| Do you get cold sores? | Do you have any problems with: |
| Do you get the flu? | Drinking? |
| Do you get colds and coughs? | Violence? |
| Do you have tuberculosis? | Depression? |
| Do you have cramped muscles or body pain? | Drug use? |
| Do you have poor sleep? | Problems with school? |
| Do you have skin problems? | Problems with work? |
| Do you suffer from stress? | People being angry? |
| Do you get migraines or headaches? | |
| Do you have other health conditions? | |

combining the items of problems with drinking, violence, depression, drug use, problems with school, problems with work and people being angry, was significantly associated with all dimensions of homelessness. By contrast, the health issue index was not associated with all dimensions of homelessness but seemed at least marginally related to lacking security of possessions, lacking privacy and lacking access to the land. Combining every dimension of homelessness together into a single index produced particularly powerful relationships to the broadest swath of problems and issues raised by respondents. Higher scores on the homelessness index were correlated with experiencing cold sores, flu, poor sleep, drinking, violence, depression, drug use, school problems and problems with people being angry. In this way, the homelessness index proved far more comprehensive than the measure of core housing need derived from the survey as roughly equivalent to CMHC measurements. Again, the core housing needs designation seems to capture some of the issues related to homelessness in Nunavut, but by no means all of them.

The significant positive correlation between the homelessness index and both the health issues index and the problem index (treated as dependent variables) persists after controlling for age, gender, presence of a partner, presence of children and schooling in OLS regression models (not shown here). By contrast, when our measure of core housing needs is introduced in the model, it does not attain significance, but the significant effect of the homelessness

**Table 4-6. Links between homelessness measures and health conditions or related problems**

|  | Significantly Positive Correlations |
|---|---|
| Lack shelter from elements | problem index, headaches, other health issues, *stress, depression, drug use* |
| Lack physical security | problem index, cold sores, violence*, drug use, *drinking, depression, anger* |
| Lack security for possessions | problem index, violence, drug use, school problems, *health issue index, cold sores, drinking* |
| Lack privacy | problem index, poor sleep, depression, *health issue index, school problems* |
| Lack belonging | problem index, drinking, violence, drug use |
| Lack access to land | problem index, violence, poor sleep, depression, work problems, anger, *health issue index, drinking* |
| Homelessness index | health issue index, problem index, cold sores, poor sleep, drinking, violence*, depression, drug use, school problems, anger, *flu* |
| Core housing need | health issue index, problem index, poor sleep, school problems, *flu* |

Note: Italicized health-related problems are marginal (0.05 < $p$ < 0.10) in the significance of their correlation.
*Listing violence as a problem related to housing is included as part of the definition of homelessness in this case.

index remains. Including each dimension of homelessness separately in regression models, treating the problem index as the dependent variable, indicates that each retains significance by itself and almost all retain significance in combination with one another. However, when treating the health issue index as the dependent variable, separate dimensions of homelessness do not attain significance. Overall, multivariate regression results support the significance of the bivariate correlations shown here and are available from the first author upon request.

## Community Perceptions of Links between Homelessness and Health

Finally, respondents in the survey were also asked directly whether or not they thought any of their health issues related to their housing circumstances. Table 4-6 summarizes the results. Headaches and tuberculosis were experienced by a very small portion of respondents but were readily linked to housing situations by those respondents. Of more common ailments, poor sleep and stress were most often linked to housing situations, but all health issues were linked to housing situations by at least some respondents. A similar question was asked about overall health, linked more specifically to whether or not respondents felt their health would be better with more space. Over half of respondents (57% weighted to Nunavut distributions) felt that their health would improve with more space.

Table 4-7 summarizes similar results for other problems. Here the wording of the question about links to housing situation was

**Table 4-7. Links between health conditions and housing situation, as perceived by respondents (weighted to Nunavut age/sex distribution)**

|  | % Experiencing | Of Those Experiencing, % Linking to Housing |
|---|---|---|
| Cold Sores | 20.3% | 20.0% |
| Flu | 46.9% | 33.1% |
| Tuberculosis | 3.6% | 48.0% |
| Cramps/Pains | 30.2% | 14.0% |
| Poor Sleep | 28.6% | 67.1% |
| Skin Issues | 7.4% | 21.8% |
| Stress | 35.5% | 48.0% |
| Headaches | 2.9% | 100.0% |
| Other Health | 8.0% | 37.0% |

**Table 4-8. Links between related problems and the number of people in the house, as perceived by respondents (weighted to Nunavut age/sex distribution)**

|  | % Experiencing | Of those Experiencing, % Linking to Number of People in House |
|---|---|---|
| Drinking | 6.8% | 70.4% |
| Violence | 10.1% | 78.8% |
| Depression | 12.4% | 49.4% |
| Drug Use | 20.3% | 20.5% |
| School Problems | 17.4% | 54.2% |
| Work Problems | 8.8% | 61.1% |
| People Being Angry | 25.6% | 51.6% |

closely tied to whether or not fewer people in the house would help the problem. Overall, problems were more consistently linked to housing situation than health issues. Problems with violence were most often thought to be fixable with fewer people in the house (over four-fifths of respondents experiencing problems with violence felt this way). By contrast, only about a fifth of respondents felt drug use problems would be fixed by fewer people.

## Conclusions

By all reliable accounts there is a housing crisis in Nunavut. The territory has the highest rate of core housing needs in Canada, well over twice its nearest competitor, the Northwest Territories (CMHC 2009a). Our analyses estimate that a shocking 87 percent of Inuit experience some form of homelessness, dimensions of which are strongly tied to the housing crisis. Dimensions of homelessness are also strongly correlated with a wide range of health problems. The costs associated with building and maintaining enough decent and affordable housing in the Eastern Arctic to ease the housing crisis have often been far outweighed by the costs of dealing with the various health problems associated with homelessness.

At the same time, the ways in which the lack of housing in Nunavut affects people are not quite the same as the way the housing crisis is measured by estimates of core housing need. Those in core housing need are often treated as being at risk of homelessness (Fiedler, Schuurman and Hyndman 2006). In the case of Inuit living in Nunavut, we suggest that most of those classified as being in core housing need are, in fact, experiencing multiple dimensions of homelessness. Strikingly, this is also true for many Nunavut residents who would not be considered in core housing need.

In Nunavut, homelessness is the result of a particular history of displacement, as well as a history of inadequate resources for housing, mapped onto a shifting cultural definition of home. Thinking about homelessness in terms of various dimensions of the meaning of home provides a powerful way to incorporate history and culture into definitions. The result of Nunavut's history and culture is that sizable portions of the population of Nunavut feel they lack shelter, security, a place to store their property, privacy, a sense of belonging and any way to feel connected to their ancestral lands and the way of life that makes them feel Inuit. In a very real sense, these are the dimensions of homelessness of relevance to the Inuit population of Nunavut. The housing problems of Nunavut are rooted in material circumstance, but these material circumstances, in turn, are culturally interpreted as they are experienced in everyday life.

Each of the dimensions of homelessness we specify and attempt to measure here were correlated with aspects of health and well-being. Each of the dimensions also remained distinct from the other dimensions of homelessness measured. It seems clear that homelessness is a multifaceted experience, at least in the context of the Eastern Arctic.

We provide only rough estimates of the size of the population in Nunavut experiencing homelessness. These estimates come with many qualifications, especially since we attempt to generalize from the experiences recorded in only one of Nunavut's 25 communities. Nevertheless, we argue that the survey analyzed here provides valuable results for the study of homelessness in Nunavut. We suggest that one of the problems encountered in studying relationships between homelessness and health is the lack of attention provided to how culture matters. The experience of home and problems associated with achieving it are culturally mediated, as ultimately are experiences of health. One particularly valuable aspect of the survey analyzed here is that it was constructed with significant input from the community members being studied. As a result, the findings of the survey better reflect local understandings of homelessness and health than would be the case for a survey designed without this input.

This is a direction that needs to be pursued further. Since the NHC was created in 2000, there have been a number of detailed studies of housing in Nunavut territory. These include the 2009–2010 Nunavut Housing Needs Survey and a report on the NHC prepared by the Auditor General of Canada and released in May of 2008. These documents do a credible job of detailing the extent of overcrowding noted in the report used to frame this chapter. The statistical information collected in these studies meets primarily the managerial needs of the NHC. Their findings are important. The recommendations made by the Auditor General of Canada include: improved training for the local housing authorities responsible for total management of social housing at the community level, ensuring that the rating system for determining priorities in the provision of social housing are actually applied, taking steps to ensure that eligibility criteria are met and updating manuals and procedures and ensuring that proper procedures are followed in maintaining and reporting on the condition of social housing stock. These are all important to making the existing system work better.

But the Inuit experience of home—what it is, how it works, what it means, how its provision might be changed and improved—merits more attention. The research presented in this chapter attempts to moves in this direction. The Nunavut housing situation is characterized by considerable need and inadequate resources. The withdrawal of CMHC maintenance funds for social housing over the next 25 years will place considerable additional financial pressure on the NHC. A report prepared by the Government of Nunavut and Nunavut Tunngavik Incorporated (2004) estimates that it would take the unlikely sum of $1.9 billion invested between 2006 and 2016 to bring housing in Nunavut up to Canadian standards. This is an unlikely investment, suggesting the need for a radically different approach to dealing with overcrowding (homelessness) in Nunavut. If 'home' is about meaning-making and belonging, if self-esteem is tied to what one accomplishes in the creation and management of space, then Inuit need both the pride and responsibility of 'ownership' in a situation where conventional ideas about ownership are unrealistic. These considerations suggests the merit of exploring radically redesigned cooperative or co-housing associations, perhaps defined in relation to extended family units involving otherwise unemployed coop members in construction, management and maintenance of units for which they have a budget and responsibility, with the NHC providing technical, managerial and related assistance. While the details and complexities of such a program are considerable, the current social housing program operating in Nunavut is unsustainable, suggesting that alternatives integrating social, cultural and health—as well as conventionally understood space-related needs—are in order.

## Notes

1. Only 12.9% of non-Inuit households in Nunavut experienced core housing need in 2006.
2. Assuming approximately two persons per household on the waiting list.

## References

Bourgeois, Annette. 1998 (January 23). "Housing Sector to Get Boost from GNWT." *Nunatsiaq News.*

_____. 1997 (June 13). "Housing Shortage Worsens in Communities." *Nunatsiaq News.*

Clark, M., P. Riben, E. Nowgesic. 2002. "The Association of Housing Density, Isolation and Tuberculosis in Canadian First Nations Communities." *International Journal of Epidemiology* 31: 940–45.

CMHC. 2009a. *Canadian Housing Observer 2009.* Ottawa: CMHC.

_____. 2009b. *Canadian Housing Observer 2009.* Supplemental Table for Nunavut. [on-line]. CMHC. http://www.cmhc.gc.ca/en/corp/about/cahoob/data/data_013.cfm [consulted April 28, 2010].

Evans, Gary. 2003. "The Built Environment and Mental Health." *Journal of Urban Health,* 80(4): 536–55.

Fiedler, R., N. Schuurman and J. Hyndman. 2006. "Hidden Homelessness: An Indicator-Based Approach for Examining the Geographies of Recent Immigrants At-Risk of Homelessness in Greater Vancouver." *Cities,* 23(3): 205–16.

Goffman, E. 1959. *The Presentation of Self in Everyday Life.* New York: Anchor Books.

Goldscheider, F. and C. Goldscheider. 1999. *The Changing Transition to Adulthood: Leaving and Returning Home.* Thousand Oaks, CA: Sage Publications.

Government of Nunavut (Nunavut Housing Corporation) and Nunavut Tunngavik Incorporated. 2004 (September). *Nunavut Ten-Year Inuit Housing Action Plan: A Proposal to the Government of Canada.* [on-line]. http://www.tunngavik.com/documents/publications/2004-09-00-Ten-Year-Inuit-Housing-Plan-English).pdf [consulted January 12, 2014].

Hill, R. 1991. "Homeless Women, Special Possessions, and the Meaning of 'Home': An Ethnographic Case Study." *Journal of Consumer Research,* 18(3): 298–310.

Hopper, K. 1997. "Homelessness Old and New: The Matter of Definition." In *Understanding Homelessness: New Policy and Research Perspectives.* Washington, DC: Fannie Mae Foundation.

Hulchanski, David. 1988. *The Evolution of Housing Policy and Programs in the Northwest Territories: An Outline History.* Draft report. Vancouver: School of Community and Regional Planning (SCARP), University of British Columbia.

Kellett, P. and J. Moore. 2003. "Routes to Home: Homelessness and Home-Making in Contrasting Societies." *Habitat International,* 27: 123–41.

Lauster, N. 2006. "A Room of One's Own or Room Enough for Two? Access to Housing and New Household Formation in Sweden, 1968–1992." *Population Research and Policy Review,* 25(4): 329–51.

Lauster, N. and F. Tester. 2010. "Culture as a Problem in Linking Material Inequality to Health: On Residential Crowding in the Arctic." *Health and Place,* 16: 523–30.

Lodge, A., P. Orr, L. Larcombe and B. Martin. 2006. "Tuberculosis in a Remote Canadian Dene Community: The Impact of Virulence, Genetic, and Environmental Factors on Epidemiology and Control." Abstract. 13th International Congress on Circumpolar Health, June 12–16, Novosibirsk, Russia, 199: 168.

Kovesi, T. and N. L. Gilbert. 2007. "Indoor Air Quality and the Risk of Lower Respiratory Tract Infection in Young Canadian Inuit Children" *Canadian Medical Association Journal,* 177: 155–60.

Mallett, S. 2004. "Understanding Home: A Critical Review of the Literature." *The Sociological Review,* 52(1): 62–89.

Moore, P. E. 1964. "Puvallutuq: An Epidemic of Tuberculosis at Eskimo Point, Northwest Territories." *Canadian Medical Association Journal,* 90(21): 1193–1202.

Northwest Territories Housing Corporation. 1997. *1996 Housing Needs Survey: Overall Results. Report No. 1.* Yellowknife: Government of the Northwest Territories.

OAG (Office of the Auditor General of Canada). 2008. *2008 May Report of the Auditor General of Canada on the Nunavut Housing Corporation.* [on-line]. http://www.oag-bvg.gc.ca/internet/English/nun_200805_e_30754.html [consulted April 28, 2010].

Paperny, Anna Mehler and Sara Minogue. 2009 (August 15). "Life on the Mean Streets of Iqaluit." *Globe and Mail,* A8.

Peressini, T., L. McDonald and D. Hulchanski. 1995. *Estimating Homelessness: Towards a Methodology for Counting the Homeless in Canada.* Ottawa: CMHC.

Springer, S. 2000. "Homelessness: A Proposal for a Global Definition and Classification." *Habitat International,* 24(4): 475–84.

Statistics Canada. 2006. "Aboriginal Population Profile for Cape Dorset, Nunavut." 2006 Census. [on-line]. http://www12.statcan.ca/census-recensement/2006/dp-pd/prof/92-594/Index.cfm?Lang=E. [consulted January 13, 2011].

Tester, F. 2006. "Iglu to Iglurjuaq: Understanding Culture, Home and History." In *After Boal: New Approaches to Arctic Anthropology,* ed. Pamela Stern and Lisa Stevenson. Lincoln: University of Nebraska.

Tester, F. and The Harvest Society. 2006. *Iglutaq (in My Room): The Implications of Homelessness for Inuit: A Case Study of Housing and Homelessness in*

*Kinngait, Nunavut Territory. Report for the National Homelessness Initiative.* Ottawa: Human Resources and Social Development, Canada.

Tester, Frank and Peter Kulchyski. 1994. *Tammarniit (Mistakes): Inuit Relocation in the Eastern Arctic, 1939–63.* Vancouver: UBC Press.

United Nations. 1998. "Principles and Recommendation for the Population and Housing Censuses." Statistical Papers, Series M, No. 67. New York: United Nations.

Windeyer, Chris. 2010a (September 23). "Housing Corp. Overspends by Another $50 Million." *Nunatsiaq News,* 1.

_____ . 2010b (May 6). "Nunavut Housing Fund Overspends by $60 Million." *Nunatsiaq News,* 1.

# CHAPTER 5

# Homeless Immigrants' and Refugees' Health over Time

Fran Klodawsky, PhD
Department of Geography and Environmental Studies, Carleton University

Tim Aubry, PhD
School of Psychology, University of Ottawa

Rebecca Nemiroff, PhD
School of Psychology, University of Ottawa

## Introduction

Gaps in health research in Canada have been noted with regard to both persons who have experienced homelessness (Frankish, Hwang and Quantz 2005) and immigrants and refugees (Beiser 2005; Dunn and Dyck 2000). Recently, some investigations have reported research on immigrants and refugees who have been homeless (Chui et al. 2009; Kappel Ramji 2002; Klodawsky et al. 2005, 2007; Paradis et al. 2008). In particular, Chui and colleagues' (2009) Toronto-based research on the health of homeless immigrants is the first peer-reviewed published research on this topic in Canada. One important question investigated in that article is whether the *healthy immigrant effect*, as noted more generally among Canada's newcomer populations, is relevant to homeless immigrants. The healthy immigrant effect is a tendency among newcomers to arrive in Canada (or the United States) healthier than their native-born peers but then for their health status to decline in proportion to the time spent as an immigrant (Ali, McDermott and Gravel 2004; Argeseanu Cunningham, Ruben and Narayan 2008; Beiser 2005; Dey and Lucas 2006; Fennelly 2007; Huh, Prause and Dooley 2008; McDonald and Kennedy 2004; Newbold 2005; Singh and Hiatt 2006). Reasons for the decline remain unclear. Explanations range from adopting lifestyles that are less healthy than those practiced in the country of origin to the adverse impact of stress related to discrimination, poverty and/or unexpected difficulties in finding suitable employment (Simich et al. 2005; Singh and Hiatt 2006). Some researchers also highlight the need to further explore the ways that the heterogeneity of immigrant backgrounds and characteristics intersects with health status, health service utilization and changes over time (Ali, McDermott and Gravel 2004; Argeseanu Cunningham, Ruben and Narayan 2008; Beiser 2005; Castro 2008; Dunn and Dyck 2000).

Chui and colleagues' analysis confirms that the healthy immigrant effect is also relevant to Toronto's homeless population, with recent immigrants being "physically and mentally healthier and less likely to have chronic conditions and substance use problems than native-born homeless individuals" (2009: 946). They note the significance of length of time since entry to Canada: "the health status of homeless individuals who immigrated more than 10 years ago is not significantly different from that of homeless non-immigrants" (946). That study is significant in that it was based on a large, representative sample of English-speaking homeless immigrants and native-born homeless persons in Toronto. Limitations include its cross-sectional nature and its inability to include refugees and immigrants who were not able to complete the survey in English.

The primary goal of this chapter is to contribute further insights to that of Chui and colleagues (2009) as well as other Canadian health research about immigrants and refugees that have experienced homelessness. Here, we report on an analysis of responses by both foreign-born and Canadian-born participants who were homeless in 2002 or 2003 and who were participants in a longitudinal study in Ottawa, Ontario: the Panel Study on Homelessness in Ottawa. The Panel Study's objective was to examine the diversity of pathways that lead people into and out of homelessness over time by following a mixed group of individuals and adults with children in Ottawa who were homeless at the beginning of the study. Additional goals were to explain factors that distinguished those who successfully exited homelessness from those who remained homeless or experienced multiple episodes of homelessness and to assess the impacts of their pathways on health (Aubry et al. 2003, 2007; Klodawsky et al. 2007). The Panel Study offers a unique opportunity to contribute knowledge about changes over time in homeless immigrants' and refugees' health status and about their use of health services in a mid-sized Canadian city. It is one of only a few Canadian longitudinal studies having to do with people who have been homeless, and it is the only extant study that offers the opportunity to examine what happens to homeless immigrants and refugees over time.

## Methods

### Setting and Study Population

Ottawa is Canada's national capital and fourth largest city, with about 1 million people located in the census metropolitan area (which includes Gatineau, Quebec). The City of Ottawa has become an attractive alternative to Toronto, Montreal and Vancouver for many newcomers. Between 1996 and 2001, Ottawa's immigrant population grew at almost twice the rate of its Canadian-born population. The 2009 report of the Community Foundation of Ottawa (CFO) observed that "foreign-born persons accounted for 22.3 percent of Ottawa's population, or 178,545 persons in 2006 compared to 21.8 percent in 2001" (CFO 2009: 3). The report also highlighted a growing gap between rich and poor, the high cost of housing and health deficiencies as areas of concern that required particular attention (CFO 2009).

The Panel Study researchers defined being homeless in a manner consistent with other North American academic literature (Susser, Moore and Link 1993) and the City of Ottawa's municipal government: "a situation in which an individual or family has no housing at all, or is staying in a temporary form of shelter" (Region of Ottawa-Carleton 1999: 2). Based on research indicating that the overwhelming majority of homeless adults in Ottawa used emergency shelters at some point (Farrell, Aubry and Reissing 2002), we decided to recruit adult participants from the emergency shelters. On the other hand, because use of emergency shelters by homeless youth was more variable (Farrell, Aubry and Reissing 2002), we specified that half the sample would be drawn from among those who were using homeless services, such as drop-ins, but were not staying in an emergency shelter.

The Panel Study's interest was in capturing a diversity of experiences of individuals who had been homeless rather than in capturing a representative sample of Ottawa's homeless population overall. As a result, we sought a representative sample from within each of five equal-sized groups of individuals who were homeless at the time of the first set of interviews: adult men, adult women, male youth, female youth and adults accompanied by at least one child under 16. Within each group, the sampling frame was based on available emergency shelter data. Sampling criteria were established as follows: length of stay, in the case of adult women and men; and citizenship status, in the case of adult women and adults with at least one child under 16. After assessing the available data, we specified that 40 percent of adults with children and 25 percent of adult women for the study would not be Canadian citizens and that cultural interpretation would be offered to reduce the likelihood of language as a barrier to being interviewed. Selective sampling was not required in the case of youth: we were able to interview all male and female youth who were eligible and who accepted an invitation to participate (see Table 5-1).

Four hundred and twelve face-to-face interviews took place between October 2002 and June 2003, and 255 individuals were interviewed again between October 2004 and June 2005. At baseline, 99 respondents were foreign-born, and 58 of them participated in follow-up interviews. The baseline interviews were carried out by 11 trained interviewers with a background in clinical psychology and/or experience in working with homeless people. These interviewers conducted 356 interviews in English, 30 in French and 14 in Somali. The services of cultural interpreters were used for 16 additional interviews (Somali, 4; Arabic, 5; Spanish, 3; Cantonese, 1;

**Table 5-1. Overview of panel study subgroups, sampling criteria, number of recruitment sites and baseline and follow-up sample size**

| Subgroup | Size of Baseline Sample (2002–2003) | Sampling Criteria | Number of Shelters and Drop-in Facilities* Involved in Recruitment | Size of Follow-up Sample (2004–2005) |
|---|---|---|---|---|
| Adult Men | 88 | length of stay | 4 | 43 |
| Adult Women | 85 | length of stay citizenship | 14 | 55 |
| Male Youth | 79 | population | 5 | 50 |
| Female Youth | 81 | population | 5 | 49 |
| Adults with Children | 83 | citizenship | 7 | 58 |
| TOTAL: | 412 | | | 255 |

*Youth were recruited at shelters and drop-in facilities in equal numbers.

Lingala, 1; Russian, 1; and Ukrainian, 1). At follow-up, there were 221 interviews in English, 13 in French and 13 in Somali. The services of cultural interpreters were used for eight other interviews (Arabic, 4; Spanish, 2; Somali, 1; and Cantonese, 1). Their countries of origin are summarized in Table 5-2.

### Interview Protocol and Content

Managers at the emergency shelters and drop-in centres that we visited and consulted with were very enthusiastic about the study. Their support was vital to the study's success since respondents were recruited with the help of staff at these facilities, who were the first point of contact. Interviewers followed up staff referrals and explained to potential respondents the purpose of the study and its informed consent provisions (as approved by the University of Ottawa Research Ethics Board for the Humanities and Social Sciences). Shelter staff also facilitated the availability of private interview spaces at the shelters. At follow-up, respondents were contacted directly by specially trained 'trackers'. In some cases, these trackers arranged interviews in advance but in many instances, the trackers conducted the interviews themselves as quickly as possible after contact had been made with an interested respondent.

These interviews took place in private spaces in a variety of locations, including community centres, emergency shelters and offices at the Centre for Research on Community Services at the University of Ottawa. The trackers contacted respondents on the basis of information gleaned from a variety of means that had been approved by respondents at baseline, including address and telephone contact information obtained through the City of Ottawa's Ontario Works files or from family and friends (Aubry et al. 2004). Typically, each interview took between 50 and 150 minutes, with an average length of about 75 minutes. At follow-up, 36 follow-up interviews took place over the phone with individuals who no longer lived in Ottawa. These interviews tended to be about 20 minutes longer than the face-to-face interviews. Individuals were paid an honorarium of $10 for the first interview and $20 for the second interview.

The interview instruments consisted of both quantitative and qualitative measures. To assess respondents' self-reported health status, we relied on a widely used instrument called the sf-36. This instrument provided a measure of physical health and mental health relative to the US general population, matched on the basis of

## Table 5-2.  Country of origin of foreign-born respondents

| Country of Origin | Foreign-Born Respondents (*n* = 98) | Immigrants (*n* = 45) | Refugees (*n* = 53) |
|---|---|---|---|
| Somalia | 22 | 6 | 16 |
| United States | 8 | 8 | |
| Haiti | 6 | 5 | 1 |
| Unknown/Missing | 6 | 4 | 2 |
| Rwanda | 5 | | 5 |
| Djibouti | 4 | | 4 |
| Zaire | 3 | 2 | 1 |
| Ethiopia | 3 | 1 | 2 |
| Columbia | 3 | | 3 |
| Congo, Dem. Rep. of | 3 | | 3 |
| Burundi | 2 | | 2 |
| Italy | 2 | 1 | 1 |
| Kenya | 2 | | 2 |
| Lebanon | 2 | 1 | 1 |
| Palestine | 2 | | 2 |
| Philippines | 2 | 1 | 1 |
| Ukraine | 2 | 2 | |
| Africa (unspecified) | 1 | | 1 |
| Angola | 1 | 1 | |
| Armenia | 1 | 1 | |
| Burkina Faso | 1 | | 1 |
| China | 1 | 1 | |
| Congo, Republic of | 1 | | 1 |
| England | 1 | 1 | |
| Eritrea | 1 | | 1 |
| Guatemala | 1 | | 1 |
| India | 1 | 1 | |
| Kuwait | 1 | 1 | |
| Poland | 1 | 1 | |
| Saudi Arabia | 1 | | 1 |
| Scotland | 1 | 1 | |
| Singapore | 1 | 1 | |
| South Korea | 1 | 1 | |

**Table 5-2.** (Continued)

| Country of Origin | Foreign-Born Respondents (n = 98) | Immigrants (n = 45) | Refugees (n = 53) |
|---|---|---|---|
| Sudan | 1 | 1 | |
| The Gambia | 1 | | 1 |
| Trinidad | 1 | 1 | |
| Vietnam | 1 | 1 | |
| Yemen | 1 | 1 | |

age and sex (Ware, Kosinski and Gandek 2002). We also asked a series of questions about chronic conditions and injuries that were part of the National Population Health Survey, a longitudinal survey of over 17,000 households across Canada about the current state of health, contact with health-related service providers and health care needs. To this we added questions about other physical health and mental health chronic conditions that were likely relevant to a population that had experienced homelessness. In order to assess the extent and severity of alcohol and drug use problems, we relied on CAGE, a four-item scale identifying the presence of alcohol use problems (Chan, Pristach and Welte 1994; Mayfield, McLeod and Hall 1974) and the Drug Abuse Screening Test (DAST), a 20-item scale identifying the presence of drug use problems (Skinner 1982). Qualitative measures were created and integrated into the interview protocol in order to provide more in-depth information and to provide participants with an opportunity to share their experiences and perceptions.

In the baseline interviews, we asked respondents whether they were Canadian citizens and whether they had been born in Canada. For those born elsewhere, we also asked when they had arrived in Canada and in Ottawa, and why they moved to Canada. During the course of an investigation of the baseline results in which we compared Canadian-born and foreign-born respondents, we realized that an important question had been missed, having to do with whether respondents had arrived as immigrants or as refugees (Klodawsky et al. 2005). To compensate for this limitation, we revisited the interviews and were able to categorize foreign-born respondents as immigrants or refugees on the basis of their qualitative responses to such questions as why they had come to Canada. In other words, we assessed their qualitative responses overall to answer the question, "does the evidence suggest that this individual came to Canada as an immigrant or a refugee, or is there insufficient evidence to make a decision either way?"

### Statistical Analyses

Our analysis of the baseline interviews revealed that the socio-demographic characteristics of refugees and immigrants in the study were distinct from their Canadian-born peers. Whereas the former were more likely to be female and living with children, Canadian-born respondents were more likely to be men on their own. The reasons for being homeless also differed, with the former more likely to be homeless for economic reasons. To address and compensate for these differences, comparisons were made on the basis of matched pairs

The matches were selected using the following criteria: (1) participation in both the baseline and follow-up interview and (2) paired matching based on age (adult or youth), sex (male or female) and family status (with or without at least one child under 16). In matching by pairs, random selection among Canadian-born participants was used within subgroups that were made up of these matching variables.

## Results

The results reported here are based on interviews with 90 respondents—45 Canadian and 45 foreign-born—who were matched according to the criteria and approach described above and who completed the follow-up interviews. These matched respondents included: 1 pair of adult men, 11 pairs of adult women, 6 pairs of female youth, 4 pairs of male youth, 12 pairs of women in families and 4 pairs of men in families.

The quantitative, health-related results of the Canadian-born and the foreign-born matched samples are summarized in Table 5-2. A series of repeated measure ANOVAS were conducted to examine for differences between the two groups, for changes across time and for interactions of group and time on health-related variables measured with continuous data. A series of chi-square analyses were conducted on data presenting the percentage of alcohol and drug use among participants of the two groups at the two time points.

Overall, foreign-born respondents reported a significantly higher level of mental health functioning than their Canadian-born peers. At follow-up, both Canadian and foreign-born respondents showed a significant and similar level of improvement in mental health functioning However, the average score of both groups of respondents on the sf-36 showed them to have poorer mental health functioning when compared with the average score of the normative sample drawn from the US general population.[1]

With regard to physical health, foreign-born participants reported a significantly higher level of physical health functioning than Canadian-born participants across the two time points. There were no changes in level of physical functioning over time with both groups showing similarly stable levels at both time points. In comparison to the US normative group, foreign-born participants demonstrated slightly better physical health than the normative American sample. In contrast, Canadian-born participants reported a similar level of physical functioning to the American sample.

In line with the differences in the level of physical health functioning, Canadian-born participants also reported having significantly more chronic health conditions at baseline and at follow-up than foreign-born participants. No changes in the number of chronic health conditions were evident over time for either of the groups. Over the two data collection points, foreign-born participants had significantly less contact with service providers in the previous 12 months than Canadian-born participants. Although the utilization of health care providers increased for foreign-born participants, the interaction between groups and time was not significant.

A significantly higher proportion of Canadian-born participants reported drug use problems at baseline than foreign-born respondents. A larger proportion of foreign-born participants (26%) reported not having a health card compared to Canadian-born participants (13%) at the baseline interview, although this difference was not statistically significant. On the other hand, a higher proportion of Canadian-born respondents (20%) indicated at baseline, when they were homeless, that they had had an experience of not receiving health care when they needed it, compared to foreign-born participants (15%). Again, these differences were not statistically significant.

The quantitative, health-related results of the immigrants and refugees making up the foreign-born participant group are presented in Table 5-3. A series of repeated measure ANOVAS were also conducted to examine for differences between the two groups, for changes across time and for interactions of group and time on health-related variables measured with continuous data. As well, a series of chi-square analyses were conducted on data presenting the percentage

**Table 5-3. Health-related quantitative results for panel study matched Canadian-born and foreign-born respondents, and immigrant and refugee respondents**

| Variables | Canadian-Born ($n$ = 45) | | Foreign-Born ($n$ = 45) | |
|---|---|---|---|---|
| | Baseline | 2-Yr. Follow-up | Baseline | 2-Yr. Follow-up |
| | Mean (SD) | | Mean (SD) | |
| sf-36: Mental Health Component Score[a, b] | 35.89 (13.83) | 40.65 (13.12) | 42.52 (10.65) | 45.75 (12.57) |
| sf-36: Physical Health Component Score[c] | 49.51 (9.19) | 49.84 (12.69) | 54.48 (7.12) | 55.96 (7.46) |
| Number of Chronic Conditions[d] | 2.47 (1.98) | 2.71 (2.27) | 0.89 (1.28) | 1.11 (1.52) |
| Number of Health Care Providers Consulted over Past Year[e] | 3.09 (1.80) | 3.14 (1.55) | 2.0 (1.24) | 2.77 (1.60) |
| | % | | % | |
| Alcohol Use Problems? | 20% | 11% | 7% | 7% |
| Drug Use Problems? | 30%[f] | 16% | 13%[f] | 7% |

[a]$F^{(Group)}$ (1, 88) = 6.79, $p$ < 0.02; [b]$F^{(Time)}$ (1, 88) = 8.06, $p$ < 0.01; [c]$F^{(Group)}$ (1, 88) = 9.01, $p$ < 0.005; [d]$F^{(Group)}$ (1, 90) = 22.01, $p$ < 0.001; [e]$F^{(Group)}$ (1, 87) = 7.41, $p$ < 0.01; [f]$Chi$-$square$ ($df$ = 1) = 4.09, $p$ < 0.05.

of alcohol and drug use among participants of the two groups at the two time points.

Our analyses found no differences across the two time points between immigrants and refugees in terms of reported levels of physical health functioning or mental health functioning, number of chronic health conditions and number of health care providers seen in the past year. There was a significant increase in the number of health care providers over time for the two groups together. There were no differences between immigrants and refugees in terms of the reported prevalence of alcohol use or drug use problems at baseline or at the two-year follow-up. Changes over time within the group were also non-significant statistically.

We also examined the health related, qualitative results of the interviews with adults in families (12 pairs) and single adult women (11 pairs). The qualitative analysis in this study was conducted with the help of ATLAS.ti, a software package for the analysis of qualitative data (http://www.atlasti.com/). ATLAS.ti is organized around the capacity to assign codes to words or phases in the qualitative data

### Table 5-4. Health-related quantitative results for immigrant and refugee respondents

| Variables | Immigrants (*n* = 23) | | Refugees (*n* = 22) | |
|---|---|---|---|---|
| | Baseline | 2-Yr. Follow-up | Baseline | 2-Yr. Follow-up |
| | Mean (SD) or % | | Mean (SD) or % | |
| SF-36: Mental Health Component Score | 41.94 (10.87) | 45.39 (11.94) | 43.12 (10.65) | 46.12 (13.45) |
| SF-36: Physical Health Component Score | 52.85 (8.01) | 56.69 (8.0) | 55.14 (6.18) | 55.22 (6.99) |
| Number of Chronic Conditions | 0.95 (1.29) | 1.04 (1.69) | 0.81 (1.30) | 1.18 (1.37) |
| Number of Health Care Providers Consulted over Past Year[a] | 2.43 (1.24) | 3.10 (1.73) | 1.55 (1.10) | 2.45 (1.44) |
| | % | | % | |
| Alcohol Use Problems? | 4% | 4% | 4.5% | 4.5% |
| Drug Use Problems? | 22% | 13% | 4.5% | 0% |

[a]$F_{(1, 42)} = 5.29$, $p < 0.05$.

that are relevant to the research questions under discussion. In this study, 33 sets of questions at baseline and six at follow-up included some qualitative elements (Aubry et al. 2007). We began by examining systematically the respondents' answers to open-ended questions that directly addressed health care to assess the extent of differences and similarities in the responses of those born in Canada and those born elsewhere. Key questions included, "Have problems with your physical health contributed to your being/becoming homeless? If yes, what are they and how have they contributed?" and "Have you ever been told by a health care professional that you had mental health problems? If yes, how were they explained to you?" In the course of this examination, it became clear that a strict interpretation of health-related codes (those having to do with discussions of one's physical and/or mental health) would be overly restrictive in terms of what respondents had to say about health-related matters, when 'health' is interpreted as having to do with well-being. In order to address this shortcoming, each respondent's file was scanned across all open-ended questions for other health-related commentary. The following questions proved to be particularly useful: "What helps you get through the rough times? What are some of the things you do to cope?"; "What is the best place you ever lived? What did you enjoy about it?"; "Do you have any advice for people who are homeless and looking for regular housing?"; and "What difference has it made for you to be in regular housing?" After this scan, we identified four additional sets of questions/topics where health-related themes were mentioned or implied. Health-related commentary was then organized for each of the respondent subgroups according to the six resulting themes (in addition to an 'other' category): (1) physical health, (2) mental health, (3) sense of control, (4) advice to others, (5) feelings and (6) particularly important services.

Among adults in families, those born in Canada were more likely than the others to report both physical and mental health problems:

> *She has fibromyalgia, asthma and bronchitis* (CDN 214).
>
> *Post-traumatic stress disorder (from childhood experiences) and depression* (CDN 225).
>
> *Being bullied throughout my public school years affected my ability to concentrate on school work and get proper education. As a result, it disturbed me mentally until today* (CDN 530).

No immigrants mentioned physical or mental health difficulties, and the reasons given by refugees for their health-related problems were specifically linked to their experiences of war and conflict:

> *The torture was worse than the war. War is just hearing the Boom Boom. It is not like having someone hold a gun to your head and your neck* (REF 124).
>
> *I have shrapnel in my leg that prevents me from climbing stairs if an emergency occurs* (REF 524).

The experiences of access to health care services were somewhat more similar. All of the adults in families reported difficulties:

> *I didn't get a doctor at Cobourg because they were not taking new patients* (CDN 519).
>
> Why did you not get care? *Transportation; couldn't get to the office; not convenient; single dad* (CDN 530).
>
> Why did you not get care? *Six months ago I tried to see a GP and made the appointment but the doctor had to cancel* (REF 545).

*Why did you not get care? When living with my husband, needed somebody to talk to and listen to—and nobody was there for me* (IMM 551).

Overall though, the adults in families did not emphasize their health status or access to health services as primary factors that explained their homelessness, although health was sometimes used to explain why they didn't have sufficient income:

*I had a mechanical back disorder, and if I wouldn't have that I would be working and making more money to avoid homelessness* (CDN 521).

*Due to my physical disability I can't obtain employment and that forced me to be on social assistance. As a result, the money doesn't allow me to rent a private accommodation* (REF 524).

Access to affordable housing (and often, escape from abuse) were the factors that generated the most response. In fact, many of the adults identified moving into the family shelter as a strategic decision:

*I was a single mother who is working and not making enough money. For a year, 85% of my earnings was going to my landlord. I couldn't continue doing that, and decided to come into the family shelter so I can find an affordable place to live. Before [that] I was living in a tent on Bank Street . . .* (CDN 518).

*I had been in an abusive relationship for 15 years and finally decided to leave, but I couldn't find an affordable place to rent and sought help in this shelter* (CDN 523).

*I was in an abusive relationship for a long time. I couldn't accept that type of abuse any longer, and sought refuge in this shelter* (IMM 527).

*I have been in this shelter for 7 months, waiting to find an affordable place to live* (IMM 509).

*My two sons and I were renting a one-bedroom apartment and paid $818 for rent, while our income was $1162 from Ontario Works. In order to avoid being homeless, I had to take a portion of our food allowance . . . to pay the rent* (REF 524).

For all of the adults in family respondents, the services that were highlighted as being of most benefit were closely tied to access to economic and/or housing resources. When health services were mentioned, it was typically as part of a broad range of services that together were perceived as helping the individual to become self-sufficient:

> How do they help you? *Welfare (Ontario Works) shelter, Native Women's group—came with me to Ontario Works, helped me get to Ottawa and into the shelter* (CDN 139).
>
> *The shelter when I had no place to stay and the food banks when I had no food* (CDN 537).
>
> How do they help you? *When we have appointments: babysit. Worker gives what I need. If I leave a message . . . he helps right away, he does job well* (IMM 229).
>
> *The shelter for housing; legal aid for immigration; the community health centre for health services* (REF 147).

In contrast to the adults in families, there were clearer distinctions among the single adult women, with Canadian-born women being much more likely than those born elsewhere to focus on health-related problems and services:

> *Self-mutilated. Bipolar disorder. Panic attacks* (CAN 109).
>
> *Alcohol addiction* (CDN 240).
>
> *I can't work—my lower back has bad pain, neck muscle spasms go all the way down my arms* (CDN 112).
>
> *I need some nursing care because of my legs. I don't know if I will need a second amputation . . .* (CDN 149).
>
> *Seeing my family doctor at Centretown Community Health Centre* (CDN 149).
>
> Do you receive help from outreach workers? *ACT Team— bring medication, my dad gives them $150/month, and they bring me $5/day; find out about housing; book doctor app'ts, drive me around, take me for coffee* (CDN 101).

The foreign-born adult women also mentioned physical and mental health problems, but their overall focus was more similar to the adults in families than they were to their single Canadian peers. For example, when asked what advice they would give to others in similar circumstances, the foreign-born women emphasized strategies that would help them exit homelessness, whereas the focus of the Canadian-born women was more on personal healing:

> *When they are in shelters they should get help and education—coun-*
> *selling, help for employment, getting a house—fill up everyday with*
> *activities. They have to follow you, push you to go out and look for*
> *work, housing . . .* (IMM 144).
>
> *You have to fight for a living and it will make you feel good; you*
> *need to work at it and never give up; there's always help* (REF 141).
>
> *Find counselling. Work things out with a counsellor. It's mostly*
> *addictions to drugs or alcohol or mental illness why people are home-*
> *less, they need to get help* (CDN 137).
>
> *Keep their appointments. Keep your act together. Don't fuck up*
> (CDN 240).

The foreign-born single women and adults in families also were similar in their responses to questions about the difference it has made to be in regular housing (that they perceived as being of good quality):

> What difference has it made for you to be in regular housing?
> *Big time difference. I am much better here* (single adult, REF 901).
>
> *I am really happy to be provided with subsidized housing. And*
> *for the social assistance that the Government provides me. English*
> *courses are free of charge. Legal aid was a turning point to stabilizing*
> *my family situation. I know for sure in Ukraine they have no social*
> *network like this* (single adult, IMM 222).
>
> What difference has it made for you to be in regular hous-
> ing? *Peace of mind. My children have become healthy kids again after*
> *residing at this address* (adult in family, CDN 517).

## Discussion

This study contributes to knowledge about the health of immigrants and refugees in Canada who have been homeless. In the analysis discussed here, the mental and physical health status of foreign-born respondents was higher than that of their matched, Canadian-born peers. But contrary to other research on immigrants' health, there was no evidence of a shrinking gap between the two groups over the two-year study period. Mental health status generally remained lower than that of the US normative sample but it did improve for all of the respondents over time. Immigrants and refugees' physical health status also was better than that of the Canadian-born respondents and, somewhat surprisingly, remained at a higher level than the US normative general population sample.

It is plausible that improvements in mental health were associated with respondents who were in stable housing at follow-up and who perceived their housing to be of good quality. The adult-in-family respondents (both Canadian and foreign-born) were almost all stably housed at follow-up. Statistical analyses of the full Panel Study sample revealed that improvements in mental health status occurred when respondents perceived their living circumstances as being of good quality (Aubry et al. 2007). In the specific case of refugees, it is also plausible that feelings of safety and security had improved as compared to their situations at the beginning of the study.

With regard to physical health status, the substantially more extensive reporting of chronic physical health conditions among the Canadian-born certainly provides one window on why there is a gap between the physical health status of those born in Canada and those born elsewhere. Although it is unsurprising that immigrants would have many fewer chronic conditions, given the extensive screening of their health status as a condition of entry, the case of refugees is more surprising, since their entry is not governed by the same health-related limitations. However, the superior health of refugees may be a testament to their resilience in surviving extremely difficult life circumstances in their home country and finding a way to escape these circumstances to a new country. Overall, our findings do provide further evidence of the healthy immigrant effect at least in terms of physical health among foreign-born adults who are homeless. Moreover, there was no evidence of a diminishment in physical health functioning among these individuals over the course of the two-year study.

The health service utilization results do suggest a move towards similar rates of use among foreign-born and Canadian-born respondents over time, but this trend raises at least as many questions as answers. Given that foreign-born respondents report better mental and physical health, are they seeking the same kinds of health services as their Canadian-born peers or are they seeking help for settlement-related issues? The higher utilization of religious leaders and similarities in the rates that they and the Canadian-born respondents report in not getting the help they needed suggest that settlement-related issues are of particular concern for those born outside the country.

The respondents' qualitative commentary revealed more similarities than differences among foreign-born and Canadian-born adults with family, but they also revealed clear distinctions between the foreign-born single women and their Canadian peers. It is likely that site-specific factors had a role to play. Among the full Panel Study sample, fully 97 percent of the adult-in-family group was stably housed at follow-up, and, of that group, 78 percent were living in subsidized housing. Given that homeless adults with children were placed on the priority list for subsidized housing in Ottawa, this trend is, at least in part, the unsurprising result of a municipal public policy choice. Among adult women, the probability of access to subsidized housing was considerably lower and depended on additional conditions such as mental health impairment or escape from domestic abuse: 73 percent were stably housed at follow-up, and, of that group, 51 percent were living in subsidized housing. Although respondents would not have been privy to the statistics presented here, the adult-in-family group might well have been aware of others who were successful in accessing subsidized housing, making the choice to move to the shelter a meaningful strategy in the search for affordable housing. The logic of using such a strategy in the case of single women would have been much less straightforward. In the case of foreign-born women, similar to the case of adults with family, it is likely that their poverty and/or domestic abuse were the driving factors in the decision to move to a shelter, whereas for the Canadian-born women, the reasons were more likely to do with interactions between mental and physical health limitations, domestic conflict and abuse and poverty.

## Strengths and Limitations

This study has several strengths. One is the Panel Study's site-specific success in re-interviewing 255 participants two years after first meeting them at an emergency shelter or drop-in in Ottawa. The Panel Study's interest in diversity and its systematic approach to capturing that diversity in a statistically rigorous manner is a second positive feature. It permitted the investigation of similarities and differences in the health status and health trajectories of matched samples of Canadian-born and foreign-born respondents living in Ottawa. The benefits of combining close-ended and open-ended questions in the interview contributed further insights into the 'healthy immigrant effect' for persons who have been homeless, and it identified additional reasons for examining the impacts of settlement-related concerns. The use of cultural interpreters and the ability to incorporate the experiences of both immigrants and those who arrived in Canada as refugees are additional significant features of the study.

Our study also had a number of limitations that need to be taken into account in interpreting the findings. The first was that the study was not representative of the overall homeless population in Ottawa; in addition, the sample did not include single adults and adults in families who were living on the street or temporarily living with friends or family. A further limitation of our sampling strategy was the reliance on shelter staff to find participants in the single adult and adult-in-families subgroups who matched specific characteristics. This process had the potential to introduce some bias toward sampling higher functioning individuals. There were also refusals by some of the individuals invited to participate. Another limitation was the level of attrition in the study, as 38 percent of the original participants were lost at follow-up. There were no differences found between participants and non-participants in the follow-up interview on all of the compared characteristics with the exception of length of residency in Ottawa (Aubry et al. 2007).

All of the information collected in the study was self-report in nature. Self-report information may be prone to inaccuracy because of faulty memory, lack of information or discomfort with self-disclosure. Related to the use of self-report measures in the Panel Study, it is important to note that the SF-36 provides a subjective assessment of physical health functioning and mental health functioning. Other limitations associated with the use of SF-36 include the potential lack of relevancy of some of the items in the measure related to inquiring about physical functioning and social functioning from people who are experiencing homelessness. As well, our use of cultural interpreters may have affected the interpretation and response of participants on some of the items. Despite these limitations, scores on the SF-36 showed the expected differences between immigrants and refugees and Canadian-born participants, with immigrants and refugees reporting better physical health functioning and mental health functioning. As well, the measure proved to be sensitive to capturing improvements in mental health functioning over time for both groups of participants.

Another limitation of our study was the relatively short length of the follow-up period (i.e., two years). It was of sufficient length to capture the housing instability experienced by a relatively large proportion of our participants. However, a longer period of time may have shown more changes in the health-related characteristics. A further limitation was the fact that no distinctions were made among the foreign-born respondents who were recent arrivals and those who had been in Canada for a longer period of time. This shortcoming may have compromised the ability to examine the healthy immigrant effect over time. A final limitation was the relatively small numbers of respondents that were compared based on matched samples.

## Conclusions

Beiser's (2005) review of extant research on the health of immigrants and refugees revealed a complex picture and lent support to his conclusion that "unexpected and paradoxical findings underline the need to take account of heterogeneity in future studies . . ." (539). The results reported here lend support to his conclusions and also raise questions about the impact of site-specific public policy measures on respondents' health status and health services utilization. Although the study results do provide support for the widely observed healthy immigrant effect, the similarities noted between immigrants and refugees raise questions about its causal roots. So too do the observations about similarities between the foreign-born and Canadian-born adults with families. These findings have implications for policy-makers, health administrators and health and social care professionals. This study suggests that the existence of a certain difference (such as country of origin) does not automatically mean a linear relationship with other distinctions (such as reasons for being homeless). In fact, our data suggest that adults with children, whether born in Canada or elsewhere, are more similar than different, whereas this is not the case among unaccompanied adult women. The data also raise further questions about the circumstances under which a healthy immigrant effect occurs and suggests that contextual factors need careful consideration before inferences are drawn on the basis of this tendency. Thus, in the case of Chui and colleagues (2009), the focus on English-speaking immigrants in Toronto homeless shelters needs to be taken into account in drawing inferences from that study. It would also be useful to investigate healthy immigrant effects among persons who have been homeless in locations other than Toronto or Ottawa.

It is clear that further research is required and that its ideal form would be both longitudinal and multi-site. The Housing and Health in Transition study, now underway in Toronto, Vancouver and Ottawa, has the potential to contribute further insights about the health of single adults, both foreign- and Canadian-born, who have been homeless or unstably housed in these three cities.

## Note

1. Standardized scores involve converting the raw score to a scaled score based on a normative sample of the 1998 general US population (ages 18–64; $n = 6742$) where the mean is 50 and the standard deviation is 10.

## References

Ali, J. S., S. McDermott and R. G. Gravel. 2004. "Recent Research on Immigrant Health from Statistics Canada's Population Surveys." *Canadian Journal of Public Health,* 95(3): I9–13.

Argeseanu Cunningham, S., J. D. Ruben and K. M. Narayan. 2008. "Health of Foreign-Born People in the United States: A Review." *Health & Place,* 14(4): 623–35.

Aubry, T., F. Klodawsky, E. Hay and S. Birnie. 2003. *Panel Study on Persons Who Are Homeless in Ottawa: Phase 1 Results.* Ottawa: Centre for Research on Community Services.

Aubry, T., F. Klodawsky, R. Nemiroff, S. Birnie and C. Bonetta. 2007. *Panel Study on Persons Who Are Homeless in Ottawa: Phase 2 Results.* Ottawa: Centre for Research on Community Services.

Aubry, T., F. Klodawsky, E. Hay, R. Nemiroff and S. Hyman. 2004. *Developing a Methodology for Tracking Persons Who are Homeless over Time. Final Report.* Ottawa: Canada Mortgage and Housing Corporation.

Beiser, M. 2005. "The Health of Immigrants and Refugees in Canada." *Canadian Journal of Public Health,* 96 (March/April): S30–S44.

Castro, F. G. 2008. "Personal and Ecological Contexts for Understanding the Health of Immigrants." *American Journal of Public Health,* 98(11): 1933.

Chan, A., E. Pristach and J. Welte. 1994. "Detection by the CAGE of Alcoholism or Heavy Drinking in Primary Care Outpatients and the General Population." *Journal of Substance Abuse,* 6: 123–35.

Chui, S., D. Redelmeier, G. Tolomiczenko, A. Kiss and S. Hwang. 2009. "The Health of Homeless Immigrants." *Journal of Epidemiology and Community Health,* 63: 943–48.

CFO (Community Foundation of Ottawa). 2009. *Ottawa's Vital Signs 2009: The City's Annual Check-Up.* Ottawa: Community Foundation of Ottawa.

Dey, A. N. and J. W. Lucas. 2006. "Physical and Mental Health Characteristics of U.S. and Foreign-Born Adults: United States, 1998–2003." *Advance Data*, (369): 1–19.

Dunn, J. and I. Dyck. 2000. "Social Determinants of Health in Canada's Immigrant Population: Results from the National Population Health Survey." *Social Science & Medicine,* 51: 1573–93.

Farrell, S., T. Aubry and E. Reissing. 2002. "Street Needs Assessment: An Investigation of the Characteristics and Service Needs of Persons Who Are Homeless and Not Currently Using Emergency Shelters in Ottawa." [on-line]. Homeless Hub. http://www.homelesshub.ca/Library/Street-Needs-Assessment-An-Investigation-of-the-Characteristics-and-Service-Needs-of-Persons-who-are-Homeless-and-not-Currently-using-Emergency-Shelters-in-Ottawa-54361.aspx [consulted January 12, 2014].

Fennelly, K. 2007. "The 'Healthy Migrant' Effect." *Minnesota Medicine,* 90(3): 51–53.

Frankish, C., S. Hwang and D. Quantz. 2005. "Homelessness and Health in Canada: Research Lessons and Priorities." *Canadian Journal of Public Health,* 96(March/April): S23–S29.

Kappel Ramji Consulting Group. 2002. *Common Occurrence: The Impact of Homelessness on Women's Health: Phase II: Community Based Action Research: Final Report Executive Summary.* Toronto: Sistering: A Woman's Place.

Klodawsky, F., T. Aubry, B. Behnia, C. Nicholson and M. Young. 2007. "Comparing Foreign-Born and Canadian-Born Respondents to the Panel Study on Homelessness (Phase 1)." *Our Diverse Cities: Ontario,* 4(Fall). Ottawa: Metropolis, 51–53.

_____. 2005. *The Panel Study on Homelessness: Secondary Data Analysis of Respondents Whose Country of Origin Is Not Canada.* Ottawa: Ottawa: National Homelessness Secretariat.

Huh, J., J. A. Prause and C. D. Dooley. 2008. "The Impact of Nativity on Chronic Diseases, Self-Rated Health and Comorbidity Status of Asian and Hispanic Immigrants." *Journal of Immigrant and Minority Health,* 10(2): 103–18.

Mayfield, D., G. McLeod, P. Hall. 1974. "The CAGE Questionnaire: Validation of a New Alcoholism Screening Instrument." *American Journal of Psychiatry,* 131(10): 1121–23.

McDonald, J. T. and S. Kennedy. 2004. "Insights into the 'Healthy Immigrant Effect': Health Status and Health Service Use of Immigrants to Canada." *Social Science & Medicine,* 59(8): 1613–27.

Newbold, B. 2005. "Health Status and Health Care of Immigrants in Canada: A Longitudinal Analysis." *Journal of Health Services & Research Policy,* 10(2): 77–83.

Paradis, E., S. Novac, M. Sarty, J. Hulchanski. 2008. *Better Off in a Shelter? A Year of Homelessness & Housing among Status Immigrant, Non-Status Migrant, & Canadian-Born Families (Research Paper 213).* Toronto: Centre for Urban and Community Studies, University of Toronto.

Region of Ottawa Carleton. 1999. *Homelessnesss in Ottawa-Carleton.* Ottawa: Region of Ottawa Carleton.

Simich, L., M. Beiser, M. Stewart and E. Mwakarimba. 2005. "Providing Social Support for Immigrants and Refugees in Canada: Challenges and Directions." *Journal of Immigrant Health,* 7(4): 259–68.

Singh, G. K. and R. A. Hiatt. 2006. "Trends and Disparities in Socioeconomic and Behavioural Characteristics, Life Expectancy, and Cause-Specific Mortality of Native-Born and Foreign-Born Populations in the United States, 1979–2003." *International Journal of Epidemiology,* 35(4): 903–19.

Skinner, H. 1982. "The Drug Abuse Screening Test." *Addictive Behaviour,* 7(4): 363–71.

Susser, E., R. Moore and B. Link. 1993. "Risk Factors for Homelessness." *American Journal of Epidemiology,* 15: 546–56.

Ware, J., M. Kosinski and B. Gandek. 2002. *SF-36 Health Survey: Manual and Interpretation Guide.* Lincoln, RI: Quality Metric Incorporated.

PART II

# POLICY & PROGRAMMATIC RESPONSES TO HOMELESSNESS & HEALTH

# CHAPTER 6

# Housing and HIV/AIDS among People Who Inject Drugs: Public Health Evidence for Effective Policy Response

Brandon D. L. Marshall, PhD
Department of Epidemiology, Brown University

Thomas Kerr, PhD
British Columbia Centre for Excellence in HIV/AIDS
Department of Medicine, University of British Columbia

## Introduction

Injection drug use is a serious public health concern in many countries, including Canada. Recent estimates suggest that between 220,000 and 375,000 Canadians, or approximately 1 to 2 percent of the general population, have ever injected an illegal drug (Mathers et al. 2008). People who inject drugs (injection drug users or IDU) represent a diverse population with a range of health needs and outcomes. In Canada, the majority of IDU are male, and persons of Aboriginal ancestry are heavily overrepresented among IDU (PHAC 2006). Initiation into injection drug use typically occurs at 20 years of age (Ompad et al. 2005); however, a significant proportion of IDU report beginning injecting in their early teens (Miller et al. 2006). Although the pathways into injection drug use are varied, heavy non-injection drug use and homelessness in the months preceding injection onset are common (Roy et al. 2003). Further, several recent studies (Kerr et al. 2009; Ompad et al. 2005) have pointed to the role that childhood maltreatment plays in increasing the risk of initiating injection drug use.

Prior to the discovery of HIV in 1982, very little research involving IDU had been conducted in Canada. However, injection drug use was prevalent across the country well in advance of the HIV pandemic. Historical documents suggest that by the mid-20th century, 4,000 Canadians were actively injecting drugs: the vast majority of these early users were from poor working-class families living in the cities of Vancouver and Toronto (Carstairs 2002). By 1989, 120 AIDS cases attributable to injection drug use had been reported to the Federal Centre for AIDS, and high rates of HIV-related risk behaviour among IDU began to garner significant public health attention (Smart 1991). In the same year, studies presented at the 5th International AIDS Conference in Montreal provided further evidence that immediate public health action was required to prevent the situation from worsening (Bruneau et al. 1989). An early study undertaken in Montreal suggested that the prevalence of HIV among IDU was approximately 4 percent (Lamothe et al. 1988). In 1997, a massive HIV epidemic, described as one of the most severe in the developed world, was observed among IDU in Vancouver (Strathdee et al. 1997). In more recent years, the proportion of HIV infections attributable to injection drug use has remained relatively constant at just under 20 percent, representing between 390 and 750 new cases of HIV infection annually (PHAC 2009). In addition to a sustained and unacceptably high rate of HIV incidence, IDU face multiple social and structural barriers to accessing appropriate HIV treatment and experience poorer clinical outcomes (Wood et al. 2008).

### Homelessness and the Risk Environment
The limited success of conventional public health interventions to reduce HIV-related morbidity and mortality among IDU has led to a new emphasis on ecological approaches that incorporate how factors exogenous to the individual impact exposure to risk and poor health. For example, the 'risk environment' model posits that social, physical and structural factors intersect to produce differential exposures to infectious disease risks and drug-related harms (Rhodes et al. 2005). These environments thus impose constraints on one's ability to mitigate risk behaviour and achieve health. Within this framework, substandard housing and homelessness have been identified as key factors that play direct roles in augmenting vulnerabilities to HIV and perpetuating health inequities among marginalized populations (Galea and Vlahov 2002). Complementary to this body of literature is a large volume of research indicating that secure and stable housing is a robust determinant of health within the general population (Hwang 2001).

Despite evidence to suggest a powerful link between lack of access to housing, HIV infection and overall health, there remains no clear policy approach to addressing housing and HIV/AIDS issues in Canada (Canadian AIDS Society 2009). Although research has shown that housing plays an important and direct role in the prevention of HIV and other health-related harms among IDU (Briggs et al. 2009), policy-makers in Canada have failed to implement housing interventions as central tenets of current HIV/AIDS strategies for this population. In order to more effectively influence the development of evidence-based policy and programs that benefit equivocally housed drug users, scientists, policy-makers and service providers must promote rigorous housing-focused research, articulate why housing and HIV/AIDS issues are closely linked and justify how the provision of supportive housing can improve the health of drug users living with HIV/AIDS (Aidala and Sumartojo 2007).

This review synthesizes evidence, primarily from a Canadian context, examining the relationship between housing and HIV/AIDS among IDU populations, compares housing interventions to reduce HIV risk behaviour and support individuals who are already living with HIV/AIDS and provides recommendations for future research to best inform the development of housing policy. Given the recent call to action by the Canadian AIDS Society to address housing as a critical component of the federal response to HIV/AIDS in Canada (Canadian AIDS Society 2009), this chapter aims to serve as a key tool for public health practitioners and other stakeholders interested in advocating for evidence-based housing interventions to improve the health of people who inject drugs.

### Housing and HIV/AIDS among Drug Users

Homeless people in Canada face significant barriers to accessing health and social services and experience a range of adverse health outcomes (Hwang 2001). Notably, homelessness is a strong predictor of premature mortality (Hwang 2000). Homelessness is extremely common among people who inject drugs, particularly those who are HIV positive (Song et al. 2000). An inability to attain safe and stable housing is known to be both a cause and consequence of drug use (Galea and Vlahov 2002). For example, studies of homeless young people have shown that drug use is often a critical factor in deciding to leave home, while many youth initiate illicit drug use only after becoming homeless (Mallett, Rosenthal and Keys 2005). It is clear

that chronic homelessness tends to exacerbate the negative consequences of drug use (and vice versa), which can result in a mutually
reinforcing pattern of complex service needs and declining overall
health (Neale 2001). Therefore, elucidating how homelessness, drug
use and HIV/AIDS intersect to produce and perpetuate health inequities is crucial for informing more effective public health strategies
to address the needs of this marginalized population.

Housing environments shape and perpetuate HIV risk among
people who inject drugs (Aidala et al. 2005). Many studies have demonstrated that homeless IDU are more likely than housed individuals to participate in sexual and injecting-related HIV risk behaviour,
including syringe sharing, shooting gallery attendance and sex work
(Coady et al. 2007; Des Jarlais, Braine and Friedmann 2007; Reyes et al.
2005; Salazar et al. 2007). Furthermore, homeless IDU are more likely
to report higher intensity drug use patterns than those with stable
housing (Lloyd-Smith et al. 2009), while higher levels of sexual risk
have been observed among drug-using youth who are equivocally
housed (Marshall et al. 2009). Among young drug users, HIV risks
tend to accumulate as the severity and frequency of homelessness
increases, indicating a dose-response relationship between HIV vulnerability and exposure to street environments (Ennett et al. 1999).
Similarly, residential transience and long-term housing instability
are important drivers of HIV risk among drug-using adults. Injection
risk behaviours are more common among adult IDU who report
frequent moves (German, Davey and Latkin 2007). Frequent relocation may also disrupt social networks and diminish one's exposure
to positive peer norms, which have been shown to be important
mitigating factors of risk behaviour among IDU (Latkin et al. 2003).
Finally, unstable housing and homelessness have been identified as
key determinants of poor treatment outcomes among HIV-positive
IDU (Knowlton et al. 2006).

Given the strong and consistent relationship between inadequate housing environments and HIV risk behaviour, it is not surprising that several studies have identified an independent association
between poor housing conditions and increased rates of HIV infection among IDU. One of the earliest studies to demonstrate this link
was conducted in Ohio, and although the overall HIV prevalence
was low (1.5%), living in a homeless shelter residence was second
only to being a man who has sex with men as the strongest correlate
of HIV infection (Siegal et al. 1991). A more recent study conducted

in Baltimore also observed a strong relationship between exposure to homelessness and both HIV prevalence at baseline and seroconversion over follow-up (Song et al. 2000). In Canada, a large prospective cohort study of injection drug users in Vancouver (i.e., the Vancouver Injection Drug Users Study) has investigated the relationship between housing status and HIV among IDU for over a decade. HIV infection was more common among IDU reporting recent homelessness or unstable living conditions at baseline, independent of other risk factors including sex work and syringe sharing (Strathdee et al. 1997). A follow-up study indicated a strong association between unstable housing and HIV incidence (Tyndall et al. 2003). This trend has continued: after eleven years of follow-up, housing status has remained a significant predictor of HIV seroconversion (see Figure 6-1).

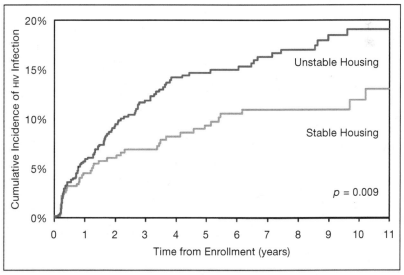

**Figure 6-1. Cumulative incidence of HIV infection among Vancouver injection drug users from 1996 to 2007, stratified by housing status at baseline**

Note: *Unstable housing* includes living in a shelter/hostel, treatment/recovery house, jail, single-room occupancy hotel or on the street. *Stable housing* was defined as living in an apartment or house.

Source: Urban Health Research Initiative, British Columbia Centre for Excellence in HIV/AIDS (2009).

### Homelessness and the Production of HIV Risk

Detailed ethnographic investigations have established the importance of place in the social-structural production of HIV risk among homeless IDU populations. For example, participant-observation studies have shown how homelessness and the extreme social marginalization experienced by many IDU result in survival strategies in which precarious income-generating activities and social relationships of mutual dependence are prioritized over HIV risk reduction practices (Bourgois 1998). Among women, homelessness also exacerbates exposure to everyday violence and subordinated positions in social hierarchies, in which the risk of HIV infection is secondary to immediate physical dangers (Epele 2002).

Ethno-epidemiological studies have also suggested that a multitude of environmental and structural factors may explain the observed relationship between housing instability and HIV vulnerabilities. For example, homeless IDU experience increased exposure to high-risk injecting environments (e.g., shooting galleries, open drug scenes), which have been shown to be settings of heightened HIV vulnerability, particularly for younger IDU (Rhodes et al. 2006). Homeless IDU who inject in public settings are also more likely to skip safer injecting practices due to fears of being intercepted by the police, physically assaulted or robbed (Small et al. 2007). Furthermore, homeless IDU frequently encounter police as a result of participation in illegal income-generating activities and are thus more likely to experience HIV risks associated with incarceration (Wood et al. 2005). At a policy level, features unique to unstable housing environments have also been shown to perpetuate HIV risks among IDU. For example, evening 're-entry fees', a common feature of single-room occupancy hotels, dissuade individuals from accessing HIV prevention and harm reduction services (Wood and Kerr 2006b) and thus may be partially responsible for the high prevalence of HIV observed among persons who live in these environments (Shannon et al. 2006).

### Barriers to Housing

IDU experience a multitude of social and structural barriers while attempting to access safe and stable housing. Many IDU are considered by housing providers as 'hard to house' for reasons including lack of stable employment and income, 'unclean' visual appearance, erratic or aggressive behaviour and the presence of co-morbidities (e.g., mental illness) associated with chronic substance use (Gurstein and Small 2005). Having a criminal history and experiencing incarceration, common among IDU, further complicates one's ability to obtain housing (Mizuno et al. 2009). Furthermore, individuals who are actively drug dependent and continue to use substances are often ineligible for abstinence-contingent housing services or will be discharged upon relapse or positive urine test (Kruas, Serge and Goldberg 2006). For many drug-using youth, the fact that many shelters are abstinence focused and adhere to a 'zero-tolerance approach' severely restricts acceptable housing options (Krüsi et al. 2010).

The ability to obtain stable housing is further complicated by inadequate access to substance abuse treatment, income support and employment opportunities. For example, IDU who are homeless are less likely to enrol in any form of addiction treatment (Wood et al. 2005) and are less likely to attain legal employment (Richardson et al. 2008) compared to those who are stably housed. Furthermore, unstable housing status has been associated with a decreased uptake of methadone maintenance therapy (MMT) among opioid users in Canada (Fischer et al. 2008). Homelessness has also been found to impact the types of addiction treatment most often accessed by people who inject drugs. A large study conducted in Massachusetts demonstrated that homeless IDU were more likely to enter detoxification and residential treatment programs but were half as likely to access MMT over the four-year study period (Lundgren et al. 2003). These short-term programs often do not lead to improved long-term housing outcomes due to a lack of integration between substance abuse treatment and housing services, insufficient or unacceptable housing options and other gaps in the continuum of care (Meschede 2010).

### Housing as HIV/AIDS Prevention, Treatment and Care

Housing programs are increasingly well recognized as an integral component of comprehensive HIV prevention strategies (Shubert and Bernstine 2007). In the United States, observational studies and randomized controlled trials have demonstrated that the provision of rental assistance and other housing supports is associated with improved health outcomes and better treatment adherence among persons living with HIV/AIDS (PLWHA) (Wolitski et al. 2010). Among homeless PLWHA, treatment compliance is complicated by competing priorities associated with homelessness (e.g., obtaining shelter, meeting dietary requirements), lack of transportation to HIV-related health care services and inability to store medications (Henry et al. 2008). The advent of single-pill regimens will likely mitigate many of these concerns, although the provision of housing should continue to be a key priority to improve HIV-related outcomes and overall health among IDU. Even with less than perfect adherence, homeless PLWHA have been shown to benefit from HIV treatment; thus, service providers should not restrict access to highly active antiretroviral therapy (HAART) on the basis of housing status alone (Wolitski, Kidder and Fenton 2007). Finally, given the evidence indicating that housing instability significantly reduces one's ability to engage effectively with HIV treatment and practice risk reduction behaviours, secondary prevention programs for PLWHA at risk for HIV transmission should include housing assistance within a package of comprehensive intervention strategies (Fisher and Smith 2009). HIV-infected persons with unsuppressed viral load (i.e., detectable levels of virus circulating in body fluids) are more likely to transmit HIV during high-risk sexual or injection-related behaviours (Attia et al. 2009). Higher levels of HIV viral load among IDU have also been associated with increased HIV incidence at the community level (Wood et al. 2009). Given that antiretroviral therapy induces viral load suppression among adherent patients (Gulick et al. 1997), the expansion of access to HAART is now thought to be an effective means to control the spread of HIV (Montaner et al. 2006). However, HIV-infected IDU who are homeless are less likely to achieve viral load suppression upon receiving HAART (Knowlton et al. 2006). Therefore, if IDU populations are to receive maximal treatment and preventive benefits of HAART expansion programs, efforts should also be made to address housing instability and other barriers to treatment initiation and compliance. Under this framework, safe and stable housing are viewed not only as a necessary prerequisite to effective HIV/AIDS management and care but also as an evidence-based public health intervention to reduce new HIV infections among drug users.

## Evidence-Based Interventions

Several interventions and models of housing assistance programs have been proposed for drug-using individuals who are homeless or are at risk for homelessness. In this section, we provide a brief discussion of several housing interventions and a review of evidence regarding the effectiveness of each program.

### Case Management

Case management has been found to facilitate access to stable housing and improve adherence and other treatment outcomes among homeless and marginally housed drug users with HIV infection (Kushel et al. 2006). Furthermore, the provision of case management can prevent individuals undergoing substance abuse treatment from relapsing and becoming unstably housed (Katz et al. 2001). However, evidence suggests that better long-term housing outcomes are achieved with more comprehensive housing support services compared to case management alone (Clark and Rich 2003). For these reasons, case management in the absence of other comprehensive interventions is not recommended as a best practice to achieve sustainable housing among people who use drugs.

### Linear Approach Programs

In the United States, linear approach programs (also called the 'continuum of care' model) are common and provide housing once an individual has completed a course of addiction treatment and has achieved abstinence (Milby et al. 2000). These programs have demonstrated efficacy in some settings, and sustained periods of abstinence have been demonstrated among individuals who achieve abstinent-contingent housing (Schumacher et al. 2007). However, many of these programs fail to recognize the chronic nature of substance abuse and thus are unable to provide appropriate support upon relapse. For example, individuals who do return to drug use after obtaining housing may be evicted, thus dramatically increasing the risk for homelessness and return to engagement in HIV risk behaviours.

A second limitation of this type of intervention is that a lack of formal linkages with placement programs and low rental stock may prevent individuals who achieve abstinence from obtaining affordable stable housing. This has been demonstrated recently by a Vancouver study showing that enrolment in addiction treatment failed to predict obtaining stable housing over four years of follow-up (Palepu et al. 2010). Improved integration of addiction treatment services with supportive housing programs for individuals who are able to maintain abstinence and those who continue drug use or experience relapse is therefore recommended.

### Housing First

A more recent model is 'Housing First', premised on the notion that housing is a basic human right and should not be requisite to abjuring substance use. Within a Housing First framework, homeless individuals with substance abuse or other co-morbidities (e.g., mental illness) are immediately provided with their own apartments without any prerequisites for treatment or sobriety (Greenwood et al. 2005). Thus, individuals are not required to be in substance abuse treatment in order to obtain or maintain housing. In addition to the provision of housing, these models often include additional support services that participants can access at their discretion, including an 'Assertive Community Treatment' team consisting of health care and social service professionals, for example (Tsemberis, Gulcur and Nakae 2004). The underlying principle of this approach is one of 'consumer choice'; that is, participants are empowered to determine the priority and order of services they receive.

Housing First programs have been shown to result in higher rates of housing stability compared to individuals receiving abstinence-contingent services and do not lead to increases in substance use among participants (Tsemberis, Gulcur and Nakae 2004). Housing First interventions have also been shown to be highly cost effective for chronically homeless persons with severe alcohol dependence (Larimer et al. 2009). These programs have also been strongly endorsed by the Canadian Mortgage and Housing Corporation (CMHC) as the preferred mode of housing homeless individuals with substance abuse or dependence. In a review of housing programs in Canada, CMHC (2006) concluded that the immediate provision of safe, independent and secure housing is one of the key factors in assisting individuals to reduce drug use and the negative health impacts of substance abuse on their lives.

Harm reduction approaches provided in *combination* with permanent, independent housing are an effective means to address the needs of homeless people with substance abuse and are thus a central tenet of the Housing First model (Tsemberis, Gulcur and Nakae 2004). *Harm reduction* refers to policies and practices that aim to reduce the risks and harmful effects associated with substance use without requiring reduced drug consumption or abstinence (Inciardi and Harrison 2000). In Canada, some housing programs have adopted a 'client-centred' harm reduction approach, which focuses on supporting individuals in meeting their housing, substance abuse and health care needs in a flexible, respectful and dignified way (Evans and Strathdee 2006). The provision of housing is increasingly viewed internationally as an evidence-based harm reduction strategy to reduce risk behaviour and prevent adverse health outcomes among people who inject drugs (Briggs et al. 2009). Evidence also exists to suggest that IDU who achieve stable housing are more likely to cease injection drug use altogether and are less likely to relapse (Shah et al. 2006). These findings provide further support for Housing First models and suggest that the immediate provision of housing should be regarded as an evidence-based pathway to drug use cessation.

## Recommendations for Research and Policy

Throughout this chapter we have argued that housing is good for health. This is particularly true for marginalized people who are equivocally housed and use drugs. The benefits of housing in terms of HIV prevention are clear: a large volume of evidence indicates that safe and stable housing is associated with reduced engagement in HIV risk behaviour and improved health outcomes for those living with HIV disease. In order to more effectively inform housing and health policy in Canada, researchers must now do more than simply state that these relationships exist. Novel lines of inquiry should be proposed and examined; for example, evidence that differentiates which modes of housing interventions are most successful at improving the health of homeless people who use drugs would be invaluable for the design and implementation of new housing programs. Examining these 'second generation' questions is only a very recent phenomenon and thus many questions remain unanswered. Although an increasing number of researchers are investigating the effectiveness of the *integration* of housing and addiction treatment services based on Housing First and harm reduction models, case studies of success, particularly in the Canadian context, are urgently needed. One example is the Dr. Peter Centre in Vancouver, which has successfully integrated an assisted-living residential program for HIV-positive IDU with harm reduction approaches, including a supervised injecting room and spaces where residents can consume non-injection drugs such as crack cocaine (Krüsi et al. 2009). The evaluation of innovative models of care for homeless people who use drugs is critical for the creation of evidence-based housing programs across the country.

It must be recognized that additional scientific evidence is on its own insufficient to enact the policy and programmatic changes that would often be required to meaningfully improve the health of homeless IDU. Controversial interventions (even those with a significant scientific evidence base such as needle exchange programs) can be met with moral and ethical arguments that in some cases have impeded their implementation and expansion (Buchanan et al. 2003). Acknowledging moralistic opposition to harm reduction-based approaches and identifying ways to engage communities and policy-makers that hold these views is critical to ensuring that future interventions are based upon the best available scientific evidence.

A second area of future research is the identification of *points of intervention* to most effectively bring homeless IDU in contact with the health and social service systems. Given that IDU are an extremely marginalized population who experience a multitude of barriers to accessing traditional primary and ancillary services (Wood and Kerr 2006a), housing programs should provide multiple points of entry and be highly flexible to diverse health needs and challenges. For example, although many IDU are completely disconnected from services, those who are unstably housed report high rates of emergency room and acute care utilization (Kerr et al. 2005). These points of contact with the primary health care system may be an important opportunity to engage and connect homeless IDU with low threshold housing support programs. The responsibility lies with service providers to identify these opportunities and with researchers to evaluate their potential to improve the health and functioning of people who use drugs.

Finally, given recent Canadian research suggesting that the use of non-injection drugs (e.g., crack and methamphetamine) among marginalized groups may be associated with elevated HIV risk (Bungay et al. 2010; DeBeck et al. 2009), future studies should seek to elucidate the intersection of homelessness and non-injection drug use in the production of HIV-related risks and harms. Importantly, there are few effective treatments for stimulant dependence (Rawson et al. 2006), and few studies have determined whether the provision of housing may improve treatment outcomes among these groups. It is clear, however, that the creation of sustainable supportive housing for non-injection drug users should be a policy and public health priority.

We wish to conclude this chapter by emphasizing that the implementation of housing interventions should proceed in tandem with improved access to and expansion of comprehensive

HIV services. Indeed, it is the *integration* of housing and homelessness prevention programs with addiction treatment, HIV treatment, health services and other HIV prevention interventions where the largest benefits to the individual and to society will likely be observed. It is our hope that this chapter will act as a call to researchers, service providers and advocates to better articulate the need for housing to assume a central role in Canadian public health strategies to improve the health of all citizens, including those who use drugs.

## References

Aidala, A. A. and E. Sumartojo. 2007. "Why Housing?" *AIDS and Behavior,* 11(Suppl 2): S1–S6.

Aidala, A. A., J. E. Cross, R. Stall, D. Harre and E. Sumartojo. 2005. "Housing Status and HIV Risk Behaviors: Implications for Prevention and Policy." *AIDS and Behavior,* 9(3): 251–65.

Attia, S., M. Egger, M. Muller, M. Zwahlen and N. Low. 2009. "Sexual Transmission of HIV According to Viral Load and Antiretroviral Therapy: Systematic Review and Meta-analysis." *AIDS,* 23(11): 1397–1404.

Bourgois, P. 1998. "The Moral Economies of Homeless Heroin Addicts: Confronting Ethnography, HIV Risk, and Everyday Violence in San Francisco Shooting Encampments." *Substance Use & Misuse,* 33(11): 2323–51.

Briggs, D., T. Rhodes, D. Marks, J. Kimber, G. Holloway and S. Jones. 2009. "Injecting Drug Use and Unstable Housing: Scope for Structural Interventions in Harm Reduction." *Drugs: Education Prevention and Policy,* 16(5): 436–50.

Bruneau, J., F. Lamothe, J. Soto, M. Brabant, J. Vincelette and M. Fauvel. 1989. "Sero-epidemiology of HIV-1 Infection among Injection Drug Users Seeking Medical Help in Montréal: 1985–1988." Paper presented at the 5th International AIDS Conference, Montreal, Canada, June 4–9.

Buchanan, D., S. Shaw, A. Ford and M. Singer. 2003. "Empirical Science Meets Moral Panic: An Analysis of the Politics of Needle Exchange." *Journal of Public Health Policy,* 24(3–4): 427–44.

Bungay, V., J. L. Johnson, C. Varcoe and S. Boyd. 2010. "Women's Health and Use of Crack Cocaine in Context: Structural and 'Everyday' Violence." *International Journal of Drug Policy,* 21(4): 321–29.

Canadian AIDS Society. 2009. "'Bring Me Home': The Canadian AIDS Society's Position Statement on Housing and HIV/AIDS." [on-line]. Canadian AIDS Society. http://www.cdnaids.ca/web/position.nsf/pages/cas-pp-0303 [consulted August 10, 2010].

Carstairs, C. 2002. "Becoming a 'Hype': Heroin Consumption, Subcultural Formation and Resistance in Canada, 1945–1951." *Contemporary Drug Problems,* 29(1): 91–115.

Clark, C. and A. R. Rich. 2003. "Outcomes of Homeless Adults with Mental Illness in a Housing Program and in Case Management Only." *Psychiatric Services,* 54(1): 78–83.

CMHC (Canada Mortgage Housing Corporation). 2006. "Homelessness, Housing, and Harm Reduction: Stable Housing for Homeless People with Substance Use Issues." [on-line]. CMHC. https://www03.cmhc-schl.gc.ca/catalog/productDetail.cfm?cat=123&itm=30&lang=en &fr=1298392802035 [consulted August 1, 2010].

Coady, M. H., M. H. Latka, H. Thiede, E. T. Golub, L. Ouellet, S. M. Hudson et al. 2007. "Housing Status and Associated Differences in HIV Risk Behaviors among Young Injection Drug Users (IDUS)." *AIDS and Behavior,* 11(6): 854–63.

DeBeck, K., T. Kerr, K. Li, B. Fischer, J. Buxton, J. Montaner et al. 2009. "Smoking of Crack Cocaine as a Risk Factor for HIV Infection among People Who Use Injection Drugs." *Canadian Medical Association Journal,* 181(9): 585–89.

Des Jarlais, D. C., N. Braine and P. Friedmann. 2007. "Unstable Housing as a Factor for Increased Injection Risk Behavior at US Syringe Exchange Programs." *AIDS and Behavior,* 11(6 Suppl): 78–84.

Ennett, S. T., E. B. Federman, S. L. Bailey, C. L. Ringwalt and M. L. Hubbard. 1999. "HIV-Risk Behaviors Associated with Homelessness Characteristics in Youth." *Journal of Adolescent Health,* 25(5): 344–53.

Epele, M. E. 2002. "Gender, Violence and HIV: Women's Survival in the Streets." *Culture Medicine and Psychiatry,* 26(1): 33–54.

Evans, L. and S. A. Strathdee. 2006. "A Roof Is Not Enough: Unstable Housing, Vulnerability to HIV Infection and the Plight of the SRO." *International Journal of Drug Policy,* 17(2): 115–17.

Fischer, B., M. F. Cruz, J. Patra and J. Rehm. 2008. "Predictors of Methadone Maintenance Treatment Utilization in a Multisite Cohort of Illicit Opioid Users (OPICAN)." *Journal of Substance Abuse Treatment,* 34(3): 340–46.

Fisher, J. D. and L. Smith. 2009. "Secondary Prevention of HIV Infection: The Current State of Prevention for Positives." *Current Opinion in HIV and AIDS,* 4(4): 279–87.

Galea, S. and D. Vlahov. 2002. "Social Determinants and the Health of Drug Users: Socioeconomic Status, Homelessness, and Incarceration." *Public Health Reports,* 117(Suppl 1): S135–45.

German, D., M. A. Davey and C. A. Latkin. 2007. "Residential Transience and HIV Risk Behaviors among Injection Drug Users." *AIDS and Behavior,* 11(6 Suppl): 21–30.

Greenwood, R. M., N. J. Schaefer-McDaniel, G. Winkel and S. J. Tsemberis. 2005. "Decreasing Psychiatric Symptoms by Increasing Choice in Services for Adults with Histories of Homelessness." *American Journal of Community Psychology*, 36(3–4): 223–38.

Gulick, R. M., J. W. Mellors, D. Havlir, J. J. Eron, C. Gonzalez, D. McMahon et al. 1997. "Treatment with Indinavir, Zidovudine, and Lamivudine in Adults with Human Immunodeficiency Virus Infection and Prior Antiretroviral Therapy." *New England Journal of Medicine*, 337(11): 734–39.

Gurstein, P. and D. Small. 2005. "From Housing to Home: Reflexive Management for Those Deemed Hard to House." *Housing Studies*, 20(5): 717–35.

Henry, R., J. L. Richardson, S. Stoyanoff, G. P. Garcia, F. Dorey, E. Iverson et al. 2008. "HIV/AIDS Health Service Utilization by People Who Have Been Homeless." *AIDS and Behavior*, 12(5): 815–21.

Hwang, S. W. 2001. "Homelessness and Health. *Canadian Medical Association Journal*, 164(2): 229–33.

_____. 2000. "Mortality among Men Using Homeless Shelters in Toronto, Ontario." *Journal of the American Medical Association*, 283(16): 2152–57.

Inciardi, J. A. and L. D. Harrison. 2000. *Harm Reduction: National and International Perspectives*. Thousand Oaks, CA: Sage.

Katz, M. H., W. E. Cunningham, J. A. Fleishman, R. M. Andersen, T. Kellogg, S. A. Bozzette et al. 2001. "Effect of Case Management on Unmet Needs and Utilization of Medical Care and Medications among HIV-Infected Persons." *Annals of Internal Medicine*, 135(8 Pt 1): 557–65.

Kerr, T., J. A. Stoltz, B. D. L. Marshall, C. Lai, S. A. Strathdee and E. Wood. 2009. "Childhood Trauma and Injection Drug Use among High-Risk Youth. *Journal of Adolescent Health*, 45(3): 300–02.

Kerr, T., E. Wood, E. Grafstein, T. Ishida, K. Shannon, C. Lai et al. 2005. "High Rates of Primary Care and Emergency Department Use among Injection Drug Users in Vancouver." *Journal of Public Health*, 27(1): 62–66.

Knowlton, A., J. Arnsten, L. Eldred, J. Wilkinson, M. Gourevitch, S. Shade et al. 2006. "Individual, Interpersonal, and Structural Correlates of Effective HAART Use among Urban Active Injection Drug Users." *Journal of Acquired Immune Deficiency Syndromes*, 41(4): 486–92.

Kruas, D., L. Serge and M. Goldberg. 2006. "Housing and Services for People with Substance Use and Mental Health Issues." [on-line]. Social Planning and Research Council (SPARC) of BC. http://www.sparc.bc.ca/resources-and-publications/doc/68-report-housing-and-services.pdf [consulted Feburary 22, 2011].

Krüsi, A., D. Fast, W. Small, E. Wood and T. Kerr. 2010. "Social and Structural Barriers to Housing among Street-Involved Youth Who Use Illicit Drugs." *Health and Social Care in the Community,* 18(3): 282–88.

Krüsi, A., W. Small, E. Wood and T. Kerr. 2009. "An Integrated Supervised Injecting Program within a Care Facility for HIV-Positive Individuals: A Qualitative Evaluation." *AIDS Care,* 21(5): 638–44.

Kushel, M. B., G. Colfax, K. Ragland, A. Heineman, H. Palacio and D. R. Bangsberg. 2006. "Case Management is Associated with Improved Antiretroviral Adherence and CD4+ Cell Counts in Homeless and Marginally Housed Individuals with HIV Infection." *Clinical Infectious Diseases,* 43(2): 234–42.

Lamothe, F., J. Bruneau, J. Soto, M. Brabant and J. Vincelette. 1988. "Prevalence of HIV-1 Infection among Injection Drug Users in Montreal, 1985–1987." *Canada Diseases Weekly Report,* 14(50): 225–27.

Larimer, M. E., D. K. Malone, M. D. Garner, D. C. Atkins, B. Burlingham, H. S. Lonczak et al. 2009. "Health Care and Public Service Use and Costs Before and After Provision of Housing for Chronically Homeless Persons with Severe Alcohol Problems." *Journal of the American Medical Association,* 301(13): 1349–57.

Latkin, C. A., V. Forman, A. Knowlton and S. Sherman. 2003. "Norms, Social Networks, and HIV-Related Risk Behaviors among Urban Disadvantaged Drug Users." *Social Science & Medicine,* 56(3): 465–76.

Lloyd-Smith, E., E. Wood, K. Li, J. S. Montaner and T. Kerr. 2009. "Incidence and Determinants of Initiation into Cocaine Injection and Correlates of Frequent Cocaine Injectors." *Drug and Alcohol Dependence,* 99(1–3): 176–82.

Lundgren, L. M., R. F. Schilling, F. Ferguson, K. Davis and M. Amodeo. 2003. "Examining Drug Treatment Program Entry of Injection Drug Users: Human Capital and Institutional Disaffiliation." *Evaluation and Program Planning,* 26(2): 123–32.

Mallett, S., D. Rosenthal and D. Keys. 2005. "Young People, Drug Use and Family Conflict: Pathways into Homelessness." *Journal of Adolescence,* 28(2): 185–99.

Marshall, B. D. L., T. Kerr, J. A. Shoveller, T. L. Patterson, J. A. Buxton and E. Wood. 2009. "Homelessness and Unstable Housing Associated with an Increased Risk of HIV and STI Transmission among Street-Involved Youth." *Health & Place,* 15(3): 753–60.

Mathers, B. M., L. Degenhardt, B. Phillips, L. Wiessing, M. Hickman, S. A. Strathdee et al. 2008. "Global Epidemiology of Injecting Drug Use and HIV among People Who Inject Drugs: A Systematic Review." *Lancet,* 372(9651): 1733–45.

Meschede, T. 2010. "Accessing Housing: Exploring the Impact of Medical and Substance Abuse Services on Housing Attainment for Chronically

Homeless Street Dwellers." *Journal of Human Behavior in the Social Environment*, 20(2): 153–69.

Milby, J. B., J. E. Schumacher, C. McNamara, D. Wallace, S. Usdan, T. McGill et al. 2000. "Initiating Abstinence in Cocaine Abusing Dually Diagnosed Homeless Persons." *Drug and Alcohol Dependence*, 60(1): 55–67.

Miller, C. L., S. A. Strathdee, T. Kerr, K. Li and E. Wood. 2006. "Factors Associated with Early Adolescent Initiation into Injection Drug Use: Implications for Intervention Programs." *Journal of Adolescent Health*, 38(4): 462–64.

Mizuno, Y., D. W. Purcell, J. Zhang, A. R. Knowlton, M. De Varona, J. H. Arnsten et al. 2009. "Predictors of Current Housing Status among HIV-Seropositive Injection Drug Users (IDUS): Results from a 1-Year Study." *AIDS and Behavior*, 13(1): 165–72.

Montaner, J. S., R. Hogg, E. Wood, T. Kerr, M. Tyndall, A. R. Levy et al. 2006. "The Case for Expanding Access to Highly Active Antiretroviral Therapy to Curb the Growth of the HIV Epidemic." *Lancet*, 368(9534): 531–36.

Neale, J. 2001. "Homelessness amongst Drug Users: A Double Jeopardy Explored." *International Journal of Drug Policy*, 12(4): 353–69.

Ompad, D. C., R. M. Ikeda, N. Shah, C. M. Fuller, S. Bailey, E. Morse et al. 2005. "Childhood Sexual Abuse and Age at Initiation of Injection Drug Use." *American Journal of Public Health*, 95(4): 703–09.

Palepu, A., B. D. L. Marshall, C. Lai, E. Wood and T. Kerr. 2010. "Addiction Treatment and Stable Housing among a Cohort of Injection Drug Users." *PLoS One*, 5(7): e11697.

PHAC (Public Health Agency of Canada). 2009. *Summary: Estimates of HIV Prevalence and Incidence in Canada, 2008.* [on-line]. Public Health Agency of Canada. http://www.phac-aspc.gc.ca/aids-sida/publication/survre port/pdf/estimat08-eng.pdf [consulted August 22, 2010].

_____. 2006. *I-Track: Enhanced Surveillance of Risk Behaviours among People Who Inject Drugs. Phase I Report, August 2006.* [on-line]. Public Health Agency of Canada. http://www.phac-aspc.gc.ca/i-track/sr-re-1/pdf/ itrack06_e.pdf [consulted March 31, 2010].

Rawson, R. A., M. J. McCann, F. Flammino, S. Shoptaw, K. Miotto, C. Reiber et al. 2006. "A Comparison of Contingency Management and Cognitive-Behavioral Approaches for Stimulant-Dependent Individuals." *Addiction*, 101(2): 267–74.

Reyes, J. C., R. R. Robles, H. M. Colón, T. D. Matos, H. A. Finlinson, C. A. Marrero et al. 2005. "Homelessness and HIV Risk Behaviors among Drug Injectors in Puerto Rico." *Journal of Urban Health*, 82(3): 446–55.

Rhodes, T., M. Singer, P. Bourgois, S. R. Friedman and S. A. Strathdee. 2005. "The Social Structural Production of HIV Risk among Injecting Drug Users." *Social Science & Medicine,* 61(5): 1026–44.

Rhodes, T., J. Kimber, W. Small, J. Fitzgerald, T. Kerr, M. Hickman et al. 2006. "Public Injecting and the Need for 'Safer Environment Interventions' in the Reduction of Drug-Related Harm." *Addiction,* 101(10): 1384–93.

Richardson, L., E. Wood, R. Zhang, J. Montaner, M. Tyndall and T. Kerr. 2008. "Employment among Users of a Medically Supervised Safer Injection Facility. *American Journal of Drug and Alcohol Abuse,* 34(5): 519–25.

Roy, E., N. Haley, P. Leclerc, L. Cedras, L. Blais and J. F. Boivin. 2003. "Drug Injection among Street Youths in Montreal: Predictors of Initiation." *Journal of Urban Health,* 80(1): 92–105.

Salazar, L. F., R. A. Crosby, D. R. Holtgrave, S. Head, B. Hadsock, J. Todd et al. 2007. "Homelessness and HIV-Associated Risk Behavior among African American Men Who Inject Drugs and Reside in the Urban South of the United States." *AIDS and Behavior,* 11(6 Suppl): 70–77.

Schumacher, J. E., J. B. Milby, D. Wallace, D. C. Meehan, S. Kertesz, R. Vuchinich et al. 2007. "Meta-analysis of Day Treatment and Contingency-Management Dismantling Research: Birmingham Homeless Cocaine Studies (1990–2006)." *Journal of Consulting and Clinical Psychology,* 75(5): 823–28.

Shah, N. G., N. Galai, D. D. Celentano, D. Vlahov and S. A. Strathdee. 2006. "Longitudinal Predictors of Injection Cessation and Subsequent Relapse among a Cohort of Injection Drug Users in Baltimore, MD, 1988–2000." *Drug and Alcohol Dependence,* 83(2): 147–56.

Shannon, K., T. Ishida, C. Lai and M. W. Tyndall. 2006. "The Impact of Unregulated Single Room Occupancy Hotels on the Health Status of Illicit Drug Users in Vancouver." *International Journal of Drug Policy,* 17(2): 107–14.

Shubert, V. and N. Bernstine. 2007. "Moving from Fact to Policy: Housing Is HIV Prevention and Health Care." *AIDS and Behavior,* 11(Suppl 2): S172–81.

Siegal, H. A., R. G. Carlson, R. Falck, L. Li, M. A. Forney, R. C. Rapp et al. 1991. "HIV Infection and Risk Behaviors among Intravenous Drug Users in Low Seroprevalence Areas in the Midwest." *American Journal of Public Health,* 81(12): 1642–44.

Small, W., T. Rhodes, E. Wood and T. Kerr. 2007. "Public Injection Settings in Vancouver: Physical Environment, Social Context and Risk." *International Journal of Drug Policy,* 18(1): 27–36.

Smart, R. G. 1991. "AIDS and Drug Abuse in Canada: Current Status and Information Needs." *Journal of Drug Issues,* 21(1): 73–82.

Song, J. Y., M. Safaeian, S. A. Strathdee, D. Vlahov and D. D. Celentano. 2000. "The Prevalence of Homelessness among Injection Drug Users With and Without HIV Infection." *Journal of Urban Health,* 77(4): 678–87.

Strathdee, S. A., D. M. Patrick, S. L. Currie, P. G. Cornelisse, M. L. Rekart, J. S. Montaner et al. 1997. "Needle Exchange Is Not Enough: Lessons from the Vancouver Injecting Drug Use Study." *AIDS,* 11(8): F59–65.

Tsemberis, S., L. Gulcur and M. Nakae. 2004. "Housing First, Consumer Choice, and Harm Reduction for Homeless Individuals with a Dual Diagnosis." *American Journal of Public Health,* 94(4): 651–56.

Tyndall, M. W., S. Currie, P. Spittal, K. Li, E. Wood, M. V. O'Shaughnessy et al. 2003. "Intensive Injection Cocaine Use as the Primary Risk Factor in the Vancouver HIV-1 Epidemic." *AIDS,* 17(6): 887–93.

Urban Health Research Initiative, British Columbia Centre for Excellence in HIV/AIDS. (2009). *Drug Situation in Vancouver.* [on-line]. Urban Health Research Initiative, UBC. http://uhri.cfenet.ubc.ca/images/documents/dsiv2009.pdf [consulted February 1, 2011].

Wolitski, R. J., D. P. Kidder and K. A. Fenton. 2007. "HIV, Homelessness, and Public Health: Critical Issues and a Call for Increased Action." *AIDS and Behavior,* 11(Suppl 2): S167–71.

Wolitski, R. J., D. P. Kidder, S. L. Pals, S. Royal, A. Aidala, R. Stall et al. 2010. "Randomized Trial of the Effects of Housing Assistance on the Health and Risk Behaviors of Homeless and Unstably Housed People Living with HIV." *AIDS and Behavior,* 14(3): 493–503.

Wood, E., and T. Kerr. 2006a. "Needle Exchange and the HIV Outbreak among Injection Drug Users in Vancouver, Canada." *Substance Use & Misuse,* 41(6–7): 841–43.

Wood, E. and T. Kerr. 2006b. "What Do You Do When You Hit Rock Bottom? Responding to Drugs in the City of Vancouver." *International Journal of Drug Policy,* 17(2): 55–60.

Wood, E., T. Kerr, M. W. Tyndall and J. S. Montaner. 2008. "A Review of Barriers and Facilitators of HIV Treatment among Injection Drug Users." *AIDS,* 22(11): 1247–56.

Wood, E., K. Li, W. Small, J. S. Montaner, M. T. Schechter and T. Kerr. 2005. "Recent Incarceration Independently Associated with Syringe Sharing by Injection Drug Users." *Public Health Reports,* 120(2): 150–56.

Wood, E., T. Kerr, B. D. L. Marshall, K. Li, R. Zhang, R. S. Hogg et al. 2009. "Longitudinal Community Plasma HIV-1 RNA Concentrations and Incidence of HIV-1 among Injecting Drug Users: Prospective Cohort Study." *British Medical Journal,* 338: b1649.

# CHAPTER 7

# Supported Housing as a Promising Housing First Approach for People with Severe and Persistent Mental Illness

Tim Aubry, PhD
School of Psychology, University of Ottawa

John Ecker, PhD candidate
School of Psychology, University of Ottawa

Jonathan Jetté, PhD candidate
School of Psychology, University of Ottawa

## Introduction

Since the 1970s, deinstitutionalization has been the main focus of mental health policies in provinces across Canada (Kirby and Keon 2006). A primary reason behind deinstitutionalization was the recognition of the negative consequences associated with long-term treatment in psychiatric institutions (Mechanic and Rochefort 1990). The main objective of deinstitutionalization has been to move people with severe and persistent mental illness from psychiatric institutions into the community by replacing institutional services with community supports. The end goal of this major transformation in psychiatric services is to assist the deinstitutionalized population in assuming normal roles and becoming integrated back into society.

Unfortunately, close to four decades after the onset of deinstitutionalization in Canada, the goal of integrating people with severe and persistent mental illness remains a work in progress. A primary reason has been the slowness in developing much-needed community services to replace institutional ones, including housing. As a consequence, a substantial number of people with severe and persistent mental illness across Canada are socially isolated, live in extreme poverty and are either homeless or at constant risk of becoming homeless (Kirby and Keon 2006).

Only one Canadian survey has been completed to estimate the prevalence rates of mental illness in the homeless population. In a study conducted in Toronto, Goering, Tolomiczenko, Sheldon, Boydell and Wasylenki (2002) used a structured diagnostic interview among the city's homeless and found an overall lifetime prevalence rate of 67 percent for mental illness and 68 percent for substance abuse or dependence. Six percent of the sample reported having had a psychiatric hospitalization in the past 12 months. The lifetime prevalence of schizophrenia among the sample was 6 percent. A comparison of individuals who were experiencing homelessness the first time and individuals having had multiple episodes found no differences in prevalence rates of mental illness or substance abuse problems or in the percentage having had a psychiatric hospitalization in the past year.

In a review of 29 different studies conducted between 1979 and 2005 on the prevalence of major mental disorders among the homeless population in seven Western countries other than Canada, Fazel, Khosla, Doll and Geddes (2008) reported a pooled prevalence rate across studies for psychotic disorders of 12.7 percent with estimates from individual studies ranging from 2.8 percent to 42.3 percent. They found a similar pooled prevalence rate of 11.4 percent for major depression, with estimates in individual studies ranging from 0 percent to 40.9 percent. Among the disorders examined in the research, alcohol dependence had the highest pooled prevalence rate across studies with over a third of surveyed individuals (37.9%) identified with the problem. In response to the high prevalence rates of homelessness among people with mental illness and substance abuse problems, the development of effective housing and supports has been a preoccupation of mental health systems in Western countries, including in Canada (Nelson 2010).

The objective of this chapter is to review the current status of supported housing, a contemporary approach that is gaining increasing interest and support throughout North America and Europe for addressing homelessness of people with severe and persistent mental illness (Nelson 2010). In the Canadian context, the Mental Health Commission of Canada is in the process of investigating the effectiveness of supported housing through a large multi-site study in which housing and support of different levels of intensity are being delivered to people with mental illness and a history of homelessness (MHCC 2011). In this chapter, we present a history of the development of housing in response to deinstitutionalization, followed by a description of the supported housing approach. Subsequently, we will review the outcome research on supported housing. Based on this review, we will present limitations of this research. The chapter will conclude with a discussion of future directions for research and implications of the current state of knowledge on policy and program development.

## History of Housing for People with Severe and Persistent Mental Illness

In the wake of deinstitutionalization, the development of housing for people with severe and persistent mental illness has involved three distinct approaches: custodial housing, supportive housing and supported housing (Nelson 2010; Trainor et al. 1993). In tracing the policy stages with regard to housing in the province of Ontario, Trainor (2008) described the first type of housing created in response to the initial stage of deinstitutionalization in the 1970s as being custodial in nature. This was followed by the development of supportive housing in the 1980s and 1990s. Over the past 15 years, supported housing has emerged increasingly as the preferred housing approach. Table 7-1 presents a comparative description of the three approaches.

Custodial housing refers to board and care homes—often for-profit, semi-institutional facilities and single-room occupancy hotels (Parkinson, Nelson and Horga 1999). The residents are typically people with disabilities and support is provided by staff on-site (Parkinson, Nelson and Horga 1999). Custodial housing was critiqued for the segregation, social isolation and dependency that it fostered among its residents. As well, the quality of custodial housing was often very poor with residents lacking privacy or control over their living situation (Nelson 2010).

In response to these critiques, supportive housing was developed with the primary objective of helping residents develop life skills through community treatment and rehabilitation (Ridgway and Zipple 1990). Supportive housing was intended to be organized in a residential continuum (e.g., quarterway houses, halfway houses, group homes, etc.) in which the intensity of rehabilitation and the amount of autonomy varied in accordance with an individual's

## Table 7-1. Description of different housing approaches implemented after deinstitutionalization

|  | Custodial Housing | Supportive Housing | Supported Housing |
|---|---|---|---|
| Definition | • Consumers receive shelter, medication and meals, but little or no rehabilitation or support. | • Consumers receive shelter and on-site rehabilitation. As their functioning improves, they move to less restrictive setting. | • Consumers choose, get and keep regular housing in the community. They often receive rent supplement; support is portable and not tied to housing. |
| Key Characteristics | • Special care homes or foster families<br>• Congregate housing<br>• Staff control<br>• In-house staff provides custodial care | • Group home or clustered apartment with common areas<br>• Shared control over household decisions<br>• In-house staff provides rehabilitation services | • Apartment or other type of independent housing<br>• Consumers are regular tenants and have control over their housing.<br>• Staff are off-site and provide supports that are individualized according to needs. |
| Strengths | • Less expensive then institutions<br>• Does not require trained staff | • Consumers have more control over housing arrangements<br>• Housing includes an individualized rehabilitation program<br>• Facilitates the development of a social network with other tenants | • Preferred housing for majority of consumers<br>• Residents have choice and control over housing and support<br>• Less expensive than other alternatives<br>• Ongoing support |

**Table 7-1.** (Continued)

|  | Custodial Housing | Supportive Housing | Supported Housing |
|---|---|---|---|
| Weaknesses | • Lack of privacy<br>• Quality of the housing is often poor<br>• Frequently fosters dependency<br>• Consumers have little control<br>• Can include people with different disabilities<br>• No individualized support provided | • Full continuum of housing often lacking<br>• Transitional housing and services lacking permanency<br>• Interpersonal demands of group living<br>• Discharge to affordable permanent housing with support may not be available | • Some consumers report being socially isolated and lonely<br>• Lacks sufficient resources for consumers to pursue leisure activities and achieve community integration<br>• Intensity of support may be insufficient |

functioning level (Nelson 2010; Parkinson, Nelson and Horga 1999). Individuals were supposed to move along the continuum until they were ready to live independently. Although considered better living situations than custodial housing, supportive housing also had its share of detractors, who noted that a full continuum of housing options were rarely created in communities, moving in and out of housing was not in the best interest of consumers and individuals rarely achieved independent living (Blanch, Carling and Ridgway 1988; Nelson 2010; Ridgway and Zipple 1990).

Beginning in the late 1980s and early 1990s, mental health advocates called for the development of supported housing, wherein individuals with severe and persistent mental illness would be provided with the necessary support to live in regular housing as tenants (Blanch, Carling and Ridgway 1988; Carling 1993, 1995; Ridgway and Zipple 1990). The type of support in this approach usually involves Assertive Community Treatment (ACT) or Intensive Case Management (ICM) or some variant of these (Tabol, Drebing and Rosenheck 2010).

Wong and Solomon (2002) identified three factors as contributing to the development of the supported housing approach: (1) the criticism of supportive housing and the residential continuum model, (2) the recognition of homelessness as a significant social problem, particularly for individuals with severe and persistent mental illness and (3) the development of effective approaches for providing treat-ment and support in the community, including ACT and ICM. Another important contributor to the ascendancy of supported housing has been the results of research on consumer preferences in relation to housing and support.

In a review of 26 studies of mental health consumers' prefer-ences for housing and support conducted between 1986 and 1992, Tanzman (1993) reported that the most preferred living arrange-ment was independent living in a house or apartment. In 20 of the 26 surveys, at least 70 percent of the sample expressed this prefer-ence. Consumers in the reviewed studies also reported a preference for living alone or with a spouse or romantic partner and not living with other mental health consumers. With regard to staff support, consumers expressed a preference for having outreach staff that are readily available but separated from their housing. A majority of the respondents in the surveys also underlined the importance of income support and rent subsidies for them to be able to afford their preferred housing.

Two other Canadian studies had very similar findings con-cerning consumer preferences as Tanzman (1993). Nelson, Hall and Forchuk (2003) surveyed 300 individuals with severe and persistent mental illness in Ontario using the same instrument used in the American studies reviewed by Tanzman (1993). Of these respondents, 79 percent reported wanting to live independently in regular housing and only 38 percent actually lived in the housing that they preferred. Similar to the results of the American surveys, a very high propor-tion of survey respondents (82%) identified greater income support as being required for them to access their preferred housing. Less than one quarter of respondents (23%) wished to live with other mental health consumers. With regard to supports, consumers preferred supports that are external to their living situation and available on an on-call basis.

More recently, Piat and colleagues (2008) evaluated the hous-ing preferences of a stratified random sample of 315 mental health consumers living in housing supervised by health and social service organizations in Montreal. Over three-quarters of the sample (77%) expressed a preference for living in their own apartment, social housing or a supervised apartment. In contrast, less than half of con-sumers' case managers (49%) chose these options for them and only 35 percent of case managers agreed with their clients' preferences.

Piat and her colleagues (2008) interpreted their results as showing that consumers preferred housing that offered them more independence than the housing in which they were currently living. Case managers also showed preferences in this direction but were generally more conservative in these preferences relative to their clients, wanting more structure and clinical involvement in the housing, such as that offered by supervised apartments. Overall, these findings show unequivocally that consumers prefer supported housing over custodial or supportive housing.

## Core Principles, Dimensions and Elements of Supported Housing

Early writings advocating a supported housing approach argued that, compared to custodial housing or supportive housing, it was most conducive to facilitating consumer empowerment, community integration and normalization (Blanch, Carling and Ridgway 1988; Carling 1992, 1993; Ridgway and Zipple 1990). This represented a paradigm shift wherein former psychiatric patients would be supported to assume the normal role of tenant in regular and integrated housing through supported housing. A fundamental assumption of the approach was that people with severe and persistent mental illnesses can succeed in independent housing without first requiring a period of rehabilitation (Rog 2004).

The adoption of supported housing as a response to the chronic homelessness experienced by individuals with severe and persistent mental illness has gained momentum in North American cities because of the very promising findings emerging from research on the Pathways to Housing program in New York City (Greenwood et al. 2005; Stefancic and Tsemberis 2007; Tsemberis 1999; Tsemberis and Eisenberg 2000; Tsemberis, Gulcur and Nakae 2004). Four studies on the Pathways program have been completed in the United States, and their findings show participants remaining stably housed despite having a chronic history of homelessness (Greenwood et al. 2005; Pearson, Montgomery and Locke 2009; Stefancic and Tsemberis 2007; Tsemberis and Eisenberg 2000). A more detailed review of this research is conducted in a later section of the chapter.

Typically, the support includes a rent subsidy and there are no requirements for treatment of their mental illness and/or addiction for consumers to move into or stay in housing. For this reason, supported housing is often referred to as 'Housing First'. It is important to note that most supported housing described in the literature is Housing First in nature. However, not all housing that is described as Housing First is necessarily supported housing since both custodial housing and supportive housing can adopt Housing First principles and not require their residents or participants to engage in treatment or remain abstinent from alcohol or drug use to qualify for the housing. We will examine the criteria of supported housing in more detail next.

Three reviews defining the core ingredients of supported housing have been conducted (Rog 2004; Tabol, Dreben and Rosenheck 2010; Wong, Filoromo and Tenille 2007). The core ingredients of supported housing identified in each of the reviews are presented in Table 7-2.

In an attempt to operationalize the supported housing approach, the Substance Abuse and Mental Health Services Administration's (SAMHSA) Centre for Mental Health Services, located in the United States, defined eight core dimensions to the approach (as cited in Rog 2004):

1. An individual owns the housing or holds a lease in his or her name as a tenant and the housing is considered permanent.
2. Housing and services are legally and functionally separate.
3. Housing is integrated in the community (i.e., regular in nature).
4. Housing is affordable (i.e., does not exceed 40% of gross income).
5. Participation in services is voluntary and not a condition of getting or keeping housing.
6. Individuals are given choice for both housing and services.
7. Services are community-based and external to the housing (i.e., no live-in or regular in-house staff).
8. Crisis services are available 24 hours per day and seven days per week.

Rog (2004) noted that descriptions of supported housing programs in research literature are frequently missing certain dimensions. As well, alternative housing programs to which supported housing is compared often are presented as having some of these dimensions.

In examining the implementation of supported housing in Philadelphia and based on a review of the literature, Wong, Filoromo

## Table 7-2. Criteria of supported housing as defined in different reviews focusing on implementation issues

| Criteria Areas | Rog (2004) | Wong et al. (2007) | Tabol et al. (2010) |
|---|---|---|---|
| Use of Regular Housing | • An individual owns the housing or holds a lease in his or her name as a tenant and the housing is considered permanent.<br>• Housing is integrated in the community.<br>• Housing is affordable (i.e., does not exceed 40% of of gross income). | • Typical and normalized housing | • Housing is affordable<br>• 'Normal' tenancy agreement<br>• Privacy over access to the unit<br>• Appearance of residence fits with neighbourhood norms<br>• Integrated with non-consumers<br>• Long-term placement/ potentially permanent housing |
| Separation of Housing and Services | • Housing and services are legally and functionally separate.<br>• Participation in services is voluntary and not a condition of getting or keeping housing.<br>• Services are community-based and external to the housing (i.e., no live-in or regular in-house staff). | • Promotes the independence and control of consumers with regard to their relationships with support providers | • Housing and services legally/ functionally separate<br>• Absence of requirements as condition of stay<br>• No live-in/ regular in-house staff |

**Table 7-2.** (Continued)

| Criteria Areas | Rog (2004) | Wong et al. (2007) | Tabol et al. (2010) |
|---|---|---|---|
| Delivery of Flexible Supports | • Crisis services are available 24 hours per day and 7 days per week. | • Housing located close to community resources<br>• Support delivered to consumers is individualized, flexible and of varying intensity based on needs | • Individualized and flexible support<br>• Crisis services available 24/7<br>• Resources in close proximity |
| Facilitation of Choice | • Individuals are given choice for both housing and services. | • Consumer choice for housing<br>• Promotes the independence and control of consumers with regard to their relationships with support providers | • Shared decision-making<br>• Choice in housing options |
| Immediate Placement | | | • Immediate placement into normal housing (i.e., no preparatory setting) |

and Tenille (2007) descried supported housing as being based on four core principles: (1) housing is a basic right for people with psychiatric disabilities, (2) people with psychiatric disabilities are to live in housing as regular tenants and community members, (3) empowerment is the practice goal for the relationship between consumers and support staff and (4) access to and the delivery of housing and mental health services are functionally separate. According to Wong, Filoromo and Tenille (2007), these principles produce five operational domains integral to supported housing and pertaining to either housing/tenancy or support/services. The first principle is ensuring 'consumer choice' particularly as it relates to the location and type of housing as well as with whom and how consumers will live. The second principle refers to consumers living in 'typical and normalized housing' that corresponds to neighbourhood norms and is located in an environment (e.g., apartment block, neighbourhood) where there are a majority of non-disabled individuals. The third principle has housing located close to community resources and facilities that can facilitate community participation and integration. The fourth principle promotes the independence and control of consumers with regard to their relationships with support providers. Finally, the fifth principle holds that support delivered to consumers be individualized, flexible and of varying intensity based on needs.

Wong, Filoromo and Tenille (2007) conducted an extensive analysis of data from housing providers and consumers to evaluate the extent that 27 housing programs for people with severe and persistent mental illness in Philadelphia demonstrated these five operational principles. Results showed substantial variations in housing and mental health support characteristics in terms of being in line with these principles. The researchers concluded that this variation reflects the existence of different versions of supported housing with some programs showing high fidelity to these principles while others deviate from them.

In a recent study, Tabol, Drebing and Rosenheck (2010) conducted a comprehensive review of the literature on supported housing programs and examined the degree of clarity of the approach and the degree of fidelity to the model in the descriptions of programs appearing in studies published in the research literature. For this review, key articles on supported housing were investigated to identify the critical elements of the model. A total of 15 elements were identified and clustered into five broader overarching categories—namely, (1) normal housing, (2) flexible supports, (3) separation of housing and services, (4) choice and (5) immediate placement (see Table 7-2). Using the identified elements in their conceptualization of supported housing, Tabol, Drebing and Rosenheck (2010) evaluated the descriptions of 38 different housing programs described in articles published in peer-reviewed journals between 1987 and 2008. In particular, they assessed if the descriptions of the programs in these articles included each of these elements and determined the extent they adhered to them. Of the 38 programs, 25 were characterized in the published articles as supported housing, seven programs as supportive housing and the remaining six programs as unlabelled or other.

Tabol, Drebing and Rosenheck's (2010) analysis found that although programs described as supported housing adhered to more elements than those defined as supportive housing or other housing, less than half of the supported program adhered to most of the 15 elements. Based on these findings, the researchers concluded that the lack of clarity of the supported housing model along with the lack of fidelity to the critical ingredients of the model in many programs has hindered the broad dissemination, implementation and evaluation of the approach. Related to these issues is the inconsistency in the community mental health sector of the use of the labels *supported housing* versus *supportive housing* to describe programs. As a result, there is confusion in the field among researchers, practitioners, policy-makers and the public about the critical ingredients of these two approaches and how to differentiate them. In the next section of the chapter, we turn our attention to the outcome research on supported housing, focusing on those programs that show adherence to the key core elements of the approach.

As yet, there is no consensus on the criteria that should be used to evaluate the validity of a supported housing approach, nor has a fidelity measure for the approach been developed. Each of the reviews used a different process to establish their criteria. Rog (2004) used the early criteria developed by SAMHSA's Center for Mental Health Services that were based on a set of interviews and surveys with key informants. Wong, Filoromo and Tennille (2007) operationalized the key dimensions of supported housing appearing in the theoretical literature as defined by Carling (1995), Hogan and Carling (1992) and Ridgway and Zipple (1990). Tabol, Drebing and Rosenheck (2010) reviewed the criteria appearing in the extant research literature, including from the two previous reviews (Rog 2004; Wong, Filoromo and Tenille 2007), and developed what they considered an exhaustive list of key criteria of supported housing.

## Review of Research on Effectiveness of Supported Housing

### Criteria for Selection of Studies

An electronic literature search was conducted of the databases of published research, PSYCINFO and MEDLINE, by entering the keywords "housing first", "supported housing", "homeless", "homeless mentally ill", "assertive community treatment", "intensive case management" and "case management". We also examined recent literature reviews on housing in the area of community mental health (Aubry, Doestaler and Baronet 2004; Coldwell and Bender 2007; Leff et al.

2009; Nelson, Aubry and Lafrance 2007; Nelson 2010; Tabol, Drebing and Rosenheck 2010).

The selection of eligible studies emerging from our literature search was based on the following criteria: (1) the study needed to be published in a refereed journal, (2) the study involved a comparison of at least two groups, of which one of the groups comprised individuals living in supported housing and (3) the study examined effectiveness using at least some quantitative measures.

In order to determine if a study included at least one group in its design in which individuals received supported housing, the description of the housing and support in the paper reporting had to include the presence of four criteria which we considered the minimum critical ingredients of the approach. These criteria were selected from Rog's (2004) critical elements of supported housing: (1) housing and supports are provided separately by different organizations, (2) individuals in the program live in regular housing that is integrated into the community, (3) individuals live in housing that is affordable, defined typically as costing 40 percent or less of their income and (4) support services are delivered separately and externally from the housing (i.e., portable rather than involving live-in support). A total of nine studies were identified.

### Description of Selected Studies

Table 7-3 presents descriptive information about the selected studies. All of the studies were conducted in cities in the United States. Of the nine studies, six adopted a true experimental design (i.e., participants were randomly assigned to different treatment conditions) and another three used a quasi-experimental design (i.e., participants of different groups were not randomly assigned but were matched on key variables instead).

In terms of comparison groups, four studies compared supported housing to a continuum model of housing (McHugo et al. 2004; O'Connell, Kasprow and Rosenheck 2009; Tsemberis 1999; Tsemberis et al. 2003), three studies compared supported housing to case management without housing or to standard care in the community (Hurlburt, Hough and Wood 1996; Rosenheck et al. 2003; Stefancic and Tsemberis 2007), one study compared supported housing to supportive housing (i.e., congregate housing with on-site case management) (Dickey et al. 1996) and one study compared supported housing to two types of housing models: (1) supportive housing and (2) multi-site

**Table 7-3. Characteristics of selected supported housing studies**

| Study | Location | Sample | Comparison Group(s) | Experimental Group | Study Type | Follow-up |
|---|---|---|---|---|---|---|
| Hurlburt, Wood & Hough (1996); Hurlburt, Hough & Wood (1996); Wood et al. (1998) | San Diego | C1: 90 C2: 91 E1: 90 E2: 91 | No Section 8 certificate with comprehensive (C1) or traditional case management (C2) | Supported housing: Section 8 certificate with either comprehensive case management (E1) or traditional case management (E2) | Experimental | 24 months |
| Dickey et al. (1996); Goldfinger et al. (1999); Seidman et al. (2003) | Boston | C:63 E: 55 | Evolving consumer households with congregate living (C) | Supported housing, independent living (E) | Experimental | 18 months |
| Tsemberis (1999); Tsemberis & Eisenberg (2000) | New York | C: 3,811 E: 139 | Residential continuum model (C) | Pathways supported housing with ACT (E) | Quasi-experimental | 36 months (Tsemberis 1999); 60 months (Tsemberis & Eisenberg 2000) |

**Table 7-3.** (Continued)

| Study | Location | Sample | Comparison Group(s) | Experimental Group | Study Type | Follow-up |
|---|---|---|---|---|---|---|
| Gulcur et al. (2003); Tsemberis et al. (2003); Tsemberis, Gulcur & Nakae (2004); Greenwood et al. (2005) | New York | C: 119 E: 87 | Residential continuum model (C) | Pathways supported housing with ACT (E) | Experimental | 24 months (Gulcur et al. 2003; Tsemberis et al. 2003; Tsemberis et al. 2004) 36 months (Greenwood et al. 2005) |
| Rosenheck et al. (2003); Cheng et al. (2007); O'Connell, Kasprow & Rosenheck (2008) | San Francisco, San Diego, New Orleans, Cleveland | C1: 90 C2: 188 E: 182 | No Section 8 certificate with case management (C1) or standard treatment (C2) | Supported housing: Section 8 certificate with intensive case management (E) | Experimental | 36 months (Rosenheck et al. 2003; Cheng et al. 2007); 60 months (O'Connell et al. 2008) |
| McHugo et al. (2004) | Washington, DC | C: 61 E: 60 | ICM with congregate housing or non scattered-site housing (C) | Supported housing with ACT (E) | Experimental | 18 months |

**Table 7-3.** (Continued)

| Study | Location | Sample | Comparison Group(s) | Experimental Group | Study Type | Follow-up |
|---|---|---|---|---|---|---|
| Stefancic & Tsemberis (2007) | New York, NY | C: 51<br>E1: 105<br>E2: 104 | Standard care (C) | Supported housing with ACT (Pathways) (E1); Consortium of treatment and housing agencies (E2) | Experimental | 20 months (E1, E2, & C); 47 months (E1, E2) |
| O'Connell, Kasprow & Rosenheck (2009) | 15 sites across the United States | C: 183<br>E: 139 | Section 8 voucher with multistage housing and case management (C) | Section 8 voucher with direct placement into independent housing and case management (E) | Quasi-experimental | 24 months |
| Pearson, Montgomery & Locke (2009) | Seattle (DESC); San Diego (REACH); New York (Pathways) | DESC : 25 (C1); REACH 29 (C2); Pathways: 26 (E) | Supportive housing (C1); Multi-site housing with modified ACT (C2) | Supported housing with ACT (E) | Quasi-experimental | 12 months |

housing with modified ACT support (Pearson, Montgomery and Locke 2009).

Some of the studies were reported in several different articles, sometimes with different sample sizes or overlapping samples. When there were overlapping samples in different reports, it was decided to count them as one study, rather than separate studies, using the article with the largest sample size reported. There was great variability in the supported housing models across the studies in terms of fidelity criteria for supported housing. A full description of the different supported housing programs examined in the literature was often lacking. As well, few studies conducted fidelity assessments to determine how adequately the program components were being implemented. In general, as Tabol, Drebing and Rosenheck (2010) reported, there was great variability in the housing programs described in the different studies in terms of fidelity to the supported housing criteria.

### Description of Population in Selected Studies
The samples of participants in the selected studies are characterized by a preponderance of non-white, middle-aged men. Only one study had a majority of white participants (Hulburt, Wood and Hough 1996) and only one study had a majority of women (McHugo et al. 2004).

Most studies targeted a population with severe and persistent mental illness as reflected by the relatively high prevalence of schizophrenia among study participants in seven of the nine studies. The remaining two studies were conducted on military veterans (O'Connell, Kasprow and Rosenheck 2009; Rosenheck et al. 2003), and less than 10 percent of participants from those studies had a diagnosis of schizophrenia. In these studies, the eligibility criteria included having a serious mental disorder (e.g., schizophrenia, psychotic disorder, depression, post-traumatic stress disorder) and/or addiction in addition to being homeless. The samples in eight of the studies show a high prevalence of substance use, indicating the presence of concurrent disorders in a majority of study participants.

A large proportion of participants in the reviewed studies had experienced lengthy periods of homelessness leading up to their participation in the study. Upon admission to the study, they were either living in emergency shelters, on the street, in transitional housing, in jail or in a psychiatric hospital.

### Findings on Outcomes

Table 7-4 presents a summary of results of studies examining the effectiveness of supported housing in relation to other housing models or to standard care. In discussing the findings, outcomes will be summarized into the categories of housing outcomes (e.g., length of time housed), service use outcomes (e.g., number of hospital admissions, length of hospitalizations and satisfaction with services), clinical outcomes (e.g., client functioning and symptoms), community adaptation (e.g., quality of life, employment, and community integration) and costs.

**Housing.** Overall, individuals placed in supported housing had better outcomes in relation to housing compared to individuals placed in residential continuum housing. In particular, supported housing resulted in superior housing outcomes including the achievement of stable housing in five of the nine studies when compared to residential continuum housing models (Tsemberis 1999; Tsemberis et al. 2003), programs providing case management without housing (Hulburt, Hough and Wood 1996; Rosenheck et al. 2003), supportive housing, and standard care (e.g., Rosenheck et al. 2003; Stefancic and Tsemberis 2007).

In one of the studies, tenants in supported housing achieved comparable housing outcomes to tenants in supportive housing and residential continuum housing but reported having fewer housing problems (Pearson, Montgomery and Locke 2009). In two of the studies, supportive housing was found to yield superior housing outcomes to supported housing (Dickey et al. 1996; McHugo et al. 2004). Finally, in the remaining study, housing outcomes were mixed, with tenants in supported housing showing a greater reduction of homelessness over 24 months than tenants in residential continuum housing (O'Connell, Kasprow and Rosenheck 2009). However, tenants in supported housing had more days of homelessness over the course of the study. The non-equivalence of the housing history of the two groups was interpreted as contributing to these differences in findings.

**Service use outcomes.** In three of the six studies that looked at service use outcomes, tenants in supported housing were found to experience less time in hospital in comparison to tenants in residential continuum housing (Gulcur et al. 2003; O'Connell, Kasprow and

**Table 7-4. Summary of outcomes in effectiveness studies on supported housing**

| Studies | Housing | Service Use Outcomes | Clinical Outcomes | Community Adaptation | Costs |
|---|---|---|---|---|---|
| Hurlburt, Hough & Wood (1996); Hurlburt, Wood & Hough (1996); Wood et al. (1998) | (+) shorter amount of time to being housed (+) % independent living at 2 yrs. | (+) greater continued contact with services | | | |
| Dickey et al. (1996); Goldfinger et al. (1999); Seidman et al. (2003) | ND % housed at 18 mos. (−) lower % experiencing homelessness, mean # of days homeless | ND hospitalizations ND use of mental health and addiction services | ND neuropsychological functioning over time (−) decreased executive functioning over time | | |
| Tsemberis (1999); Tsemberis & Eisenberg (2000) | (+) % housed at 5 yrs. | | | | |
| Gulcur et al. (2003); Tsemberis et al. (2003); Tsemberis, Gulcur & Nakae (2004); Greenwood et al. (2005) | (+) time stably housed | (+) less time in hospital (−) substance abuse treatment | NC drug use, alcohol use, psychiatric symptoms | ND self-esteem, ND quality of life | (+) lesser hospitalization/ housing/shelter costs |

**Table 7-4.** (Continued)

| Studies | Housing | Service Use Outcomes | Clinical Outcomes | Community Adaptation | Costs |
|---|---|---|---|---|---|
| Rosenheck et al. (2003); Cheng et al. (2007); O'Connell, Kasprow & Rosenheck (2008) | (+) days housed at 36 mos., housing satisfaction, retention at 60 mos. <br> (+) fewer days homeless | (+) fewer days institutionalized <br> (+) greater use of mental health services | (+) fewer days of alcohol use <br> (+) fewer days intoxicated, days using drugs, drug index score <br> (+) reduced alcohol index score | (+) greater housing satisfaction, social network, quality family relations <br> (+) fewer housing problems employment, legal involvement and income | (−) lesser societal costs |
| McHugo et al. (2004) | ND % in stable housing at 18 mos. <br> (−) increased time in stable housing, decreased homelessness <br> ND housing satisfaction <br> ND neighbourhood satisfaction | ND medical or dental care, treatment for alcohol and drug use, psychiatric services | ND decreased psychiatric symptoms over time <br> (−) fewer psychiatric symptoms <br> ND days of alcohol use & days of drug use | ND exposure to community violence <br> ND increased life satisfaction over time <br> (−) greater life satisfaction | |
| Stefancic & Tsemberis (2007) | (+) % retention of housing at 2 yrs. | | | | (+) lesser program costs vs. emergency shelter costs |

**Table 7-4. (Continued)**

| Studies | Housing | Service Use Outcomes | Clinical Outcomes | Community Adaptation | Costs |
|---|---|---|---|---|---|
| O'Connell, Kasprow & Rosenheck (2009) | (−) fewer days homeless<br>ND increased days housed in past 90 days<br>(+) decreased days homeless over time | (+) fewer days institutionalized<br>(+) fewer days institutionalized over time<br>(+) greater use of outpatient services | ND decreased psychiatric symptoms and substance abuse over time | ND increased employment, quality of life, income, social network, days of drug use over time<br>ND decreased minor and major crimes over time<br>(−) increased employment over time | (+) lesser health care costs |
| Pearson, Montgomery & Locke (2009) | ND % housed at 12 mos.<br>(+) fewer housing problems | | | | |

Note. (+) outcomes in favour of supported housing, (−) outcomes in favour of comparison group, ND = no difference, NC = no change over the treatment time.

Rosenheck 2009) or those receiving case management or standard care (O'Connell Kasprow and Rosenheck 2008). With regard to participation in substance abuse treatment, individuals in the residential continuum group reported significantly greater participation in substance abuse treatment programs than individuals living in supported housing (Tsemberis, Gulcur and Nakae 2004). In terms of utilization of outpatient services, supported housing tenants showed greater utilization in comparison to tenants living in a residential continuum program (O'Connell, Kasprow and Rosenheck 2009). Finally, two studies found no differences between tenants of supported housing group and those in a residential continuum program with regard to overall health care utilization (Dickey et al. 1996; McHugo et al. 2004).

**Clinical outcomes.** Of the five studies evaluating clinical outcomes, mixed results were found. Two studies found no differences in changes over time in the severity of psychiatric symptoms or substance use between supported housing and residential continuum housing tenants (O'Connell, Kasprow and Rosenheck 2009; Tsemberis, Gulcur and Nakae 2004). McHugo and colleagues (2004) and O'Connell, Kasprow and Rosenheck (2009) also report no group differences in psychiatric symptoms or substance use between individuals in supported housing and individuals in residential continuum program, but McHugo and colleagues (2004) did find that the residential continuum group had significantly greater improvements in their psychiatric functioning. Pearson, Montgomery and Locke (2009) report that although individuals experienced month-to-month variation in their levels of impairment, there were no significant decreases in psychiatric impairment or substance use over the course of the first year in either of the three housing programs (i.e., supported housing, supportive housing, multi-site housing with modified ACT support).

The Rosenheck set of studies found perhaps the most compelling results. In particular, Cheng, Lin, Kasprow and Rosenheck (2007) found that the group of individuals receiving supported housing had substantially and significantly fewer days of alcohol and drug use, fewer days on which they drank to intoxication and lower scores on a composite drug problem index than the groups receiving either case management or standard care. O'Connell, Kasprow and Rosenheck (2008) also report lower scores on alcohol and drug scales for their supported housing clients, as well as less money spent on substances.

Seidman and his colleagues (2003) looked at different clinical outcomes than the other studies. They assessed the neuropsychological functioning of tenants in supported housing and supportive housing. Overall, neuropsychological functioning improved significantly across both groups from baseline to 18 months. However, the executive functioning of the tenants in supported housing had a significant decline across the study period, while supportive housing tenants had a slight, but non-significant, increase in their executive functioning.

**Community adaptation.** The studies assessing community adaptation outcomes also yielded mixed results. Specifically, tenants of supported housing were found to either have achieved superior outcomes in this area or showed no difference from consumers receiving services from other programs. Tenants of supported housing perceived their choices to be more numerous than did tenants in a residential continuum program (Tsemberis, Gulcur and Nakae 2004). Supported housing tenants also reported fewer housing problems, larger social networks and greater satisfaction with their family relationships in comparison to consumers receiving case management or standard care (Rosenheck et al. 2003). As well, tenants in the supported housing group reported higher quality of life scores in terms of their overall life, their finances, their health and their social relations in comparison to consumers receiving case management (Rosenheck et al. 2003). There were no differences in the same study between tenants in supported housing and consumers receiving standard care.

On the other hand, there were no differences found between consumers in supported housing and consumers in residential continuum programs with regard to increases in self-esteem (Tsemberis et al. 2003), improvements in family relations (Wood et al. 1998), size of social networks (O'Connell, Kasprow and Rosenheck 2009), increases in satisfaction with neighbourhood, decreases in exposure to community violence (McHugo et al. 2004) or increases in quality of life (O'Connell, Kasprow and Rosenheck 2009; Tsemberis et al. 2003).

In terms of employment, individuals living in residential continuum housing had higher than average scores on an employment index and a greater number of days worked in comparison to individuals in supported housing (O'Connell, Kasprow and Rosenheck 2009); however, both groups reported significant increases in the number of days worked in the past 30 days and in their total income. With regard to legal involvement, one study found no significant differences among individuals in supported housing, case management only or standard care (Rosenheck et al. 2003). O'Connell, Kasprow and Rosenheck (2009) report that although no differences were found between their groups, both the residential continuum and the supported housing tenants demonstrated decreases in occurrences of minor and major crimes.

**Costs.** In relation to costs, tenants in supported housing were evaluated as having hospitalization, residential and shelter costs that were lower than tenants in residential continuum programs (Gulcur et al. 2003), program costs that were lower than emergency shelter costs for individuals in standard care (Stefancic and Tsemberis 2007) and health care costs that were lower than for tenants in residential continuum housing (O'Connell, Kasprow and Rosenheck 2009). In contrast to supported housing tenants having lower costs relative to other approaches, one study found the opposite, with services consumed by supported housing tenants costing more than those for consumers receiving case management or standard care (Rosenheck et al. 2003). However, unlike the other studies, which conducted costing on a limited range of health and social services, this latter study used a comprehensive costing to assess societal costs associated with a full range of services consumed by individuals.

### Limitations of Research to Date
Based on our review of the extant research literature, an important limitation is the relatively small number of studies that have been conducted on supported housing to date. Our review of the peer-reviewed literature found only nine studies, even though liberal criteria were set for programs being considered supported housing. Of those studies examined in our review, several of them had small samples, limiting the power to detect differences between groups. In fact, three of the nine studies had groups with fewer than 65 participants (Dickey et al. 1996; McHugo et al. 2004; Pearson, Montgomery and Locke 2009). Another limitation to the samples of studies in our review was the over-representation of participants who are male, non-white and diagnosed with schizophrenia and substance use problems.

As noted by Tabol, Drebing and Rosenheck (2010) and Wong, Filoromo and Tenille (2007), the definition of supported housing varies in the research literature, with programs described in this way being implemented in different ways in different locales. Some programs appear to adopt criteria that make them a hybrid of supported and supportive housing. Other programs adopt only some of what are considered critical ingredients of supported housing. We purposely kept in our review only programs that had these critical ingredients. However, the description of housing programs in published studies does not always provide enough information to accurately identify if critical ingredients of supported housing are present or not. Moreover, a majority of the outcome studies we reviewed did not report having undertaken an evaluation of program implementation or an assessment of program fidelity in terms of the criteria of supported housing.

Another limitation of the research in this area is the narrow range of outcomes that have been examined in the majority of studies. In particular, studies have relied heavily on housing, service use and clinical outcomes in examining the effectiveness of supported housing programs. Limiting outcomes to just these areas is inconsistent with the goals of recovery-oriented programs such as supported housing, which are intended to assist individuals with severe mental illness to live successfully in the community in a manner similar to that of non-disabled persons.

As presented in our review, the variety of comparison groups used in the small number of studies, which included standard care, case management without housing and supportive housing, limit the conclusions that can be drawn at this point from the literature. As well, the examined outcomes vary across the studies making it difficult to compare them to each other or draw reliable conclusions about the effectiveness of supported housing in relation to different outcomes. Also related to outcomes, most of the outcomes were measured in the studies through the use of self-report measures.

A further limitation of research conducted in this area is the relatively short follow-up period for many of the studies. Given the complex needs of persons with severe mental illness with a history of homelessness, an examination of outcomes over periods longer than two years seems necessary to capture the full range of positive benefits experienced by participants over time. Early treatment often focuses on engaging participants, building a trusting relationship and stabilizing functioning (Foster, LeFauve, Kresky-Wolff and Rickards 2010). Once progress has been made in these areas, treatment can focused on improving an individual's quality of life in the community.

Finally, the large majority of studies we reviewed were conducted in large cities in the United States. Given the differences in the mental health systems of the United States and other Western countries such as Canada, findings from American studies are not necessarily generalizable. A major difference in the delivery of health care between the United States and Canada is the universal coverage provided in Canada, including in the area of mental health services. Other contextual differences between the United States and Canada that may limit generalizability include the larger size of cities in the United States and the different racial and ethnic origins of urban populations in the two countries.

### Future Directions for Research

Based on these limitations, a number of suggestions for future research are indicated. Firstly, there is a clear need for studies with larger and more diverse samples. The use of multi-site research designs can provide the necessary power and diversity to examine effectiveness and cost-effectiveness as well as identifying the types of individuals who benefit from the approach. A large multi-site trial that is currently being conducted in five cities in Canada testing a number of different supported housing approaches adapted to local needs can be expected to address limitations related to sample size and sample makeup as well as knowledge gaps (MHCC 2011). Given the eligibility criteria for participation in this study, which includes having mental health diagnoses of psychotic disorders or non-psychotic disorders, including affective disorders and some anxiety disorders, it is expected that this study will extend our understanding of with whom supported housing can be effective.

In our reviewed studies, there are a minority of individuals placed in supported housing who fail to achieve housing stability and return to homelessness. In a critique of the Housing First approach including supported housing, Kertesz, Crouch, Milby, Cusimano and Schumacher (2009) question the effectiveness of the approach for people with active and severe addictions. The researchers note that the approach has been tested on individuals with severe mental illness whose addictions are at a low to moderate level. Consequently, they conclude that the current state of the evidence on supported housing is not strong enough for it to be applied as a singular strategy for people with active and severe addictions. Instead, they recommend the continued need for residential treatment programs such as therapeutic communities that adopt a residential continuum approach to promote recovery for this subpopulation.

Secondly, there is a need for studies on supported housing to use fidelity scales and report in a clear manner how programs being examined meet the criteria of supported housing. The work of Tabol, Drebing and Rosenheck (2010) that outlines 15 criteria characterizing supported housing can be very helpful in guiding fidelity assessments. It would probably be helpful if the criteria for supportive housing could also be defined in a similarly distinct and detailed manner.

Thirdly, future research needs to examine how supported housing can be combined with vocational services, peer support and integrated concurrent disorders treatment. To date, research shows that the most prevalent outcome produced by supported housing is the achievement of housing stability. Outcomes in other areas such as participation in work or school, community integration and reduction in alcohol or drug use have not been achieved, at least not consistently, across studies. A likely reason for this inconsistency in outcomes in these areas is that they have not been targeted in a systematic manner in many of the investigated supported housing programs.

Further rigorous studies comparing the outcomes of supported and supportive housing are also needed. The research to date indicates that supportive housing produces positive outcomes including housing stability (Nelson 2010; Nelson, Aubry and Lafrance 2007). In fact, the two studies from our review in which supported housing had inferior housing outcomes involved comparisons to supportive housing (Dickey et al. 1996; McHugo et al. 2004). In a 16-year follow-up of participants in the study by Dickey and colleagues (1996), Schutt (2011) reports that tenants of supportive housing experienced a higher level of housing retention than tenants of supported housing.

To date, as reported in our review, only a small number of studies have evaluated the costs of supported housing with only one study using a comprehensive costing method, which produced mixed findings. Future research is required to examine the cost–benefit and cost-effectiveness of supported housing using a comprehensive costing methodology.

It is recommended that future studies follow participants for greater lengths of time. In addition to determining if the housing stability achieved by participants is enduring, longer study periods will also determine if outcomes in areas other than housing are achieved as a result of individuals receiving long-term support.

Finally, most of the studies on supported housing have relied on self-report measures to evaluate outcomes. The combination of self-report measures and observational measures can strengthen the conclusions that can be drawn from studies on the effectiveness of supported housing, particularly as it relates to severity of mental health symptoms, functioning and substance use.

### Implications for Policy and Program Development

Our review of the small number of studies focusing on supported housing suggests that it is effective for what it targets—namely, the exiting from homelessness and the achievement of housing stability. The combination of these findings favouring supported housing with the values promoted by the approach and the fact that it is the type of housing preferred by a vast majority of consumers make it an attractive intervention for mental health policy development in Canada. In addition, the nature of the approach, which relies on private market housing, lends itself to being implemented in communities in a rapid manner As well, it does not require the major capital outlay associated with building residential facilities. This is particularly important in the Canadian context, where there has been a paucity of investments over the last two decades by provincial governments and the federal government in the creation of affordable housing including social housing (Hulchanski 2002).

Although communities throughout North America are implementing supported housing as a Housing First strategy to address chronic homelessness, custodial housing continues to be very prevalent in mental health systems, particularly in Canada (Trainor 2008); however, there are examples of communities in Canada shifting housing from custodial housing to supported housing (Nelson 2010). This shift is an important policy direction for systems to take up in order to finally integrate people with severe and persistent mental illness fully into the community. Of course, in order for supported housing to be in sufficient supply to meet the demand, the development of an affordable housing stock is needed, something that is sorely lacking and which has contributed to the growing homeless population in cities across Canada (Hulchanski 2002).

Overall, our review of research on supported housing found relatively little evidence of supported housing achieving superior outcomes than other housing approaches in terms of reducing psychiatric symptoms or substance use or improving community adaptation. These findings are not surprising given that the support provided in most of the programs studied through ACT or ICM is generic in nature. As suggested in the section on future research directions, it would seem important that supported housing evolve so that more targeted support be integrated in the approach that is intended to address substance use, vocational needs, leisure needs and social support needs. The development and evaluation of the effectiveness of treatments and supports addressing these need areas are an important part of the multi-city trial of supported housing currently being conducted in Canada (MHCC 2011).

As discussed, supported housing originated from the mental health field in response to the deinstitutionalization of people with severe and persistent mental illness. In the context of high levels of homelessness throughout Canada, supported housing is now being applied increasingly as a response for people who are experiencing chronic homelessness, most of whom have a severe mental illness and substance use problem. Although they use a high proportion of shelter beds, the latter group makes up only a small minority of the homeless population (Kuhn and Culhane 1998; Aubry et al. 2013). Given the success of supported housing at achieving housing stability, it makes sense that variants of it could be developed in response to homelessness of other groups in Canada such as youth, families, and individuals with less severe mental health problems. In particular, the intensity and length of support provided could be shaped in response to the needs of these different homeless groups.

## Conclusion

Supported housing has been heralded as representing a transformative change of the mental health system and with how we assist people with severe and persistent mental illness to become fully integrated into the community (Nelson 2010). The approach alters the view of individuals from being patients or clients to being seen as tenants and neighbours with the same housing rights and responsibilities as other citizens. Based on our review of the research on the effectiveness of the approach, we conclude that supported housing is a promising approach to ending homelessness for individuals with severe and persistent mental health problems who have experienced chronic homelessness.

Specifically, the research evidence to date is indicative of supported housing being effective in assisting a majority of this population to achieve housing stability. Although all of the studies on supported housing to date involve relatively small samples and have been conducted in the United States, the large multi-site demonstration research project being conducted in five cities by the Mental Health Commission of Canada will provide a rigorous evaluation of its effectiveness in the Canadian context. We also believe that supported housing has the potential to serve as a platform on which housing and support can be evolved to help other subgroups within the homeless population who require assistance to exit homelessness and achieve stable housing.

## References

Aubry, T., T. Doestaler and A. M. Baronet. 2004. "Revue des etudes empiriques sur l'efficacité du suivi communautaire." In *Le suivi communautaire: Une invitation à se bâtir une vie*, ed. R. Emard and T. Aubry. Ottawa: University of Ottawa Press, 129–202.

Aubry, T., S. Farrell, S. Hwang and M. Calhoun. 2013. "Identifying Patterns of Emergency Shelter Stays of Single Individuals in Canadian Cities of Different Sizes." *Housing Studies*, 28(6): 910–27. doi: 10.1080/02673037.2013.773585.

Blanch, A. K., P. Carling and P. Ridgway. 1988. "Normal Housing with Specialized Supports: A Psychiatric Approach to Living in the Community." *Rehabilitation Psychology*, 33: 47–55.

Carling, P. J. 1995. *Return to Community: Building Support Systems for People with Psychiatric Disabilities*. New York: Guilford Press.

_____. 1993. "Housing and Supports for Persons with Mental Illness: Emerging Approaches to Research and Practice." *Hospital and Community Psychiatry*, 44: 439–49.

_____. 1992. "Homes or Group Homes? Future Approaches to Housing, Support, and Integration for People with Psychiatric Disabilities." *Adult Residential Care Journal*, 6: 87–96.

Cheng, A., H. Lin, W. Kasprow and R. A. Rosenheck. 2007. "Impact of Supported Housing on Clinical Outcomes: Analysis of a Randomized Trial Using Multiple Imputation Technique." *Journal of Nervous and Mental Disease*, 195: 83–88.

Coldwell, C. M. and W. S. Bender. 2007. "The Effectiveness of Assertive Community Treatment for Homeless Populations with Severe Mental Illness: A Meta-analysis." *American Journal of Psychiatry*, 164: 393–99.

Dickey, B., O. Gonzalez, E. Latimer, K. Powers, R. K. Schutt and S. M. Goldfinger. 1996. "Use of Mental Health Services by Formerly Homeless Adults Residing in Group and Independent Housing." *Psychiatric Services*, 47: 152–58.

Fazel, S., V. Khosla, H. Doll and J. Geddes. 2008. "The Prevalence of Mental Disorders among the Homeless in Western Countries: Systematic Review and Meta-Regression Analysis." *PLoS Medicine*, 5(12): e225. doi: 10.1371/journal.pmed.0050225.

Foster, S., C. LeFauve, M. Kresky-Wolff and L. D. Rickard. 2010. "Services and Supports for Individuals with Co-occurring Disorders and Long-Term Homelessness." *Journal of Behavioral Health Services & Research*, 37: 239–251.

Goering, P., G. Tolomiczenko, T. Sheldon, K. Boydell and D. Wasylenki. 2002. "Characteristics of Persons Who Are Homeless for the First Time." *Psychiatric Services*, 53: 1472–74.

Goldfinger, S. M., R. K. Schutt, G. S. Tolomiczenko, L. Seidman, W. E. Penk, W. Turner and B. Caplan. 1999. "Housing Placement and Subsequent Days Homeless among Formerly Homeless Adults with Mental Illness." *Psychiatric Services*, 50(5): 674–79.

Greenwood, R. M., N. J. Schaefer-McDaniel, G. Winkel and S. J. Tsemberis. 2005. "Decreasing Psychiatric Symptoms by Increasing Choice in Services for Adults with Histories of Homelessness." *American Journal of Community Psychology*, 36: 223–38.

Gulcur, L., A. Stefancic, M. Shinn, S. Tsemberis and S. N. Fischer. 2003. "Housing, Hospitalization and Cost Outcomes for Homeless Individuals with Psychiatric Disabilities Participating in Continuum of Care and Housing First Programmes." *Journal of Community & Applied Social Psychology*, 13: 171–86.

Hogan, M. F., and P. J. Carling. 1992. "Normal Housing: A Key Element of a Supported Housing Approach for People with Psychiatric Disabilities." *Community Mental Health Journal*, 28(3): 215–26.

Hulchanski, J. D. 2002. *Housing Policy for Tomorrow's Cities*. Discussion Paper F27. Family Network. Ottawa: Canadian Policy Research Networks Inc.

Hurlburt, M. S., R. L. Hough and P. A. Wood. 1996. "Effects of Substance Abuse on Housing Stability of Homeless Mentally Ill Persons in Supported Housing." *Psychiatric Services*, 47: 731–36.

Hurlburt, M. S., P. A. Wood and R. L. Hough. 1996. "Providing Independent Housing for the Homeless Mentally Ill: A Novel Approach to Evaluating Long-Term Longitudinal Housing Patterns." *Journal of Community Psychology*, 24(3): 291–310.

Kertesz, S. G., K. Crouch, J. B. Milby, R. E. Cusimano and J. E. Schumacher. 2009. "Housing First for Homeless Persons with Active Addiction: Are We Overreaching?" *Milbank Quarterly*, 87: 495–534.

Kirby, M. J. and W. K. Keon. 2006. *Out of the Shadows at Last: Highlights and Recommendations of the Final Report on Mental Health, Mental Illness and Addictions.* Ottawa: The Standing Senate Committee on Social Affairs, Science and Technology.

Kuhn, R. and D. P. Culhane. 1998. "Applying Cluster Analysis to Test a Typology of Homelessness by Pattern of Shelter Utilization: Results from the Analysis of Administrative Data." *American Journal of Community Psychology*, 26: 207–32.

Leff, H. S., C. M. Chow, R. Pepin, J. Conley, I. E. Allen and C. A. Seaman. 2009. "One Size Fit All? What We Can and Can't Learn from a Meta-analysis of Housing Models for Persons with Mental Illness." *Psychiatric Services*, 60: 473–82.

Mechanic, D. and D. A. Rochefort. 1990. "Deinstitutionalization: An Appraisal of Reform." *Annual Review of Sociology*, 16: 301–27.

McHugo, G. J., R. R. Bebout, M. Harris, S. Cleghorn, G. Herring, H. Xie et al. 2004. "A Randomized Controlled Trial of Integrated versus Parallel Housing Services for Homeless Adults with Severe Mental Illness." *Schizophrenia Bulletin*, 30: 969–82.

MHCC (Mental Health Commission of Canada). 2011. "At Home." In Initiatives and Projects [on-line]. Mental Health Commission of Canada. http://www.mentalhealthcommission.ca/English/Pages/homelessness.aspx [consulted June 15, 2013].

Nelson, G. 2010. "Housing for People with Serious Mental Illness: Approaches, Evidence, and Transformative Change." *Journal of Sociology and Social Welfare*, 37: 123–46.

Nelson, G., T. Aubry and A. Lafrance. 2007. "A Review of the Literature on the Effectiveness of Housing and Support, Assertive Community Treatment, and Intensive Case Management Interventions for Persons with Mental Illness Who Have Been Homeless." *American Journal of Orthopsychiatry*, 77: 350–61.

Nelson, G., G. B. Hall and C. Forchuk. 2003. "Current and Preferred Housing of Psychiatric Consumer/Survivors." *Canadian Journal of Community Mental Health*, 22: 5–19.

O'Connell, M. J., W. Kasprow and R. Rosenheck. 2009. "Direct Placement versus Multistage Models of Supported Housing in a Population of Veterans Who Are Homeless." *Psychological Services*, 6: 190–201.

_____. 2008. "Rates and Risk Factors for Homelessness after Successful Housing in a Sample of Formerly Homeless Veterans." *Psychiatric Services*, 59: 268–75.

Parkinson, S., G. Nelson and S. Horga. 1999. "From Housing to Homes: A Review of the Literature on Housing Approaches for Psychiatric Consumer/Survivors." *Canadian Journal of Community Mental Health,* 17: 145–64.

Pearson, C., A. E. Montgomery and G. Locke. 2009. "Housing Stability among Homeless Individuals with Serious Mental Illness Participating in Housing First Programs." *Journal of Community Psychology,* 37: 404–17.

Piat, M., A. Lesage, R. Boyer, H. Dorvil, A. Courure, G. Grenier and D. Bloom. 2008. "Housing for Persons with Serious Mental Illness: Consumer and Service Provider Preferences." *Psychiatric Services,* 59: 1011–17.

Ridgway, P. and A. M. Zipple. 1990. "Challenges and Strategies for Implementing Supported Housing." *Psychosocial Rehabilitation Journal,* 13: 115–20.

Rog, D. J. 2004. "The Evidence on Supported Housing." *Psychiatric Rehabilitation Journal,* 27: 334–44.

Rosenheck, R. A., W. Kasprow, L. Frisman and W. Liu-Mares. 2003. "Cost-Effectiveness of Supported Housing for Homeless Persons with Mental Illness." *Archives of General Psychiatry,* 60: 940–51.

Schutt, R. K. 2011. *Homelessness, Housing and Mental Illness.* Cambridge, MA: Harvard University Press.

Seidman, L. J., R. K. Schutt, B. Caplan, G. S. Tolomiczenko, W. M. Turner and S. M. Goldfinger. 2003. "The Effect of Housing Interventions on Neuropsychological Functioning among Homeless Persons with Mental Illness." *Psychiatric Services,* 54: 905–08.

Stefancic, A. and S. Tsemberis. 2007. "Housing First for Long-Term Shelter Dwellers with Psychiatric Disabilities in a Suburban County: A Four-Year Study of Housing Access and Retention." *Journal of Primary Prevention,* 28: 265–79.

Tabol, C., C. Drebing and R. A. Rosenheck. 2010. "Studies of 'Supported' and 'Supportive' Housing: A Comprehensive Review of Model Descriptions and Measurement." *Evaluation and Program Planning,* 33: 446–56.

Tanzman, B. 1993. "An Overview of Surveys of Mental Health Consumers' Preferences for Housing and Support Services." *Hospital and Community Psychiatry,* 44, 450–455.

Trainor, J. N. 2008. "Housing and the Development of a Personal Resource Base." In *Hébergement, logement et rétablissement en santé mental,* ed. J-F. Pelletier, M. Piat, S. Côte and H. Dorvil. Boisbriand, QC: Prologue, 33–51.

Trainor, J. N., T. L. Morrell Bellai, R. Ballantyne and K. M. Boydell. 1993. "Housing for People with Mental Illnesses: A Comparison of Models and an Examination of the Growth of Alternative Housing in Canada." *Canadian Journal of Psychiatry,* 38: 494–501.

Tsemberis, S. 1999. "From Streets to Homes: An Innovative Approach to Supported Housing for Homeless Adults with Psychiatric Disabilities." *Journal of Community Psychology,* 27: 225–41.

Tsemberis, S. and R. F. Eisenberg. 2000. "Pathways to Housing: Supported Housing for Street-Dwelling Homeless Individuals with Psychiatric Disabilities." *Psychiatric Services,* 51: 487–93.

Tsemberis, S., L. Gulcur and M. Nakae. 2004. "Housing First, Consumer Choice, and Harm Reduction for Homeless Individuals with a Dual Diagnosis." *American Journal of Public Health,* 94: 651–56.

Tsemberis, S. J., L. Moran, M. Shinn, S. M. Asmussen and D. L. Shern. 2003. "Consumer Preference Programs for Individuals Who Are Homeless and Have Psychiatric Disabilities: A Drop-in Center and a Supported Housing Program." *American Journal of Community Psychology,* 32: 305–17.

Wong, Y. I. and P. L. Solomon. 2002. "Community Integration of Persons with Psychiatric Disabilities in Supportive Independent Housing: A Conceptual Model and Methodological Considerations." *Mental Health Services Research,* 4: 13–28.

Wong, Y. I., M. Filoromo and J. Tennille. 2007. "From Principles to Practice: A Study of Implementation of Supported Housing for Psychiatric Consumers." *Administration and Policy in Mental Health and Mental Health Services Research,* 34: 13–28.

Wood, P. A., M. S. Hurlburt, R. L. Hough and C. R. Hofstetter. 1998. "Longitudinal Assessment of Family Support among Homeless Mentally Ill Participants in a Supported Housing Program." *Journal of Community Psychology,* 26: 327–44.

# CHAPTER 8

# Homelessness and Oral Health

Bruce Wallace, MSW, PhD
Centre for Addictions Research of British Columbia, University of Victoria

Rafael Figueiredo, DDS
Faculty of Dentistry, University of Toronto

Michael MacEntee, LDS(I), PhD
Faculty of Dentistry, University of British Columbia

Carlos Quiñonez, DMD, PhD
Faculty of Dentistry, University of Toronto

## Introduction

In Canada, dentistry is generally funded as an employment-based benefit or as an out-of-pocket expense rather than via the public health care system. Consequently, socioeconomic status heavily influences access to dental treatment. In this system, persons experiencing poverty and homelessness face significant barriers to oral health care. The links between poverty and poor oral health are well documented, as is the importance of good oral health to overall health and well-being. However, less is known about how to reduce the barriers to oral health care faced by persons experiencing poverty and homelessness.

Dentists often seek to meet the needs of homeless persons and other low-income populations through charitable donations of their services. However, there are strong opinions that charity offers little more than a 'band-aid solution' to a complicated set of social problems (Crall 2006; De Palma and Nordenram 2005; Frankish, Hwang and Quantz 2005; Hwang 2001, 2002; Moore, Gerdtz and Manias 2007; Mouradian 2006). The British Dental Association (2003), for example, states that charitable dentistry by unpaid volunteers "is clearly no substitute for a coherent and properly-funded dental access strategy for homeless people", and adds "that homeless people, just as much as any other section of the community, are entitled to adequate and accessible dental care as a right, and should not be forced to rely on charity" (37).

The issue of access to dental care is gaining more prominence as a health policy issue in Canada. Social and professional pressure has mounted on governments for renewed investments in dental care, and some provincial and municipal governments have responded (Quiñonez et al. 2010). However, policy-makers and service providers lack a definite strategy to respond to the numerous groups and challenges associated with oral health and oral health care inequalities (Quiñonez, Figueiredo and Locker 2009a). Meanwhile, governments and local health authorities continue to reduce health care spending and to encourage shifts of public health care into the private realm (Quiñonez, Figueiredo and Locker 2009a). Therefore, it appears that dental care reform is not a priority at present (Birch and Anderson 2005) and that dentistry is likely to remain outside the Canadian national health care system for the foreseeable future. In this context, the oral health needs of homeless persons are often ignored and excluded in service plans or policies that address access to dental care, and similarly in those that address homelessness and health in general.

Improvements to oral health policies and practices for homeless populations are most likely to occur through the inclusion of oral health within national, provincial and local strategies to reduce poverty and homelessness. Provincial poverty reduction plans with measurable goals and timelines have been developed as a proactive response to regressive 'welfare reform', which has dismantled the public safety net significantly over the last few decades. In some cases, the strategies have recommended increased public dental benefits. For example, the Ontario Poverty Reduction Strategy contains a Low-Income Dental Program that includes building community capacity to deliver prevention and treatment services for low-income Ontarians (Province of Ontario 2008). New Brunswick's poverty reduction plan includes a plan to provide dental care to children in low-income families and the extension of dental benefits for individuals leaving welfare for work for three years as part of an overall goal of a comprehensive system of supplementary health care for low-income people (Government of New Brunswick 2010).

Homeless action plans have become a standard response to homelessness. Again, the inclusion of dental care in these strategies is a possible approach to ensure that oral health is not excluded from health care for the homeless. The report of the Mayor's Homelessness Action Task Force from Toronto (Golden et al. 1999) notes that many people who are homeless cannot access dental care and that we must first ensure that all homeless persons get dental benefits and then expand the number of accessible clinics where people can walk in and receive basic dental care along with other health and social services (Golden et al. 1999). Victoria's Mayor's Task Force on Breaking the Cycle of Mental Illness, Addiction and Homelessness (City of Victoria 2007) led to the creation of the Greater Victoria Coalition to End Homelessness. Calgary developed a 10-Year Plan to End Homelessness (Calgary Committee to End Homelessness 2008) and Ottawa also has a Community Action Plan on Homelessness—and there are similar examples of more local poverty responses in other Canadian urban areas.

Meanwhile, communities are seeing the immediate needs and, on a local basis, are responding in unique ways. There are now numerous examples of treatment alternatives helping homeless persons and persons living in extreme poverty get the dental care they need (Leake 2005, 2006; Main, Leake and Burman 2006). The literature on community dental clinics in Canada and the United States shows that they can play a unique and valuable role as a source of dental care for groups with traditional access barriers (Byck, Cooksey and Russinof 2005; Geller, Taylor and Scott 2004; Gooch, Griffin and Malvitz 2006). Indeed, they have been deemed by some as a 'mandatory' health service due to the shortcomings of the existing dental care delivery system and the overwhelming unmet dental health needs of the underserved (Byck, Cooksey and Russinof 2005).

Community dental clinics in many parts of Canada are expanding dental care for underserved populations, including homeless populations. Inner-city community health centres (CHCs), in particular, provide an avenue to address the health care needs of vulnerable and marginalized populations, yet most of them do not have dental clinics. To advance discussion in this area, we will describe the oral health care needs of homeless populations, the barriers they face to accessing these services and the growing role that community dental clinics play in improving access to care.

## Oral Health and Homelessness

Studies of homelessness and oral health (Table 8-1) are few and usually limited to small sample sizes (Blackmore et al. 1995; Chi and Milgrom 2008; Collins and Freeman 2007; Conte et al. 2006; Daly, Newton and Batchelor 2009; De Palma and Nordenram 2005; De Palma et al. 2005; De Palma 2007; Gibson et al. 2008; Jago, Sterberg and Westerman 1984; Kahabuka and Mbawalla 2006; Kaste and Bolden 1995; Lee, Gaetz and Goettler 1994; Luo and McGrath 2006; Pizem et al. 1994; Waplington, Morris and Bradnock 2000). Overall, they show that homelessness has a direct association with poor oral health (Bolden and Kaste 1995; Clarke et al. 1996; Conte et al. 2006; De Palma and Nordenram 2005; De Palma et al. 2005; De Palma 2007; Dogan et al. 2006; Gaetz and Lee 1995; Gelberg, Lin and Rosenberg 1988; Gibson et al. 2003; Han, Wells and Taylor 2003; Jago, Sterberg and Westerman 1984; Kaste and Bolden 1995; Lee, Gaetz and Goettler 1994; Luo and McGrath 2006; Pizem et al. 1994). Homeless persons have poor oral health, such as missing and decayed teeth, oral pain, gum disease and related conditions in need of urgent attention (Allukian 1995; City of Toronto 2000; Clarke et al. 1996; Collins and Freeman 2007; Hwang 2001, 2002; King and Gibson 2003). For example, 91 percent of clients of a dental program associated with homeless shelters in Boston had a very high need for preventive and restorative dentistry due to caries (Kaste and Bolden 1995). They reported difficulty accessing dental care and caring for their teeth due to a lack of oral hygiene products and adequate restroom facilities. Similar observations were made in Brisbane, Australia, where homeless individuals had thick calculus deposits on their teeth and seemed to accept tooth loss without complaint or obvious concern, although they did state that dentists were reluctant to treat them (Jago, Sterberg and Westerman 1984).

Research published as early as the 1990s shows that Canada's homeless populations have fared no better. In Montreal, in 1994, Pizem and colleagues (1994) reported that 61 percent of the homeless population needed dental treatment. In Toronto, 50.6 percent of the homeless youth (14 to 25 years old) reported toothache and 74.1 percent expressed willingness to visit a dentist, but among those one-third did not know where to go (Lee et al. 1994). Also in North York, Ontario, 29.4 percent of the homeless youth needed dental restorative treatment and 72.7 percent had moderate to severe gingivitis (Clarke et al. 1996).

## Table 8-1.  Select published studies of the oral health status of homeless people

| Author | Location | Sample Size | Age Range in Years | Finding |
|--------|----------|-------------|--------------------|---------|
| Jago, Sterberg & Westerman 1984 | Brisbane, Australia | 162 | 15–85 | 34.6% needed urgent treatment for one or more of the following conditions: toothache, oral infection, endodontic problems, large carious lesions, fractured teeth. |
| Gelberg, Lin & Rosenberg 1988 | Los Angeles, USA | 529 | 18–78 | 56% observed to have at least one grossly decayed tooth and 27% reported a toothache during the previous month. |
| Lee, Gaetz & Goettler 1994 | Toronto, Canada | 174 | 14–25 | 40.8% had not been to the dentist in the previous two years. |
| Kaste & Bolden 1995 | Boston, USA | 73 | 19–64 | 91.4% had untreated caries and 88.6% were missing some teeth. |
| Blackmore et al. 1995 | Leeds, UK | 101 | 18–75 | 59% of the dentulous men had 12 or more missing teeth, and 69% need some dental intervention. |
| Clarke et al. 1996 | North York, Canada | 155 | 14–20 | 59% had not been to the dentist in the previous year, and 18% had toothache in the previous four weeks. |
| Waplingon, Morris & Bradnock 2000 | Birmingham, UK | 70 | 19–94 | 54% had caries involving the pulp. |
| Gibson et al. 2003 | US national survey | 1,152 | 24–79 | 68.1% reported need for dental care. |

**Table 8-1.  (Continued)**

| Author | Location | Sample Size | Age Range in Years | Finding |
|---|---|---|---|---|
| De Palma et al. 2005 | Stockholm, Sweden | 147 | 20–79 | Almost 100% had calculus and considerable plaque accumulation. |
| Luo & McGrath 2006 | Hong Kong, China | 147 | 21–75 | 53% considered their oral health poor or very poor, and 52% had dental pain in the previous year. |
| Conte et al. 2006 | Newark, USA | 46 | 40.4 (mean age) | 66.7% reported oral facial pain during the previous year. |
| Collins & Freeman 2007 | North and West Belfast, Ireland | 317 | 16–91 | 75% had bleeding gums and calculus. |
| Chi & Milgrom 2008 | Seattle, USA | 45 | 14–28 | 29% self-rated their oral health as "very bad" or "bad" and 38.5% reported a toothache. |
| Daly, Newton & Batchelor 2009 | London, UK | 201 | 25–54 | 71% required treatment for dental decay, recurrent decay, and root caries. |
| Robbins et al. 2010 | San Francisco, USA | 340 | 42.8 (mean age) | 64% of homeless injection drug users (IDUS) reported need for dental care. |
| Daly et al. 2010 | London, UK | 102 | 19–77 | 76% required treatment for dental decay, root caries, recurrent decayed teeth and 80% required oral hygiene and periodontal treatment. |

A recent report from Toronto found similarly high distributions of oral pain and poor self-rated oral health (Khandor and Mason 2007). The report also notes that many of those interviewed were without teeth or dentures because social assistance in Ontario would only pay to have their teeth extracted (Khandor and Mason 2007). Moreover, nearly half (43%) of respondents stated that they could not afford dental care and had not been to a dentist in the past three years due to poverty (Khandor and Mason 2007). Homeless persons in Vancouver and Victoria also made little use of dental services compared to other health services, especially emergency departments of local hospitals (sparc-bc 2008; Victoria Cool Aid Society 2007). Homeless persons in Victoria identified dental problems as a barrier to finding work (Victoria Cool Aid Society 2007), and they feel that public dental benefits from welfare programs do not cover extensive treatment needs (Klein et al. 2008).

Many factors contribute to poor oral health of homeless people:

- a chaotic lifestyle and more pressing 'survival needs' prevent routines of eating and personal hygiene;
- acceptance of poor dental health and appearance;
- limited access to washing facilities, toothbrush and toothpaste;
- poverty;
- lack of awareness of diet and oral hygiene issues;
- mental health problems and substance misuse (British Dental Association 2003: 13).

People with dental pain or who have no teeth often eat only soft foods, such as the day-old pastries and coffee offered by drop-in day-programs and other social service agencies (Gelberg, Lin and Rosenberg 1988). Frequent consumption of refined carbohydrates and other sugary foods, especially when oral hygiene is poor, quickly leads to rampant caries (Bolden and Kaste 1995; Gaetz and Lee 1995; Han, Wells and Taylor 2003). Undoubtedly, many people who are homeless are acutely aware of the consequences of poor oral hygiene. As one homeless youth in Gaetz and Lee's (1995) study reported: *"I left home two weeks ago and I haven't been able to brush my teeth since. I hate that feeling—my teeth all furry. It's kind of embarrassing"* (34).

Tobacco, alcohol and illicit drug use are widespread among homeless people and can have a devastating impact on oral health, with problems such as 'meth mouth' from inhaling crystal meth

(Gelberg, Lin and Rosenberg 1988; Conte et al. 2006; Blackmore et al. 1995; Chi and Milgrom 2008). Other studies (Robbins et al. 2010), however, questioned the supposed impacts of 'meth mouth' with the view that the oral diseases might be related more to poverty, homelessness and poor hygiene than to crystal meth. Dental problems are common among injection drug users who are homeless in San Francisco, where 64 percent of participants in a recent study reported a need for oral health care in the past six months (Robbins et al. 2010). Methadone has also been associated with increased incidence of caries, whilst untreated oral disease adds to the complications of HIV and hepatitis C. Frequent substance use can suppress dental pain and therefore mask awareness of dental problems, which explains why the self-assessed need for dental care is usually low in this population (Daly, Newton and Batchelor 2009). Mental health challenges can also lead to a chaotic lifestyle, low priority for oral health care and cravings for sugar and tobacco. Furthermore, dry mouth is a side effect of many medications used to treat mental health challenges. Finally, homeless individuals are at greater risks of trauma generally, and teeth can be knocked out as a consequence of such experiences (Gaetz and Lee 1995; King and Gibson 2003).

## Barriers to Access

It is difficult to access primary health care, including oral health care, if you are homeless (Hwang, Tolomiczenko, Kouyoumdjian and Garner 2005). Access to dentistry is complicated by the private service model that demands direct out-of-pocket payments for service. Consequently, minor problems are often ignored because of treatment costs and, when untreated, lead to pain, infection, swelling and even more costly care (Bolden and Kaste 1995; Gibson et al. 2003; King and Gibson 2003). People in dire poverty may use over-the-counter analgesics for quite severe toothache rather than seek the services of a dentist (Bedos et al. 2003; Bedos et al. 2005), and some people have even been driven to extract painful teeth with household pliers and use other domestic remedies (Cohen et al. 2009; Bedos et al. 2003).

Hospital emergency departments are used all too frequently by people who are unable to pay for a visit to a dentist (Cohen et al. 2009). Yet emergency departments are not usually prepared or suitably equipped to tackle dental emergencies involving endodontics and are even less prepared for routine restorative dental care and prosthodontics (Daiski 2007; Hwang 2001; Schanzer et al. 2007). Indeed, the level of dental care in emergency rooms rarely involves much more than symptomatic advice or prescriptions for antibiotics and painkillers.

### Financial Barriers

Dentistry is not covered by Canada's system of national health benefits and is available as a tax-based benefit only to Aboriginal peoples, recipients of social assistance, some children, the armed forces and Royal Canadian Mounted Police, veterans of the armed forces and some elderly populations in the Yukon (Health Canada 2011). Approximately 4 percent of Canadians use public dental benefits when paying for dental treatment (Leake 2006), and dental benefits available to homeless people are typically provided through provincial social assistance. Poverty and poor oral health are very closely linked, in part because low incomes limit access to dental care in North America (Lawrence and Leake 2001; Locker 2000; MacEntee, Harrison and Wyatt 2001; Quiñonez et al. 2009b).

Public dental benefits in North America have been criticized as overly restrictive, burdened by red tape and based on payment fees significantly below the fees received by dentists in private practice (Gaetz and Lee 1995; Han, Wells and Taylor 2003). Improving public dental benefits might reduce the financial barriers to accessing dental care by encouraging more dentists to participate in the service (Altieri et al. 2002; Birch and Anderson 2005; Dharamsi and MacEntee 2002; Kalebjian and Murphy-Tong 2001; Patrick et al. 2006; U.S. General Accounting Office 2000). However, people experiencing poverty and homelessness confront many barriers to accessing treatment in general dental practices. Improved public dental benefits might help, but other types of barriers to accessing dental care would likely remain.

### Patient-Related Barriers

Homeless persons have continual difficulties obtaining food, shelter, safety and money. Consequently, dentistry is rarely a priority until a problem surfaces in or around the mouth. Competing priorities are often interpreted as general apathy or a lack of motivation rather than a sign of adaptation to unpleasantness and chaos (Daiski 2007; De Palma and Nordenram 2005; Gelberg, Lin and Rosenberg 1988). Yet this adaptation is usually a source of social embarrassment sufficient to inhibit the search for care.

A high level of dental anxiety has been reported within home-less populations, for reasons that are not altogether clear but prob-ably relate to personal trauma and mental health issues (Clarke et al. 1996; Kaste and Bolden 1995; King and Gibson 2003; Lee, Gaetz and Goettler 1994; Luo and McGrath 2006; Pizem et al. 1994; Collins and Freeman 2007). Just as a chaotic lifestyle predisposes the individual to poor oral health, it is also makes it all but impossible for them to access care. Keeping appointments is a challenge without a daily routine, a watch, an alarm clock or a daily planner—even more so when confounded by substance use or mental health problems.

There is a wide gulf of distrust between people living in poverty and the system of dental care around them, as well as a perception among homeless people that dentists will not accept them as patients (Bedos et al. 2003; British Dental Association 2003; Greenberg, Kumar and Stevenson 2008). This can include being very critical of dentists, whom they see as rich, unsympathetic, at the opposite end of the social scale and motivated professionally by money (Daiski 2007; Frankish, Hwang and Quantz 2005; Han, Wells and Taylor 2003). Consequently, when they encounter dental problems, they prefer community dental clinics rather than private dental practices (Bedos et al. 2003).

### Private Practice Dentistry

While 81 percent of Canadian dentists surveyed report supporting government spending on dental benefits, most (70%) report that less than 10 percent of their patients are publicly insureds (Quiñonez, Figueiredo and Locker 2009a; Quiñonez et al. 2010). Similarly, many people on low incomes in Canada feel that their access to dental care is likely to improve only when their relationship with dentists improves (Quiñonez et al., 2009b). Dental care providers often hold misconceptions and negative stereotypes about people receiving social assistance (Bedos et al. 2005; Quiñonez et al. 2010). In defence of this position, dentists cite financial risks, low reimbursement rates, excessive and complicated paperwork, broken appointments, unpredictably disruptive behaviour and a general disregard for oral health as reasons for refusing to accept patients with public dental benefits (Greenberg, Kumar and Stevenson 2008; Levesque et al. 2009; Patrick et al. 2006).

The reluctance among dentists to accept homeless patients is not just stereotyping, then, but includes a pragmatic awareness of the challenges involved in providing appropriate care to a population facing multiple psychological, social and biological barriers. Patients with mental health or substance use problems can be unpredictable and socially disruptive (Muirhead et al. 2009) and, consequently, tend to be shunned by dentists (Allukian 1995; Clarke et al. 1996; De Palma and Nordenram 2005; Falvo 2009; Lee, Gaetz and Goettler 1994; McCormack and MacIntosh 2001; Pizem et al. 1994).

## Community Dental Clinics

Concern regarding the extent of untreated dental pain and oral infection has led to a growing interest in the potential of community dental clinics (British Dental Association 2003; Leake 2005; Melanson 2008; Wallace 2008). With limited funds available from governments, these clinics are often dependent on the charity of dental volunteers. Typically, they have developed locally, independently of similar experiences elsewhere (Wallace 2008). Some of them operate with charitable donations of time and professional skill to provide emergency care for a few hours each month. Others pay full-time staff members to provide a comprehensive range of dental treatments in well-equipped clinics. However, the financial risks increase as the services expand, because of the relatively low income generated from the low professional fees they must charge to meet the needs of low-income patients (Quiñonez et al. 2010).

Community dental clinics in Canada have emerged with little documentation or scrutiny, other than the observations that they are either run as a charity or on a not-for-profit basis, and in community drop-in centres and health care centres (Wallace 2009). Many dentists also provide charitable dentistry in private practice as well as in teaching clinics for dental personnel attached to colleges and universities in larger cities.

### Charitable Volunteer-Operated Dental Clinics

The dental services provided by charitable clinics vary greatly around the country, but they usually limit their activities to relief of pain and gross infection by extracting teeth. The Calgary Urban Project Society, for example, offers free emergency dentistry with volunteer staff and supplies donated by local supply companies. In Toronto, the Shout Clinic and Evergreen Health Centre for Street Youth were established and serviced by volunteer dentists to provide dentistry for minimal professional fees. The Ottawa Mission Dental Clinic is also an active volunteer-based clinic providing a range of preventive and restorative treatments. Likewise, in British Columbia, the population in Vancouver's Downtown Eastside can get relief of pain and infection without charge by the East Side Walk-In Dental Clinic. The Kelowna Gospel Mission opened a free dental clinic with funds from the national Homelessness Strategy, while dental volunteers in Prince George operate a community dental clinic several evenings a month without charge, to relieve dental pain for low-income residents. The most compelling concern about the limited services provided by most charitable clinics is that they might become the basic and legitimate standard of care for low-income and vulnerable populations, which some believe is an unacceptable breach of human rights and tiering of an important health service (Dharamsi and MacEntee 2002; McNally 2003).

### Non-profit Dental Clinics

Community dental clinics resemble community health centres (CHCs) and are often part of integrated health settings focused on providing primary health care that is accessible, affordable, comprehensive and well-integrated. There is very little information available on how these clinics operate, other than that they usually have full-time hours and employ dentists and other dental professionals to provide a full range of emergency and comprehensive treatments including prevention. These clinics can have relatively large operating expenses, which require secure funding. Some operate in part with government funding to supplement pro bono treatment. However, most of them rely on reduced fees paid by patients. Therefore, these are social enterprises operating as non-profit businesses with significant financial risks. Examples of non-profit dental clinics are Edmonton's Boyle McCauley Community Health Centre; Winnipeg's Mount Carmel Clinic; Toronto's Queen West Community Health Centre and Regent Park Community Health Centre; Vancouver's REACH Community Health Centre, Mid-Main Community Health Centre and Strathcona Community Dental Clinic; and Victoria's Cool Aid Community Health Centre. While most operate within integrated health settings such as a CHC, some are integrated within other settings. For example, the Strathcona Clinic operates within an inner-city school, while the Portland Clinic is administered as part of Vancouver's Downtown Eastside housing projects and supervised drug consumption service.

### Teaching Clinics

In cities with teaching clinics for students of dentistry, dental hygiene, denturism or dental assisting, there is opportunity for oral care from students at a reduced fee. All of the dental schools in Canada offer students opportunities for community service learning (Brothwell 2008; Brondani et al. 2008). Consequently, teaching clinics are an integral part of the oral health care system in Canada as in most other industrial countries.

The Centre Local de Services Communautaires (CLSC) des Faubourges Clinic operated by L'Universite de Montreal provides preventive and restorative dental care to young homeless persons in Montreal and is integrated with other health and social services for homeless youth in the city (Allison, Allington and Stern 2004; Wallace 2008). The University of Manitoba operates the Centre for Community Oral Health (CCOH), which provides dental care for inner-city poor. The University of British Columbia operates on- and off-campus teaching clinics for dental and dental hygiene students, while the general practice residency program rotates young dentists through various community clinics in the province. Although they offer care at reduced fees, teaching clinics rarely operate without professional fees, and frequently these can exceed the financial resources of people in extreme poverty.

## Future Research

While existing research confirms that homelessness is directly associated with poor oral health and a lack of access to oral health care, future research should inform responses to address these inequities. One recent exploratory study of the oral health of the homeless population in Toronto (Figueiredo, Hwang and Quiñonez 2013) recommends future research that includes mixed method study designs with adequately large sample sizes in order to explore all subgroups of the homeless population and, most importantly, to investigate the potential for alternative models of service provision for this population. Currently, though, there remains a dearth of evidence to inform responses to best meet the complex needs of these populations and no evaluations of alternative care models in Canada.

## Conclusions

Non-profit dental clinics serving homeless communities have the capacity to:

- *Reduce the financial barriers to accessing dental care for patients who have low incomes and are uninsured or without public dental benefits:* Community dental clinics address the financial barriers to accessing dental care by reducing the fees for individuals who lack dental coverage and the ability to pay private practice dental fees. For individuals with public dental benefits, the clinics are able to subsidize additional care at lower rates by billing public benefit plans. Still, while fees are reduced and pro bono services provided when possible, even at these reduced fees the costs can be prohibitive, notably for significant procedures such as root canals or dentures.

- *Provide dental care within integrated care settings to reduce barriers to care within the general social and health needs of this population:* In addition to addressing the financial barriers experienced by most patients of community clinics, there are additional barriers that community clinics must address to effectively meet the diverse needs of specific vulnerable groups. Community dental clinics are often integrated within community health centres, providing a medical and dental home for persons who are homeless and facilitating the delivery of complex oral health care that can often be associated with other medical co-morbidities.

- *Provide a full range of dental diagnostic and restorative services similar to the distribution of services available from private dental practices:* Volunteer-charitable clinics are demonstrating the value in providing emergency, relief-of-pain dental treatment (notably extractions) for free. Meanwhile, the other model of community dental clinics is demonstrating the ability to provide a full range of diagnostic and restorative services; the distribution of services provided are similar to the distribution of services in private practices.

- *Accommodate a high frequency of missed appointments and emergency needs:* Private practice dentistry is challenged to accommodate the high numbers of missed appointments that can be expected when treating individuals in crisis and facing significant challenges to self-sufficiency. The clinics similarly report a high rate of missed appointments; however, there is also high demand for unscheduled emergency treatments. These challenges actually complement each other, and the clinics can keep their clinicians very busy despite the broken appointments.

- *Sustain a pool of dental professionals employed in community-based dentistry and paid competitive salaries:* It appears that recruitment and retention of dental staff may be challenging but not an absolute barrier. If community treatment alternatives are to expand, it would be beneficial if the curriculum for dental professionals could support the development of dental graduates with the interest and skills to work in these settings.

Charitable dentistry by unpaid volunteers cannot adequately address the enormity and complexity of unmet dental needs experienced by those who are experiencing dire poverty. These 'band-aid' responses, while valuable and laudable, risk becoming an accepted standard of care for low-income populations. The financial sustainability of community-based clinics depends on relatively small but regular financial subsidies from government combined with some fees recovered from patients with public dental benefits. The recommendation to support and expand community dental clinics is vital, yet limited. While clinics can play a critical role in a response to the oral health needs of people experiencing homelessness, the safety net they provide has limited capacity to overcome the overwhelming barriers to accessing dental care (Slott 2005). Ultimately, the social determinants of oral health of homeless persons must provide the framework to locate the various components of a comprehensive response.

## References

Allison, P., C. Allington and J. Stern. 2004. *Access to Dental Care for Under-Privileged People in Quebec.* Montreal: Faculty of Dentistry, McGill University.

Allukian, M., Jr. 1995. "Oral Health: An Essential Service for the Homeless." *Journal of Public Health Dentistry,* 55(1): 8–9.

Altieri, J. P., S. M. Bruce, J. J. Crall, S. A. Eklund, J. L. Parrish, D. A. Schneider et al. 2002. "Future of Dentistry: Access to Care. Today's Vision:

Tomorrow's Reality." *Journal of the American Dental Association*, 133(10): 1408–24.

Bedos, C., J. Brodeur, A. Levine, L. Richard, L. Boucheron and W. Mereus. 2005. "Perception of Dental Illness among Persons Receiving Public Assistance in Montreal." *American Journal of Public Health*, 95(8): 1340–44.

Bedos, C., J. Brodeur, L. Boucheron, L. Richard, M. Benigeri, M. Olivier et al. 2003. "The Dental Care Pathway of Welfare Recipients in Quebec." *Social Science & Medicine*, 57(11): 2089–99.

Birch, S. and R. Anderson. 2005. "Financing and Delivering Oral Health Care: What Can We Learn from Other Countries." *Journal of the Canadian Dental Association*, 71(4): 243.

Blackmore, T., S. A. Williams, M. J. Prendergast and J. E. Pope. 1995. "The Dental Health of Single Male Hostel Dwellers in Leeds." *Community Dental Health*, 12(2): 104–09.

Bolden, A. J. and L. M. Kaste. 1995. "Considerations in Establishing a Dental Program for the Homeless." *Journal of Public Health Dentistry*, 55(1): 28–33.

British Dental Association. 2003. *Dental Care for Homeless People*. London: British Dental Association.

Brondani, M. A., C. Clark, L. Rossoff and J. Aleksejuniene. 2008. "An Evolving Community-Based Course on Professionalism and Community Service." *Journal of Dental Education*, 72(10): 1160–68,

Brothwell, D. J. 2008. "Outreach and Service Learning: Manitoba's Centre for Community Oral Health." *Journal of the Canadian Dental Association*, 74(10): 879–81.

Byck, G., J. Cooksey and H. Russinof. 2005. "Safety-Net Dental Clinics." *Journal of the American Dental Association*, 136(7): 1013–21.

Calgary Committee to End Homelessness. 2008. *10 Year Plan to End Homelessness*. Calgary, AB: Calgary Committee to End Homelessness.

Chi, D., and P. Milgrom. 2008. "The Oral Health of Homeless Adolescents and Young Adults and Determinants of Oral Health: Preliminary Findings." *Special Care in Dentistry*, 28(6): 237–42.

City of Toronto. 2000. *Toronto Report Card on Homelessness 2000*. Toronto: City of Toronto.

City of Victoria. 2007 (October 19). *Mayor's Task Force on Breaking the Cycle of Mental Illness, Addiction and Homelessness: Report of the Expert Panel*. [on-line]. Victoria, BC: City of Victoria. http://www.victoria.ca/assets/ City~Hall/Documents/tskfrc_brcycl_exprtp.pdf [consulted January 22, 2014].

Clarke, M., D. Locker, H. Murray and B. Payne. 1996. "The Oral Health of Disadvantaged Adolescents in North York, Ontario." *Canadian Journal of Public Health*, 87(4): 261–63.

Cohen, L. A., A. J. Bonito, D. R. Akin, R. J. Manski, M. D. Macek, R. R. Edwards et al. 2009. "Toothache Pain: Behavioral Impact and Self-Care Strategies." *Special Care in Dentistry*, 29(2): 85–95.

Collins, J. and R. Freeman. 2007. "Homeless in North and West Belfast: An Oral Health Needs Assessment." *British Dental Journal*, 202(12): E31.

Conte, M., H. L. Broder, G. Jenkins, R. Reed and M. N. Janal. 2006. "Oral Health, Related Behaviors and Oral Health Impacts among Homeless Adults." *Journal of Public Health Dentistry*, 66(4): 276–78.

Crall, J. J. 2006. "Access to Oral Health Care: Professional and Societal Considerations." *Journal of Dental Education*, 70(11): 1133–38.

Daiski, I. 2007. "Perspectives of Homeless People on Their Health and Health Needs Priorities." *Journal of Advanced Nursing*, 58(3): 273–81.

Daly, B., J. T. Newton and P. Batchelor. 2009. "Patterns of Dental Service Use among Homeless People Using a Targeted Service." *Journal of Public Health Dentistry*, 70(1): 45–51.

Daly, B., T. Newton, P. Batchelor and K. Jones. 2010. "Oral Health Care Needs and Oral Health-Related Quality of Life (OHIP-14) in Homeless People." *Community Dentistry and Oral Epidemiology*, 38(2): 136–44.

De Palma, P. 2007. *Oral Health among a Group of Homeless Individuals from Dental Professional's and Patient's Perspective.* Stockholm: Karolinska Institutet, Department of Periodontology, Institute of Odontology.

De Palma, P. and G. Nordenram. 2005. "The Perceptions of Homeless People in Stockholm Concerning Oral Health and Consequences of Dental Treatment: A Qualitative Study." *Special Care in Dentistry*, 25(6): 289–95.

De Palma, P., L. Frithiof, L. Persson, B. Klinge, J. Halldin and U. Beijer. 2005. "Oral Health of Homeless Adults in Stockholm, Sweden." *Acta Odontologica Scandinavica*, 63(1): 50–55.

Dharamsi, S. and M. I. MacEntee. 2002. "Dentistry and Distributive Justice." *Social Science & Medicine*, 55(2): 323–29.

Dogan, M. C., M. C. Haytac, O. Ozali, G. Seydaoglu, O. Yoldas and H. Oztunc. 2006. "The Oral Health Status of Street Children in Adana, Turkey." *International Dental Journal*, 56(2): 92–96.

Falvo, N. 2009. *Homelessness, Program Responses, and an Assessment of Toronto's Streets to Homes Program.* Ottawa: Canadian Policy Research Networks.

Figueiredo, R. L. F., S. W. Hwang and C. Quiñonez. 2013. "Dental Health of Homeless Adults in Toronto, Canada." *Journal of Public Health Dentistry*, 73: 74–78.

Frankish, C. J., S. W. Hwang and D. Quantz. 2005. "Homelessness and Health in Canada." *Canadian Journal of Public Health*, 96: 23–29.

Gaetz, S. and J. Lee. 1995. "Developing Dental Services for Street Youth." *Ontario Dentist*, 72(9): 34–37.

Gelberg, L., L. S. Lin and D. J. Rosenberg. 1988. "Dental Health of Homeless Adults." *Special Care in Dentistry*, 8(4): 167–72.

Geller, S., B. M. Taylor and H. D. Scott. 2004. "Free Clinics Helping to Patch the Safety Net." *Journal of Health Care for the Poor and Underserved,* 15(1): 42–51.

Gibson, G., E. F. Reifenstahl, C. J. Wehler, S. E. Rich, N. R. Kressin, T. B. King et al. 2008. "Dental Treatment Improves Self-Rated Oral Health in Homeless Veterans—A Brief Communication." *Journal of Public Health Dentistry,* 68(2): 111–15.

Gibson, G., R. Rosenheck, J. B. Tullner, R. M. Grimes, C. L. Seibyl, A. Rivera-Torres et al. 2003. "A National Survey of the Oral Health Status of Homeless Veterans." *Journal of Public Health Dentistry,* 63(1): 30–37.

Golden, A., W. Currie, E. Greaves and J. Latimer. 1999. *Taking Responsibility for Homelessness: An Action Plan for Toronto.* Toronto: Report of the Mayor's Homelessness Action Task Force.

Gooch, B. F., S. O. Griffin and D. M. Malvitz. 2006. "The Role of Evidence in Formulating Public Health Programs to Prevent Oral Disease and Promote Oral Health in the United States." *Journal of Evidence-Based Dental Practice,* 6(1): 85–89.

Government of New Brunswick. 2010. *Overcoming Poverty Together: The New Brunswick Economic and Social Inclusion Plan.* New Brunswick: Government of New Brunswick.

Greenberg, B. J. S., J. V. Kumar and H. Stevenson. 2008. "Dental Case Management: Increasing Access to Oral Health Care for Families and Children with Low Incomes." *Journal of the American Dental Association,* 139(8): 1114–21.

Han, B., B. L. Wells and A. M. Taylor. 2003. "Use of the Healthcare for the Homeless Program Services and Other Healthcare Services by Homeless Adults." *Journal of Health Care for the Poor and Underserved,* 14(1): 87–99.

Health Canada, Office of the Chief Dental Officer. 2011. [on-line]. Health Canada. http://hc-sc.gc.ca/ahc-asc/branch-dirgen/fnihb-dgspni/ocdo-bdc/project-eng.php [consulted June 13, 2013].

Hwang, S. W. 2002. "Is Homelessness Hazardous to Your Health? Obstacles to the Demonstration of a Causal Relationship." *Canadian Journal of Public Health,* 93(6): 407–10.

_____. 2001. "Homelessness and Health." *Canadian Medical Association Journal,* 164(2): 229.

Hwang, S. W., G. Tolomiczenko, F. G. Kouyoumdjian and R. E. Garner. 2005. "Interventions to Improve the Health of the Homeless: A Systematic Review." *American Journal of Preventive Medicine,* 29(4): 311.

Jago, J. D., G. S. Sternberg and B. Westerman. 1984. "Oral Health Status of Homeless Men in Brisbane." *Australian Dental Journal,* 29(3): 184–88.

Kahabuka, F. K. and H. S. Mbawalla. 2006. "Oral Health Knowledge and Practices among Dar es Salaam Institutionalized Former Street Children Aged 7–16 Years." *International Journal of Dental Hygiene,* 4(4): 174–78.

Kalebjian, D. M. and C. A. Murphy-Tong. 2001. "A Focus on the Institutionalized Aged and Special Care Patient for Today's Practice." *Journal of the California Dental Association,* 29(6): 408–14.

Kaste, L. M. and A. J. Bolden. 1995. "Dental Caries in Homeless Adults in Boston." *Journal of Public Health Dentistry,* 55(1): 34–36.

Khandor, E. and K. Mason. 2007. *The Street Health Report 2007.* Toronto: Street Health.

King, T. B. and G. Gibson. 2003. "Oral Health Needs and Access to Dental Care of Homeless Adults in the United States: A Review." *Special Care in Dentistry,* 23(4): 143–47.

Klein, S., M. G. Cohen, T. Garner, I. Ivanova, M. Lee, B. Wallace et al. 2008. *A Poverty Reduction Plan for BC.* Vancouver: Canadian Centre for Policy Alternatives, BC Office.

Lawrence, H. P. and J. L. Leake. 2001. "The US Surgeon General's Report on Oral Health in America: A Canadian Perspective." *Journal of the Canadian Dental Association,* 67(10): 587.

Leake, J. L. 2006. "Why Do We Need an Oral Health Care Policy in Canada?" *Journal of the Canadian Dental Association,* 72(4): 317.

———. 2005. "Access and Care: Reports from Canadian Dental Education and Care Agencies." *Journal of the Canadian Dental Association,* 71(7): 469–71.

Lee, J., S. Gaetz and F. Goettler. 1994. "The Oral Health of Toronto's Street Youth." *Journal of the Canadian Dental Association,* 60(6): 545–48.

Levesque, M. C., S. Dupere, C. Loignon, A. Levine, I. Laurin, A. Charbonneau et al. 2009. "Bridging the Poverty Gap in Dental Education: How Can People Living in Poverty Help Us?" *Journal of Dental Education,* 73(9): 1043–54.

Locker, D. 2000. "Deprivation and Oral Health: A Review." *Commissioned Review,* 28(3): 161–69.

Luo, Y. and C. McGrath. 2006. "Oral Health Status of Homeless People in Hong Kong." *Special Care in Dentistry,* 26(4): 150–54.

MacEntee, M. I., R. Harrison and C. Wyatt. 2001. *Strategies to Enhance the Oral Health of British Columbians, Specifically Aboriginal Peoples, Tobacco-Users and Those of Low Socioeconomic Background.* Vancouver: UBC Faculty of Dentistry.

Main, P., J. Leake and D. Burman. 2006. "Oral Health Care in Canada— A View from the Trenches." *Journal of the Canadian Dental Association,* 72(4): 319.

McCormack, D., and J. MacIntosh. 2001. "Research with Homeless People Uncovers a Model of Health." *Western Journal of Nursing Research,* 23(7): 679.

McNally, M. 2003. "Rights Access and Justice in Oral Health Care: Justice toward Underserved Patient Populations—The Elderly." *Journal of the American College of Dentists*, 70: 56–60.

Melanson, S. L. 2008. "Establishing a Social Dental Clinic: Addressing Unmet Dental Needs." *Canadian Journal of Dental Hygiene*, 42(4): 185–93.

Moore, G., M. Gerdtz and E. Manias. 2007. "Homelessness, Health Status and Emergency Department Use: An Integrated Review of the Literature." *Australasian Emergency Nursing Journal*, 10(4): 178–85.

Mouradian, W. E. 2006. "Band-Aid Solutions to the Dental Access Crisis: Conceptually Flawed—A Response to Dr. David H. Smith." *Journal of Dental Education*, 70(11): 1174.

Muirhead, V., C. Quiñonez, R. Figueiredo and D. Locker. 2009. "Predictors of Dental Care Utilization among Working Poor Canadians." *Community Dentistry and Oral Epidemiology*, 37(3): 199–208.

Patrick, D., R. Lee, M. Nucci, D. Grembowski, C. Jolles and P. Milgrom. 2006. "Reducing Oral Health Disparities: A Focus on Social and Cultural Determinants." *BMC Oral Health*, 6(Suppl 1): S4.

Pizem, P., P. Massicotte, J. R. Vincent and R. Y. Barolet. 1994. "The State of Oral and Dental Health of the Homeless and Vagrant Population of Montreal." *Journal Canadian Dental Association*, 60(12): 1061–65.

Province of Ontario. 2008. *Breaking the Cycle: Ontario's Poverty Reduction Strategy*. Ontario: Province of Ontario.

Quiñonez, C. R., R. Figueiredo and D. Locker. 2009a. "Canadian Dentists' Opinions on Publicly Financed Dental Care." *Journal of Public Health Dentistry*, 69(2): 64–73.

Quiñonez, C., D. Gibson, A. Jokovic and D. Locker. 2009b. "Emergency Department Visits for Dental Care of Nontraumatic Origin." *Community Dentistry and Oral Epidemiology*, 37(4): 366–71.

Quiñonez, C., R. Figueiredo, A. Azarpazhooh and D. Locker. 2010. "Public Preferences for Seeking Publicly Financed Dental Care and Professional Preferences for Structuring It." *Community Dentistry and Oral Epidemiology*, 38(2): 152–58.

Robbins, J. L., L. Wenger, J. Lorvick, C. Shiboski and A. H. Kral. 2010. "Health and Oral Health Care Needs and Health Care–Seeking Behavior among Homeless Injection Drug Users in San Francisco." *Journal of Urban Health*, 87(6): 1–11.

Schanzer, B., B. Dominguez, P. E. Shrout and C. L. M. Caton. 2007. "Homelessness, Health Status, and Health Care Use." *American Journal of Public Health*, 97(3): 464.

Slott, S. D. 2005. "The Role of Free Dental Programs in Care Provision for the Underserved." *North Carolina Medical Journal*, 66(6): 471–74.

SPARC-BC. 2008. *Still on Our Streets . . . . Results of the 2008 Metro Vancouver Homeless Count.* Vancouver: Greater Vancouver Regional Steering Committee on Homelessness.

U.S. General Accounting Office. 2000. *Oral Health: Factors Contributing to Low Use of Dental Services by Low-Income Populations—Report to Congressional Requestors.* No. GAO publication HEHS-00-149. Washington: U.S. General Accounting Office.

Victoria Cool Aid Society. 2007. *Homelessness Needs Survey: Housing First: Plus Supports.* Victoria, BC: Victoria Cool Aid Society.

Wallace, B. 2009. *A Case Study of Five Community Dental Clinics in British Columbia.* Victoria, BC: Victoria Cool Aid Society.

_____. 2008. *Improving Access to Dental Services for Low-Income Adults in BC.* Victoria, BC: Victoria Cool Aid Society and Vancouver Island Public Interest Research Group.

Waplington, J., J. Morris and G. Bradnock. 2000. "The Dental Needs, Demands and Attitudes of a Group of Homeless People with Mental Health Problems." *Community Dental Health,* 17(3): 134–37.

# CHAPTER 9

# Close to the Street:
# Nursing Practice with People
# Marginalized by Homelessness
# and Substance Use

Bernadette Pauly, RN, PhD
School of Nursing, University of Victoria
Centre for Addictions Research of British Columbia, University of Victoria

## Introduction

Nurses are often an initial and ongoing point of contact for persons marginalized by homelessness and substance use in health care settings. As such, nurses are uniquely positioned to facilitate access to health care for people who have poor health and face multiple barriers to care. In particular, persons marginalized by homelessness and substance use often encounter stigma and discrimination when accessing health care. Professional standards for ethical nursing practice include promoting health and well-being, preserving dignity and promoting justice and health equity (Canadian Nurses Association 2008). The promotion of justice means that nurses do not discriminate in the provision of care on any basis and refrain from judging and stigmatizing behaviours. However, specific concerns related to exclusionary 'othering', in which others are differentiated on the basis of class, race, gender or some other aspect, contribute to negative processes of engagement and are prevalent in health care (Canales 2000; MacCallum 2002; Peternelj-Taylor 2004; Varcoe 2004). Further, nurses have a specific professional commitment to the promotion of equity in health and health services.

This chapter discusses findings from an ethnographic study exploring access to health care for people marginalized by homelessness and substance use within nurse–patient interactions and

the environment in which these interactions took place. A key finding was that forging a chain of trust in a climate of distrust fosters
access to health care. This chain of trust is triple-linked, consisting
of interlocking interpersonal, organizational and systemic linkages.
Health care access is negatively impacted when these links are weak
or broken. Strategies for enhancing access to health care for people
marginalized by homelessness and substance use through enhancement of ethical nursing practice are also discussed.

## Stigmatization, Discrimination and Health Care Encounters

People impacted by homelessness and substance use often encounter stigma and discrimination when accessing health care services
(Butters and Erickson 2003; Crockett and Gifford 2004; Gelberg
et al. 2004; Lloyd 2010; McLaughlin et al. 2006; Stajduhar et al. 2004;
Trevana, Simpson and Nutbeam 2003; Wen, Hudak and Hwang 2007).
Negative attitudes of health care providers have been implicated in
the development of stigmatizing experiences and discriminatory
practices associated with class, substance use, disease conditions or
other factors such as race or ethnicity.

Stigma is the outcome of social processes that result in social
devaluing and spoiled identity in which individuals are marked on
the basis of negative attributes (Goffman 1963). Stigmatization results
in either *enacted stigma,* where individuals are actively discriminated
against, or *perceived or felt stigma,* where stigmatized individuals inter-
nalize negative beliefs (Goffman 1963). Stigma is highly contingent on
an individual's social location and "entirely dependent on social, political and economic power" with power imbalances between those who
are the subject of stigma and those who stigmatize (Link and Phelan
2001). Stuber, Meyer and Link (2008) argue that stigmatization and discrimination share common features, "including exposure to negative
attitudes, structural and interpersonal experiences of discrimination
or unfair treatment and violence perpetrated against persons who
belong to disadvantaged social groups" (351). Further, people may be
subject to intersecting stigmas associated with age, sex, gender, sexual
orientation, race, ethnicity socioeconomic status or disease (Benoit and
Shumka 2009; Wailoo 2006). For example, the stigma associated with
homelessness may combine with other stigmatizing conditions, such as
mental illness, HIV/AIDS, hepatitis C and substance use, and contribute to
discrimination (Harter et al. 2005; Takahashi 1997; Wolitski et al. 2009).

Researchers have reported that homeless persons often encounter negative experiences or judgments when accessing health care (Ensign and Planke 2002; Gelberg et al. 2004; Stajduhar et al. 2004). For example, Wen, Hudak and Hwang (2007) found that homeless persons either implicitly or explicitly connected unwelcomeness with feelings of discrimination. The stigma associated with drug use has contributed to negative experiences in health care settings for this population (Butters and Erickson 2003; Crockett and Gifford 2004; Lloyd 2010). Stigma and discrimination decrease the likelihood that individuals will access health care in the future and may contribute to further marginalization and feelings of low self-worth and may also manifest in physical and mental health concerns (Bird, Bogart and Delahanty 2004; Browne et al. 2002; Dinos et al. 2004; Krieger 1999; Wen, Hudak and Hwang 2007; Zickmund et al. 2003).

In contrast, several studies have found that registered nurses providing primary care outreach and provision of care in community health centres are perceived more positively by marginalized populations (Hilton et al. 2001; Politzer et al. 2004). For example, a Vancouver evaluation of the street nurse program was found to foster the development of relationships and enhance access to heath care. However, there is limited understanding of ethical nursing practice and strategies within nurse–patient interactions that might provide insight into reducing barriers and fostering access to health care services for those marginalized by homelessness and substance use.

## Methodology and Methods

An ethnographic approach that drew on critical and feminist perspectives was used to examine access to health care and ethical nursing practice in interactions between nurses and persons experiencing homelessness and/or substance use and the environment in which these interactions occur. The specific research objectives were to: (1) describe the nature of interactions and the development of relationships between nurses and marginalized populations, (2) explicate the underlying factors (social, political, economic and historical) supporting and limiting the enactment of professional standards and practice by nurses within these relationships, (3) explore the impact on access to health care and (4) identify the insights of clients and nurses that would contribute to the development of more equitable access to health care services. A detailed description of the methodology is provided elsewhere (Pauly 2008b).

Data collection methods included qualitative interviews with 26 primary participants (13 registered nurses, four people accessing health care, nine non-nursing health care staff) and 203 hours of participant observation at two community health care centres (CHCs) and one emergency department (ED). Interviews and participant observation were conducted over a period of 10 months. All interviews and field notes were audio recorded and transcribed verbatim. Both the CHCs and the ED were located in western Canada and were identified as serving an inner-city population in areas associated with poverty, homelessness and substance use. Data collection and analysis occurred concurrently. Inductive methods of data analysis as described by Lincoln and Guba (1985) were used. Immersion in the transcripts and field notes through multiple readings contributed to the identification of activities, events and conversations that provided insight into nurse–patient interactions within the social context that facilitated or inhibited access to health care. Consistent with feminist approaches, nurse participants were actively consulted at various points to clarify and extend the analysis. Criteria for reliability and validity in feminist research including dependability, adequacy, reflexivity and catalytic validity were employed to ensure rigour in the study (Hall and Stevens 1991; Lather 1991).

Ethical approval for the study was granted by each site as well as the University of Victoria. Initial information sessions were conducted in both CHCs to inform staff about the study. Written consent was obtained from all primary participants for interviews and observations. Throughout the study, staff members in each setting were informed about the study when observations were conducted. Verbal consent was obtained from individuals who were observed during nursing care delivery.

## Findings

All participants emphasized that people marginalized by homelessness and substance use were often distrustful of mainstream health care services and expressed an avoidance or reluctance to access health care, particularly in hospitals. One participant echoed the feelings of many: *"I'm not going to go, I don't go to hospital unless I absolutely, desperately have to go, unless I am on my deathbed."* Client participants relayed a range reasons for avoiding hospital care, including fears of being overlooked, prejudged and treated like garbage by a system that focuses on addressing acute concerns and getting people through quickly (Pauly 2005). Distrust was exacerbated by a 'culture of fixing' in the emergency department and embedded in personal experiences of past trauma and being on the street, where "trust is a lousy survival tactic" (Pauly 2008b). In this climate of distrust, re-establishing trust with people experiencing homelessness and substance use was central to the work nurses did to facilitate access to health care services. Rebuilding trust occurred on three interrelated levels: interpersonal, organizational and systemic.

### Interpersonal Linkages

**Building trusting relationships over time.** In this study, nurses felt that each client interaction was an opportunity to build trust that could facilitate access to health and ancillary services. A nurse describes:

> It is a process over time. Yeah. It doesn't . . . it certainly doesn't happen on the first visit. It certainly takes a while, and sometimes the first visit is . . . just meeting their immediate needs but letting them know that the door is open . . . Really . . . the basis of providing access to care is that relationship and that sense of trust.

Multiple interactions build interpersonal trust over time and are necessary to facilitate access to health care services. Some key features of building interpersonal trust were preserving respect, not brushing concerns off and sensitivity to life circumstances.

**Preserving respect.** Client participants' fears of being "overlooked", "prejudged" and "treated like garbage" highlight the lack of respect they often experience in health care relationships. All participants noted the importance of respect in health care encounters and relationships and a desire to be treated "like a real person". One client participant remarked, "*I just want a doctor that respects me and treats me like a person.*" This client participant continued:

> You know, [the street nurse] has seen me when I've been so stoned I could hardly walk or talk or anything, gibbled, or you know, doing the chicken or whatever they call it, flailing away. And he doesn't degrade me for it. Like you know [the street nurse] accepts the fact that I'm a

*junkie and I'm going to be a junkie the rest of my life. But I'm still a
good person inside. I mean I have compassion for people. I try and help
people out. You know he understands I have compassion for people.*

Nurses and health professional participants endeavoured to see their
clients as persons with unique value and worth, not as 'addicts',
'junkies' or 'the homeless'. Some nurses described their clients as
'survivors' and admired them for how they coped with daunting
life experiences and the daily challenges of homelessness, poverty
and life on the street.

As suggested by the quote above, a key to respecting clients
was the ability to move beyond judgments and stereotypes. One
nurse describes how it was easy to fall into the trap of thinking of
her clients in stereotypical ways:

*I think what I do is that I'm able to split my thoughts and how I react
to these guys. When I'm on [the street] Christmas shopping and when
I'm having my glass of wine in a wine bar, I do think of my clients as
scumbags, addicts, who broke into my car. Get an f'in life, go to work
. . . I do think of it that way. And when I come here and I'm actually
physically caring for them . . . and I'm actually wiping the purulent
discharge from the horrible festering cellulitis all over their body and
they're telling me how hungry they are because they've only had this
whatever it is. I can chit chat with them and really feel for them. So
again, it's overcoming all these prejudices, right? Also, you know . . .
it's the environment that's along with it . . . you live the middle-class
life, it's so totally removed. . . . Actually physically doing it without
having this colonial attitude that I'm doing good for these poor little
souls and helping them.*

This nurse describes how one has to navigate judgments about personal responsibility that are part of societal norms while not taking
up an attitude of servitude and charity and striving to find genuine
compassion.

In light of past experiences and the hypervigilance necessary
for survival on the streets, nurses were aware that clients were both
hypervigiliant and attuned to negative judgments when accessing
health care. One nurse describes, *"You know I think they are so sensitive about everything because they've been so bruised and so damaged and
everything is seen as a reprimand, a spank, put in the corner. They're not*

*able to decipher that out."* In response, nurses described being hyper-vigilant and super sensitive to non-verbal and verbal behaviour that might communicate negative judgments. One nurse noted:

> *You always have to be checking yourself doing a mental check, saying oh, because now I'm more aware of it than I was. So that's why yesterday I thought, I'm getting my back up, I need to take a deep breath because I'm not going to be able to help this guy if I'm feeling defensive. It's just a question of breathing through it and recognizing what it is that's triggering me.*

This excerpt demonstrates the challenges of being self-aware and recognizing when one is being triggered by a client's behaviour and monitoring potentially negative responses that could reduce access to care.

While health care interactions are a precious opportunity to show respect, nurses described the challenge of maintaining respect in the face of disrespect. For example, one nurse observed:

> *It means you have to constantly find respect for people that constantly step on you and don't do what it is you're there to help them do. . . . And you secretly lose respect for someone that yells at you from the door. You can't help it . . . when somebody says, Fuck off! Well okay, I will fuck off. You know. And it's very hard not to develop that attitude and just take yourself out of it.*

'Taking yourself out of it' could mean withdrawal from the person or situation or refusing to take it personally. One social worker indicated it would have been easy to say something harsh to someone who was being verbally abusive but recommended a more respectful approach:

> *But it was that kind of behaviour [respect] that would throw people off more than. And [I] got to let you know this isn't okay but the last thing I'm going to do is do this dance with you. I'm going to take every opportunity I can to model something different. You're deserving of respect, I'm deserving of respect. So, let's work on that.*

When respecting a client became difficult, often due to violent behaviour, nurses and other health professionals emphasized the importance of preserving and respecting a client's right to receive health care services without judgment. Several participants expressed the belief that the CHC was the last stop for health care and that it would be ethically wrong to limit care even in the face of challenging behaviours. In preserving a client right to access health care, nurses had to navigate two tensions: (1) management of health care resources and (2) perceived threats to personal safety and security (Pauly 2008b).

**Not brushing people off.** Nurses listened and acknowledged clients concerns and sought to never 'brush clients off'. Nurses strived to view all presenting concerns as serious and worthy of time and attention. For example:

> A man came into the exam room and told the nurse he thought he had glass in his scalp from a broken bottle. As he pulled and picked at his hair, the nurse put on disposable rubber gloves and explained she would have a look and patiently began parting his hair and examining his scalp. After a few minutes, she said, "I can't see anything." The interaction ended abruptly as he jumped up and said, "Well okay, I must have gotten it all out." Later, the nurse explained that he has come in many times before with the same complaint and that he often picks his scalp until it bleeds. She suspected it was a side effect of cocaine use. As I had watched the interaction, I had assumed from the nurse's behaviour, that she had taken seriously his request to see if there was any broken glass in his scalp.

Nurses were attentive to the presenting concerns regardless of their perceived validity. Such an approach can become a tangible way of showing respect to clients who are frequently 'brushed off' not just in health care services but every day.

In their interactions with nurses, clients frequently expressed anger and frustration at their life situations, such as conflicts with family and friends, housing difficulties and money problems. Nurses listened patiently to these concerns and, once clients had expressed their frustrations and the client was ready to move on, nurses would often calmly ask about the reason for their visit and what assistance they needed. One client describes the powerful impact this has:

> I've been in rages sometimes and gone and see the . . . nurse and totally calmed down because I got everything off my chest in five minutes, right. From a totally raging animal to nice mellow guy again in

*five minutes. I talk to the [nurse], I tell him you haven't got the golden pill but you've got the golden ear. . . . You know just getting things off my chest. And if I didn't see [the nurse] there, I probably would have gone downtown and got in a fight and took my rage out on somebody else right rather than talking to the [nurse]. A lot of times it's just the listening part means the whole world of difference from freakin' out and going totally ballistic. You know when you're right on the edge, maybe haven't made money for a day or so and somebody's in jail and you're trying to get her out of jail. And you're right on the edge, you know, you're full of rage. You can talk to the [street nurse] for five minutes or the other girl and you know you get it all off your chest.*

After a few minutes of expressing their frustration, clients were frequently observed to experience a shift in demeanor from anger or frustration to calm. Not brushing these concerns off did not imply agreement or necessarily require additional action by the nurse. Rather, listening conveyed respect and helped build relationships that were essential to facilitating access to and provision of nursing care. Some nurses expressed a view that listening to clients about whatever was on their mind helped them to get to know them better, what their worries and concerns were.

**Sensitivity to life circumstances.** Sensitivity to life circumstances helped to contextualize individual behaviours and choices and foster respect for clients. One nurse noted that clients often felt embarrassed and apologized for the odour of their feet when they take their socks off for an exam. Rather than judging them as a "rude stinky street person", she observed that being on the street makes it difficult for people to shower every day and they don't always have access to clean socks. Thus, rather than judging them for their appearance and cleanliness, the nurse situated these encounters within the context of life on the street, specifically lack of access to showers and resources to promote personal hygiene. Another nurse noted:

*Trying to put yourself in their shoes and understanding the issues that they're talking about and sometimes it's the hardest thing because it's hard for them to communicate their reality and it's hard for you to understand them because the living situations are so different. . . . One patient told me the [medication she is on] and I told her it's important to drink lots of water to minimize side effects. And I asked her how many glasses of water she drinks and she says, "Well, I just drink coffee in the pharmacy where I pick up my methadone then maybe I buy a coffee in McDonald's. But I don't drink water in my A hotel. It's undrinkable. It's disgusting." So to get to the bottom of these details is crucial for people's treatment. You need time and you have to then think of solutions that . . . you would not otherwise think in any other situation.*

Recognizing that clients' decisions are shaped by the context in which they live and recognizing that the life circumstances of their clients was different than their own provided an avenue to avoid judging behaviours and fostered provision of care that was situated and relevant to the life circumstances of the client. As illustrated above, telling someone to drink water when they do not have access to water is ineffective and would not promote proper medication administration. It is necessary to constantly think in terms of 'what would this be like if I didn't have housing and access to taken for granted privileges such as water, showers, privacy and so on?'

Individuals' ability to care for their health is profoundly shaped by their individual living situations, social position and access to resources. Some nurses were quick to caution that you may never know a client's whole story or could only understand to degrees the effect of poverty, addiction and violence on clients' behaviours and choices. Rather than expecting individuals to share their life story, nurses assumed there was also more to individual client situations than they might ever know, need to know or understand.

### Organizational Linkages in Building a Chain of Trust
Organizational linkages are vitally important in building a chain of trust. Key organizational linkages in creating a climate of trust that fostered access to health care were harm reduction, outreach and inter-agency trust. The absence of these conditions inhibited access to health care for those marginalized by homelessness and substance use.

**Harm reduction: meeting people where they are.** Nurses working in CHCS recognized harm reduction as an organizational philosophy, a set of strategies and a practical approach to working with homeless and substance using populations. They described harm reduction as integral to ethical nursing practice, the development of relationships with clients and the consequent increased access to health services. Harm reduction created a relational space in which relationships between health professionals and clients could develop without judgments related to substance use. The context of health care delivery shifted from a 'culture of fixing' substance use to accepting that people 'fix'. Some of the nurses and other participants in the study described harm reduction as taking the pressure off trying to fix people and instead putting the focus on keeping them safe. A philosophy of harm reduction shifted moral values to (1) focus on reducing harm associated with substance use and living conditions, (2) emphasize the moral worth of clients and (3) enhance the decision-making capacity of clients (Pauly 2008b). For CHC nurses, harm reduction meant being ready for change but not expecting it and not giving up. One nurse noted, *"Ethical practice is when the person can keep coming back without judgments, without recriminations"*. Another nurse stated, *"We don't fire people and we don't give up on them"*. Nurses consistently tried to minimize harm not only from substance use but also the other harms associated with homelessness and street-involvement that might impact health and well-being. Reducing harm became a moral imperative for guiding ethical nursing practice.

**Outreach: meeting people on their turf.** Outreach from the CHC provided an important organizational linkage to help rebuild the chain of trust. Nurses and health professional participants described the importance of meeting clients 'on their turf'. One outreach nurse noted:

> *Outreach is a golden opportunity to be able to intervene and change the situation. Although you've had many no gos, no shows, whatever, you can't ever assume that you're going to be able to turn that around. That's what we wait for, that golden opportunity and it happens. It happens and you have to be there. You have to actually be there where they are to make it happen and that's why our model of being in shelters being like we set it up in the [downtown hotel], being at the shelter. We run the clinic there. You know, we need to do much more of that.*

Outreach helped to provide care to clients reluctant to access health services or unable to access health services due to competing survival needs.

Outreach provided nurses with an opportunity to get to know and build trust with clients outside of clinical settings and allowed them to become an initial point of contact for health information, education, counselling, assessment and referral. 'Curbside consults' were common as outreach nurses moved agency to agency. Although nurses were primarily employed by CHCs, clients considered them to be 'street nurses' because of their outreach role. Nurse outreach to homeless and drop-in shelters was considered an important component of services at one of the CHCs. One nurse noted:

> When you've been [there] consistently, clients recognize that. They go, 'Oh, I've seen you around before.' And they'll talk to you. Frontline workers who've been there for a long time . . . you've become a consistent presence for them too, so they'll start advocating and pull people in to come and see you. So I'll go up to [one shelter] and often there's a frontline worker [who will] say, 'We told them you'd keep coming around and you're okay.' So they'll see you. So that's really important, the consistency.

Those CHC nurses who did outreach consistently were able to build trust with both drop-in staff and clients. They were directly linked to the CHC and could facilitate the development of trust with the CHC, thereby facilitating access that fostered earlier intervention and treatment for people who often avoid and delay health care.

**Inter-provider trust.** Trusting relationships between nurses and other team members in their health settings facilitated access to a broader range of health services. Nurses who had established relationships with health professionals in their setting helped to extend the chain of trust for clients and achieve access to a broader range of services. For example, an outreach nurse noted:

> Often what I'll do is if I think someone really would benefit from counselling, then well, I'm coming in and I'm talking with you. I say, 'Yeah that's fine but I think you're at a point where you would really benefit from someone that has expertise that I don't have.' And then I'll go and see if [the counsellor] is free and then I'll bring them down and say, 'Let me introduce you to the [counsellor]. If you feel this is someone that you could talk to, that you feel comfortable with, then this will be great.' So sometimes, just initiating contact and bringing them down.

*Then they put a face to the [counsellor]. . . . If you know, he doesn't have anybody, he'll sit down with them for five minutes and go, 'Well, what's going on? We'll make an appointment. . . .' Then people tend to follow him through then with that [i.e., the appointment]. . . . I'm always advocating for the other practitioners too. 'Oh, you've got an appointment coming up with Dr. So and So.' 'Well I don't really like doctors.' 'Yeah, I don't either, but you know [laughs] this is a good one. I think you'll like this one.'*

By establishing trusting relationships with other professionals in her organization, this nurse was able to facilitate access to a wider range of health services for her client. Nurses stressed that working with like-minded colleagues was particularly important to the development of inter-provider trust. Where team approaches were valued and the role of nurses was understood and respected, health care teams facilitated client transitions between health care providers. In the absence of trust and respect for other roles, access was inhibited.

Working in physical proximity as part of an interdisciplinary team provided multiple opportunities for hallway consults and referrals. In the presence of trust, this fostered a shared care approach, which improved the ability of team members to address multiple and complex client health needs. One client noted:

*I can get in quickly when I need to. I can see the nurse and she consults the doctor so I don't need an appointment with the doctor. This is the whole package. I can get my drugs here even have my blood drawn (But not have X-rays). Much better than going to emergency where you have to wait five hours.*

Clients highly valued coming to one location and having access to an integrated team of health care providers. Health centre managers were integral to fostering the development of teams that are supportive and able to work together. For example, in one centre, the manager played a central role in establishing the values of the centre, reminding the team of their mandate and keeping everyone on track, especially in difficult situations. An additional benefit of shared care approaches is that nurses were not left to deal with challenging clients alone. Nurses cautioned against hiring nurses and making them solely responsible for caring for homeless and street-involved populations, as this would potentially lead to burnout.

### Systemic Trust: Disrupting Negative Judgments and Missing Linkages

To rebuild trust in the health care system, CHC nurses disrupted negative chains of judgment and worked to build inter-agency trust. However, there were often fundamental links missing that limited nurses' ability to facilitate access to health and social services.

**Disrupting negative chains of judgment.** Negative chains of judgment—that is, negative labels passed from one provider to another—led to adverse experiences and limited access to health services. For example, one nurse explains:

> *You're seeing how other staff, treat certain clients, so you can see that domino effect. . . . I mean, when I worked emerg, it was amazing that the ambulance guys would come in and go, oh yeah, so and so again; blah, blah, blah and then that is passed on to the triage nurse and then passed on to the nurses you're giving report to. . . . And you're passing that on to the doctor and so that judgment is all the way down and it was something that it took me a long time to realize. . . . Then all of a sudden you're at the bedside and someone shows up, like a family member or a friend, and they're giving you a different take on what the parmedics picked up. And all of sudden it's like, oh, I feel bad because we had that judgment happening and so we've been treating that person a certain way and there's actually something else much more complicated going on and we're compromising care because of that. . . . And you see that often with overdoses and things like that. Oh, you're bringing in another overdose. You know. How to break that chain. So that's something that you have to be aware of.*

This example highlights how judgments are played out in health care systems. Societal beliefs that individuals are at fault of their poor health are at the root of these judgments and have the tendency to blame individuals for their current situations. Participating nurses attempted to break negative chains of judgments by facilitating access to health care in emergency departments and hospitals. One nurse described calling the ED to facilitate the admission of a client living with HIV:

> *His hemoglobin just dropped in his boots and he just showed up one day, like, so white he was yellow, short of breath, just standing there but did not want to go to the hospital because he was always mistreated.*

*I was the one who ended up calling the emerg doc, and right away, he's well, how come I'm talking to the nurse not to the doctor [i.e., referring physician]. I said, well right now I've got a man with a hemoglobin of 30. He needs to come in and I'm giving you a heads up. And I said, now he's going to swear, you're all fuckin' assholes and idiots and he hates doctors, but that's just who he is and we love him [laughs]. And so the emergency room doctor actually laughed. The patient stayed there for a couple of days, got some transfusion and came out and said, they treated me really well. They even fed me.*

This client returned several times and was willing to do so because of his initial positive experience. The referring nurse indicated that her goal was to help the physician focus on how sick the client was and shift away from viewing the client as only a 'homeless person' or 'drug user'.

**Inter-agency trust.** Trust between nurses, health care providers and agencies is integral to enhancing access to health and social services. Access becomes compromised when there is little or no trust between agencies. One nurse manager noted:

*I think the agencies themselves need to trust each other and to know about each other. Extremely challenging [here]. There's so much history. . . . Everybody has some kind of historical view of where they're working and who their next door neighbours are and what they doing and how they're doing it. . . . Everybody thinks that they're . . . doing the right thing and everyone else is doing it wrong. And, if only the other person over here could understand that this is the way it should be done, we could save the population, which of course isn't true. Because, if we could save this population, if someone has the answer . . . we'd know that because all of the people would be all better, cured and going off and that is not happening. . . . Nobody seems to want to see that and to really look and see that maybe there is more than one [route to take]. . . . Maybe sharing what I'm doing, instead of holding onto it tightly, would be a good thing.*

When there is a lack of trust between providers and agencies, providers may refuse to refer individuals to those agencies because of fears that their clients will be mistreated. In such situations, agencies became distrustful of each other and services were more likely to be fragmented and marginalized. When linkages of trust between agencies were developed, there was an increased capacity to foster access to needed services for clients. Inter-agency meetings and collaboration on projects provided opportunities to develop relationships, but such opportunities were rare and often not formalized due to limited time and resources.

**Missing and absent linkages.** There were frequently missing linkages, barriers or gaps that prevented clients from accessing needed services. Of particular concern, there were missing linkages with detoxification programs, hospitals, prisons and housing. Clients were repeatedly unable to gain timely access to detoxification services simply because such services were not accessible. One nurse explained:

> *Ready for detox and you fill out the forms and you fax it and tell [them to wait]. You want to do the best for people who have decided that now's the time and want to detox, [the best] would be to take them there, put them in a cab right now. While they're ready.*

Wait times averaged four to six weeks, and if the client was admitted after two weeks, they were required to fill out the form again. After being told this, one client replied, *"I can't wait a month, I don't know if I can wait a week."* He turned around and walked out and the nurse did not fill out the form. Nurse and health professional participants grew weary of filling out these forms, which led to the false impression that there was a decreased demand for these services.

There was a lack of linkages with hospitals, prisons, community resources and housing. A specific concern was clients being 'dumped into the community'—that is, discharged to the shelters or community directly from hospitals or prisons without any discharge planning around housing and community supports. As one social worker said, *"Discharge to a shelter is not a discharge plan."* Nurses pointed out that being discharged to the shelter is very different than being discharged to home where one can rest and convalesce in a safe place. In a shelter, clients may not be able to access their rooms during the day to rest.

Central to the problem of 'dumping' is the lack of affordable housing in the community. Attempts to link individuals to housing were often unsuccessful due to high costs of rent and low vacancy rates in the cities where the research was conducted. In particular, there was lack of access to housing that tolerated drug and alcohol use. In one city, low-cost supportive housing had policies that restricted access even to individuals currently on methadone. Thus, individuals frequently returned to the shelters even after going through detox and rehabilitation only to re-enter the cycle of homelessness and drug use. Further access to affordable housing was impacted by welfare reform and shelter rates that prevented those on social assistance in finding affordable housing.

## Discussion

Access to health care services for persons who are marginalized due to homelessness and substance use is facilitated by the rebuilding of trust at three interrelated levels: interpersonal, organizational and systemic. Trust in health care is often taken for granted but is at issue when there is uncertainty about another's behaviour and how one might be treated (Smith 2005). Lack of trust can negatively impact access to health care. Trust is most often understood at the interpersonal level and reflects a moral concern for the other (Smith 2005). Rebuilding interpersonal trust between nurses and clients is the first link in building a chain of trust that can facilitate access to the health and social services needed to address complex health and social care challenges. Organizational policies supporting harm reduction and outreach enabled nurses to meet people 'where they were at' and 'on their own turf' and contributed to development of trust. Inter-provider trust fostered access to broader range of health and social services within CHCs. Disrupting negative chains of judgment and building inter-agency trust fostered access but highlighted gaps and missing systemic linkages. These findings suggest that health care providers rebuild trust not only interpersonally but organizationally and systemically to enhance access to health care.

The importance of respect for persons regardless of their behaviours is underscored and strategies for conveying respect highlighted. The importance of being treated as a person and not being brushed off are similar to the findings of Wen, Hudak and Hwang's (2007) discussion of welcomeness and unwelcomeness in health care encounters for homeless persons. These findings extend this discussion by providing insight into strategies nurses use to facilitate welcoming encounters. Guirguis-Younger, McNeil and Runnels (2009) found that past experiences, having a client-centred approach and engaging in inter-professional knowledge exchange were important strategies in caring for homeless populations. This study provides further insight into the professional knowledge that nurses use in enhancing access and delivery of care as well as the importance of inter-provider and inter-agency trust to delivery of services.

While respectful behaviours foster trust and access, they also ensure that health issues are not overlooked because the person is a 'frequent flyer' or seen as less deserving (Corley and Goren 1998; Malone 1996). Of particular interest is the importance of health care providers being able to see patients in an appropriate life context in order to overcome judgments and plan care appropriately. This suggests that knowledge of the life circumstances of clients is important and that potential insights from fields of study such as cultural safety may be important areas for exploration (Anderson et al. 2003; Browne et al., 2009). Cultural safety is, in part, a means of engaging nurses in reflexive praxis and the development of situated knowledge that promotes awareness of stereotypical discourses that impact the provision of health care to various groups.

Registered nurses have dual professional and ethical commitments to respect the dignity of all persons through provision of care on the basis of need regardless of race, ethnicity, gender or other conditions and to promote social justice through the development of equitable health care policies (Canadian Nurses Association 2008). Harm reduction is consistent with professional and ethical nursing standards of practice (Lightfoot et al. 2009; Pauly et al. 2007). Although harm reduction is a partial approach to tackling health inequities among those marginalized by homelessness, nurses can embrace and advocate for harm reduction as part of their commitment to social justice and reducing inequities (Pauly 2008a).

Although not solely responsible for creating the conditions in which trust is fostered at organizational and systemic levels, nurses, through their actions, can disrupt prevailing negative judgments and promote inter-provider and inter-agency trust to facilitate access to health care. Further, nurses can seek and use opportunities to raise issues related to inter-agency collaboration, lack of discharge planning and missing linkages to managers and other leaders. Nurses have unique knowledge of missing linkages and the way in which lack of access to services and housing negatively impact health. Through engagement and participation in team, organizational and community activities nurses can bring such issues to the fore and inform solutions. Advocating for primary health care, harm reduction and housing are consistent with promotion of social justice and equity for those marginalized by homelessness and substance use.

## References

Anderson, J., J. Perry, C. Blue, A. Browne, A. Henderson, K. B. Khan et al. 2003. "'Rewriting' Cultural Safety within the Postcolonial and Postnational Feminist Project: Toward New Epistemologies of Healing." *Advances in Nursing Science,* 26(3): 196–214.

Benoit, C. and L. Shumka. 2009. *Stigma and the Health of Vulnerable Women.* Research brief. Vancouver: Women's Health Research Network.

Bird, S. T., L. Bogart and D. Delahanty. 2004. "Health-Related Correlates of Perceived Discrimination in HIV Care." *AIDS Patient Care and STDS,* 18(1): 19–26.

Browne, A. J., J. L. Johnson, J. L. Bottorf, S. Grewal and B. A. Hilton. 2002. "Recognizing Discrimination in Nursing Practice." *Canadian Nurse,* 98(5): 24–27.

Browne, A., C. Varcoe, V. Smye, S. Reimer Kirkham, J. Lynam and S. Wong. 2009. "Cultural Safety and the Challenges of Translating Critically Oriented Knowledge in Practice." *Nursing Philosophy,* 10: 167–79.

Butters, J. and P. G. Erickson. 2003. "Meeting the Health Care Needs of Female Crack Users: A Canadian Example." *Women and Health,* 37(3): 1–17.

Canadian Nurses Association. 2008. "Code of Ethics for Registered Nurses." [on-line]. Canadian Nurses Association. http://www.cna-nurses.ca/CNA/practice/ethics/code/default_e.aspx [consulted October 30, 2008].

Canales, M. K. 2000. "Othering: Toward an Understanding of Difference." *Advances in Nursing Science,* 22(4): 16–31.

Corley, M. and S. Goren. 1998. "The Dark Side of Nursing: Impact of Stigmatizing Responses on Patients." *Scholarly Inquiry for Nursing Practice,* 12(2): 99–118.

Crockett, B. and S. M. Gifford. 2004. "'Eyes Wide Shut': Narratives of Women Living with Hepatitis C in Australia." *Women and Health,* 39(4): 117–37.

Dinos, S., S. Stevens, M. Serfaty, S. Weich and M. King. 2004. "Stigma: The Feelings and Experiences of 46 People with Mental Illness." *British Journal of Psychiatry,* 184: 176–81.

Ensign, J. and A. Planke. 2002. "Barriers and Bridges to Care: Voices of Homeless Female Adolescent Youth in Seattle, Washington, USA." *Journal of Advanced Nursing,* 37(2): 166–72.

Gelberg, L., C. H. Browner, E. Lejano and L. Arangua. 2004. "Access to Women's Health Care: A Qualitative Study of Barriers Perceived by Homeless Women." *Women and Health*, 40(2): 87–100.

Goffman, E. 1963. *Stigma: Notes on the Management of Spoiled Identity*. Englewood Cliffs, NJ: Prentice Hall.

Guirguis-Younger, M., R. McNeil and V. Runnels. 2009. "Learning and Knowledge-Integration Strategies of Nurses and Client Care Workers Serving Homeless People." *Canadian Journal of Nursing Research*, 41(2): 20–34.

Hall, J. and P. Stevens. 1991. "Rigor in Feminist Research." *Advances in Nursing Science*, 13(3): 16.

Harter, L., C. Berquist, B. Scott Titsworth, D. Novak, T. Brokaw and C. Tobutt. 2005. "The Structuring of Invisibility among the Hidden Homeless: The Politics of Space, Stigma, and Identity Construction." *Journal of Applied Communication Research*, 33(4): 305–27.

Hilton, B. A., R. Thompson, L. Moore-Dempsey and K. Hutchinson. 2001. "Urban Outpost Nursing: The Nature of the Nurses' Work in the AIDS Prevention Street Nurse Program." *Public Health Nursing*, 18(4): 273–80.

Krieger, N. 1999. "Embodying Inequality: A Review of Concepts, Measures, and Methods for Studying Health Consequences of Discrimination." *International Journal of Health Services*, 29(2): 295.

Lather, P. A. 1991. *Getting Smart: Feminist Research and Pedagogy with/in the Postmodern*. New York: Routledge.

Lightfoot, B., C. Panessa, S. Hayden, M. Thumath, I. Goldstone and B. Pauly. 2009. "Gaining Insite: Harm Reduction in Nursing Practice." *Canadian Nurse*, 105(4): 16–22.

Lincoln, Y. S. and E. C. Guba. 1985. *Naturalistic Inquiry*. Beverly Hills, CA: Sage.

Link, B. and J. Phelan. 2001. "Conceptualizing Stigma." *Annual Review of Sociology*, 27: 363–85.

Lloyd, C. 2010. *Sinning and Sinned Against: The Stigmatization of Problem Drug Users*. London: U.K. Drug Policy Commission.

MacCallum, E. J. 2002. "Othering and Psychiatric Nursing." *Journal of Psychiatric and Mental Health Nursing*, 9(87): 94.

Malone, R. 1996. "Almost 'Like Family': Emergency Nurses and 'Frequent Flyers'." *Journal of Emergency Nursing*, 22: 176.

McLaughlin, D., H. McKenna, J. Leslie, K. Moore and J. Robinson. 2006. "Illicit Drug Users in Northern Ireland: Perceptions and Experiences of Health and Social Care Professionals." *Journal of Psychiatric and Mental Health Nursing*, 13(6): 682–86.

Pauly, B. 2008a. "Harm Reduction through a Social Justice Lens." *International Journal of Drug Policy*, 19: 4–10.

_____. 2008b. "Shifting Moral Values to Enhance Access to Health Care: Harm Reduction as a Context for Ethical Nursing Practice." *International Journal of Drug Policy,* 19: 195–204.

_____. 2005. "Close to the Street: The Ethics of Access to Health Care." PhD dissertation, University of Victoria.

Pauly, B., I. Goldstone, J. McCall, F. Gold and S. Payne. 2007. "The Ethical, Legal and Social Context of Harm Reduction." *Canadian Nurse,* 103(8): 19–23.

Peternelj-Taylor, C. 2004. "An Exploration of Othering in Forensic Psychiatric and Correctional Nursing." *Canadian Journal of Nursing Research,* 36(4): 130.

Politzer, R., A. Schempf, B. Starfield and L. Shi. 2004. "The Future Role of Health Centers in Improving National Health." *Journal of Public Health Policy,* 24(3/4): 296–306.

Smith, C. 2005. "Understanding Trust and Confidence: Two Paradigms and Their Significance for Health and Social Care." *Journal of Applied Philosophy,* 22(3): 299–316.

Stajduhar, K. I., L. Poffenroth, E. Wong, C. P. Archibald, D. Sutherland and M. Rekart. 2004. "Missed Opportunities: Injection Drug Use and HIV/AIDS in Victoria, Canada." *International Journal of Drug Policy,* 15(3): 171–81.

Stuber, J., I. Meyer and B. Link. 2008. "Stigma, Prejudice, Discrmination and Health." *Social Science & Medicine,* 67: 351–57.

Takahashi, L. 1997. "The Socio-spatial Stigmatization of Homeless and HIV/AIDS: Towards an Explanation of the NIMBY Syndrome." *Social Science & Medicine,* 45(6): 903–14.

Trevana, L. J., J. M. Simpson and D. Nutbeam. 2003. "Soup Kitchen Consumer Perspectives on the Quality and Frequency of Health Service Interactions." *International Journal of Quality in Health Care,* 15(6): 495.

Varcoe, C. 2004. "Widening the Scope of Ethical Theory, Practice, and Policy: Violence against Women as an Illustration." In *Toward a Moral Horizon: Nursing Ethics for Leadership and Practice,* ed. J. Storch, P. Rodney and R. Starzomski. Toronto: Pearson-Prentice Hall, 414–432.

Wailoo, K. 2006. "Stigma, Race, and Disease in 20th Century America." *Lancet,* 367: 531–33.

Wen, C., P. Hudak and S. Hwang. 2007. "Homeless Peoples' Perceptions of Welcomeness and Unwelcomeness in Health Care Encounters." *Journal of General Internal Medicine,* 22: 1011–17.

Wolitski, R., S. Pals, D. Kidder, C. Courtenay-Quirk and D. Holtgrave. 2009. "The Effects of HIV Stigma on Health, Disclosure of HIV Status, and Risk Behavior of Homeless and Unstably Housed Persons Living with HIV." *AIDS Behavior,* 13(1): 1222–32.

Zickmund, S., E. Ho, M. Masuda, L. Ippolito and D. LaBrecque. 2003. "They Treated Me Like a Leper: Stigmatization and the Quality of Life of Patients with Hepatitis C." *Journal of General Internal Medicine,* 18: 835.

# CHAPTER 10

# Dignity in Design: The Siting and Design of Community and Shelter-Based Health Facilities for Homeless Persons

Ryan McNeil, PhD
British Columbia Centre for Excellence in HIV/AIDS
Faculty of Health Sciences, Simon Fraser University

Manal Guirguis-Younger, PhD
Faculty of Human Sciences, Saint Paul University

## Introduction

Community and shelter-based health services have emerged as one of the main strategies for improving the health of homeless persons in Canada. One of the earliest shelter-based health services, the Seaton House Annex Harm Reduction program in Toronto, has been in operation since 1997, and community and shelter-based health services have since followed in cities across Canada. These services are intended to reduce the impact of barriers preventing homeless persons from accessing services in hospitals and community clinics, such as geographic isolation, lack of identification cards and family physicians, feelings of unwelcomeness and long wait times (Hwang 2001; Podymow et al. 2006b; Podymow, Turnbull and Coyle 2006a; Wen, Hudak and Hwang 2007). Community and shelter-based health services have also been demonstrated to improve treatment compliance and health outcomes while reducing hospital stays and emergency room visits (Podymow et al. 2006b; Podymow, Turnbull and Coyle 2006a; Schwarz et al. 2008; Stergiopoulos et al. 2008) and play an increasingly prominent role in health services delivery in many Canadian cities. As a consequence, health services are now located in many settings not traditionally associated with health care delivery. This raises many questions for health and social services providers. For example, what are the perceived benefits of community and shelter-based health services delivery? How are community and shelter-based settings adapted in order to accommodate health services delivery? And what factors influence the design of community and shelter-based health facilities?

Although researchers have increasingly turned their attention toward the relationship between urban planning, design and health and human services delivery to homeless persons (Takahashi and Dear 1997; Graham, Walsh, and Sandalack 2008), these questions remain unanswered. A growing body of research has examined the impact of community opposition to health and human services facilities for homeless persons (see, e.g., Dear and Wolch 1987; Takahashi and Dear 1997; Strike, Myers and Millson 2004); factors affecting the siting of emergency shelters and facilities serving homeless clients, such as AIDS service organizations and needle exchange programs (see, e.g., Chiotti and Joseph 1995; Takahashi 1997; Takahashi and Dear 1997; Brinegar 2003; Datta 2005); and, lastly, the characteristics of optimum emergency shelter design (see, e.g., Davis 2004; Shier, Walsh and Graham 2007; Graham, Walsh and Sandalack 2008). Yet relatively little attention has been paid to how the social, political and built environment impact the siting *and* design of community and shelter-based health facilities, despite the steady growth in the number of these facilities over the past decade.

This chapter examines the interplay of the siting and design of community and shelter-based health facilities across Canada. It looks at the perceived benefits of community and shelter-based health facilities, including increased access to health services and responsiveness to the day-to-day challenges in shelters. It explores the siting of these facilities within the context of categories of urban space (see, e.g., Duncan 1978; Snow and Anderson 1993; Snow and Mulcahy 2001) to shed light on the factors that contain these facilities, as well as how agencies resist containment. It then considers the characteristics of community and shelter-based health facility design, drawing on previous research on emergency shelter design (see, e.g., Davis 2004; Shier, Walsh and Graham 2007; Graham, Walsh and Sandalack 2008). Lastly, this chapter discusses the implications of these findings for those involved in the development of these facilities. It is hoped that this chapter will help to improve the design of community and shelter-based health facilities and, as a result, health services delivery.

## Methods

The authors collected data between April 2007 and July 2008 as part of a study on health and end-of-life care services delivery to homeless persons. Homeless persons receive health services in a range of settings, including hospitals, community health clinics, emergency shelters and harm reduction facilities. The availability of these services is often affected by the local social, cultural and political context, which might or might not support the delivery of health services to this population. This study focused on identifying the characteristics that improved health services delivery to homeless persons, including the design of community and shelter-based health facilities. A section of the questionnaire included the questions about the impact of facility location and building design on health services delivery and clinical practice.

The authors collected data in Halifax, Hamilton, Ottawa, Thunder Bay, Toronto and Winnipeg. Existing relationships with health and social services providers in Ottawa and Toronto helped to facilitate participant recruitment in those cities. Research assistants developed an annotated directory of organizations providing health and social services to homeless persons in Halifax, Hamilton, Thunder Bay and Winnipeg that helped the authors identify key informants in those cities. Potential participants were sent letters outlining the study and inviting them to participate. Fifty-four individuals agreed to participate in this study, including physicians, nurses, social workers, mental health professionals and program directors. All participants worked either full- or part-time in community or shelter-based settings. Semi-structured interviews were conducted with participants at their place of employment or off-site, if they preferred to be interviewed elsewhere. One section of the interview guide concentrated on facility design. Participants were invited to discuss the development of their organizations, how their facilities help or do not help them work effectively with homeless persons and how their facilities may be modified to improve health services delivery. These questions were structured so as to address the questions raised in the chapter introduction. Interviews ranged in length between forty-five minutes and two hours. Informed consent was obtained at the time of the interview.

Interviews were audio recorded and transcribed verbatim. Data were coded using NVivo qualitative data analysis software (version 8) to identify preliminary themes. Analysis focused on the siting and design of community and shelter-based health facilities, as well as their impact on health services delivery to homeless persons. A coding tree was developed based on these preliminary themes and used to recode data. Hard copies of the coding summaries were reviewed by the authors and used to make further refinements to the coding tree in order to better explicate themes. Once the final categories were established, the authors recoded a section of the data to verify theoretical validity.

The authors identified the perceived benefits of community and shelter-based health services delivery to homeless persons. They then identified two general categories: (1) the siting of community and shelter-based health facilities and (2) the design of community and shelter-based health facilities. Each of these categories includes several sub-categories that identify characteristics that might optimize the design of health facilities and contextualize the challenges that health and social services providers encounter in planning and developing them.

## Findings

### Perceived Benefits of Community and Shelter-Based Health Facilities

Community and shelter-based health services delivery was perceived as an important strategy for improving access to health services for homeless persons. Participants described how community and shelter-based services reduced geographical barriers to health services for homeless persons, as well as responded to the day-to-day challenges encountered by homeless service organizations. In addition, participants indicated that community and shelter-based health services facilitated the development of interdisciplinary strategies to meet the health and social care needs of homeless persons.

**Strategy to overcome geographical barriers to health services.** Participants described how community and shelter-based health services allowed them to overcome many of the geographical barriers that prevent homeless persons from accessing health services. One of the main barriers that many participants identified was the inaccessibility of hospitals and clinics. Many participants observed that hospitals in their communities were located in residential or isolated areas. They noted that many homeless persons were unable to access services because they had reduced mobility or were not healthy enough to walk to hospitals or clinics and could not afford to take public transit. One emergency shelter director recalled:

> I remember several years ago in our old place, watching an elderly gentleman that had taken his socks off. I saw his bare feet. He was suffering from diabetes and his feet looked like black clubs. I said, "You need to go to the hospital and get those looked at." He just refused. And one level in my naïveté I thought, what happened if I had feet like that? Would I walk to the hospital?

These neighbourhoods also lacked services used by homeless persons to meet daily survival needs, such as soup kitchens and emergency shelters. Participants observed that community and shelter-based health services, on the other hand, had the potential to minimize these barriers because these services were already a part of the daily patterns of homeless persons. These services were thus perceived as a strategy to overcome geographical barriers by, as one nurse stated, "Meeting clients where they are, wherever they are comfortable."

**Responding to day-to-day challenges in shelter settings.** Integrating health services into emergency shelters was not only identified as an optimum strategy for addressing the complex health and social care needs of homeless persons but also as a necessity due to the health challenges of the homeless population. Participants reported that emergency shelter clients had complex health needs—or, as one nurse practitioner observed, were the "sickest of the sick"—that shelter staff lacked the training to address. This contributed to adverse outcomes, including client deaths. An agency director recalled:

> Agency Director: They'd come here at night and we'd find, we'd find a dead body at least once a month, in the beds here. They'd be people that would be sick, and the other thing they'd do is that they'd either take a whole bunch of pills some nights, so some of them would just overdose and say 'I'm out of here'. Some of them would just drink, and drink, and drink. Some of them would mix the two, and I'm sure their deaths were accidental. But people who were sick would just not go to the hospital then.
>
> Interviewer: How did you deal with that at the time?

> Agency Director: *It was really hard on staff. The cleaners got so they wouldn't want to go upstairs. I mean really, it was really difficult. . . . We were doing this work and nobody was trained. I don't even think we did a good grieving piece after. Some young cleaner finding two bodies in a month and saying to him, "Are you okay?"*

One factor that exacerbated this situation was poor discharge planning—or, to be more specific, the practice at some hospitals of discharging homeless patients directly to shelters or the street. Many participants reported that this commonly happened, despite the fact that many emergency shelters lacked the capacity to care for these clients. Another agency director recalled:

> *We recently had a death here at the shelter of a gentleman who came to us mentally ill. He was really a mess. He was discharged [from hospital] to us at 11 p.m. on a Friday evening and he was not well at all. My staff had big concerns with him, but they kept him here. He was exhibiting signs of his mental illness and he was dead by 1 a.m. the next morning. He went and committed suicide over here.*

Participants identified cases such as these as one of the driving forces behind the development of shelter-based health services.

Furthermore, several participants reported that community and shelter-based health services responded to clients' desire to receive health services in shelter settings. An agency director recalled, "*[The client] came and asked if he could die here. He knew he had AIDS. He knew he was going to be dying, and he did not want to go into the hospital.*" Previous research has, likewise, suggested that emergency shelters are a preferred site of usual care for homeless persons and result in higher levels of satisfaction with care received (O'Toole et al. 1999). However, participants of this study went further and reported that shelters were often a preferred site for receiving palliative care because clients considered dying in the shelter to be dying at home. As a consequence, many participants felt that it was important to develop these services in order to accommodate these wishes.

**Harmonizing health and social services delivery.** Integrating health services into community and shelter-based settings harmonized health and social services delivery, allowing both health and social services providers to benefit from greater access to potential clients.

Many participants reported that they were able to gain access to new clients and provide them with services responsive to their needs, while maintaining continuity with health or social services received in other settings. For example, participants referred clients directly to services delivered on-site—or by nearby community agencies—and had clients referred to them by these services. One of the added benefits of this, according to participants, is that they were able to better respond to changes in the health status of clients. For example, a program manager observed:

> *Often with our Managed Alcohol people, they will do very poorly. If we can't care for them in that setting, we will move them to the hospice and then often stabilize them. I'd say 50 percent of them stabilize enough to come back.*

Participants observed of this continuity helped them to develop interdisciplinary strategies to address client needs and implement these strategies across settings.

### Siting Health Facilities for Homeless Persons

The siting of community and shelter-based health facilities is impacted by the interplay of community values, health systems, infrastructure and the distribution of homeless persons. This interplay is most evident in the factors that contribute to the siting of community and shelter-based health facilities in prime and marginal spaces—that is, areas that have use value to the majority of community members and areas that have little or no use value to the majority of community members, respectively (Duncan 1978; Snow and Anderson 1993). It is useful, then, as a point of departure, to identify the strategies that contribute to the successful siting of community and shelter-based health facilities in each these categories of urban space, as well as the challenges encountered.

**Siting facilities in marginal spaces.** Marginal spaces have little or no use or economic value to the majority of community members and, as a consequence, are largely abandoned to homeless persons and other marginalized populations (Duncan 1978; Snow and Anderson 1993; Snow and Mulcahy 2001). Many of the common characteristics of marginal spaces, such as high concentrations of homeless service organizations, single-room occupancy hotels and abandoned buildings (Snow and Anderson 1993; Snow and Mulcahy 2001), were apparent in neighbourhoods with community and shelter-based health facilities. In fact, the majority of community and shelter-based health facilities surveyed in this study were concentrated in marginal spaces—or, to be more specific, in impoverished inner-city neighbourhoods or near industrial areas. But what accounts for the concentration of these facilities in these spaces?

In many cases, participants reported that these were the only spaces available to them for facilities due to community opposition to their facilities in other neighbourhoods. One participant, for example, remarked that when his organization attempted to move to a downtown area, local business owners persuaded the city to deny their re-zoning application. Another participant noted that the only site that the city agreed to zone for the facility was in a poor neighbourhood, adjacent to a highway on-ramp. Participants, however, noted that these locations were not without their benefits. They reported that the siting of community and shelter-based health facilities in marginal spaces often improved their capacity to deliver health services to homeless persons—whom they reported were largely concentrated in these areas—while minimizing community opposition. One of the key benefits of siting community and shelter-based facilities in marginal spaces, according to participants, is that they are most likely to be frequented by homeless persons. Participants believed that this increased their visibility and, hence, their accessibility to clients and potential clients. For example, many participants reported that they were better able to provide services to clients on the street, as well as advertise their services to potential clients, due to their location. A nurse recalled:

> We walk our catchment area with harm reduction kits. We hand out kits, socks, whatever, but we're also there to advertise the nursing clinics. We'll walk by most, if not all, of the shelters at some point in our outreach, plus we'll do alleys and places we know people are—parks in the summer—so in that way we're able to advertise our clinic and what we do and it's all within walking distance.

Other participants reported that their close proximity to single-room occupancy hotels and low-cost housing helped them provide services to clients at risk of homeless and, in several cases, provide them with health services that helped them maintain housing. Another nurse noted:

*We've had palliative people in [the social housing complex] right beside us, which is this big high rise. Those are people who are going to come to us, but are still able to remain in their own home. CCAC [Community Care Access Centre] alerts us of those people, or the community agencies will.*

Another key benefit, according to participants, is that siting community and shelter-based health facilities in marginal spaces results in reduced community opposition. Participants reported little opposition to their facilities and, in some cases, noted that their cities seemed most receptive to siting their facilities in these areas. This echoes previous research suggesting that these neighbourhoods are least opposed to homeless service organizations, but, while this research—and, indeed, several participants—warns that this might result in service-dependent ghettos (Wolch and Dear 1993), the majority of participants emphasized the benefits of increased access to clients and lower rent and property costs. Several participants suggested that low rent and property costs played a crucial role in allowing them to expand and diversify their services in order to increase their responsiveness to the needs of their target population. An agency director of a recently relocated inner-city shelter recalled:

*When we bought this building, we bought it with the idea that it could do a lot of programs that weren't being done. As we developed the first floor, our architect drew up the floor plans and he had a large space that was supposed to be used for storage for our clothing bank. But, as our construction guys were building it, I said just leave that space alone because someday I am going to have a health centre there.*

**Siting facilities in prime space.** A small number of community and shelter-based facilities in cities surveyed in this study were located in prime space—that is, areas with use or exchange value to most community members, including spaces used for residential, economic and navigational purposes (Duncan 1978; Snow and Anderson 1993). These organizations typically had long histories—in some cases, reaching back more than one hundred years—and remained in their locations even as the surrounding areas gentrified, while others were affiliated with hospitals or community health clinics. Participants reported community opposition to these facilities was most likely due to negative attitudes toward homeless persons among people living in these neighbourhoods, which is a well-documented dynamic of community opposition to homeless services facilities (Takahashi and Dear 1997; Takahashi 1997). However, they also identified strategies that minimized the impact of community opposition. One of the key strategies involved shifting the terms of the debate by emphasizing that the organizations provided health services, not emergency housing. A nurse at a community-based health facility recalled:

> Nurse: *[Community members] were afraid that this was going to be a shelter and there would be lots of homeless people roaming the neighbourhood, possibly breaking into their houses. That was what their greatest concern was and, note, today we haven't had a single complaint in fifteen months.*
>
> Interviewer: *What were some strategies that were used to overcome that perception?*
>
> Nurse: *We held a community meeting where about 300 people showed up. The Executive Director of [Community Ministry Organization] spoke. The program manager of [the proposed facility] spoke about the program. I spoke about the program and the alderman of the neighbourhood spoke in favour of the program. He got it and explained to his constituents that it's not a shelter, it's a residential facility.*

Another strategy was to site health services in existing facilities—or, to be more specific, to integrate health services into emergency shelters. Participants reported that doing so allowed their organizations to expand and diversify their services, while avoiding applications for re-zoning and community opposition.

### Designing Community and Shelter-Based Health Facilities

Participants reported that the design of community and shelter-based health facilities has a significant impact on the delivery of health services to homeless persons. Participants identified design features of the community and shelter-based health facilities that improved the delivery of services to their target populations, as well as shortcomings that prevented some clients from accessing services.

**Using building design to promote client confidentiality.** Participants reported that buildings ought to promote client confidentiality by blending in with the surrounding neighbourhoods. Many of the buildings visited by the authors were consistent with the architectural style of their neighbourhoods, because existing buildings had been renovated to accommodate health and social services delivery, while newer buildings had been designed to blend in with their surroundings. Participants believed that this consistency with neighbourhood design helped to promote client confidentiality by making it less obvious to passersby that clients entering and exiting the building were homeless. Participants reported additional design features that helped clients remain anonymous—something that, according to participants, is particularly important when providing services to stigmatized populations, such as persons living with HIV/AIDS, sex workers and injection drug users. For example, many buildings did not post signs on their property identifying their organization. One social worker remarked:

> If you notice outside of the building, there are no signs that say HIV and AIDS. Some people feel comfortable coming here and we're kind of out of the area of the HIV circle. Most of it is on [street name]. Well we're a little outside of it so people do feel comfortable coming here.

Nondescript entrances helped clients to retain anonymity. A harm reduction specialist noted that having separate entrances at a community clinic allowed clients to access harm reduction services while remaining anonymous to clients receiving other services. The use of one-way glass also ensured that these clients could not be seen by passersby.

**Improving accessibility for clients.** Participants reported that physical disabilities might decrease the ability of homeless persons to access their facilities, if appropriate actions were not taken improve accessibility. Many buildings included ramps, automatic doors, elevators and wide doorways. Participants reported that these mobility aids helped them work with clients. A nurse explained how these mobility aids improved client care:

> They have a wheelchair right in the shower—everything now is so user-friendly and easy. Before, how were we to get a person down the stairs to shower them? That's what we were faced with. You took them into the bathroom and pretty much hosed them down in the bathroom and sponged bathed them. It has only been in the last few years that we

*have had an elevator. You used to have to go down a very steep flight to the bathroom, so it wasn't about [the client's] problems. . . . We needed a place that is full serviced, that provides all the level of care of all the other agencies.*

Several of the facilities the authors toured were less accessible, and participants reported challenges providing care to clients. Participants drew attention to the fact that they had difficulty providing services to clients in wheelchairs and, in some cases, could not provide them with services. The challenges of an intake coordinator and outreach worker illustrate the challenges faced:

Intake coordinator: *There are certain things I have to think about in this house. Because three of the rooms at the back of the house have four steep steps to get to them, those ones can only be used by people who are mobile enough to get up the stairs to the elevator. I have to look at mobility.*

Outreach worker: *We just don't have the resources to be as inclusive as we'd like. As you notice there's no ramp out front but we do have actually several clients that are confined to wheelchairs. There are so many different types of sex workers.*

**Using safety precautions and security systems to ensure staff safety.** Another important consideration is staff safety, which many participants identified as a chief concern. These participants reported that, due to the high incidence of mental illness and addiction among clients, they believed that safety precautions needed to be taken. Many of the facilities had complex security systems, including security cameras and safety buttons, and sightlines allowing staff to monitor the facilities. Several participants indicated that this minimized the likelihood of disruptions, as well as the impact of these events. Several facilities, however, lacked safety precautions, and participants in these settings reported concerns about personal safety. For example, a physician explained:

*There's a safety concern amongst physicians on an individual level, which I think can be a pretty intimidating environment to step into. You're dealing with a pretty rough clientele and you're in a setting that is fairly variable. The offices we work in aren't set up with individual safety in mind. When you work in isolation many of the times, we can't just have someone in the room when we're dealing with sensitive issues. The office that I work in is at the end of a hallway behind two closed doors and I've asked over and over again for a safety button to be put in there to call for help.*

Participants who perceived themselves as being at risk due to the absence of safety precautions and security reported higher levels of stress—in some cases, implying a link to staff burnout.

**Improving the design of clinical spaces.** Participants reported that, because of the wide range of functions carried out in their settings, clinical spaces needed to provide sufficient space and flexibility to serve multiple purposes. Many of these spaces were originally intended only for treatment and rehabilitation but also needed to address unanticipated health and social care needs. A nursing station at a shelter-based facility, for example, had originally been intended to serve mainly clinical functions, such as intake, charting and dispensing medication, but in practice served a variety of other functions, including preparing meals, organizing social activities and, often, monitoring the movement of clients in and out of the shelter. When the facility was later redesigned, the nursing station was expanded in order to better accommodate this wide range of functions. Other clinical spaces, including exam rooms and offices, often had to be flexible in order to meet client needs and address emergency situations. Participants reported that the space and flexibility to move equipment, including beds and medical equipment, in and out of rooms improved the efficiency and efficacy of clinical spaces.

**Using private rooms to help clients feel 'at home'.** Multiple participants reported that the design of their facilities helped clients feel 'at home'. Many of these facilities not only had a home-like atmosphere—that is, they were located in formerly residential buildings—but also provided clients with private or semi-private rooms. Participants indicated that providing clients, many of whom had lived on the streets and in shelters for decades, with private and semi-private rooms helped them feel 'at home', leading to greater satisfaction with care. Participants explained that clients were often pleasantly surprised to find out that they would have a private room and, in some cases, expressed that they wished they had arrived there sooner. A nurse remarked:

*Some of them would think that our hospice is like heaven—I mean, it's just beautiful. They're amazed that they have a private room and they're amazed they have a TV. They're amazed they've got a beautiful dresser to put their things in and that there's endless juice and there's endless coffee, you know.*

Furthermore, multiple participants observed that, because palliative clients considered their facilities to be their home, they wanted them to be their place of death. A program manager observed:

*What we have really noticed is that some of our long-term residents— who have been with our organization for the last 10 or 15 years—don't necessarily want to go. We have been trying to do our very best in maintaining a place of dignity for them during their last days, but it is not easy.*

Participants, therefore, suggested that private rooms and a welcoming environment allowed clients to construct home spaces.

**Using common areas to create a social atmosphere.** Participants reported that common areas, such as television rooms and lounges, improved the atmosphere in residential care settings by allowing staff to host social activities, as well as facilitating relationship-building among clients and staff. Many of the facilities that provided complex long-term care had multiple common areas. Common areas allowed participants to host a range of social activities, including teas, movie nights and games, as well as provide a venue for unstructured interaction between clients. One clinical manager explained how this helped to create a caring atmosphere among clients:

*I watched them play bingo the other day and I thought this is so much more than bingo. Bingo is one thing, but the fact that they're all together in the room, that they're respectful of the caller, that they're quietly playing bingo, that it's something to test their mind, right, their ability to connect. One of the guys in the room he's mentally ill, he has dementia and he has HIV, and they set him up and he has a card and he has a dabber and he has a snack and he can't dab the numbers but he's there with them. And so she'll bring out a prize and maybe they'll be two prizes and one of them is like a chocolate bar and she'll say to the group, "Can [client name] have the chocolate bar?" And they'll all say, "Yeah that's okay." Like he didn't win it but he can have it, so then they give the chocolate bar to him.*

But also, multiple participants described how creating a caring atmosphere improved the self-efficacy of clients. They reported several ways in which clients became increasingly engaged in the day-to-day operations in their setting by volunteering, helping each other and taking a leadership role in social programming. One program coordinator observed:

*I think that the atmosphere now is a very uplifting, very positive atmosphere. It is a very family-like atmosphere. It has come a long way over the last seven years. We have a resident mayor. So, they elect their own mayor. They have resident meetings. If they have any issues, they will go the mayor. The mayor will come to us. As I mentioned with Social Initiative the volunteering is very important part of the program. They have certain residents that make breakfast every day with staff supervision. Make lunch, make dinner, do all of the laundry, clean the sheets, and disinfect the mattresses. They really have taken a sense of ownership of their own program.*

**Aligning design with organizational values.** Participants explained that the design of health care facilities should be congruent with the values of their organizations. This included mandates to provide homeless persons with the same quality of care as the housed population received but in a way that is congruent with organizational values and the experiences of homeless persons. One health administrator observed:

*We just painted our office. It's freshly painted and we put new rugs down. For the first five years that we were here, we just had primer on the walls. We've never had paint before. It's a big symbolic thing, to get paint but, you know, that is how our clients live. It's very hand to mouth and it hasn't done us any harm. I do think that there's a certain way that a program that works with the clinically homeless needs to be. We can't have big fancy offices. It is just incongruent with the work that we're doing.*

## Summary and Implications

Community and shelter-based health services are an important strategy for improving the health of homeless persons in Canada and, as the recent growth in the number of these services suggests, they play an increasingly vital role in health services delivery to this population. In this chapter, the authors have explored the context of community and shelter-based health services delivery, drawing attention to the fact that it developed out of necessity to address the dire situation in many emergency shelters and offered an opportunity to overcome barriers that homeless persons face to accessing traditional services. Previous research echoes these claims and points also to the demonstrated cultural competence that community and shelter-based health services have in providing care to homeless persons (Podymow et al. 2006b; Podymow, Turnbull and Coyle 2006a; Guirguis-Younger, McNeil and Runnels 2009).

This chapter also examines the impact of community opposition to the siting of facilities serving homeless clients and, as a result, can be situated within the growing literature on this topic (Wolch and Dear 1993; Takahashi 1997; Brinegar 2003; Strike, Myers and Millson 2004; DeVerteuil 2006). Previous research has charted the evolution of the 'Not In My Backyard' (NIMBY) syndrome and discrimination against homeless persons on the basis that they are dangerous, undeserving of services and hurt property values (Takahashi 1997; Takahashi and Dear 1997). This body of research has drawn attention to strategies that communities have used to limit the development and expansion of health and human services facilities, such as the use of zoning by-laws, echoing statements made by study participants (Smith 1998; Brinegar 2003; Ranasinge and Valverde 2006). But, as is the case when the need is so great, these facilities are built and this chapter has outlined some of the considerations of the siting of these facilities. Of note, although facilities are often pushed into marginal spaces, they might benefit from closer proximity to potential clients. Also, siting health facilities in shelters might allow organizations to circumvent community opposition.

Lastly, this chapter explored the characteristics that might improve the design of community and shelter-based health facilities. Several of these characteristics have been previous described in the literature on emergency shelter design (Davis 2004; Shier, Walsh and Graham 2007; Graham, Walsh and Sandalack 2008). This research identified several characteristics of optimum shelter design that were also described in this chapter, including using building design to promote client confidentiality and improving accessibility for clients (Shier, Walsh and Graham 2007; Graham, Walsh and Sandalack 2008). This chapter, however, is the first to describe these characteristics within the context of health facilities for homeless persons and consequently identified previously overlooked characteristics. These include the characteristics that improve clinical services and increase client satisfaction and self-efficacy, such as flexible clinical spaces, private rooms and social spaces. Together, these findings have several key implications for decision-makers and future research.

First, this chapter documents some of the factors that have contributed to the evolution of shelter and community-based health services in Canada. It situates their emergence within the context of the health needs of the client population, as well as the Canadian social and political environment. This is an important factor that helps us better understand *why* these facilities emerged and the problems that they were intended to address.

Second, these findings have the potential to inform the development of community and shelter-based health facilities. They identify characteristics that planners, designers and decision-makers might want to consider in order to optimize the design of these facilities. For example, what impact would health services have on the operations of the shelter? What changes need to be made to the building to accommodate health services? Is community opposition to the proposed facility expected and, if so, what can be done to minimize its impact? Is the proposed facility accessible to potential clients? Does the building promote client confidentiality? And does the facility account for the personal and social needs of potential clients?

Lastly, this research opens up the possibility for future research on the design of facilities intended for use by homeless and marginalized populations. There are many questions regarding the impact of health facility design on the health of homeless and marginalized populations that go unanswered. For example, how do private rooms affect the health of homeless clients? What characteristics do clients feel are most important about these facilities? What changes do they feel would improve them? It is hoped that this chapter represents a step in this direction and will pave the way for future improvements in the design of community and shelter-based health facilities.

## References

Brinegar, S. 2003. "The Social Construction of Homeless Shelters in the Phoenix Area." *Urban Geography,* 24(1): 61–74.

Chiotti, Q. P. and A. E. Joseph. 1995. "Casey House: Interpreting the Location of a Toronto AIDS Hospice." *Social Science & Medicine,* 41(1): 131–40.

Datta, A. 2005. "'Homed' in Arizona: The Architecture of Emergency Shelters." *Urban Geography,* 26(6): 536–57.

Davis, S. 2004. *Designing for the Homeless: Architecture That Works.* Berkeley, CA: University of California Press.

Dear, M. J. and J. R. Wolch. 1987. *Landscapes of Despair: From Deinstitutionalization to Homelessness.* Cambridge: Polity Press.

DeVerteuil, G. 2006. "The Local State and Homeless Shelters: Beyond Revanchism?" *Cities,* 23(2): 109–20.

Duncan, J. 1978. "Men without Property: The Tramp's Classification and Use of Urban Space." *Antipode,* 10: 24–34.

Graham, J. R., C. Walsh and B. Sandalack. 2008. *Design Considerations for Shelters for the Homeless.* Calgary: Detselig Enterprises Ltd..

Guirguis-Younger, M., R. McNeil and V. Runnels. 2009. "Learning and Knowledge Integration Strategies of Nurses and Client Care Workers Serving Homeless Persons." *Canadian Journal of Nursing Research,* 41(2): 20–34.

Hwang, S. W. 2001. "Homelessness and Health." *Canadian Medical Association Journal,* 164(2): 229–33.

O'Toole, T. P., J. L. Gibbon, B. H. Hanusa and M. J. Fine. 1999. "Preferences for Sites of Care among Urban Homeless and Housed Poor Adults." *Journal of General Internal Medicine,* 14: 599–605.

Podymow, T., J. Turnbull and D. Coyle. 2006a. "Shelter-Based Palliative Care for the Homeless Terminally Ill." *Palliative Medicine,* 20(2): 81–86.

Podymow, T., J. Turnbull, D. Coyle, E. Yetisir and G. Wells. 2006b. "Shelter-Based Managed Alcohol Administration to Chronically Homeless People Addicted to Alcohol." *Canadian Medical Association Journal,* 174(1): 45–49.

Ranasinghe, P. and M. Valverde. 2006. "Governing Homelessness through Land-Use: A Sociolegal Study of the Toronto Shelter Zoning By-Law." *Canadian Journal of Sociology,* 31(3): 325–49.

Schwarz, K., B. Garrett, J. Lee, D. Thompson, T. Thiel et al. 2008. "Positive Impact of a Shelter-Based Hepatitis B Vaccine Program in Homeless Baltimore Children and Adolescents." *Journal of Urban Health,* 85(2): 228–38.

Shier, M., C. A. Walsh and J. R. Graham. 2007. "Conceptualizing Optimum Homeless Shelter Service Delivery: The Interconnection between

Programming, Community, and the Built Environment." *Canadian Journal of Urban Studies,* 16(1): 58–75.

Smith, N. 1998. "Giuliani Time: The Revanchist 1990s." *Social Text,* 57: 1–20.

Snow, D. A. and L. Anderson. 1993. *Down on Their Luck: A Study of Homeless Street People.* Berkeley, CA: University of California Press.

Snow, D. A. and M. Mulcahy. 2001. "Space, Politics, and Survival Strategies of the Homeless." *American Behavioral Scientist,* 45(1): 149–69.

Stergiopoulos, V., C. S. Dewa, K. Rouleau, S. Yoder and N. Chau. 2008. "Collaborative Mental Health Care for the Homeless: The Role of Psychiatry in Positive Housing and Mental Health Outcomes." *Canadian Journal of Psychiatry,* 53(1): 61–67.

Strike, C. J., T. Myers and M. Millson. 2004. "Finding a Place for Needle Exchange Programs." *Critical Public Health,* 14(3): 261–75.

Takahashi, L. M. 1997. "The Socio-spatial Stigmatization of Homelessness and HIV/AIDS: Toward an Explanation of the NIMBY Syndrome." *Social Science & Medicine,* 45(6): 903–14.

Takahashi, L. M. and M. J. Dear. 1997. "The Changing Dynamics of Community Opposition to Human Service Facilities." *Journal of the American Planning Association,* 63(1): 79–93.

Wen, C., P. Hudak and S. W. Hwang. 2007. "Homeless People's Perceptions of Welcomeness and Unwelcomeness in Healthcare Encounters." *Journal of General Internal Medicine,* 22(7): 1011–17.

Wolch, J. and M. J. Dear. 1993. *Malign Neglect: Homelessness in an American City.* San Francisco, CA: Jossey Bass Publishers.

PART III

# NEW APPROACHES: INNOVATIONS TO ADDRESS HOMELESSNESS & HEALTH

# CHAPTER 11

# An Examination of the Delivery of Psychiatric Services within a Shelter-Based Management of Alcohol Program for Homeless Adults

Susan Farrell, PhD, CPsych
Royal Ottawa Health Care Group

Beth Wood, MScN, ACNP
Royal Ottawa Health Care Group

Heather King-Andrews, PhD candidate
Institute of Population Health, University of Ottawa

Donna Lougheed, MD, FRCPC
Royal Ottawa Health Care Group

Wendy Muckle, RN, MHA
Ottawa Inner City Health

Lynn Burnett, RN
Ottawa Inner City Health

Jeff Turnbull, MD
Ottawa Inner City Health
The Ottawa Hospital

## Introduction

Approximately one in five Canadians will have a dual disorder (mental illness and substance use disorder, commonly termed 'concurrent disorder' in Canada) in their lifetime (CAMH 2001). Yet there is a paucity of research on the delivery of, or measurement of the impact of, efficacious concurrent treatment (Drake et al. 1998; Mercier and Beaucage 1997; RachBeisel, Scott and Dixon 1999). Rates of concurrent disorders among the homeless population in Ottawa are estimated at 60 to 70 percent of the population (Farrell 2003;

Farrell et al. 2000), in comparison to incidence estimates of 18 percent in the housed population (CAMH 2001). Persons with concurrent disorders are one of the fastest growing groups of the homeless population as the rates of substance use and the detection of mental illness are increasing (Barreira et al. 2000; Mayes and Handley 2005; Nuttbrock et al. 1998; Rosenblum et al. 2002). This population represents an extensive cost to the health care system due to their frequent need for acute health care and their demonstrated difficulty accessing and remaining attached to existing models of service delivery (Burnam et al. 1995; Tsemberis, Gulcur and Nakae 2004).

Treatment programs for homeless persons with substance abuse problems have been found to be effective for those whose goal is abstaining from substance use (Hwang et al. 2005). However, it remains a challenge to work with persons who wish to address but not stop their substance use. Harm reduction is the focus of treatment used most often for those who do not wish to stop substance use (Baer, Peterson and Wells 2004). *Harm reduction* is an umbrella term for the variety of practices used to reduce the negative consequences of substance use and promote improved quality of life while incorporating a spectrum of strategies from safer use to managed use to abstinence (Harm Reduction Coalition 2003). Marlatt and Witkiewitz (2010) note that the primary goal of harm reduction is to minimize the harmful effects of behaviours related to substance use. These may include health risks, psychosocial risks or criminal involvement. As noted by Pauly and colleagues (2007), the adoption of a harm reduction philosophy has been primarily within street outreach, inner-city health care centres, needle exchange programs and, more recently, supervised injection sites. This chapter focuses on harm reduction within an emergency shelter, particularly on persons who have a concurrent disorder of alcohol dependence and mental illness.

Harm reduction programs with a housing focus such as Housing First have been implemented to assist homeless individuals with psychiatric illness and substance abuse problems to attain a residence (Gulcur et al. 2003; Tsemberis, Gulcur and Nakae 2004; Tsemberis et al. 2003). Some housing programs had aids to sustain housing, such as substance abuse and/or mental health treatments (Bebout 1999; Blankertz and Cnaan 1994). Other harm reduction programs that have been developed and implemented for homeless individuals have been mental health and substance abuse treatments (Tsemberis et al. 2003).

Despite literature on the key principles of harm reduction being pragmatism, humanistic values, focus on harms, balancing costs and benefits and hierarchy of goals (Riley et al. 1999), which should be agreed-upon principles within universal health care, harm reduction has been a controversial issue. Harm reduction has been described by its critics as promoting continued substance use (Buchanan et al. 2003). Advocates of harm reduction, by contrast, support it as a model for reducing the detrimental effects of substance abuse rather than promoting abstinence from substances (Davis et al. 2006; Pauly et al. 2007). Harm reduction strategies have been most prominent in initiatives for injection drug users (Wood et al. 2004), although the need for harm reduction strategies for persons with alcohol abuse has been recognized (Health Canada 2001). Interestingly, although there has been some initial opposition to harm reduction practices for alcohol use (Svoboda 2009), this has not been considered as controversial as harm reduction practices and programs for injection drug use (MacPhee 2006/2007; Wood et al. 2003), despite several studies showing evaluation results for safe injection sites including social and health-related improvements and no detrimental effects for users or the community. Although the reasons are not clearly known, a possible explanation for the decreased level of controversy for harm reduction for alcohol is that alcohol use is not illegal, unlike injection drug use. Similar evaluations of the effects of harm reduction for alcohol use programs are less common and none to date have focused on the partnership of harm reduction and psychiatric services to address concurrent disorders (Hass 2001; Podymow et al. 2006).

Harm reduction for alcohol (or managed alcohol) programs for homeless persons exist within a few emergency shelters in Canadian cities. As noted by Svoboda (2009), a coroner's inquest into the death of three homeless men in Toronto who had uncontrolled heavy alcohol use and mental illness in 1996 led to jury recommendations for a 24-hour-in-shelter harm reduction program to be provided within an emergency shelter. Known as The Annex, and located within Toronto's largest homeless shelter (Seaton House), this managed alcohol program has been found to reduce emergency room and detoxification unit visits, as well as police interactions (Svobodoa 2010). What has not been investigated within the Canadian harm reduction literature is the impact on client characteristics of offering concurrent psychiatric treatment for concurrent disorders within a management of alcohol model program. This is the focus of the present chapter, which examines the Ottawa Inner City Health (OICH) Managed Alcohol Program (MAP), in which individuals who are homeless with substance dependence reside within a shelter in a closed harm reduction program and receive concurrent psychiatric services.

## Ottawa Inner City Health—Management of Alcohol Program (MAP)

Ottawa Inner City was developed in 2001 as a unique model of providing health care to persons who are homeless with complex health needs (Podymow et al. 2006). One of the component programs of Ottawa Inner City Health is the Management of Alcohol Program (MAP), which is a 25-bed residential harm-reduction program located on a separated unit within an emergency shelter. The program is designed for persons who are homeless and have a long history of alcohol use and limited success with other attempts to control their drinking, plus frequent or prolonged experiences of homelessness, and who are identified as a frequent disruption in the community (as defined by frequent contact with police or disruption to local merchants or residents due to public intoxication). Clients reside in a designated floor of the emergency shelter that is staffed by client care workers and has a medical staff of physicians and nurses available for 24-hour care. Clients are served a regulated amount of wine during the day (one standard serving per hour, 13.6 grams of alcohol) in an attempt to both regulate their alcohol consumption (70% of clients reported daily or weekly binge drinking before admission to MAP) and as a harm reduction approach to decrease their consumption of non-beverage alcohol (e.g., mouthwash, aftershave, hair spray) (Hass 2001). Both substituting a less dangerous ingested substance and monitoring the intake of the substance contribute to minimizing personal harm and adverse social effects from substance use (Hass 2001). The first small sample outcome study of MAP ('before and after' design of 17 participants) found a significant decrease in the number of emergency room visits and encounters with police for clients after admission to the program (Podymow et al. 2006). However, the initial study did not account for whether MAP clients had been diagnosed with mental illness.

Shortly after the inception of MAP, program staff recognized that many of the clients had symptoms of concurrent psychiatric illnesses (mainly psychotic and depressive disorders). At that point, psychiatric services (offered by an Advance Practice Nurse, Psychiatry, of the Psychiatric Outreach Team of the Royal Ottawa Health Care Group) were introduced into the program. The Psychiatric Outreach Team is a multidisciplinary team developed to provide specialized mental health services directly to individuals with serious mental illness and/or concurrent disorders who are homeless. The advance practice nurse (APN) role was designed to deliver psychiatric services (under the medical directives of the team psychiatrist) to provide assessment, pharmacological treatment and education to clients and staff about mental illness and concurrent disorders. This was the first known on-site delivery of psychiatric services within a residential management of alcohol program. This unique model of introducing psychiatric services to a management of alcohol program, therefore, requires further investigation and evaluation. Health Canada (2001) identified the need to understand best practices in concurrent disorders for vulnerable, underserved populations such as persons who were homeless, yet noted that this evaluation research was not available in Canada.

The purpose of the present study was to examine the effects of delivering psychiatric services within a shelter-based management of alcohol program for homeless adults. Given this new area for investigation, outcomes for investigation were selected in consultation with an advisory committee that consisted of program staff, client representatives and community service providers. The effects of delivering concurrent psychiatric services in a MAP was examined by investigating the effects of program participation on changes over time in psychiatric symptoms, mental status, global functioning, aggression, quality of life and consumption of alcohol and alcohol substitutes for participants in the MAP.

Directional hypotheses were assumed for each of the clinical outcomes over time. Specifically, it was hypothesized that: (1) Clients receiving psychiatric services during their residence in the MAP will have a decrease in the severity of their psychiatric symptoms (as measured by the Brief Psychiatric Rating Scale [BPRS]); (2) Clients receiving psychiatric services during their residence in the MAP will have an increase in their cognitive functioning (as measured by the Mini Mental State Examination [MMSE]); (3) Clients receiving psychiatric services during their residence in the MAP will have an increase in their mental health–related functioning (as measured by the Global

Assessment of Functioning [GAF]); (4) Clients receiving psychiatric services during their residence in the MAP will have a decrease in the frequency of their aggressive behaviour (as measured by the Cohen-Mansfield Agitation Inventory [CMAI]); (5) Clients receiving psychiatric services during their residence in the MAP will have an increase in both their subjective quality of life (client ratings of domains) and providers' perception of their quality of life (as rated by the Wisconsin Quality of Life Index, client and provider forms [W-QLI]); (6) Clients receiving psychiatric services during their residence in the MAP will have a decrease in their consumption of alcohol and alcohol substitutes.

## Methods

### Participants
All clients of the Ottawa Inner City Health's MAP were considered for the project. All participants in this study were already admitted to MAP when approached for their consent to participate in this study. For the duration of the study, all participants resided within the MAP in a specialized unit of a homeless shelter. As noted above, inclusion criteria for the study were based on acceptance to the MAP, in the absence of exclusion criteria, which included a diagnosis of dementia, acquired brain injury or previous head injury—due to the cognitive demands of the measure completion. Only two people were excluded based on these criteria. Four additional people did not consent to participate due to the range of information collected.

### Procedure
The project protocol was developed in collaboration with Ottawa Inner City Health staff and approved by the Royal Ottawa Health Care Group Research Ethics Board. Informed consent for participation was obtained by MAP staff approaching all clients upon admission with a prepared script describing the project. If interested, participants met with project staff to complete a consent form and discuss the project (to accommodate a range of literacy levels in clients) and then review a written consent form. Participants were informed that participation in the project had no effect on receiving full MAP services.

Data collection occurred at admission and at six months following admission to MAP. MAP clients are admitted individually as this is not a structured group treatment program. Therefore, given the variation in intake date for each client, a follow-up calendar method was used to determine the required timing for each phase of data collection. All measures were completed within three to five days of the required interval and were always collected before noon to ensure consistency in clients' alcohol consumption at each interval.

All data were collected by trained staff at admission and follow-up. In addition, an independent reviewer, who is a psychiatrist working with persons who are homeless and have concurrent disorder, saw each participant at both time intervals. The independent review consisted of a psychiatric interview, completion of a mental status exam and rating of global functioning (see Measures section). The independent reviewer conducted the evaluation session using the same procedure mentioned above within the premises of MAP.

### Measures
**Brief Psychiatric Rating Scale-Expanded.** The Brief Psychiatric Rating Scale-Expanded (BPRS-E) was used (by trained raters) as a measure of psychiatric symptoms (Rhoades and Overall 1988). The BPRS-E provides a seven-point Likert-scale rating of the severity of symptoms related to 14 diagnostic categories and 10 clusters of behavioural patterns. The BPRS is the most commonly used measure of psychiatric symptoms in evaluation research of persons involved in community-based treatment programs and has been demonstrated to have sufficient sensitivity to detect symptom change within brief intervals in a treatment program. Past research has demonstrated estimates of inter-rater reliability ranging from $r = 0.53$ to $0.98$ (Gabbard et al. 1987; Tarrell and Schultz 1988; Ventura et al. 1993).

**Mini mental state examination.** The mini mental state examination (MMSE) was used by the independent raters as an objective and short assessment of an individual's cognitive state. It is mostly used as a determinant of cognitive dysfunction at any time, as well as measuring changes in treatment effects (Folstein, Folstein and McHugh 1975; Psychological Assessment Resources 2005). There are two parts to the MMSE: (1) assessment of attention, orientation and memory performed orally and (2) assessment of labelling, following orders, composing a sentence and duplicating a polygon. The MMSE has also demonstrated strong inter-rater reliability ($r = 0.83$) as well test–retest reliability ($r = 0.98$) (Folstein, Folstein and McHugh 1975). In essence, adequate reliability and validity has been confirmed with the MMSE among multiple populations with mental health concerns.

**Global assessment of functioning.** From the rating scale provided in the DSM-IV-TR, a global assessment of functioning (GAF) score was provided by the independent rater at each time interval. The GAF score is a scale from 0 to 100 that rates an individual's overall psychological, social and occupational functioning and is used to track clinical progress of individuals in global terms (APA 2000). The GAF scale is divided into 10 ranges of functioning and each range has two components: symptom severity and functioning. A single score is derived for functioning in the current time period (a period of five days was used for the current project).

**Cohen-Mansfield Agitation Inventory.** The Cohen-Mansfield Agitation Inventory (CMAI) was used as a measure of aggressive behaviour and is completed by trained staff raters (Cohen-Mansfield, Marx and Rosenthal 1989). Decreases in aggressive behaviour (both physical and verbal) and related agitation symptoms are often related to improved mental health of clients (Koss et al. 1997). The CMAI provides a rating of the severity and frequency of physical aggressive, physical non-aggressive, verbal aggressive and verbal non-aggressive behaviours. The measure is completed by staff who observed the client over the past week. Estimates of inter-rater reliability range from $r = 0.88$ to 0.92 (Cohen-Mansfield, Marx and Rosenthal 1989; Koss et al. 1997).

**Wisconsin Quality of Life Index, client.** The Wisconsin Quality of Life Index (client form) was used as a measure of subjective and other ratings of quality of life (Becker, Diamond and Sainfort 1993). The client form was used (completed in interview format with trained staff raters) to provide ratings of subjective quality of life and satisfaction with physical and psychological health and social relations (Maspero 1998; Sainfort, Becker and Diamond 1996). The measure has been previously used in Canadian studies of quality of life for persons with serious and persistent mental illness (Diaz, Mercier and Caron 2000; Diaz et al. 1999; Diaz and Mercier 1996). The test–retest coefficient of this instrument was noted to be 0.82 and high criterion related validity coefficients were observed between the QLI-MH and the Quality of Life Index (0.91), client ratings (0.68) and provider ratings (0.80) (Becker, Diamond and Sainfort 1993).

**Advanced practice nurse practitioner service inventory.** This measure was created for the current study to record the frequency and type of activity provided in each contact by the Advance Practice Nurse (Psychiatry) with participants. The inventory included a record of dates and foci for initial and all subsequent intervention.

**Consumption record.** The consumption record was created for the study and consists of a daily log of alcohol consumption for each client of the managed alcohol program, including both the type of alcohol consumed (i.e., beverage or non-beverage alcohol) and the location of consumption (i.e., inside or outside of the program). This record is already a part of the daily OICHP daily record keeping protocol.

## Results

### Demographic Characteristics

The final sample consisted of 80 participants in Time 1 and 63 in Time 2 over a six-month period. Demographic characteristics of the full sample are shown in Table 11-1. There were no significant differences found in demographic characteristics between those who did and did not complete both testing times. The reasons for non-completion were participant leaving the program by his/her own intention ($n$ = 12), being discharged from the program ($n$ = 3) for medical or behavioural issues or no longer wishing to participate in the study ($n$ = 2). Those participants who completed both time intervals were included in the analysis of clinical outcome measures.

As shown in Table 11-1, the sample was mostly male (88%) with a mean age of 49.73 years (range: 30–70 years). Three quarters of clients (75%) had not completed formal education beyond secondary school, almost all (97%) had past involvement with the legal system and 40 percent had current involvement. The details of legal system involvement were not available. The range of medical conditions reported in the past two years and currently is shown in Table 11-1. However, less than a quarter (24%) reported having been hospitalized or in an emergency department in the past 12 or 24 months. The most common mental health diagnosis among the sample was depression (71%) and 88 percent reported substance use other than alcohol (predominantly marijuana, crack and cocaine).

Most participants had independent functioning in the areas of personal care, ambulation and communication. However, most (88%)

required partial assistance (dispensing support) for daily medication adherence.

### Advanced Practice Nurse Practitioner Service Inventory

Review of the advance practice nurse practitioner service inventory suggests that the most frequently completed clinical activities of the APN were assessment (initial, 100%; monitoring, 95%), medication prescription and monitoring (80%), staff education (75%) and client education (65%). Assessment activities involved psychodiagnostic interviewing and symptom monitoring. Medication interventions were prescription and monitoring of medication effects and side effects. Staff education consisted of formal teaching and informal case discussion about concurrent disorders, the effects of mental illness on behaviour and information on medication interventions. Client education covered the same topics as staff education but was delivered in informal one-to-one sessions delivered in a manner corresponding to the client's cognitive abilities. As shown in the frequency distribution of activities, all clients were seen initially by the advance practice nurse and most remained in follow-up services. The number of interventions provided in the six-month time frame was $M = 13$ (range = 1–35).

### Clinical Outcomes

Comparison analyses of clinical outcome measures were conducted using parametric and non-parametric tests. Total scores were used for symptom rating scales (BPRS-E, CMAI, MMSE and GAF) and domain scores were used for the quality of life measure, selected on the basis of clinical relevance.

As shown in Table 11-2, to determine significant change in clinical outcomes over time, a paired-samples t-test was conducted for the CMAI, BPRS and MMSE total scores and the GAF score. Results indicated that there was a significant change in the severity of psychiatric illness symptoms (as measured by the BPRS), and in the frequency of aggression observed (as measured by the CMAI) between Time 1 and Time 2. There was also a significant improvement reported in the assessed mental status of participants between Time 1 and Time 2, but not in ratings of their global assessment of functioning.

Quality of life, as rated from the client and staff perspectives, was assessed for changes over time using non-parametric statistics. Statistically significant differences were found for the provider

## Table 11-1.  Demographic characteristics of study sample

|  | Frequency | Mean (Standard Deviation) |
|---|---|---|
| **Sex** | | |
| Male | 88.4 | |
| Female | 11.6 | |
| **Age** | | 49.73 (7.85) |
| **Level of Education** | | |
| Primary | 26.6 | |
| Secondary | 48.3 | |
| University | 13.4 | |
| Other Post-secondary | 11.7 | |
| **Legal System Involvement** | | |
| Past | 97.1 | |
| Current | 40.2 | |
| **Mental Health Diagnoses** (primary, excluding substance abuse) | | |
| Depression | 71.2 | |
| Bipolar disorder | 10.1 | |
| Schizophrenia | 9.2 | |
| Anxiety disorder | 6.1 | |
| Personality disorder | 4.5 | |
| **Use of Other Substances** | 88.2 | |
| **Use of Emergency Room** | | |
| Past 12 months | 23.8 | |
| Past 24 months | 22.6 | |
| **Primary Medical Condition** (at time of admission to MAP) | | |
| Hepititis C | 18.4 | |
| HIV/AIDS | 7.8 | |
| Broken bones/fractures | 9.2 | |
| Seizure disorder | 5.3 | |
| Skin disorders | 5.3 | |
| Arthritis | 4.9 | |
| Asthma | 3.9 | |
| Anemia | 2.6 | |
| **Level of Functioning, Personal Care** | | |
| Independent | 70.1 | |
| Partial assistance | 27.3 | |
| Complete assistance | 2.6 | |

Table 11-1.  (Continued)

| | Frequency | Mean (Standard Deviation) |
|---|---|---|
| **Level of Functioning, Medication** | | |
| Independent | 7.9 | |
| Partial assistance | 88.2 | |
| Complete assistance | 3.9 | |
| **Level of Functioning, Ambulation** | | |
| Independent | 82.9 | |
| Partial assistance | 14.5 | |
| Complete assistance | 2.6 | |
| **Level of Functioning, Communication** | | |
| Independent | 96.0 | |
| Partial assistance | 1.3 | |
| Complete assistance | 2.7 | |

ratings of: (1) psychological health: $\chi2 = 14.8$, $p < 0.01$; (2) physical health: $\chi2 = 6.97$, $p < 0.05$; (3) quality of relations with family: $\chi2 = 60.1$, $p < 0.001$ and (4) quality of life (overall): $\chi2 = 39.5$, $p < 0.001$. Client ratings of perceived quality of life were significant for change over time for physical health: $\chi2 = 23.3$, $p < 0.001$.

Related to substance use, review of the consumption record at Time 2 stated that there was no longer recorded ingestion of non-alcohol substances by participants. This is a clinically significant change in substance use patterns, but statistically significant change cannot be calculated because reliable estimates of ingestion could not be provided at Time 1 (admission to program), since they were solely based on participant recall. Alcohol consumption at Time 1 was not reliable because it was also based on participant recall. However, the amount of alcohol consumption remained constant between admission and Time 2 as it was regulated within the MAP protocol, and although it is decreased for some MAP clients, it was not for this sample.

## Discussion

The purpose of this study was to examine the effects of delivering psychiatric services within a shelter-based management of alcohol program for homeless adults. The effects of delivering concurrent psychiatric services was examined by investigating changes for MAP

## Table 11-2. Changes in clinical outcomes

| | Time 1 | Time 2 | Significance Test |
|---|---|---|---|
| Psychiatric Symptoms (BPRS) | 51.29 (17.4) | 48.71 (16.3) | $t = 5.31$* |
| Mental Status (MMSE) | 22.8 (4.6) | 25.1 (3.2) | $t = 2.20$* |
| Global Assessment of Functioning (GAF) | 36.95 (9.3) | 37.29 (7.0) | NS |
| Aggression (CMAI) | 65.71 (16.9) | 55.1 (21.1) | $t = 3.11$* |

*$p < 0.05$.

participants in their psychiatric symptoms, mental status, global functioning, aggression, quality of life and consumption of alcohol and alcohol substitutes. The hypotheses of the study were that clients of the MAP who were receiving concurrent psychiatric services would have a decrease in the severity of their psychiatric symptoms, an improvement in mental status, an increase in their mental health-related functioning and a decrease in the frequency of their aggressive behaviour. It was also hypothesized that clients would have an increase in both their own subjective quality of life (client ratings of domains) and in providers' perception of their quality of life, as well as a decrease in consumption of alcohol and alcohol substitutes.

Results of the study demonstrated mixed support for the hypotheses. There was statistically significant improvement in severity of psychiatric symptoms, mental status and frequency of aggressive behaviour, but not in a global rating of mental health-related functioning.

The lack of significant change in global functioning may be due to many of the elements of a GAF rating not being changed within participation in the MAP. The global assessment of functioning (GAF) provides a composite score based on psychological, social and occupational functioning, in addition to symptom severity (APA 2000). Since social and occupational functioning are outside the purview of the MAP, a composite score of functioning may not be sufficiently sensitive to detect change for MAP clients. Psychiatric interventions in the MAP focused on symptom identification, medication treatment and education. These interventions were expected to decrease symptoms, improve mental status (by reduction of interfering symptoms) and decrease behavioural disturbance, but not necessarily change global functioning in some clients. The regulation of alcohol consumption is also expected to have contributed to improved mental status and decreased behavioural disturbance.

Findings of improved psychiatric symptomatology in this study are consistent with other studies that found a decrease in psychiatric symptoms for homeless individuals with a dual diagnosis (concurrent disorder) as a result of receiving treatment interventions to help them attain sobriety and build work-related and social skills (Drake, Yoveitch and Bebout 1997). Additionally, in another study that compared a Housing First and continuum of care group, it was found that psychiatric symptom improvement was associated with perceived choice and mediated by beliefs of empowerment that was associated with the Housing First model of service (Tsemberis et al. 2003; Tsemeris, Gulcur and Nakae 2004). As noted above, the differences in these approaches, with a focus on building additional skills or improved empowerment, may account for some differences in overall clinical functioning from those observed in the current study, in which clients reside in the shelter and are in earlier stages of engaging in vocational or other types of skill building.

Changes to ratings of quality of life had mixed results. Service providers rated more positive changes in participants' lives with increases in psychological health, physical health, quality of relations with family and overall quality of life. Conversely, participants rated significant improvement in only their physical health. This may be explained by participants being able to first detect (and report) changes in their physical health, due to changes from the time of admission, when they may have been using non-alcohol substances, to the management of alcohol approach with pre-selected administration of alcohol and other health care needs addressed by MAP medical staff. Participants' ratings of psychological health, quality of relations with family and overall quality of life did improve over the time interval, but the change was not statistically significant. This may mean that although change had (or was starting to) occur, it was insufficient during the measured time interval to the perception of participants. This may explain the non-significant finding in client and provider ratings in other areas of quality of life such as occupational, social and domestic areas, as these areas may not have changed while in a shelter-based program. Drake, Yovetich and Bebout (1997) found increased ratings of quality of life in the areas of social contact and social relations for homeless clients with a dual diagnosis in an integrated treatment approach (psychiatric and substance use treatment) as compared to a standard treatment group. The focus of that approach, however, had more emphasis on quality of life and assessed participants over a longer time interval. This suggests that with the program being studied, ratings of change in domains of quality of life should be assessed over a longer time interval, such as following residential placement upon successful completion of the MAP. It may also suggest that domains of quality of life should become a focus of intervention or skill building within the program once participants' initial symptoms are stabilized.

The incomplete findings related to a decrease in the consumption of alcohol and alcohol substitutes was due to the lack of reliable information at the time of admission to the program, although the reported decrease and ceasing of use of alcohol substitutes represented clinically significant change. Elongation of the length of the follow-up intervals would have allowed for improved examination of consumption patterns within the program.

There are limitations in this study of the areas of participants' lives measured and the methods used. As noted, not all aspects of quality of life or functioning were addressed within the MAP. As for study methodology, the duration between time intervals of investigation in this study is a limitation of the study. Some variables under investigation may not have had sufficient time or been sufficiently a focus of service to have undergone significant change during the course of this study. With the finding that 85 percent of services delivered focused on pharmacological treatment, change measured in psychiatric symptoms, aggressive behaviour and mental status may have been detected because of the high number of participants receiving pharmacological and behavioural interventions targeted to these issues. Since all persons in the MAP were considered for this study, there is the limitation of having no control group against which to compare the clinical outcomes attained by this group. Insufficient detection of change may also be due to the shortened time intervals between ratings, the lack of focus on the domain during intervention or the heightened acuity of initial symptoms, such that the time frame was not sufficient to detect clinically observable change.

Client attrition from the final sample also limits sample size and the scope of the investigation. For this sample, clinical outcomes were measured for all clients receiving psychiatric services, but due to sample size constraints, the relationship between service intensity and clinical outcomes was not assessed. In a larger sample it would be of value to investigate difference between clients receiving different levels of service intensity and focus. This study also examined clinical outcomes only while clients resided in a shelter-based program. A longer longitudinal measure of their outcomes achieved, or maintained, upon program discharge and transition into housing would be valuable.

Findings of this study indicate that the introduction of psychiatric services, focused on assessment, pharmacological intervention and education and education to staff and clients can be an important addition to a management of alcohol program, delivered in a concurrent model of service delivery. The extent to which the influence of the characteristics of these clients (their mental health diagnoses, levels of aggressive behaviour, mental status) on the outcomes are not known, but this study suggests that a concurrent model of service delivery (of psychiatric and harm reduction services) for underserved homeless clients, such as these who would not otherwise access traditional models of treatment, should be considered for effective service delivery. The model of management of alcohol within a shelter for homeless persons should also continue to be replicated as a responsive and appropriate service model for persons with substance dependence. It is within this model that concurrent psychiatric services are also well applied to deliver concurrent disorder services for this underserved population. This model of concurrent service delivery should also be replicated for other shelter-based populations to address their mental health issues, substance use and quality of life. The philosophies of many service agencies may present challenges to the further development of concurrent service delivery (since many require abstinence from substances); a broader understanding of need for introducing harm reduction principles while delivering psychiatric services is required. In addition, the use of the concurrent service delivery model that offers harm reduction for other substances should be considered to provide innovative service delivery for the growing rates of concurrent disorder in the homeless population.

# References

APA (American Psychiatric Association). 2000. *Diagnostic and Statistical Manual of Mental Disorders: Fourth Edition, Text Revision.* Washington, DC: American Psychiatric Association.

Baer, J., P. Peterson and E. Wells. 2004. "Rationale and Design of a Brief Substance Use Intervention for Homeless Adolescents." *Addiction Research and Theory,* 12(4): 317–34.

Barreira, P., B. Espy, R. Fishbein et al. 2000. "Linking Substance Abuse and Serious Mental Illness Service Delivery Systems: Initiating a State-Wide Collaboration." *Journal of Behavioral Health Services and Research,* 27: 107–13.

Bebout, R. 1999. "Housing Solutions: The Community Connections Housing Program: Preventing Homelessness by Integrating Housing and Supports." *Alcoholism Treatment Quarterly,* 17(1–2): 93–112.

Becker, M., R. Diamond and F. A. Sainfort. 1993. "A New Patient Focused Index for Measuring Quality of Life in Persons with Severe and Persistent Mental Illness." *Quality of Life Research,* 2: 239–51.

Blankertz, L. and R. Cnann. 1994. "Assessing the Impact of Two Residential Programs for Dually Diagnosed Homeless Individuals." *Social Service Review,* 68(4): 536–60.

Buchanan, D., S. Shaw, A. Ford and M. Singer. 2003. "Empirical Science Meets Moral Panic: An Analysis of the Politics of Needle Exchange." *Journal of Public Health Policy,* 24: 427–44.

Burnam, M., S. Morton, E. McGlynn et al. 1995. "An Experimental Evaluation of Residential and Nonresidential Treatment for Dually Diagnosed Homeless Adults." *Journal of Addictive Diseases,* 14(4): 111–34.

CAMH (Centre for Addiction and Mental Health). 2001. *Best Practices: Concurrent Mental Health and Substance Use Disorders.* Ottawa: Health Canada.

Cohen-Mansfield, J., M. S. Marx and A. S. Rosenthal. 1989. "A Description of Agitation in a Nursing Home." *Journal of Gerontology,* 44: 77–84.

Davis, K., T. Devitt, A. Rollins, S. O'Neill, D. Pavick and B. Harding. 2006. "Integrated Residential Treatment for Persons with Severe and Persistent Mental Illness: Lessons in Recovery." *Journal of Psychoactive Drugs,* 38: 263–72.

Diaz, P. and C. Mercier. 1996. "An Evaluation of the Wisconsin Quality of Life Questionnaire for Clinical Application and Research in Canada." *Quality of Life Newsletter,* 16: 11–12.

Diaz, P., C. Mercier and J. Caron. 2000. "The Wisconsin Quality of Life Index (W-QLI): Overview of Research in Canada." *Quality of Life Newsletter,* 20: 25.

Diaz, P., C. Mercier, R. Hachey et al. 1999. "An Evaluation of the Psychometric Properties of the Client's Questionnaire of the Wisconsin Quality of Life Index." *Quality of Life Research*, 8: 509–14.

Drake, R., C. Mercer-McFadden, K. Mueser et al. 1998. "Review of Integrated Mental Health and Substance Abuse Treatment for Patients with Dual Disorders." *Schizophrenia Bulletin*, 24: 589–608.

Drake, R., N. Yovetich and R. Bebout. 1997. "Integrated Treatment for Dually Diagnosed Homeless Adults." *Journal of Nervous and Mental Disease*, 185(5): 298–305.

Farrell, S. 2003. *Annual Report of the Psychiatric Outreach Team.* Ottawa: Royal Ottawa Health Care Group.

Farrell, S., T. Aubry, F. Klodawsky et al. 2000. *Describing the Homeless Population of Ottawa-Carleton: Selected Fact Sheets.* Ottawa: University of Ottawa.

Folstein, M. F., S. E. Folstein and P. R. McHugh. 1975. "Mini-Mental State: A Practical Method for Grading and Cognitive State of Patients for the Clinician." *Journal of Psychiatric Research*, 12: 189–98.

Gabbard, G. O., L. L. Kennedy, C. D. Deering et al. 1987. "Interrater Reliability in the Use of the Brief Psychiatric Rating Scale." *Bulletin of the Meninger Clinic*, 51(6): 519–31.

Gulcur, L., A. Stefanic, M. Shinn et al. 2003. "Housing, Hospitalization, and Cost Outcomes for Homeless Individuals with Psychiatric Disabilities Participating in Continuum of Care and Housing First Programmes." *Journal of Community and Applied Social Psychology*, 13: 171–86.

Harm Reduction Coalition. 2003 (August). "Principles of Harm Reduction." [on-line]. Harm Reduction Coalition. http://harmreduction.org/about-us/principles-of-harm-reduction/ [consulted June 26, 2013].

Hass, J. 2001. "Harm Reduction Initiative Provides Alcohol to Ottawa's Street Alcoholics." *Canadian Medical Association Journal*, 165(7): 937.

Health Canada. 2001. *Harm Reduction and Injection Drug Use: An International Comparative Study of Contextual Factors Influencing the Development and Implementation of Relevant Policies and Programs.* Ottawa: Health Canada.

Hwang, S. W., G. Tolomiczenko, F. G. Kouyoumdijan et al. 2005. "Interventions to Improve the Health of the Homeless: A Systematic Review." *American Journal of Preventative Medicine*, 29: 311–19.

Koss, E., M. Weiner, C. Ernesto et al. 1997. "Assessing Patterns of Agitation in Alzheimer's Disease Patients with the Cohen-Mansfield Agitation Inventory." *Alzheimer Disease and Associated Disorders*, 11: S45–50.

MacPhee, M. C. 2006/2007. "Harm Reduction Facility Faces Renewal Challenge." *Canadian Women's Health Network*, 9(1–2): 5–9.

Marlatt, G. A. and K. Witkiewitz. 2010. "Update on Harm Reduction Policy and Intervention Research." *Annual Review of Clinical Psychology*, 6: 591–606.

Maspero, S. 1998. "Measuring Quality of Life in People with a Serious Mental Disorder/Illness." *Quality of Life Newsletter*, 20: 2.

Mayes, J. and S. Handley. 2005. "Evolving a Model for Integrated Treatment in a Residential Setting for People with Psychiatric and Substance Use Disorders." *Psychiatric Rehabilitation Journal,* 29(1): 59–63.

Mercier, C. and B. Beaucage. 1997. *Toxicomanie et problèmes sévères de santé mentale: recension des écrits et état de situation pour le Québec.* Montréal, QC: Comité permanent de lutte à la toxicomanie.

Nuttbrock, L., M. Rahav, J. Rivera et al. 1998. "Outcomes of Homeless Mentally Ill Chemical Abusers in Community Residences and a Therapeutic Community." *Psychiatric Services,* 49: 68–76.

Pauly, B., I. Goldstone, J. McCall, F. Gold and S. Payne. 2007. "The Ethical, Legal and Social Context of Harm Reduction." *Canadian Nurse,* 103(8): 19–23.

Podymow, T., J. Turnbull, D. Coyle et al. 2006. "Shelter-Based Managed Alcohol Administration to Chronically Homeless People Addicted to Alcohol." *Canadian Medical Association Journal,* 174: 45–49.

Psychological Assessment Resources. 2005. "Mini Mental State Examination (MMSE)." Clinical guide and test materials]. [on-line]. http://www3.parinc.com/products/product.aspx?Productid=MMSE [consulted November 13, 2008].

RachBeisel, J., J. Scott and L. Dixon. 1999. "Co-occurring Severe Mental Illness and Substance Use Disorders: A Review of Recent Research." *Psychiatric Services,* 50: 1427–34.

Rhoades, H. M. and J. E. Overall. 1988. "The Semi-structured BPRS Interview and Rating Guide." *Psychology Bulletin,* 24: 101–04.

Riley, D., E. Sawka, P. Conley, D. Hewitt, W. Mitic, C. Poulin . . . and J. Topp. 1999. "Harm Reduction: Concepts and Practice. A Policy Discussion Paper." *Substance Use & Misuse,* 34(1): 9–24.

Rosenblum, A., L. Nuttbrock, H. McQuistion et al. 2002. "Medical Outreach to Homeless Substance Users in New York City: Preliminary Results." *Substance Use & Misuse,* 37: 1269–73.

Sainfort, F., M. Becker and R. Diamond. 1996. "Judgements of Quality of Life in Individuals with Severe Mental Disorders: Patient Self-Report versus Provider Perspectives." *American Journal of Psychiatry,* 153: 497–501.

Svoboda, T. 2009. "Message in a Bottle: Wet Shelters Employ True Harm Reduction Approach." In blog for *CrossCurrents: The Journal of Addiction and Mental Health.* [on-line]. http://www.camhcrosscurrents.net/the lastword/2009/03/message-in-a-bottle.html [consulted June 2010].

Tarrell, J. D. and S. C. Schultz. 1988. "Nursing Assessment Using the BPRS: A Structured Interview." *Psychology Bulletin,* 2: 105–11.

Tsemberis, S., L. Gulcur and M. Nakae. 2004. "Housing First, Consumer Choice, and Harm Reduction for Homeless Individuals with a Dual Diagnosis." *American Journal of Public Health,* 94(4): 651–56.

Tsemberis, S., L. Moran, M. Shinn et al. 2003. "Consumer Preference Programs for Individuals Who Are Homeless and Have Psychiatric Disabilities: A Drop-in Center and a Supported Housing Program." *American Journal of Community Psychology,* 32(3–4): 305–17.

Ventura, J., M. F. Green, A. Shaner et al. 1993. "Training and Quality Assurance with the Brief Psychiatric Rating Scale: 'The Drift Busters'." *International Journal of Methods in Psychiatric Research,* 3: 221–44.

Wood, E., M. Tyndall, J. Montaner and T. Kerr. 2004. "Summary of Findings from the Evaluation of a Pilot Medically Supervised Safer Injection Facility." *Canadian Medical Association Journal,* 175: 1399–1404.

Wood, E., M. W. Tyndall, P. M. Spittal, M. V. O'Shaughnessy and M. T. Schechter. 2003. "The Health Care and Fiscal Costs of the Illicit Drug Use Epidemic: The Impact of Conventional Drug Control Strategies, and the Potential of a Comprehensive Approach." *BC Medical Journal,* 45: 128–34.

Wood, E., M. W. Tyndall, R. Zhang et al. 2006. "Attendance at Supervised Injecting Facilities and Use of Detoxification Services." *New England Journal of Medicine,* 354: 2512–14.

# CHAPTER 12

# Collaborative Approaches to Community-Based Mental Health Care for Homeless People: Toronto's Inner City Health Associates

Vicky Stergiopoulos, MD
Keenan Research Centre of the
Li Ka Shing Knowledge Institute, St. Michael's Hospital
Department of Psychiatry, University of Toronto

## Introduction

Several recent reports have reviewed the health consequences and costs of homelessness in Canada (CIHI 2007; Patterson et al. 2008). Homeless persons in Western countries have high rates of mental health challenges and addiction and approximately one-third have a severe mental illness (CIHI 2007). A recent systematic review and meta-analysis of mental disorders among homeless persons in Western countries reported pooled prevalence rates of 12.7 percent for psychotic disorders, 11.4 percent for major depression, 37.9 percent for alcohol dependence and 24.4 percent for drug dependence (Fazel et al. 2008). Furthermore 4 percent to 7 percent of homeless persons experience global cognitive deficits, and many more experience focal deficits in verbal or visual memory, attention, executive function and speed of cognitive processing (Burra, Stergiopoulos and Rourke 2009). These rates are much higher than mean prevalence rates reported for these conditions in the general population.

Not surprisingly, the risk of homelessness among individuals with serious mental illness is 10 to 20 times higher than the general population, and 4 percent to 36 percent of psychiatric hospital patients experience homelessness before or after their hospital stay (Susser et al. 1997; Kuno et al. 2000). Homeless persons with mental illness and addictions are at increased risk of experiencing chronic homelessness and utilize more health and social services than others experiencing homelessness (Aubry, Klodawsky and Hay 2003; CIHI 2007). Furthermore, many chronically homeless persons with mental illness have multiple and complex physical health needs including infectious diseases, chronic medical conditions and physical disabilities (Hwang 2001). In addition to mental and physical illness, homeless persons experience high stress levels and low self-esteem and report poor coping skills and suicidal behaviours (CIHI 2007). Mortality among homeless persons is much higher than the general population, and many unexpected deaths among homeless people in Canada are related to mental disorders and suicides (Hwang 2000; Hwang et al. 2009).

Toronto is home to Canada's largest homeless population, with over 5,000 people experiencing homelessness on any given night (City of Toronto 2009). More than three-quarters (79%) of those live in shelters, 8 percent live on the street, 6 percent in correctional facilities, 4 percent in health care or treatment facilities and another 3 percent in transition shelters for women who have experienced domestic violence. Over the course of the year, approximately 28,000 unique individuals use homeless shelters in Toronto (City of Toronto 2009). Similar to those in other jurisdictions, homeless persons in Toronto have complex health needs. A 1998 study reported that 67 percent of a representative sample of shelter users in Toronto have a lifetime diagnosis of a mental illness (Mental Health Policy Research Group 1997; CIHI 2007). The more recent 2007 *Street Health Report* (Khandor and Mason 2007) identified that 35 percent of Toronto homeless respondents had been previously diagnosed with a mental illness, with the most common diagnoses reported being depression (17%), anxiety (11%), bipolar affective disorder (8%), schizophrenia (5%) and post-traumatic stress disorder (5%). Approximately 25 percent of respondents reported a concurrent mental health and substance use disorder.

Despite Canada's universal health care system, few homeless persons in Toronto are connected to a regular health care provider. Furthermore, it is estimated that 75 percent of those diagnosed with a mental illness have not had a psychiatric outpatient contact in the previous year (CIHI 2007). Even those accessing health services have a high rate of unmet needs, as they often receive services that do not match the level of care they require (Stergiopoulos et al. 2010a). A study at Ontario's largest shelter for homeless men revealed that

38 percent of the clients required intensive case management or assertive community treatment and 9 percent required 24-hour supervision in a residential care facility. Despite the presence of primary care services on site, half the men did not have their service needs met (Stergiopoulos et al. 2010a).

Finally, unlike major US urban centres, Toronto has not developed a coordinated approach to homeless health service provision. Local services for homeless persons include a range of supportive and alternative housing, emergency shelters, drop-ins, street outreach teams, housing help and eviction prevention services, meal programs and a nurse led health bus, funded by both government and non-profit organizations. More recently, the City of Toronto launched a Streets to Homes program, which focuses on moving homeless individuals living outdoors into housing (City of Toronto, Shelter, Support and Housing Administration 2009). In addition to these homeless specific services, there is a resource-rich health service network accessible to both homeless and housed individuals, including nurse and physician primary care providers, community health centres, in-patient and outpatient specialty care, case management, assertive community treatment, early intervention for psychosis programs, court support services and mobile crisis intervention teams, amongst others.

Despite the large range of services and supports, homeless persons with mental illness and addictions face major barriers to accessing services that can meet their needs. Access to comprehensive care is limited, discharge planning from hospitals is poor and coordination and collaboration among service providers and service sectors, including housing, income support and health programs, is lacking (Goering et al. 2004). Physician care specifically remains challenging to access because medical and hospital care require a valid provincial health card, which many homeless persons do not possess. Furthermore, physicians are remunerated on a fee for service model, which fails to adequately compensate for much of the indirect and complex care involved in addressing the health needs of this population.

To effectively address these barriers and support the complex health needs of homeless people with mental health and addiction problems, comprehensive interventions that address their needs and preferences must be designed and implemented (Stefancic and Tsemberis 2007). This chapter describes the efforts of Toronto's Inner

City Health Associates (ICHA) to address some of these challenges through targeted placement of physicians in frontline homeless service settings and through the development of innovative collaborative models of service delivery in partnership with frontline health and social service providers. It also discusses the lessons learned in the efforts to build community capacity and to promote hospital and community integration and the integration of health and social service delivery. These lessons may be instructive for other jurisdictions facing similar barriers to accessing comprehensive care for homeless people with mental health and addictions problems and can support efforts to improve care for this vulnerable population.

## Toronto's Inner City Health Associates (ICHA)

St. Michael's Hospital, Toronto's urban teaching hospital, has a long history of working and planning collaboratively with local community partners to improve care for the poor and the underserved. Following persistent advocacy efforts by a small group of St. Michael's physicians and administrators, the Ontario Ministry of Health and Long Term Care negotiated an alternate payment plan to facilitate recruitment of family physicians, psychiatrists and other specialists into frontline homeless service settings, many of which are located within blocks of the hospital. To our knowledge, this was the first such alternate payment plan in Canada. The funding addressed physician compensation, a barrier to recruitment in the past, but provided no administrative or other health provider infrastructure. This limitation necessitated building extensive inter-agency and inter-sectoral partnerships and collaborations to coordinate medical care with frontline homeless social services and other health supports through innovative, collaborative models of service delivery.

In recent years, there has been increased interest in community participation in the design of health services, in an effort to improve the quality of health care (Institute of Medicine 2004). Using the principles of community-based participatory research, the efforts of health planners and policy-makers have increasingly focused on including local stakeholders, patients and their families in the redesign of local systems of care for the purpose of system improvement. Keyser and colleagues (2010) have recently outlined the steps taken for mobilizing a region to redesign its local system of care. Action steps in their efforts have included forging partnerships with local funders and policy-makers; involving all relevant system players in the collaborative change process; prioritizing community goals for system change; understanding barriers and issues faced by local providers and program staff who work in the system; learning from national and local programs; identifying potential policy levels and, finally, developing a blueprint for community action and sustainability (Keyser et al. 2010). In a similar fashion, given its intent to act on behalf of the community it serves, ICHA organized internally and aimed to set the stage for planned local system change through three broad approaches: (1) developing partnerships with local stakeholders, (2) collaborative planning and program development and (3) collaborative organizational program structures. Planning had a clear focus on addressing access to health care for homeless people and frontline social service providers and recognized the diversity of needs and perspectives of local stakeholders. It relied on frequent communication, commitment to optimal use of expertise and resources and regular review and evaluation. The framework for change was clearly set by community-driven needs assessment efforts and was informed by an extensive review of the literature.

Previous local studies have documented multiple unmet health needs among homeless persons, with less than one-third of homeless persons with mental illness in Toronto receiving treatment (Mental Health Policy Research Group 1997; Stergiopoulos et al. 2010a). Furthermore, an assessment of the health, mental health and addiction treatment needs of people using emergency shelters in Toronto highlighted the lack of coordination and collaboration among health and social service providers, leading to fragmentation, duplication and gaps in services (Goering et al. 2004).

Drawing on the findings and recommendations of these needs assessments, ICHA identified two key domains upon which to focus initial change efforts: (1) community engagement and (2) care coordination/service integration. ICHA program planning began with extensive consultations with the City of Toronto's Shelter, Support and Housing Administration Division, the Toronto Drop-In Network and several local health and social services planning groups to ensure homeless health care needs were addressed across geographical areas and service- and population-specific sectors. ICHA embarked on further extensive local needs assessments, including individual and focus group interviews of program planners, service providers and people with lived experience of homelessness, to identify perceived strengths, weaknesses and opportunities in each geographic area within the city, service priorities and needs of clients and service providers and directions for effective and inclusive planning and communication, including the principles upon which to base partnership development, planning and collaboration.

Different models of frontline health care provision were developed, depending on client needs and resources available at each service site. Models ranging from integrative and consultative collaborative care models (Stergiopoulos, Rouleau and Yoder 2007; Tam 2010) to intensive case management and assertive community treatment team models (Stergiopoulos et al. 2010a) were developed to facilitate access to the different levels of care that homeless clients with complex health needs require. Given that ICHA only has access to physician funding and that health services for homeless persons remain un-integrated and poorly coordinated, these models depended on successful partnerships and collaboration with a range of other health and social services providers, including shelter and drop-in counsellors, homecare nurses and community mental health case managers.

ICHA currently numbers 65 physicians, including 32 psychiatrists, 29 family physicians and 4 other specialists, and provides medical and psychiatric care to more than 40 frontline homeless service agencies, including men, women, family and youth shelters, drop-ins, street outreach teams and select supportive housing agencies serving homeless persons with complex health needs. The group served more than 1,700 people in 2010, providing approximately 5,700 hours of primary care and 8,700 hours of psychiatric care. ICHA physicians provide direct and indirect care, advise frontline staff on service and case management plans, and teach on selected topics in efforts to build community capacity. They also advocate to different service sectors to help coordinate care and ultimately connect homeless people to mainstream services and supports. ICHA physicians are recruited to provide recovery-oriented care from a harm reduction framework, focusing on the determinants of community health. They prioritize housing, income and social support in their treatment plan. In addition to direct and indirect care to homeless people with complex health needs and development of community capacity, ICHA has identified student and resident education as a priority. A number of elective, selective, career-track and research opportunities for medical and other health discipline students, residents and fellows have been made available. Most ICHA physicians are affiliated with the University of Toronto and have primary appointments at one of the affiliated teaching hospitals, spending only a small portion of their clinical time in homeless service settings. They also advocate, within their mainstream service settings, for services that are respectful and responsive to the needs of clients who experience homelessness or housing instability.

This approach is unlike other attempts to organize care for homeless persons, in advocating for better use or coordination of existing services and supports though integrated planning and collaboration, rather than creating a parallel system of homeless health care. ICHA services aim to create a gateway to mainstream services and supports by engaging and providing a healing relationship to patients who may have experienced stigma and discrimination in past health encounters and by developing the capacity of both mainstream health and frontline homeless social service providers to address the complex needs of homeless persons comprehensively, developing and using best practice models.

## Bringing Services Together through Partnerships and Collaborations

ICHA program development addresses needs for preventive care, management of acute illness and comprehensive management of chronic complex health needs. The following sections describe some of the programs developed through partnerships and collaborations over the past seven years.

### Shelter and Drop-in Based Collaborative Mental Health Care Teams

Collaborative mental health care is an important component of health care reform in many countries (Craven and Bland 2006). This term refers to models of practice in which patients, their caregivers and health providers from a variety of primary care and mental health settings work together to provide timely and better-coordinated services for individuals with mental health problems. Given the complex physical, mental health and social service needs of homeless persons, collaborative mental health care is an intuitively appealing service model. Since 2005, both consultative and integrative models of collaborative mental health care have been developed in the largest men, women and youth shelters and drop-ins in Toronto. These enable rapid evaluation and treatment of patients with a wide range of mental health problems, improve the ability of shelter and drop-in staff to manage them, improve the education of shelter staff and trainees on the needs of homeless persons and reduce reliance on emergency department visits and hospitalizations for unmet mental health needs.

Fusion of Care, developed at Seaton House, one of Canada's largest shelters for homeless men, is an integrated collaborative care model with on-site medical support and a flexible referral process. In this model, shelter staff and ICHA physicians work as a single team. The impetus for adopting this model of service delivery was the communication breakdown and lack of coordination in care delivery experienced when case management or medical care of clients was brokered to external agencies (Stergiopoulos, Rouleau and Yoder 2007). The Fusion of Care Team provides medical care and in-house case management to the clients of the 240-bed Hostel Program, one of Seaton House's seven programs, and has the capacity to serve 40 clients at any one time. The team consists of a client service worker, a counsellor, a nurse and a team leader/counsellor, all Seaton House full-time staff, as well as a family physician and a psychiatrist. The two ICHA physicians offer concurrent clinics at the shelter for a half day every week, working collaboratively through both direct and indirect consultations.

The target population is chronically homeless persons whose health needs exceed the hostel's resources and who are unable to access community-based services. Once a client is identified by hostel staff as a candidate for the program, the client meets with a counsellor for one hour to set goals and complete a comprehensive psychosocial assessment. The client subsequently meets with the team nurse for a comprehensive health assessment. Once the main health issues are identified, the client is referred, depending on the complexity and acuity of health needs, to either a family physician or a psychiatrist. A comprehensive care plan is developed during weekly multidisciplinary team rounds for each client. The client service worker facilitates adherence to the plan by escorting clients to appointments off site and provides team members feedback and information about the client's function, hygiene and behaviour. Medications are dispensed daily to clients by the team's nurse. Although a rigorous evaluation is under way, preliminary program evaluation results are promising. A chart review of 73 clients referred over a 12-month period revealed that six months after intake into the program 35.3 percent had improved clinically and 48.5 percent were housed. Factors associated with positive outcomes included the number of visits with a psychiatrist and treatment adherence (Stergiopoulos et al. 2008).

Consultative rather than integrative collaborative care models have been developed in other settings not resourced to support integrated teams. For example, at Agincourt Community Services, a community centre serving homeless and under-housed people at the city's east end, a psychiatrist provides consultation services to the agency's housing and outreach programs, working closely with drop-in staff. Agency case managers frequently attend appointments to ensure care is seamless and coordinated. In addition to supporting frontline staff and clients, the psychiatrist, in collaboration with Toronto Social Services, completes disability assessments to facilitate access to income support for eligible homeless persons (Tam 2010).

### Multidisciplinary Outreach Team (MDOT)
An inter-agency, multidisciplinary street outreach team—the first such team in Canada—was designed in 2007 to enable rapid evaluation and treatment of street homeless clients with a wide range of disorders, to improve the ability of street outreach staff to manage these disorders and to contribute towards ending street homelessness related to illness and disability by streamlining access to housing, entitlements and health care. The development of the clinical street outreach team was an initiative undertaken by the City of Toronto's Streets to Homes program (City of Toronto 2009) to complement the network of city-funded programs providing street outreach.

MDOT consists of two part-time psychiatrists, one full-time nurse case manager, one full-time housing case manager, one full-time street outreach case manager and one part-time concurrent disorders specialist. This team composition was thought to include the content expertise and organizational resources required to address the needs of this population. Additional program partners include a community health centre that offers comprehensive primary care services and the provincially funded Ontario Disability Support Program that provides priority access to adjudication for income supports. MDOT follows a Housing First philosophy, developed to meet the housing and treatment needs of the chronically homeless population (Shern et al. 2000; Tsemberis, Gulcur and Nakae 2004). Housing First views housing as a human right and involves providing homeless persons with immediate access to subsidized housing and case management supports. No preconditions, such as bringing substance abuse under control or being stabilized on medications, are imposed. Housing First supports access to housing concurrently with addressing immediate needs in other areas.

Unlike the Pathways Housing First model, MDOT does not provide long-term assertive community treatment, but rather offers transitional intensive case management until clients are housed and referred to appropriate long-term health services. This approach reserves the team expertise and resources for the engagement, housing and community connection of street homeless persons, transferring care to other agencies once these goals are achieved. This approach facilitates ongoing access to this highly specialized team for the street dwelling population. The team accepts referrals for clients whose needs exceed other street outreach teams' expertise and resources and who have unmet needs in one or more of the following areas: severe mental illness including severe substance abuse, developmental challenge or other acute medical needs.

Outreach and client engagement focus on frequent contact with clients to identify and address immediate needs and a client-centred approach to service provision. Client assessment and case management are integrated and multidisciplinary. Each client is assigned to a primary case manager at intake but accesses team resources and expertise according to identified needs. The team of providers from different home agencies and professional backgrounds shares an integrated clinical record. Communication and collaboration between team members is fostered through regular team meetings. Clients are directed to one of the two partner hospitals for their acute care needs. Discharge planning is facilitated and coordinated by a close working relationship with hospital discharge planners of the partner hospitals. The team provides ongoing support to clients after housing placement until other community partners are able to engage them successfully into the appropriate level of long-term treatment, often many months after the original intake to the program.

### Coordinated Access to Care for the Homeless (CATCH)

In the absence of appropriate community-based health services, many homeless persons rely on hospital emergency department visits or in-patient hospitalizations for health care (Salit et al. 1998; McNiel and

Binder 2005; D'Amore et al. 2001), which are not designed to address their needs comprehensively. When admitted to hospital, homeless persons have longer hospital stays with higher costs (Salit et al. 1998; Hwang et al. 2011). Unsurprisingly, the 2007 CIHI report on *Mental Health and Homelessness* confirmed that mental illness and addictions were the most common reasons for homeless clients visiting emergency rooms or necessitating in-patient care in Canada (CIHI 2007).

Leveraging additional funding to address both local health priorities to decrease emergency room wait times and lengths of stay in hospital, as well as community-identified needs for better discharge planning and integration of hospital and community care, ICHA led the development of a coordinated access to care for the homeless program (CATCH). The program offers a centralized referral process for community-based health services for homeless persons presenting to hospital who are not able to access other services. CATCH aims to improve access to medical care, psychiatric care, peer support and case management and facilitate appropriate discharge planning of homeless persons with complex health needs. An additional program goal is to relieve pressure from emergency departments and in-patient units by coordinating hospital-based care with community-based homeless clinical and social services. The program, in addition to streamlining access to primary and psychiatric care, offers access to nursing, personal, peer support and transitional case management in partnership with other agencies, including a large community mental health agency, a homeless shelter and a consumer-driven community centre. It also leverages partnerships to offer facilitated access to disability income support to hospitalized homeless persons and a discharge planning checklist as a guide to hospital-based discharge planners.

The program improves service coordination and hospital community integration and provides assertive outreach, transitional case management and linkage to the apporpriate level of needed support. Program participants are supported in navigating the complex system of services and supports already available to them and are linked to additional needed services as soon as it is feasible. CATCH clinicians provide transitional supports over a period of four to six months in most cases. The project team includes four full-time staff: an ICHA administrative coordinator/agency liaison, who processes referrals to the team members, and three transitional case managers, who provide outreach to three emergency department and in-patient units in downtown Toronto and the team physicians. The program enjoys the support of peer support workers, who accompany clients to appointments as needed.

## Barriers and Facilitators

ICHA strategies for creating local system change have included nurturing community partnerships, building community capacity, influencing the health care system and linking sectors and resources. Over time, several factors contributed to the growth of the association and collaborative program development, including physician funding on a competitive hourly remuneration rate, institutional support from the University of Toronto and St. Michael's Hospital, which facilitated physician recruitment and educational and research activities, and a shared vision with the City of Toronto's Support and Housing Administrative Division, the Toronto Drop-In Network and Toronto Social Services for enhanced access to comprehensive health services.

Despite program growth, several barriers to program development emerged over the years, including a diverse and poorly resourced group of frontline homeless service providers; long standing tensions between health and community-based social services; lack of central planning for the various service components that homeless persons require access to; different privacy legislations binding health information custodians and social services providers; and cultural differences in some frontline homeless service settings, who offer institutional rather than recovery-oriented care by frontline staff with very limited mental health training or supervision.

Despite these barriers, ICHA has been very successful in meeting its operational goals and priorities. Several strategies were successfully utilized for that purpose. To overcome resistance by social service providers, relationship building with frontline homeless service providers, their managers and service planners was an early ICHA priority. Extensive consultations and joint planning and program development, both within individual agencies and local homeless planning committees ensured buy-in for hosting clinics in key frontline agencies, as well as operational support for clinics by frontline agency staff. Partnerships were nurtured based on shared values, with the belief that each partner makes a unique and valuable contribution, resulting in power sharing and mutual benefit. Furthermore, ICHA leadership engaged municipal and provincial levels of government and local health networks to ensure planning meets and facilitates government identified priorities and contributes to overall system effectiveness. Helping align client centred care, frontline homeless agency needs and government priorities was very helpful in fostering partnerships and collaborations for innovative programming that spanned different sectors that do not traditionally work together. The ability to translate research findings into clinical programs was a critical aspect of developing effective relationships with these key stakeholders, informing system priorities and capitalizing on funding opportunities.

To address different privacy requirements in the frontline settings served, careful planning and rollout of a web-based electronic medical record (EMR) system, which provides role-based access to clinical notes, was undertaken. Finally, to address cultural differences in some settings, and further build community capacity, ICHA members strove to develop training seminars and workshops on a range of behavioural health topics and to provide a toolkit of knowledge and skills for frontline service providers who may have limited mental health training and supervision.

In addition to these barriers, inter-professional team building, not only at the different clinic sites, but within the ICHA leadership team, was a significant early challenge. Team members, in light of their different training and experiences, held very diverse views of system priorities and strategies for system change or for meeting homeless clients' complex health and support needs. Learning to appreciate and embrace those differences, and creating organizational structures that allow for problem solving and transparent decision-making, have been instrumental for fostering healthy teams and programs, as has the commitment to high quality, evidence-informed care.

## Lessons Learned and Future Directions

Designing effective programs and minimizing barriers to access for homeless persons with mental illness continue to be major challenges for health service systems, which are plagued by limited resources and a high degree of fragmentation. ICHA has attempted to address some of these challenges through collaborative planning and program development, partnerships with stakeholders from various sectors and collaborative organizational program structures, with little new investment. Unlike traditional health care approaches, this effort to bring local system change has required collaboration by all key stakeholders, responsiveness to community identified priorities and focused efforts on frontline social service agency staff empowerment and capacity building. It has fostered relationships that involve mutual respect, equity and inclusiveness, recognizing the community as a resource and aiming for shared leadership and power in health program development. Lessons learned through these efforts are generalizable in many urban settings facing similar challenges.

There are several advantages to the approach described above for planned system change. First, partnerships and collaborations can lead to improved access to a continuum of health, housing and income supports. Second, integrating primary and specialist mental health care in the frontline homeless settings addresses several system barriers: it avoids long waiting lists for mental health services; it improves coordination of primary care and mental health services and integration of medical care with social work and other frontline social services; it builds on the strengths of the partners, relieving pressures from other parts of the health care system; and it promotes academic–medical linkages and community development.

Our efforts to date have highlighted the need for widespread system change and the important role that communities and researchers can play in this effort through joint exploration of system barriers and working collaboratively to identify the evidence base for guiding the systems change process. In addition to drawing attention to homeless health as a priority for reform in a system that values health equity, future directions in planning an appropriate and effective mix of treatment and support services for homeless persons with mental illness should consider several complimentary approaches. First, standardized and detailed needs assessments of social, clinical and rehabilitative problems should be conducted to identify the need for mental health services (Acosta and Toro 2000; Salize et al. 2001; Stergiopoulos et al. 2010b). Second, evidence-based practices should be integrated into housing and support services, such as Housing First approaches and Assertive Community Treatment (Shern et al. 2000; Tsembersis, Gulcur and Nakae 2004; Goldwell and Bender 2007). Last, but not least, systems-level coordination should be pursued to promote hospital–community integration, the integration of mental health with addictions treatment and the integration of mental health services with the rest of the health care system (Rosenheck, Resnick and Morrissey 2003; Durbin et al. 2006).

Greater collaboration between agencies and sectors will be instrumental to better meet the goal of providing client-centred care to homeless persons with complex support needs. Finally, alternative funding models for medical care, to address the limitations of fee for service models for this population, should be considered across jurisdictions.

## References

Acosta, O. and P. A. Toro. 2000. "Let's Ask the Homeless People Themselves: A Needs Assessment Based on a Probability Sample of Adults." *American Journal of Community Psychology*, 28: 343–66.

Aubry, T., F. Klodawsky and E. Hay. 2003. *Panel Study on Persons Who Are Homeless in Ottawa: Phase 1 Results.* Ottawa: Centre for Research on Community Services, University of Ottawa.

Burra, T., V. Stergiopoulos and S. Rourke. 2009. "A Systematic Review of Cognitive Deficits in Homeless Adults: Implications for Service Delivery." *Canadian Journal of Psychiatry*, 54(2): 123–33.

CIHI (Canadian Institute for Health Information). 2007. *Improving the Health of Canadians: Mental Health and Homelessness.* Ottawa: CIHI.

City of Toronto. 2009. "Total Number of Unique Individuals Using the Shelter System 2000–2008." [on-line]. City of Toronto. http://www.toronto.ca/legdocs/mmis/2009/cd/bgrd/backgroundfile-24924.pdf [consulted July 20, 2013].

City of Toronto, Shelter, Support and Housing Administration. *2009 Street Needs Assessment: Results and Observations.* [on-line]. City of Toronto. http://www.toronto.ca/legdocs/mmis/2010/cd/bgrd/backgroundfile-29122.pdf [consulted July 20, 2013].

Craven, M. A. and R. Bland. 2006. "Better Practices in Collaborative Mental Health Care: An Analysis of the Evidence Base." *Canadian Journal of Psychiatry*, 51(1): 7S–72S.

D'Amore, J., O. Hung, W. Chiang and L. Goldfrank. 2001. "The Epidemiology of the Homeless Population and Its Impact on an Urban Emergency Department." *Academic Emergency Medicine*, 8: 1051–55.

Durbin, J., P. Goering, D. L. Streiner and G. Pink. 2006. "Does Systems Integration Affect Continuity of Mental Health Care?" *Administration and Policy in Mental Health*, 33: 705–17.

Fazel, S., V. Khosla, H. Doll and J. Geddes. 2008. "The Prevalence of Mental Disorders among the Homeless in Western Countries: Systematic Review and Meta-regression Analysis." *PLoS*, 5(12): e225.

Goering, P., J. Pyke, H. Bullock, J. Hoch, S. Hwang, S. Lindsay et al. 2004. *Health, Mental Health and Addiction Treatment Needs of People Using Emergency Shelters in Toronto.* Toronto: City of Toronto.

Goldwell, C. M. and W. S. Bender. 2007. "The Effectiveness of Assertive Community Treatment for Homeless Populations with Severe Mental Illness: A Meta Analysis." *American Journal of Psychiatry,* 164: 393–99.

Hwang, S. W. 2001. "Homelessness and Health." *Canadian Medical Association Journal,* 164: 229–33.

_____. 2000. "Mortality among Men Using Homeless Shelters in Toronto, Ontario." *Journal of American Medical Association,* 283: 2152–57.

Hwang, S. W., J. Weaver, T. Aubry and J. Hoch. 2011. "Hospital Costs and Length of Stay among Homeless Patients Admitted to Medical, Surgical, and Psychiatric Services." *Medical Care,* 49(4): 350–54.

Hwang S. W., R. Wilkins, M. Tjepkema, P. J. O'Campo and J. R. Dunn. 2009. "Mortality among Residents of Shelters, Rooming Houses and Hotels in Canada: An 11-Year Follow-up Study." *British Medical Journal,* 339: b4036.

Institute of Medicine. 2004. *1st Annual Crossing the Quality Chasm Summit: A Focus on Communities.* Washington, DC: National Academies Press.

Keyser, D., H. A. Pincus, S. B. Thomas, N. Castle, J. Dembosky, M. Greenberg et al. 2010. "Mobilizing a Region to Redesign a Local System of Care: Lessons Learned from a Community Based Learning Collaborative." *Family and Community,* 33(3): 216–27.

Khandor, E. and K. Mason. 2007. *The Street Health Report 2007.* Toronto: Street Health.

Kuno, E., A. B. Rothbard, J. Averyt and D. Culhane. 2000. "Homelessness among Persons with Serious Mental Illness in an Enhanced Community-Based Mental Health System." *Psychiatric Services,* 51(8): 1012–16.

McNiel, D. E. and R. L. Binder. 2005. "Psychiatric Emergency Service Use and Homelessness, Mental Disorder, and Violence." *Psychiatric Services,* 56: 699–704.

Mental Health Policy Research Group. 1997. "Mental Illness and Pathways into Homelessness: Findings and Implications." Paper presented at the Mental Illness and Pathways into Homelessness Conference, Toronto, November 3.

Patterson, M., J. M. Somers, K. McIntosh, A. Shiell and C. J. Frankish. 2008. *Housing and Supports for Adults with Severe Addictions and/or Mental Illness in British Columbia.* Vancouver: Centre for Applied Research in Mental Health and Addiction, Simon Fraser University.

Rosenheck, R.A., S. Resnick and J. P. Morrissey. 2003. "Closing Service System Gaps for Homeless Clients with a Dual Diagnosis: Integrated Teams and Interagency Cooperation." *Journal of Mental Health Policy and Economics,* 6: 77–87.

Salit, S. A., E. M. Kuhn, A. J. Hartz, J. M. Vu and A. L. Mosso. 1998. "Hospitalization Costs Associated with Homelessness in New York City." *New England Journal of Medicine,* 338, 1734–40.

Salize, H. J., A. Horst, C. Dillmann-Lange, U. Killmann, G. Stern, I. Wolf et al. 2001. "Needs for Mental Health Care and Service Provision in Single Homeless People." *Social Psychiatry and Psychiatric Epidemiology,* 36: 207–16.

Shern, D. L., S. Tsemberis, W. Anthony, A. M. Lovell, L. Richmond, C. J. Felton et al. 2000. "Serving Street Dwelling Individuals with Psychiatric Disabilities: Outcomes of a Psychiatric Rehabilitation Clinical Trial." *American Journal of Public Health,* 90: 1873–78.

Stefancic, A. and S. Tsemberis. 2007. "Housing First for Long-Term Shelter Dwellers with Psychiatric Disabilities in a Suburban County: A Four-Year Study of Housing Access and Retention." *Journal of Primary Prevention,* 28: 265–79.

Stergiopoulos, V., K. Rouleau and S. Yoder. 2007. "Shelter Based Collaborative Mental Health Care for the Homeless." *Psychiatric Times,* 24(8): 23–26.

Stergiopoulos, V., C. Dewa, J. Durbin, N. Chau and T. Svoboda. 2010a. "Assessing the Mental Health Service Needs of the Homeless: A Level of Care Approach." *Journal of Health Care for the Poor and the Underserved,* 21: 1031–45.

Stergiopoulos, V., C. Dewa, K. Rouleau, S. Yoder and N. Chau. 2008. "Collaborative Mental Health Care for the Homeless: The Role of Psychiatry in Positive Housing and Mental Health Outcomes." *Canadian Journal of Psychiatry,* 53(1): 61–67.

Stergiopoulos, V., C. Dewa, G. Tanner, N. Chau, M. Pett and J. Connelly. 2010b. "Addressing the Needs of the Street Homeless: A Collaborative Approach." *International Journal of Mental Health,* 39(1): 3–15.

Susser, E. S., E. Valencia, S. A. Conover, A. Felix, W. Y. Tsai and R. J. Wyatt. 1997. "Preventing Recurrent Homelessness among Mentally Ill Men: A 'Critical Time' Intervention after Discharge from a Shelter." *American Journal of Public Health,* 87: 256–62.

Tam, C. 2010. "Case Studies in Public-Sector Leadership: Developing Collaborative Mental Health Care for Homeless Persons at a Drop-in Center." *Psychiatric Services,* 61(6): 549–51.

Tsemberis, S., L. Gulcur and M. Nakae. 2004. "Housing First, Consumer Choice, and Harm Reduction for Homeless Individuals with a Dual Diagnosis." *American Journal of Psychiatry,* 94(4): 651–56.

# CHAPTER 13

# The Development and Operational Context of an Emergency Shelter–Based Hospice in Ottawa, Ontario: A Qualitative Study

Manal Guirguis-Younger, PhD
Faculty of Human Sciences, Saint Paul University

Ryan McNeil, PhD candidate
British Columbia Centre for Excellence in HIV/AIDS
Faculty of Health Sciences, Simon Fraser University

## Introduction

In Canada and internationally, there is growing recognition that homelessness is a significant public health challenge (Hwang 2001), with homeless persons experiencing high levels of morbidity and mortality (Cheung and Hwang 2004; Hwang 2000; Garibaldi, Conde-Martel and O'Toole 2005). Over the past two decades, research has demonstrated that homeless persons experience high incidences of chronic and infectious diseases, such as HIV/AIDS (Culhane et al. 2001; Robertson et al. 2004), hepatitis C (Nyamathi, Dixon and Robbins 2002; Roy et al. 2001), respiratory diseases (Snyder and Eisner 2004) and diabetes (Hwang and Bugeja 2000). In addition to these challenges, homeless persons frequently have co-morbid mental health or substance use challenges (Fisher and Breakey 1991; Grinman et al. 2010) that increase the complexity of care and, in many cases, serve as a barrier to medical care (Gelberg et al. 1997; Hwang 2001).

As the number of homeless older adults increases (Hahn et al. 2006; Stergiopoulos and Herrmann 2003), there will be a growing need to adapt services to the needs of this population and, in particular, to provide palliative care (i.e., end-of-life care oriented toward managing pain and symptoms, rather than curative treatment). This is especially true given the cumulative burden of disease experienced by this population (Cohen 1999). However, in spite of the growing need for palliative care services among this population, the palliative care system has been slow to develop strategies to ensure that homeless persons are able to access needed care at end of life (Cagle 2009; McNeil, Guirguis-Younger and Dilley 2012a).

Previous research has noted that the palliative care system has largely been developed in accordance with a series of assumptions (i.e., that prospective clients are housed, supported by caregivers and, in many cases, have the financial resources to pay for supplementary care) that do not reflect the circumstances of homeless populations (Cagle 2009; McNeil, Guirguis-Younger and Dilley 2012a; McNeil et al. 2012b). Furthermore, while homeless populations have high levels of alcohol and/or illicit drug use, palliative care services typically operate under abstinence-only policies that constrain access to care (McNeil and Guirguis-Younger 2012). Accordingly, homeless persons are typically unable to access much needed care at the end of life, often dying alone and unsupported (Hwang 2001).

In Ottawa, a coalition of community leaders began working toward developing palliative care services for homeless persons in the early 2000s. This effort culminated in the opening of the Ottawa Mission Hospice in 2002, Canada's first emergency shelter–based hospice. The Ottawa Mission Hospice is a 16-bed palliative care program integrated into an emergency shelter in downtown Ottawa and is operated in conjunction with Ottawa Inner City Health, a homeless health care organization that coordinates health care services delivery to homeless persons in multiple shelter-based locations. The Ottawa Mission Hospice provides palliative and supportive care to homeless individuals and, in recognition of high levels of substance use among this population, operates under a harm reduction policy that permits managed alcohol use and off-site illicit drug use. An evaluation of the impact of this facility has shown that it reduces overall costs to the health care system by minimizing hospital stays and admission, while increasing overall satisfaction with care among homeless persons (Podymow, Turnbull and Coyle 2006).

This initiative represents a significant innovation in the care of homeless persons who are dying, in that it is a unique palliative care model that aims to provide care in a community context that is familiar with and accustomed to serving this population. Furthermore, given that it has been demonstrated to produce positive outcomes, there is a need to document its development so as to inform the continued evolution of palliative care services for those who are socially marginalized in Canada. This chapter provides an account of the development of end-of-life care services for persons who are homeless in Ottawa, and in particular the Ottawa Mission Hospice, based on qualitative interviews with those involved in its development and ongoing operation. Specifically, it explores the factors that led to the development of this service, as well as the current structures that support its ongoing operation.

## Methods

We undertook qualitative interviews with health and social services professionals over a five-month period (April to August 2007) as part of a case study of palliative care services delivery to homeless populations in Ottawa, focusing on the Ottawa Mission Hospice. We used a qualitative case study design to facilitate the study of the development of the Ottawa Mission Hospice and the individual, social and structural factors that shape palliative care services delivery in that setting (Yin 2003).

We relied upon a purposive sample of health and social services professionals involved in palliative care services delivery to homeless persons in Ottawa, all of whom worked directly for or in collaboration with the Ottawa Mission Hospice. We drew upon the expertise of an advisory committee made up of local and regional experts (e.g., senior health and social services administrators) to identify potential participants. In addition, the lead author (Manal Guirguis-Younger) had previously undertaken research on the palliative care needs of homeless persons in Ottawa (Guirguis-Younger, Runnels, Aubry and Turnbull 2006) and thus drew upon existing contacts with health and social services providers. Thirty individuals were sent a letter or email that outlined the study and study procedures and invited them to participate in an interview. Twenty-one individuals agreed to participate and represented a wide range of professional backgrounds, including health and social services administrators, physicians, nurses, social workers and personal support workers. Approximately half of our participants were employed by the Ottawa Mission Hospice or Ottawa Inner City Health, while the remaining participants worked collaboratively with this organization to provide palliative care to homeless persons.

An interview topic guide was used to facilitate interviews with participants. This interview topic guide was designed to encourage conversation regarding the individual, social and structural dimensions of palliative care services delivery to homeless populations. Given our interest in exploring palliative care services delivery at the Ottawa Mission Hospice, this interview guide included sections focusing on a range of topics related to palliative care services delivery in this setting, including but not limited to: (1) how the Ottawa Mission Hospice was developed, (2) how it was situated within the larger landscape of health care services for homeless persons in Ottawa, and (3) how organizations collaborated with the Ottawa Mission Hospice. Interviews ranged in duration from 45 to 120 minutes, were audio recorded and later transcribed verbatim by research assistants. One of us (Ryan McNeil) reviewed the transcripts while listening to the accompanying audio recordings to ensure the quality of the transcription and make any necessary changes.

Our analysis focused on factors that shaped the development and delivery of palliative care services to homeless individuals at the Ottawa Mission Hospice. We imported the interview transcripts into NVivo qualitative data analysis software (version 8) to facilitate coding. We drew upon constant comparative analysis methods to code the data, whereby we identified emerging categories and expanded them by constantly comparing the data (Strauss and Corbin 1990; Glaser and Strauss 1967). We developed a coding tree inductively, and revisions to this coding tree were made on a continuous basis as the data were coded. Once the final thematic categories were established, the lead author recoded sections of the data to check the credibility of these categories and ensure reliability.

This study was approved by the institutional research ethics boards at Saint Paul University and the University of British Columbia. We obtained informed consent prior to interviews, and participants were given a duplicate copy of the informed consent protocol for their records.

## Results

### Pioneering Work: Identifying and Responding to Unmet Palliative Care Needs

The Ottawa Mission led efforts to develop palliative care services for homeless populations in recognition that homelessness is a significant barrier to accessing mainstream palliative care services. The Ottawa Mission and partnering organizations acknowledged the complexity of the issues surrounding palliative care in the context of homelessness and identified the need to develop an alternative service delivery model responsive to the needs of this population. Two critical factors shaped the initial planning of palliative care services for homeless persons in Ottawa. First, key stakeholders identified factors contributing to a gap in palliative care services for homeless populations. Second, those involved in developing the Ottawa Mission Hospice shared a philosophy of providing compassionate palliation responsive to the unique needs of homeless persons.

### Incompatibility of Homelessness and Mainstream Palliative Care Services

The palliative care system has been developed in accordance with a series of assumptions regarding the social and structural context of service delivery (Lewis et al. 2011). Participant accounts indicated that many of these assumptions did not reflect the needs and circumstances of homeless populations. Specifically, participants noted that, while the palliative care system assumed that its clients were older adults with housing and caregiver support, these assumptions did not reflect the experiences of homeless persons. In this context, participants emphasized that homeless persons had vastly different experiences and needs due to intersecting individual characteristics (e.g., high levels of substance use and mental illness) and structural factors (e.g., homelessness, poverty, food insufficiency, etc.). For example:

> [There was] an appreciation in the community that there was a group of people that were chronically homeless, with complicated health problems, and not a really good understanding of whether the chronic homelessness was a cause or an effect of the physical health. . . . But, basically, the community deciding that, on some level, it doesn't really

*matter. You have to address the problem and that's really where Inner*
*City Health came from . . . to look at the chronically homeless and see*
*if we could find better health care.*

        – Administrator, Emergency Shelter

In the local context, key stakeholders identified the need to develop an innovative approach to providing palliative care services to homeless persons and, given the promise that emergency shelter–based health services have shown elsewhere, identified an emergency shelter–based hospice as a potential model. Participants reported that this model of care was identified as having the potential to minimize barriers to palliative care services for homeless populations, such as stigmatization of homeless persons and substance-use or behavioural policies. In addition, those involved in the development of this service perceived a shelter-based service delivery model as having other benefits, notably that staff have demonstrated cultural competence in providing care to this population. For example, one participant noted:

*[Homeless persons] deserve a way to die that represents the way they*
*lived. They are uncomfortable in the traditional hospital care, where*
*their friends are not allowed in. They are uncomfortable being told what*
*[the] parameters of their dying are. They really need their own model.*
*We are ready to house that model and see if it works.*

        – Executive Director, Emergency Shelter

### Ensure Basic Rights around Death and Dying

Mainstream palliative care services are a part of a long tradition that aims to meet the health and social needs of dying individuals and their families (Chochinov 2002). In this context, considerable attention has been paid to how to best develop respectful services that allow individuals to die with dignity (Sepulveda et al. 2002). Given that these are the cornerstone philosophies of palliative care, they were identified by local stakeholders as guiding principles to inform the development of palliative care services for homeless individuals. Participants articulated that, in addition to pain and symptom management, promoting dignity and respect was a critical component to providing shelter-based palliative care services and countering the widespread discrimination experienced by this population in other palliative care settings. Participants emphasized that it was important to foster an environment in which clients could receive social, emotional and spiritual support and that promoted social inclusion and self-worth:

> They have been faceless and nameless for long periods of their lives. One thing, which has been very important, is to give people a place to be acknowledged.
>
> – Mental Health Worker

> The biggest thing is supporting them . . . praying for them, and then they don't die alone.
>
> – Outreach Worker

### Respecting the Unique Social and Personal Needs of Persons Who Are Homeless

Participants indicated that identifying the unique needs and life circumstances of homeless populations was critical to the development of the Ottawa Mission Hospice. Those involved in planning this health care service consulted with community stakeholders and homeless persons to identify unique challenges that shape palliative care services delivery to this population. This ongoing dialogue focused on how to ensure that this model was responsive to the needs of this population. In this context, it was critical that services account for issues typically associated with palliative care (e.g., pain and symptom management), while also accounting for challenges associated with providing care to homeless persons (e.g., substance use, mental illness, etc.). For example, participants emphasized that there was a need to take a different approach to substance use than the abstinence-only approaches common in health care settings. For example:

> At the end of the day, we are all part of one community. . . . The more you marginalize people, the less safe the community is for everybody. . . . Where we have some common ground is there. . . . For example, injection drug users. . . . It's not like they think that the wild and crazy behaviour and injection drug use is a good thing. They don't. . . . I think, we have the opportunity, if we can get past that [i.e., injection drug use], there is some common ground.
>
> – Administrator, Emergency Shelter

One of the anticipated challenges posed by providing palliative care to people who use drugs was managing pain and symptoms associated with terminal illness. For example, participants indicated that administering the recommended dosages of pain medication (e.g., narcotics, opioids, etc.) were insufficient in managing pain among those with histories of drug dependence. In this context, participants indicated that they identified a need to tailor their strategies to the individual needs of clients and, in some cases, exceed recommended dosage levels. Participant accounts indicated that this was a delicate balancing act, whereby they had to weigh the client's needs against the potential risks:

> We weren't one hundred percent sure of the volume of dying homeless and some of the complexities of managing [their health needs], like people who are addicted to narcotics and you have to control their pain. How much [pain medication] do you give? What is pain? What is addiction?
>
> – Physician

In addition to these challenges, participants indicated that homeless persons may exercise individual agency and thereby choose to forgo treatment. Participants acknowledged that there were many reasons why individuals may make this decision, including concerns regarding potential adverse side effects (e.g., pain, nausea, etc.) and fears that they would be sedated. For example:

> If somebody [i.e., a client] looks at me and says, "Don't try to give me any of those wacko-pills or make me into a zombie," that is the end of it. Fair enough, you don't want medication. That is the answer. End of story.
>
> – Mental Health Nurse

Some participants indicated that, while they acknowledged the importance of promoting agency among clients, it was often difficult for them to understand choices that had potentially negative health consequences:

> He's an adult and he makes choices for himself. We support him in whatever those choices are. The choice about whether or not he goes into housing is not mine and it's not yours.
>
> – Administrator, Health Services

### Recognizing the Non-linear Trajectory of End of Life among Homeless Persons

Participant accounts emphasized that homeless persons had end-of-life trajectories far different than those of individuals receiving care in mainstream palliative care settings, who are typically in their final hours or days of life. On the contrary, participants indicated that palliative care for the homeless potentially prolonged life because of treating previously unmanaged health conditions (e.g., HIV, hepatitis C, etc.). As one participant noted,

> We have a guy, he was supposed to die five years ago. He hasn't. He had bipolar [disorder] that had never been treated. He went on medications for his hepatitis C and HIV. He looks like the walking dead, but he's still here.
>
> – Mental Health Nurse

In this regard, participants indicated that palliative care in the context of homelessness was akin to long-term or continuing care in that it often (although not always) lasted longer than palliative care provided in mainstream settings. Participants identified this as a potential benefit because it allowed them to build trust and rapport with clients and thus improve the overall quality of care. This was especially important given that homeless persons often lacked the support of family and friends. Whereas participants noted that it was important to attempt to reunite clients with family, they also needed to provide care and support in the absence of this. For example:

> Talking with them, spending time with them, playing cards with them. Bringing them down to the big TV room, taking them out for a walk. Making them happy. They feel safe.
>
> – Care Worker

### Maintaining Compassionate Palliation in the Context of Homelessness

**Addressing the complex social care needs.** Participants reported that, in addition to palliative care needs, homeless persons have complex social care requirements. Participants noted that, because homeless persons have difficulty meeting everyday survival needs (i.e., obtaining food and shelter), palliative care services need to address these needs and, moreover, foster a safe environment. For example:

*He told me, before he came here, that at times he had nothing to eat.*
*. . . That was hard, but then I said to him, "Now you are here and now*
*we are going to take care of you and try to let you have as less pain*
*possible. You will have food and you will have clothing. You will have*
*what you need."*

– Client Care Worker

In addition, participants noted that, due to the absence of caregiver support, homeless persons were in need of social support:

*As a nurse, you're spending all the time in the evening helping the*
*client go through whatever emotional things they need to go through.*
*Or, they might come back drunk or they maybe in pain and you have*
*got to deal with pain management.*

– Nurse

**Commitment to minimizing suffering at the end of life from a harm reduction perspective.** Participants emphasized that it was important to integrate harm reduction strategies into palliative care so that clients would not face barriers to necessary care as a result of continued substance use. In this regard, harm reduction programming was identified as a form of palliation insofar as it minimized the potential suffering associated with withdrawal. As one participant noted,

*I could have a patient who is dying, who requires end-of-life care who*
*still wishes to drink. They can drink, but what we do is we decide with*
*the patient how much he can have in a day and we will dispense it as*
*medication.*

– Nurse

Although abstinence should not be the goal, participants identified that it was important to provide support to those who wished to discontinue drug or alcohol use. Accordingly, it was felt that palliative care should also include detoxification programs:

*We have a protocol here for detox. If we have to detox them, if they're*
*in withdrawal, then we have a protocol to help them with their alcohol*
*withdrawal. We also have a protocol for drug withdrawal.*

– Nurse

### Building a System of Services

Three major themes emerged in regards to the development of palliative care services at the Ottawa Mission Hospice: (1) consultations with clients and community stakeholders, (2) partnership building with Ottawa Inner City Health and researcher and educators and (3) defining the operational principles of palliative care services.

**Consulting with clients.** The Ottawa Mission Hospice emerged out of a dialogue between the organization and a group of emergency shelter clients. These consultations were critical in ensuring that homeless persons had a voice in the development of palliative care services, which had the potential of increasing the ability of these services to meet their needs. Specifically, following the death of a longtime shelter resident, the Ottawa Mission's executive leadership consulted with a group of peers who provided support to that individual. These consultations aimed to identify the parameters of services focused on the unique needs and wishes of people who are homeless.

> *[The client's friends] sat with him until he died. It was a moment that they hadn't experienced—that dignity that they were allowed to have with somebody who was on the streets. . . . After that, I met with those five people and I said, "Do we need a place like this for people to die?" They said, "Yes."*
> – Emergency Shelter Director

This consultation provided a foundation for launching culturally competent services. In addition to this early dialogue, the conversation around the nature and implementation of these services continued with the clients, specifically around the structure and governance of service.

> *I said, "What would the rules be?" Because I knew they wouldn't be regular rules. We chatted back and forth and decided [that] we needed respect and dignity for the person. [Friends and visitors] couldn't come in high. They couldn't bring alcohol or drugs to the person. They were part of the caregiving team. They wanted to be able to talk to the doctor.*
> – Emergency Shelter Director

The involvement of clients in their own care took place in many levels. The ongoing nature of this dialogue is an important feature in the ultimate success of building services that work and extending these services into multiple areas of the death and dying experience.

**Consultation with community stakeholders.** Following initial consultations with emergency shelter clients, the Ottawa Mission brought the issue of palliative care for homeless persons to the larger community of service providers, with the goal of increasing awareness of the need for an alternative palliative care services delivery model. The Ottawa Mission identified that it was advantageous to involve the local hospitals and academic institutions in order to build support within the community and encourage the development of a shelter-based hospice.

> *I started becoming part of every advisory group I could find that was talking about palliative care. . . . I sat in on, I cannot tell you how many meetings—medical meetings. I kept giving the message: these people deserve dignity.*
> – Emergency Shelter Director

One of the most difficult issues to reconcile among organizations was incorporating harm reduction strategies as part of palliative care. This became an important point of consideration in terms of finding a way to work together. Discussions took place to ensure that no one organization has to compromise its ideology or philosophy of care, while at the same time ensuring that services met the needs of those who used alcohol or drugs at the end of life.

> *[Some agencies] do not allow alcohol, but they weren't doing palliative care. They were doing convalescent care. [Other agencies] had managed alcohol programs. That was the whole idea. If you prescribed alcohol, they didn't have to drink Listerine. It's a range of harm reduction. We are always struggling, trying to find a middle ground. There's a set of rules now that we each can work by and understand where everybody is.*
> – Emergency Shelter Director

**Partnership with Ottawa Inner City Health.** Whereas the Ottawa Mission had extensive experience providing emergency shelter services, it lacked experience providing health care services, and thus sought out opportunities to formally partner with a health care organization. In this context, the Ottawa Mission developed a symbiotic relationship with Ottawa Inner City Health, an organization with a mandate to provide care to homeless persons in the Ottawa region. The Ottawa Mission would provide the infrastructure, resources and staffing, including the program administrators, while Ottawa Inner City Health would provide health care services in coordination with its partnering agencies (i.e., a network of shelter-based health services, local hospitals and other community agencies). An important benefit of this approach is that it situated the shelter-based hospice within the larger context of health care services available to homeless persons in Ottawa. For example:

> *There was sort of an understanding that we needed to integrate across the [health and social care] system. Other partners were gradually brought on board. [Ottawa Inner City Health] was a pilot project. The focus was primarily on a set of deliverables: palliative care, short stay convalescent care and alcohol addiction. Those were picked by the community as being the three priorities.*
>
> – Administrator, Health Services

The Ottawa Mission and Ottawa Inner City Health would share in the decision-making on matters relating to the shelter-based hospice. In this regard, while there was a need to maintain some continuity between the hospice and emergency shelter in general, there was a recognition that a different set of rules were needed for the hospice due to its unique demands.

> *We had to really be very respectful around what [the Mission's] constraints were. There are some people who would say, "Well, they're dying. Anything they want to do is fine." Well, that would be what a health care provider would say but that's not what you say if you're running a shelter that has two hundred other people. You basically have to say, "Yes, this person's going to get a lot more leeway than anybody else because of the situation that they're in but, if they're disrupting the operations of the Mission, if they're threatening or injuring the staff and other clients, these are the conditions under which we can and can't take care of them."*
>
> – Administrator, Health Services

Because the Ottawa Mission was well-established within the community, it was able to generate financial support for the hospice through donors that was critical in establishing this service. As a registered non-profit and heath care organization, Ottawa Inner City Health was able to secure funding for health care services from a variety of sources, including the local health authority and the provincial government.

> *Every organization that's part of Inner City Health has, in fact, not just given what they originally said that they would give, but everybody has given more. Ottawa Inner City Health process, to some extent, was just bringing people together around the table to figure out who can offer what.*
>
> – Administrator, Health Services

> *It was a partnership between the Mission and the Ottawa Inner City Health. It grew out of that initial meeting where the Mission, all the other shoulders were together, we knew that we needed palliative care services as a group. We agreed to bring in the health piece of it and the Mission was kind enough to bring the infrastructure side of it. They fundraised, they developed a beautiful wing, and provided excellent facilities for us, and we provide the health care.*
>
> – Physician

**Community–academic partnerships.** Partnering with universities provided the opportunity for research and program evaluations, which lent credibility to the work undertaken by the Ottawa Mission Hospice. In this regard, Ottawa Inner City Health first emerged as a pilot research program operated in conjunction with the University of Ottawa, with the expectation that all of its programs be evaluated, including the hospice. A pilot study was undertaken to look at the efficacy of programs across the Ottawa Inner City Health system, which included an evaluation of the Ottawa Mission Hospice. The evaluation indicated that the Ottawa Mission Hospice was successful in decreasing health care costs, while increasing the quality of and satisfaction with care. This positive evaluation helped to validate the benefits of this service delivery model. As one participant noted:

> *There is a great deal of scientific evidence that supports what we're doing . . . . [There was] an independent evaluation, which produced very promising results. You've spent a very small amount of money and in fact you're showing good results.*
>
> – Administrator, Health Services

**Continuity of care in palliative care services.** The partnership with Ottawa Inner City Health was critical to facilitating continuity of care across services providing care to homeless persons in Ottawa. This continuity was important due to the complex co-morbidities experienced by most hospice clients. In particular, because medical personnel typically worked in multiple locations across the Ottawa Inner City Health system and regularly met to discuss patient care, they were knowledgeable of the overall needs of their clients. For example:

> *We have rounds here at the office every week and there are patient reviews. Anybody who we have that's new, we get the whole history and the story and hear about things on an ongoing basis.*
> – Administrator, Health Services

Given the special needs created by homelessness, one of the operational principles of effective service provision became a flexible delivery of what is necessary at various points of service contact. That is, individuals did not need to be physically at the hospice or imminently dying to receive palliative care.

> *We do palliative care in other places [i.e., partnering agencies] besides the [Ottawa Mission Hospice]. Not everybody that is palliative is necessarily at the [Ottawa Mission Hospice]. People can go where they want to be and receive services, as long as we can do it safely.*
> – Administrator, Health Services

## Discussion

Clearly identifying the factors contributing to service gaps in palliative care for those who are homeless and marginalized was a crucial step toward a more equitable service delivery model. Consistent with other studies (Cagle 2009; Lewis et al. 2011; McNeil, Guirguis-Younger and Dilley 2012a), our data suggest that the mainstream palliative care system is not suitable to address the needs of homeless persons due to its structure and parameters of service delivery (e.g., abstinence-only approaches). Our participants associated homelessness with many social barriers that constrained access to equitable health care, including but not limited to stigma, poverty, substance use and complex co-morbidities. Homeless service organizations and allied health organizations were uniquely positioned to identify the nature and dynamics of these barriers and to propose an alternative service delivery model. Accordingly, the Ottawa Mission Hospice may be understood to be the product of the desire of these organizations to help homeless persons die with dignity and access to best care.

In this context, two factors informed the development of the Ottawa Mission. First, key stakeholders acknowledged that palliative care services would best respond to the needs of homeless individuals if they were integrated into services already accessed by this population (i.e., an emergency shelter). Second, there was recognition that palliative care services needed to incorporate a wider range of social care services to address the complex needs of this population, especially given the non-linear nature of their end-of-life trajectories. Specifically, the Ottawa Mission Hospice identified a need to combine compassionate palliation and harm reduction strategies (i.e., providing managed alcohol consumption services, providing harm reduction paraphernalia and allowing off-site illicit drug use) and situate this service within a larger network of homeless health care services. Participants believed that this was necessary to facilitate access to services and ensure continuity of care, echoing the findings of other studies emphasizing the important role that public health services should play in palliative care services delivery to underserved populations (McNeil et al. 2012b; McNeil, Guirguis-Younger, Dilley 2012a).

Importantly, the Ottawa Mission Hospice demonstrates how community leaders and the affected community (i.e., homeless persons) can work together to develop and implement innovative solutions to community challenges. Whereas service providers, researchers and administrators spearheaded the development phase, early consultations with homeless persons were critical in informing the development of this initiative. Involving potential clients in defining the parameters of palliative care service delivery helped to ensure that the resulting service delivery model was client centred. Equally important was the consultation and brainstorming that took place with community organizations involved in the delivery of health and social services to homeless persons, given that palliative care may be initiated outside of the Ottawa Mission Hospice. Those concerned with developing palliative care services responsive to the needs of homeless populations in their community would benefit from similarly involving diverse partners and homeless persons in the planning of these services.

An important element in maintaining the momentum of this initiative was building partnerships, and in particular formally partnering with Ottawa Inner City Health. Ottawa Inner City Health played a critical role in mediating relationships across a range of health and social care services that enhanced continuity of care. Many of Ottawa Inner City Health's partnering organizations developed formal and informal service agreements with one another with respect to the provision of palliative care. Furthermore, Ottawa Inner City Health continued to serve as the backbone of service integration in that it coordinated the delivery of health care services across this system. While a complete description of the operational context of Ottawa Inner City Health is beyond the scope of this chapter, it should be noted that a great deal of organization development was necessary to ensure the continued success of this service and that partnering organizations, including the Ottawa Mission, informed its development.

The partnership with educational institutions and with mainstream services (e.g., hospitals) provided some infrastructure at the inception of the corporation and allowed the use of existing resources and procedures. The involvement of researchers allowed the rigorous evaluation of palliative care services, notably their impact on clinical outcomes and cost effectiveness (Podymow, Turnbull and Coyle 2006). A partnership that comprises academic NGOs, community-based NGOs and clients would be a formidable voice in eliminating health inequities and generating information for evidence-based public health practice (Robinson et al. 2007). Documenting the various stages of this process can serve as a guide for other communities looking for some direction on how to develop palliative care services for homeless or underserved groups.

The lessons learned in the development of the Ottawa Mission Hospice are instructive to all those who may wish to develop innovative service delivery models to meet the needs of homeless persons in their community. Accordingly, the processes outlined in this chapter, while focused on palliative care services delivery in a particular case, are likely transferable to other settings. Although communities and their challenges vary widely in accordance with the unique social, political and economic factors within those communities, our findings demonstrate that, if there is agreement around fundamental service goals, then it is possible to develop innovative services responsive to the needs of homeless populations.

## References

Cagle, J. 2009. "Weathering the Storm: Palliative Care for the Elderly Homeless." *Journal of Housing for the Elderly*, 23: 29–46.

Cheung, A. M. and S. W. Hwang. 2004. "Risk of Death among Homeless Women: A Cohort Study and Review of the Literature." *Canadian Medical Association Journal*, 170(8): 1243–47.

Chochinov, H. M. 2002. "Dignity-Conserving Care: A New Model for Palliative Care." *Journal of the American Medical Association*, 287(17): 2253–60.

Cohen, C. I. 1999. "Aging and Homelessness." *The Gerontologist*, 39(1): 5–15.

Culhane, D. P., E. Gollub, R. Kuhn and M. Schpaner. 2001. "The Co-occurrence of AIDS and Homelessness: Results from the Integration of Administrative Databases for AIDS Surveillance and Public Shelter Utilization in Philadelphia." *Journal of Epidemiology & Community Health*, 55(7): 515–20.

Fisher, P. J. and W. R. Breakey. 1991. "The Epidemiology of Alcohol, Drug, and Mental Disorders among Homeless Persons." *American Psychologist*, 46(11): 1115–28.

Garibaldi, B., A. Conde-Martel and T. P. O'Toole. 2005. "Self-Reported Comorbidities, Perceived Needs, and Sources for Usual Care for Older and Younger Homeless Adults." *Journal of General Internal Medicine*, 20(8), 726–730.

Gelberg, L., T. C. Gallagher, R. M. Andersen and P. Koegel. 1997. "Competing Priorities as a Barrier to Medical Care among Homeless Adults in Los Angeles." *American Journal of Public Health*, 87(2): 217–20.

Glaser, B. and A. Strauss. 1967. *The Discovery of Grounded Theory: Strategies for Qualitative Research*. New York: Aldine.

Grinman, M., S. Chiu, D. A. Rederlmeier, W. Levinson, A. Kiss, G. Tolomiczenko et al. 2010. "Drug Problems among Homeless Individuals in Toronto, Canada: Prevalence, Drugs of Choice, and Relation to Health Status." *BMC Public Health*, 10: 94.

Guirguis-Younger, M., V. Runnels, T. Aubry and J. Turnbull. 2006. "Carrying Out a Social Autopsy on Persons Who Are Homeless." *Evaluation and Program Planning*, 29(1): 44–54.

Hahn, J. A., M. B. Kushel, D. R. Bangsberg, E. Riley and A. R. Moss. 2006. "The Aging of the Homeless Population: Fourteen-Year Trends in San Francisco." *Journal of General Internal Medicine*, 21(7): 775–78.

Hwang, S. W. 2001. "Homelessness and Health." *Canadian Medical Association Journal*, 164(2): 229–33.

———. 2000. "Mortality among Men Using Homeless Shelters in Toronto, Ontario." *Journal of the American Medical Association*, 283(16): 2152–57.

Hwang, S. W. and A. L. Bugeja. 2000. "Barriers to Appropriate Diabetes Management among Homeless People in Toronto." *Canadian Medical Association Journal,* 163: 161–65.

Lewis, J. M., M. DiGiacomo, D. C. Currow and P. M. Davidson. 2011. "Dying in the Margins: Understanding Palliative Care and Socioeconomic Deprivation in the Developed World." *Journal of Pain and Symptom Management,* 42(1): 105–18.

McNeil, R., and M. Guirguis-Younger. 2012. "Illicit Drug Use as a Challenge to the Delivery of End-of-Life Care Services to Homeless Persons: Perceptions of Health and Social Services Professionals." *Palliative Medicine,* 26(4): 350–59.

McNeil, R., M. Guirguis-Younger and L. Dilley. 2012a. "Recommendations to Improve the End-of-Life Care System for Homeless Populations: A Qualitative Study of the Views of Canadian Health and Social Services Professionals." *BMC Palliative Care,* 11: 14.

McNeil, R., M. Guirguis-Younger, L. Dilley, T. D. Aubry, J. Turnbull and S. W. Hwang. 2012b. "Harm Reduction Services as a Point-of-Entry to and Source of End-of-Life Care and Support for Homeless and Marginally Housed Persons Who Use Alcohol and/or Illicit Drugs: A Qualitative Analysis." *BMC Public Health,* 12: 312.

Nyamathi A. M., E. L. Dixon, W. Robbins et al. 2002. "Risk Factors for Hepatitis C Infection among Homeless Adults." *Journal of General Internal Medicine,* 17(2): 134–43.

Podymow, T., J. Turnbull and D. Coyle. 2006. "Shelter-Based Palliative Care for the Homeless Terminally Ill." *Palliative Medicine,* 20(2): 81–86.

Robertson, M. J., R. A. Clark, E. D. Charlebois, J. Tulsky, H. L. Long, D. R. Bangsberg and A. R. Moss. 2004. "HIV Seroprevalence among Homeless and Marginally Housed Adults in San Francisco." *American Journal of Public Health,* 94(7): 1207–17.

Robinson, V., P. Tugell, P. Walker et al. 2007. "Creating and Testing the Concept of an Academic NGO for Enhancing Health Equity: A New Mode of Knowledge Production." *Education for Health,* 20(2): 1–17.

Roy, E., N. Haley, P. Leclerc, J. F. Boivin, L. Cedras and J. Vincelette. 2001. "Risk Factors for Hepatitis C Virus Infection among Street Youths." *Canadian Medical Association Journal,* 165: 557–60.

Sepulveda, C., A. Marlin, T. Yoshida and A. Ullrich. 2002. "Palliative Care: The World Health Organization's Global Perspective." *Journal of Pain and Symptom Management,* 24(2): 91–96.

Snyder L. D. and M. D. Eisner. 2004. "Obstructive Lung Disease among the Urban Homeless." *Chest,* 125(50): 1719–25.

Stergiopoulos, V. and N. Herrmann. 2003. "Old and Homeless: A Review and Survey of Older Adults Who Use Shelters in an Urban Setting." *Canadian Journal of Psychiatry,* 48: 374–80.

Strauss, A. and J. Corbin. 1990. *Basics of Qualitative Research: Grounded Theory Procedures and Techniques*. Thousand Oaks, CA: Sage Publications.

Yin, R. K. 2003. *Case Study Research: Design and Methods*. Thousand Oaks, CA: Sage Publications.

# Contributors

**Billie Allan, MSW,** is a PhD candidate at the Factor-Inwentash Faculty of Social Work, where her doctoral research focuses on the health and well-being of urban Aboriginal women. Her research interests include Aboriginal peoples' health, Aboriginal approaches to research and pedagogy and how social work education and knowledge can better respect and reflect the knowledge(s) of communities served by social workers. Ms. Allan is a member of Shabot Obaadjiwan First Nation.

**Tim Aubry, PhD,** is a Professor in the School of Psychology and Director of the Centre for Research on Educational and Community Services at the University of Ottawa. Dr. Aubry's research is focused in the areas of community mental health, homelessness and program evaluation of health and social services for marginalized populations. He is member of the National Research Team and the Co-Lead of the At Home/Chez Moi research demonstration project in Moncton and a Co-Principal Investigator of the Homelessness and Health in Transition study.

**Lynn Burnett, RN, BScN,** is a Care Coordinator at Ottawa Inner City Health. She provides comprehensive care to the homeless population with addictions and health challenges with a particular focus on women's health. She preceptors medical and nursing students and educates frontline staff in the shelters.

**John Ecker, MA,** is a doctoral candidate in the School of Psychology at the University of Ottawa.

**Susan Farrell, PhD, CPsych,** is a clinical psychologist and the Clinical Director of the Community Mental Health Program of the Royal Ottawa Health Care Group. She provides psychological assessment and consultation services to persons who are homeless and supervises graduate students in this area of research and clinical practice.

**Rafael Figueiredo, DDS,** is a dentist currently researching the oral health of the homeless in Toronto for a master of science in Dentistry degree at the University of Toronto.

**Manal Guirguis-Younger, PhD,** is Full Professor in the Faculty of Human Sciences at Saint Paul University and an affiliated researcher with the Centre for Research on Educational and Community Services at the University of Ottawa. Dr. Guirguis-Younger's research focuses on the delivery of palliative and supportive care to homeless and marginalized populations.

**Trevor A. Hart, PhD, CPsych,** is an Associate Professor in the Department of Psychology at Ryerson University and an Adjunct Faculty at the Dalla Lana School of Public Health at the University of Toronto. Dr. Hart is the Director of the HIV Prevention Lab, which examines risk factors for poor sexual health outcomes among populations at high risk for HIV and the creation and evaluation of HIV prevention and sexual health promotion interventions for these populations.

**Stephen W. Hwang, MD, MPH,** is the Research Chair in Homelessness, Housing and Health at the Centre for Research on Inner City Health in the Keenan Research Centre for the Li Ka Shing Knowledge Institute of St. Michael's Hospital and Associate Professor in the Department of Medicine and Director of the Division of General Internal Medicine at the University of Toronto. Dr. Hwang is widely considered to be one of North America's leading experts on homelessness and health. His current research projects include a longitudinal observational study of homeless populations in Toronto, Ottawa and Vancouver and a randomized controlled trial of a Housing First program for homeless persons with mental health challenges. In addition, Dr. Hwang is a staff physician at St. Michael's Hospital with more than twenty years of experience providing front-line care to homeless persons.

**Carolyn A. James, MA,** is a doctoral candidate in clinical psychology at York University. Carolyn's research focuses on predictors of adolescent health risk behaviours, with a particular focus on sexual health and prevention of sexual risk behaviours. Her doctoral research is examining the relationship between child sexual abuse and adolescent health risk behaviours (sexual risk behaviours and substance use) among homeless youth.

**Jonathan Jetté, MA,** is a doctoral candidate in the School of Psychology at the University of Ottawa.

**Jeff Karabanow, PhD,** is a Professor of Social Work at Dalhousie University. He has worked with homeless young people in Toronto, Montreal, Halifax and Guatemala. He has published numerous academic articles about housing stability, service delivery systems, street health and homeless youth culture. He has also completed a film documentary looking at the plight of street youth in Guatemala City and several animated shorts on Canadian street culture. His most recent book, *Leaving the Streets: Stories of Canadian Youth* (Fernwood Press), was released in fall 2010.

**Thomas Kerr, PhD,** is Director of the Urban Health Research Initiative at the British Columbia Centre for Excellence in HIV/AIDS and an Associate Professor in the Faculty of Medicine at the University of British Columbia (Division of AIDS). Dr. Kerr has extensive research experience in the areas of health psychology, behavioural science, community-based research and public health, especially in evaluating programs and treatments designed to address addiction, injection drug use and HIV/AIDS.

**Sean Kidd, PhD, CPsych,** is the Head of the Psychology Service in the Centre for Addiction and Mental Health's Schizophrenia Program and is an Assistant Professor with the McMaster and University of Toronto Departments of Psychiatry. His research interests include examining mechanisms of resilience among marginalized persons and the effectiveness of psychiatric rehabilitation interventions. His past work has focused on Assertive Community Treatment, policy and service development for homeless youths and the delivery of recovery-oriented services.

**Heather King-Andrews, MEd,** is a PhD candidate in the population health program with the Institute of Population Health at the University of Ottawa. Her current research interests consist of the epidemiological, psychological and social determinants of opposition defiance in very young children.

**Fran Klodawsky, PhD,** is a Professor in the Department of Geography and Environmental Studies at Carleton University. Her areas of expertise include public policy and social inclusion/exclusion in cities and feminist perspectives on cities, community organizing, housing and homelessness. She was the Co-Principal Investigator of the Panel Study on Homelessness in Ottawa, the first large-scale longitudinal survey of homeless persons in Canada. Her work uses both quantitative and qualitative methods within a collaborative, community-based framework.

**Nathanael Lauster, PhD,** is an Associate Professor of sociology at the University of British Columbia. His research focuses on social aspects of the built environment, especially as it concerns the use of housing. In addition to work on crowding, housing and health in Nunavut, he has published many articles on the interrelationships between family formation and housing and recently co-edited a book, *The End of Children? Changing Trends in Childbearing and Childhood* (UBC Press).

**Donna Lougheed, MSc, MD, FRCPC,** is an Assistant Professor in psychiatry at the University of Ottawa and a former family physician. She has worked in a clinical capacity for over 10 years with homeless and marginally housed adults with mental illness and substance use problems through the Royal Ottawa Health Care Group and has developed an 'underserved populations' clinical rotation for psychiatric residents.

**Michael MacEntee, LDS(I), PhD, FRCD(C),** is a Professor of prosthodontics and dental geriatrics with the Faculty of Dentistry at the University of British Columbia. He is past President of the Royal College of Dentists of Canada. Dr. MacEntee received the Distinguished Scientist Geriatric Oral Research Award from the International Association for Dental Research and is the senior editor of the book *Oral Healthcare and the Frail Elder: A Clinical Perspective* (Wiley).

**Brandon D. L. Marshall, PhD,** is an Assistant Professor in the Department of Epidemiology at the Brown University School of Public Health. Dr. Marshall completed his doctoral degree in epidemiology at the University of British Columbia School of Population and Public Health and postdoctoral training in the Department of Epidemiology at the Columbia University Mailman School of Public Health. His research interests focus on substance use epidemiology and the social, environmental and structural determinants of health among vulnerable populations.

**Ryan McNeil, PhD,** is a Postdoctoral Fellow at the British Columbia Centre for Excellence in HIV/AIDS and Faculty of Health Sciences at Simon Fraser University. His current research focuses on the social-structural production of harm among drug-using populations. His previous work explored the intersection of homelessness and health, and in particular interventions to improve health outcomes among homeless populations.

**Wendy Muckle RN, BScN, MHA,** has been the Executive Director of Ottawa Inner City Health since its beginning in February 2001. Her areas of interest are poverty and health, homelessness, HIV/AIDS, harm reduction and medical education.

**Rebecca Nemiroff, PhD,** earned her PhD in clinical psychology from the University of Ottawa in 2010. Her doctoral research focused on the community integration of women who have experienced homelessness. She currently works as a school and clinical psychologist in Gatineau, Quebec and is an Associate of the Centre for Treatment of Sexual Abuse and Childhood Trauma in Ottawa.

**Bernadette Pauly, RN, PhD,** is an Associate Professor in the School of Nursing at the University of Victoria and a Scientist in the Centre for Addictions Research of British Columbia. Her research focuses on health equity, homelessness and substance use. She has conducted research related to ethical nursing practice in the context of homelessness and substance use, needle exchange services and effectiveness of transitional housing in breaking the cycle of homelessness for people recovering from substance use problems.

**Carlos Quiñonez, DMD, PhD, FRCD(C),** is an Assistant Professor in the Faculty of Dentistry at the University of Toronto and Associate Researcher with the Centre for Research on Inner City Health at St. Michael's Hospital. His research explores dental health services, with an emphasis on barriers to dental care among marginalized populations.

**Izumi Sakamoto, PhD,** is a former Fulbright Scholar and is Associate Professor, Factor-Inwentash Faculty of Social Work, University of Toronto. She was the lead researcher of the research project (Coming Together project) presented herein, for which she and the team received the Community-Based Research Award of Merit Honourable Mention in 2007 by the Centre for Urban Health Initiatives and the Wellesley Institute. Subsequently, Dr. Sakamoto led the SSHRC-funded collaborative of eight arts-informed, community-based research projects.

**Danielle R. Schwartz, MA,** is a doctoral candidate in clinical psychology at Ryerson University. She completed her undergraduate degree at McGill University and her master's degree at Ryerson University. Ms. Schwartz's research examines the sexual health of high-risk populations, including homeless and LGBT youth. She is particularly interested in the impact of adverse childhood experiences on sexual health outcomes, including sexual risk behaviours and sexual functioning.

**Vicky Stergiopoulos, MD, MHSc, FRCPC,** is the Psychiatrist-in-Chief at St. Michael's Hospital and scientist at the Centre for Research on inner-city health in Toronto. Dr. Stergiopoulos's research focuses on the development and evaluation of community-based interventions to improve health outcomes among people who are homeless, and in particular those who frequently access mental health services.

**Frank Tester, PhD,** is a Professor of social work at UBC and Adjunct Professor of Native Studies, University of Manitoba. His research focuses on Nunavut and the Inuit of the Canadian Arctic. He is co-author of *Tammarniit (Mistakes): Inuit Relocation in the Eastern Arctic 1939–62* and *Kiumajut (Talking Back): Game Management and Inuit Rights 1900–70,* both published by UBC Press. Dr. Tester is a recipient of the Gustavus Myers Award for the Study of Human Rights in North America and the Erminie Wheeler-Voegelin Prize from the America Society for Ethnohistory, Cornell University.

**Jeffrey Turnbull, MD, FRCPC, MEd,** is co-founder and Medical Director of Ottawa Inner City Health. Dr. Turnbull is currently Chief of Staff at the Ottawa Hospital and past President of the Canadian Medical Association. He is a dedicated medical educator with an interest in poverty and health inequity.

**Anne C. Wagner, MA,** is a doctoral candidate in clinical psychology at Ryerson University. She completed her undergraduate degree at the University of Western Ontario and her master's degree at Ryerson University. Ms. Wagner's research focuses on individual and structural factors associated with HIV stigma, sexual risk behaviours for HIV/AIDS and quality of life for HIV-positive individuals.

**Bruce Wallace, MSW, PhD,** is a Postdoctoral Fellow with the Centre for Addictions Research of British Columbia. His primary research focus is the role of community health centre (CHC) dental clinics in improving access to dental care. As a social worker who has been actively engaged in community-based research focused on the issues of homelessness, poverty, health and equity, Dr. Wallace brings a unique interdisciplinary perspective to oral health issues

**Beth Wood, RN, MScN, APN (Psych),** works on the Psychiatric Outreach Team of the Community Mental Health Program at the Royal Ottawa Mental Health Centre. She provides assessment, diagnosis and treatment to concurrently disordered clients who are homeless. One of the agencies she works with is Ottawa Inner City Health.